The Complete Learning Center Book, Revised

Acknowledgments

The centers included in my first edition were an outgrowth of years of working with two very creative teachers in the Child Study Center, Susu Floyd and Vera Peters. Since that time, the teachers and staff in the Child Study Center, on the campus of East Tennessee State University in Johnson City, Tennessee, have continued to assist me in the development, photography, and setup of learning centers. For this revised edition, I offer my thanks to Lynn Lodien, Joy Matson, Gloria Reilly, Sara Lewis, Kathy Carter, Ann Marie Clancy Cornelison, Yolanda Steadman, and Erin Rudd, who have allowed us to use their classrooms as testing grounds for the new and revised learning centers that are an exciting addition to this book.

Many other amazing people have contributed to the creation of this book. Sheila P. Smith is the expert and detail-oriented person who supports my writing. Her ability to read my mind as well as my creative spelling makes her the essential person in making the content clear and precise. Two graduate students in early childhood education, Hillary Hundley and Roxanne Keele, have worked extensively on the related children's books, photographs, and references needed in the book. Michael Talley's wonderful photographs make the centers visible through his contribution of high-quality professional photographs of young children as they work in centers.

To all of these wonderful people, I offer my deepest appreciation.

Special thanks to Leah Curry-Rood and Larry Rood who believed, along with me, that a revised edition was needed of this book that has become a classic in the field of early childhood education. To Kathy Charner, both friend and editor, thanks for encouraging me to be creative and giving me the freedom to follow my ideas.

All these people have helped make this revised edition happen, and each has contributed a unique aspect to making this book an effective resource. Thanks to all the amazing preschool teachers who work so hard every day to include learning centers in their classroom that will nurture the development of their young children.

Additional Gryphon House Books written by Rebecca Isbell

Sensory Integration: A Guide for Preschool Teachers, with Christy Isbell

The Inclusive Learning Center Book: For Preschool Children with Special Needs, with Christy Isbell

The Complete Learning Spaces Book for Infants and Toddlers, with Christy Isbell

Early Learning Environments That Work, with Betty Exelby

Tell It Again!: Easy-to-Tell Stories with Activities for Young Children, with Shirley Raines

Tell It Again! 2: Easy-to-Tell Stories with Activities for Young Children, with Shirley Raines

An Illustrated Guide for 40 Different
Early Childhood Learning Centers

The Complete
Learning Center
Book

Rebecca Isbell

Illustrated by Deborah C. Johnson

© 2008 Rebecca T. Isbell
Printed in the United States of America.

Published by Gryphon House, Inc.
PO Box 10, Lewisville, NC 27023
800.638.0928 (toll-free); 877.638.7576 (fax)

Visit us on the web at www.gryphonhouse.com

Illustrations: Deborah C. Johnson

Reprinted April 2018

Library of Congress Cataloging-in-Publication Data

Isbell, Rebecca T.
  The complete learning center book, revised ed. / by Rebecca T. Isbell.
    p. cm.
  ISBN 978-0-87659-064-5
  1. Early childhood education--United States. 2. Classroom learning centers--United States. I. Title.
  LB1139.35.A37I83 2008
  372.21--dc22
  2007047967

Bulk purchase

Gryphon House books are available for special premiums and sales promotions as well as for fund-raising use. Special editions or book excerpts also can be created to specification. For details, contact the Director of Marketing at Gryphon House.

Disclaimer

Gryphon House, Inc. and the authors cannot be held responsible for damage, mishap, or injury incurred during the use of or because of activities in this book. Appropriate and reasonable caution and adult supervision of children involved in activities and corresponding to the age and capability of each child involved, is recommended at all times. Do not leave children unattended at any time. Observe safety and caution at all times.

Every effort has been made to locate copyright and permission information.

Table of Contents

3 Sociodramatic Centers: Encouraging Role-Playing and Cooperative Play

4 Unique Centers: Creative Additions to the Classroom

5 Outdoor Centers: A New Place for Centers

6 Evaluation of Centers and of Children in Centers

CD Table of Contents

The attached CD contains 40 separate pdf files, one for each learning center. Each file contains the following materials:

Illustration of the Center
Center Icons (large and small)
Letter to Families
Web of Integrated Learning
Form: Children's Center Choices
Form: Individual Center Time Observation
Form: Observation of Literacy Behaviors in
    Specific Learning Centers
Form: Individual Observation of Child's Play
    in a Center
Form: Evaluation of the Center
Form: Observation of the Individual Child in
    the Center

The CD also contains a folder of usable tif versions of the small and large icons for each center.

Introduction

This revised edition of *The Complete Learning Center Book* is for early childhood teachers who want their classrooms to be exciting learning places for young children. It is for teachers who want to include new centers that will expand learning opportunities for the young children in their classrooms. It is for teachers who understand that children learn best in an active environment where they can design, choose, implement, and influence the activities. It is also for creative teachers who have used traditional centers but would like to add a creative "spark" to their classrooms.

What's New in the Revised Edition?

This expanded edition includes 40 exciting new and revised centers, more than 400 easy-to-create props and related activities, and over 250 suggested books for use in learning centers. Every center has new literacy opportunities that will nurture young children's growing abilities in this area.

An important new section for each center is the Observation of the Individual Child, which includes questions to help in recording observations of children in the classroom. Center time is the ideal time to observe, record, and evaluate young children as they participate in meaningful play. By observing children's play in the centers, it is possible to document how a child is using language, developing skills, and working with others. These observations can provide information that may help teachers to determine the child's strengths, needs, and interests. It can also provide specific information needed to plan for the child, discuss the child's progress with family members, and include in a portfolio of learning.

This edition also includes a CD with the following elements: forms to evaluate the effectiveness of each center and to evaluate the children's learning in each center; letters to families for each center; copies of the webs of integrated learning for each center; color photographs of children in each center; and icons for each center. These icons can be used on the choice board to represent the centers that the children can select. The icons can also be placed on the entrance to the center, on center sign-in boards, or on writing/literacy activities that related to a specific center. It will be helpful to use both the icon and the written name of the center to help children with different levels of literacy understanding.

Learning in Centers

Young children are active learners who touch, feel, experiment, and create. The effectively designed center relates to this world of active learners and encourages their involvement. Young children are interested in the world in which they live; centers are a symbolic representation of their world. In this "center world," children can try out many ideas and rearrange happenings to fit their level of understanding. In this environment, they can build their confidence and begin to believe that they are capable learners.

In centers, small groups of children work together, enabling children to interact more frequently than in large groups. Children work cooperatively while getting immediate response to their ideas, communication, and work. This integrated environment captures their interest and encourages them to use their learning in meaningful ways.

The Value of Play

Play is an essential component of a quality early childhood program; play is children's work and children want to play. In play, children develop problem-solving skills by trying different ways of doing things and determining the best approach. In play, children use language while talking with and listening to the other children. When playing, they learn about other people as they try out different roles and adjust to working together. Play nurtures children's intellectual, social/emotional, and physical development.

Curriculum for Different Ability Levels

One of the most difficult tasks for the early childhood teacher is designing effective curricula for the different ability levels of children within the classroom. Centers, by the nature of their design, allow each child to work at his or her individual developmental level. For example, the flexible design of centers allows two children to examine the kitchen utensils in the Home Living Center as they learn the names and uses of the tools. The child who has more experience with kitchen tools can scaffold the other child to a higher level of thinking by sharing information and asking questions. Two other children in the same center may discuss the ingredients needed to prepare a pizza while "reading" a recipe for muffins. As these children participate in the center, they learn from each other in many ways. They share vocabulary and are excited about learning a new word that a friend used. They ask questions when a child talks about something they don't understand. Through interactions, they learn to make changes and adjustments in their activities, as they begin to cooperate during center play. Working with children of different abilities in learning centers encourages an increased understanding and appreciation for others. In the centers, children's different ability levels are accepted, and this builds their self-confidence.

The Flexibility of Centers

The design of an early childhood classroom environment nurtures the total development of young children. Classroom activities provide opportunities for children to participate individually, in teams, and in small groups. Both teacher- and child-directed activities are included for use throughout the day. Centers are a special component, allowing children to participate in self-directed play activities. In centers, there are opportunities to interact with different children. In centers, the child works individually or with a partner, helping him or her become more independent or learn to work cooperatively. The versatility of centers makes them an essential ingredient in an appropriately designed and effective early childhood classroom. In centers, children are able to learn and use skills.

When playing in centers, young children

- Make choices, developing confidence in their problem-solving abilities.
- Expand their oral language, combining words with their activity.
- Enhance their creative abilities, determining the direction of their play and selecting materials.
- Develop social skills as they work with others.
- Understand others as they try out roles and participate in related play sequences.
- Develop responsibility as they care for and build with the materials they are using.
- Learn how to make plans and follow through to completion, developing persistence on a task.
- Move into more advanced play as they develop roles, sequencing, and working cooperatively with others in the episodes.
- Develop longer attention spans as they increase the length of time they work in centers and participate in activities that interest them.
- Develop their understanding of symbols as they use concrete items in their play and move to imaginative representations.
- Enhance their self-image as they learn that they can influence their world while participating in the center.
- Experience integrated learning as they use all areas of the curriculum in meaningful ways.

Teacher-directed activities, such as circle or group time, can proceed into center time, which is child-directed. Alternating teacher- and child-directed activities provides variation while helping children learn to control their own behavior. They can focus better on the teacher-directed activity when they know that center time will follow and they can choose the activity. Centers also provide an opportunity to rotate active and quiet periods during the day. For example, have the children work actively in centers following a quiet time, such as listening to a story.

Making the Literacy Connection in Centers

The early years are a critical time for literacy development. During these first years, young children establish the foundation for reading and writing. Young children need many opportunities to use these emerging abilities and enjoy their experiences with literature. Positive encounters with books and other printed materials help children become literate and learn to read and write for enjoyment. The addition of books and other printed materials to centers provides another stimulating literacy environment in the early childhood classroom. For example, informational books added to the Pet Store Center clearly demonstrate to children what they can learn about animals from books.

The addition of writing materials to centers allows children to understand the value of written communication. Leave a note on the refrigerator that says "Out of Milk" or a notepad and pencil beside the telephone for taking orders in the Restaurant Center. A sign-in sheet in each center is another opportunity to record names and choices. These simple additions to centers increase opportunities for literacy development in young children.

In the Block Center, a book may spark an idea for a new structure or inspire a bridge where a troll could hide. A phonebook in the Mall Center encourages placing orders and demonstrates the usefulness of printed materials. An "Open/Closed" sign in the Doctor's Office Center communicates when the children can choose that center.

In early childhood classrooms that use theme-based curricula, teachers can select a learning center that supports the study. For example, the Fitness Center would be appropriate when the focus is on healthy eating. Children's books can also inspire a center, such as a Hat Center, which includes many wonderful books about hats. In this center, children create, construct, model, and sell hats, using books as their inspiration. Rather than experiencing learning as isolated and unrelated, centers integrate the learning into meaningful, related activities.

Integrated Learning

Centers are integrated learning at its best. Children talk (oral language); use small motor skills (physical coordination); work together on a shared project (social skills); sort dishes as they put them away (math); discover how to make bubble bath for babies (science); follow the picture directions for storing blocks (reading); and make a grocery list (writing). Learning occurs in meaningful ways in all areas during center time, which is appropriate for the young learner.

A Consistent Plan for Organizing Centers

This book includes many suggestions to help busy teacher meet the challenges of developing effective centers for young children. It provides ideas for centers: the enrichment of traditional centers, designing new dramatic centers, ideas for unique centers, and centers that are suitable for use outdoors and indoors.

Chapter 1 describes how to plan, design, and set up centers. It covers many topics, including how to select centers for the classroom, manage the operations, establish boundaries within the classroom, and plan for children's choices in centers.

Chapters 2, 3, 4, and 5 include detailed plans for centers. These plans are easy to follow and include all the necessary ingredients for setting up wonderful centers that will invite young children to participate.

Each center plan includes the following:
- Introduction
- Learning Objectives for Children in the Center
- Time Frame for the Center
- Letter to Parents or Guardians
- Layout of the Center (illustration)
- Vocabulary Enrichment
- Family- or Teacher-Collected Props for the Center
- Web of Integrated Learning for the Center
- Child-Created Props for the Center
- Activities for the Center
- Adding Spark to the Center
- The Essential Literacy Connection
  - Reading/Writing Opportunities
  - Other Printed Materials
  - Books for the Center
- Evaluation of the Center
- Observation of the Individual Child

Learning objectives are the foundation for planning the center and indicate some of the learning that can occur. Each center plan includes an illustration of the arrangement of equipment and materials. In addition, each plan provides a list of materials (Family- or Teacher-Collected Props) and suggested items to set up the center.

Included in each center plan is a letter to send home to parents or guardians to collect items for the center, or it may include ways to share the work the children have created in the center. The suggestions will help teachers successfully make an important connection with parents. The letters for all of the centers are on the CD.

Each plan includes techniques for introducing young children to the center, for enriching vocabulary, and for extending the focus into other classroom activities. Many ideas and variations allow teachers to choose the suggestions that work best with their special group of children.

An important component of each center plan includes descriptions of the child-created props. These activities involve young children in making some of the items for the center. When children help construct and use their materials in play, they develop a feeling of ownership of the center and responsibility for care of the props.

Curriculum connections (Web of Integrated Learning) visually show how each center contributes to the integration of the curriculum, as well as demonstrating the many different areas that center play can enrich. Centers provide a wonderful avenue for integrated learning.

An important section of each center plan is the Essential Literacy Connection, which indicates ways for making each center a more literate environment. These sections include an annotated listing of appropriate books related to centers that children can "read" as they participate in the center and that teachers can use in facilitating center time with young children. This section also includes ideas for expanding reading and writing opportunities in the center.

Questions at the end of each center plan enable teachers to evaluate the center and assess the involvement of the children in the open-ended activities. These observations help teachers determine the effectiveness of the center and learn what is occurring.

A new addition for each center is the Observation of the Individual Child. This includes questions that can assist teachers as they observe a specific child working in a center and document important information they can use to evaluate the child's strengths, needs, and personal interests. These observations may help determine the child's use of specific skills, and teachers may use them for assessment, evaluation, and conferences with parents or guardians. Forms for the observation of individual children in each center are on the CD that comes with this book.

Chapter 6 helps teachers evaluate the effectiveness of the center and children's involvement in the center by using practical observation tools. Review the simple-to-use checklists to determine when to add items to the center or close a center for "renovation." The checklists are useful for all of the centers included in the book. Also included in this section are several suggestions for assessing the participation of an individual child, while he or she plays in the center. These observations assist teachers in determining a child's level of play, language use, social skills, coordination, and many other areas of development. Center time is an excellent time for teachers to collect helpful information about a specific child. These observations can help in assessing a child's development and in planning appropriate activities, both in centers and in other areas of the curriculum. All forms referenced in Chapter 6 are included on the CD that comes with this book.

Planning, Designing, and Setting Up Centers

The Importance of Play

Early childhood educators, developmental experts, and psychologists have long recognized the value of play. Play is an essential element in the lives of young children. It helps them adapt to their world and create new learning. Play is child-initiated, child-powered, and intrinsically motivated.

In the past 10 years, some early childhood programs have increased their emphasis on academic content or more teacher-directed learning—sometimes going so far as to eliminate play as an educational component. Some educators and programs rationalize this shift by saying that children are "learning" rather than "playing." But those knowledgeable of child development recognize that play is how young children learn. Play is not a waste of time. Rather, play is the means by which children learn during the early years.

Forces That Negatively Impact Healthy Play

- Increasing pressure on 3- to 6-year-olds to sit still for directed, academic teaching.
- Administering standardized testing in the early years.
- Allowing children too much "screen time," whether it is in the form of television, computers, or video games. (Real play is child-powered and child-initiated.)
- Decreasing in the number of safe outdoor spaces in which children can explore and play.
- Increasing rushed and overscheduled lives, often built around adult-organized activities.

These factors are putting play at risk. The Alliance for Childhood, a partnership of outstanding educators, health care professionals, and researchers, is working to improve the lives of children by reversing this trend. This panel of experts is leading a national movement to restore play in every program that includes young children. The alliance includes many well-known developmental experts:

T. Barry Brazelton, renowned professor of pediatrics, Harvard Medical School
David Elkind, professor of child development, Tufts University
Jane Healy, Ph.D. educational psychologist and learning specialist
Jerome and Dorothy Singer, professors of psychology and senior researchers at Yale University
Edward Zigler, founder of Head Start and director of the Center for Child Development

Research on Brain Development and Learning

Recent research on brain development and learning reemphasizes the importance of play (Jensen, 2000; Shore, 1997). This research shows that active brains make permanent neurological connections during the early years, a critical period of learning. Brain researchers have demonstrated that play is a scaffold for development, a way of increasing neural structures, and a means for practicing skills needed in later life. Researchers repeatedly determine that play is a powerful influence on learning and is necessary for young children to learn (Bergen, 2002; Christie, 2003; Frost, Wortham, & Reifel, 2001). It is time to revisit the importance of play in the lives of young children. Decades of research have clearly demonstrated that childhood play, especially "pretend" (sociodramatic) play, boosts children's development intellectually, socially, emotionally, and physically.

Ways We Can Revive Play in the Lives of Young Children

- **Provide enriched learning centers in every early childhood classroom**. In these centers, young children can participate in exploratory play, sociodramatic play, problem solving, and language-rich experiences as well as discover how to participate in their social world. They direct their play and focus on topics of interest to them.

- **Include many opportunities for physical play**. These experiences will activate young children, help develop large motor abilities, and decrease childhood obesity. Outdoor centers like those in Chapter 5 are designed to inspire movement and expand young children's physical development.

- **Encourage appropriate play that makes academic learning meaningful**. In centers, young children can learn math and science (Sand and Water Center), connect literacy in meaningful play (Restaurant Center), and solve problems creatively (Construction or Block Center). These centers help young children make connections between play and their world. All of these centers include "reading" and "writing" activities, so young children can experience the kinds of communication and language skills they will need in their lives.

- **Increase opportunities for playing with others**. In learning centers, small groups of young children increase their ability to collaborate, cooperate, empathize, reduce aggression, and make social and emotional adjustments. While playing with others in centers, children develop important social skills that will help them to work cooperatively. While role-playing, children begin to empathize with others, recognize how they feel, and learn to respect the other children in their lives.

- **Provide simple toys, props, and natural materials**. The inclusion of simple toys invites children to create their own play. These materials allow children to think, imagine, and activate their learning, rather than allow them to be passive observers who only watch the actions of their toys. When using simple props, children actively engage in creative thinking and symbolic representation while determining what the props can be, how to use them, and how to include them in their play.

- **Help family members and administrators understand that learning occurs during play.** It is important that educators be able to explain the learning that occurs in centers and outdoor areas. Each learning center in this book includes learning objectives, webs of learning that can help in this discussion, and a letter (all are on the attached CD) to family members and guardians. Displaying documentation and pictures of what the children are doing will also help support the family members' and administrators' understanding of play's educational value.

- **Let children know you value play.** Provide play environments, talk with the children about their play, and encourage their creative efforts. The panel for Alliance for Childhood, after thorough review of research and writings, concludes that "the benefits of play are so impressive that every day of childhood should be a day of play" (Dettore, 2007).

Pediatric Report

A new report from the American Academy of Pediatrics, "The Importance of Play in Promoting Healthy Child Development and Maintaining Strong Parent-Child Bonds" (2007), concludes that unstructured play is essential for helping children reach important social, emotional, and cognitive developmental milestones, as well as helping them mange stress and become resilient. The ability to cope with problems and issues can be strengthening, because young children have the opportunity to play with possibilities and adjust to the circumstances.

Importance of Sociodramatic Play

Sociodramatic play is pretending in a social environment (Smilanksy, 1968). Piaget defined sociodramatic play as the most highly developed form of symbolic play. During play, children elaborate on themes, use objects as symbols, take on roles, collaborate on ideas, and persist in activities. Participating in sociodramatic play is critical for both intellectual development and social development of young children. In addition, this high-level play can provide a rich environment for the powerful combination of language and play.

Vygotsky (1967) stated that play provides a way for understanding symbolic representation, such as when a block stands for a truck, which is a precursor for reading and writing with abstract symbols. He also emphasized that sociodramatic play develops through interactions with other children. In this play, children learn rules and try out behaviors that relate to specific situations. Other children and adults can move a child to higher levels of thinking during the scaffolding experiences that occur so frequently during play.

Other studies indicate that children need ample time to move into sociodramatic play. Christie (1998, 2003), Ferguson (1999), and others recognize that children need at least 30 minutes to move into this higher level of play. Short periods of play do not allow children to move into sociodramatic play, select materials, determine the situation, select roles, or communicate about the happenings.

Learning centers provide the necessary stimulus for participating in sociodramatic play. An effective center includes a selection of materials that support a theme or concrete experiences. For example, a Camping Center set up in a preschool classroom will encourage nature study, roles of hiker or cook, and conversations about camping supplies. Maps, first-aid kits, and lists of supplies can encourage the use and understanding of print and literacy.

Child-Initiated and Child-Constructed Play

Young children can contribute to the development of learning centers. They can assist in selecting a center that matches their interests and experiences. In addition, they can build props, select related books, and collect items for the center. When centers relate to the children's experiences and they are able to contribute to the design, they develop a sense of ownership toward the center.

Literacy-Rich Environments

Learning centers provide a rich environment where young children can explore, use, and practice their emergent literacy skills. Literacy-rich learning centers contain theme-related reading and writing materials. For example, in the Doctor's Office Center, children may use pencils, pens, prescriptions pads, appointment books, patient folders, and a sign-in chart on the wall. Children can create labels and signs and "read" books that relate to themes from their sociodramatic play. As children use these literacy materials in their play, they are mastering their understanding of how print communicates, extending their vocabulary and participating in personally meaningful ways (Ferguson, 1999).

Findings from a 2001 longitudinal study show that using rich oral language in play has a positive impact on literacy development. The research illustrates the consistent relationship between the language that children use in play and their performances in literacy and language measures. (Dickinson & Tabors, 2001).

A literacy-enriched classroom should include a library center and author/illustrator center. Each of these centers is designed to include the tools for literacy learning. These centers focus on providing meaningful literacy opportunities that allow children to play, read, and write at their own level. In these centers, they are able to collaborate and scaffold, increasing children's language and knowledge of the functions of literacy (Roskos, 2001).

Theme-related learning centers provide an environment where children can use more complex language and interact with their playmates around topics they have experienced. Socio-dramatic play, which includes taking on roles and using language, encourages children to refine their communication skills. This play talk accompanies meaningful activity and provides immediate feedback that allows children to evaluate and refine their conversations. Organizing play props, literacy materials, and related equipment helps children understand and practice early literacy skills. In each center included in this book, there are many ideas for props, books, printed materials, and writing tools that will help establish a literacy-rich environment that will nurture the young children in your classroom.

Guided Play

For many years, educators have used the term "free play" to describe many different kinds of activities in early childhood classrooms. This label may mistakenly characterize play as unfocused, unimportant, and nothing more than children running wild. The phrase "guided play" is perhaps a more accurate description of the play that occurs in indoor and outdoor early childhood program learning centers.

In guided play, with children's input, adults select the centers to set up in the classroom and the props that will support the center's theme. The learning center guides children's learning though play by determining the theme, objects, and the space they will use. In learning centers, children still make choices, determine which materials they will use, what roles individuals will play, and the specific activity that will occur in the area. They also participate in the care and maintenance of the center, building their sense of responsibility.

Selection of Centers for the Classroom

First, select centers that are appropriate for your classroom and the diverse children it serves. A common recommendation is to provide twice the number of spaces available in centers as there are children using the centers. Most centers function best with four to six children in the center space, although some centers, such as the Construction Center, may work best with fewer children. If a preschool class has 15 children, the classroom should accommodate approximately four to five centers. The size of the room and materials available also affect the decision to include more or fewer centers. To have more choices available, some teachers share classroom space during center time, increasing the number of centers accessible to their children.

Understanding the backgrounds of the children in the class helps teachers determine which Traditional Centers (Chapter 2) to set up, as well as which props to include in those centers. It can also help in the selection of Unique Centers (Chapter 4). One classroom may contain children who have never been to a grocery store, while another may have children who have traveled extensively. Most classrooms, however, have children from diverse backgrounds and varying developmental levels, which necessitates providing a range of centers. The use of Traditional Centers (Chapter 2), Sociodramatic Centers (Chapter 3), Outdoor Centers (Chapter 5), and a sprinkling of Unique Centers (Chapter 4) provides enough variety for most early childhood classrooms. Outdoor centers provide a new way to include play and increase physical activity.

In centers, children learn while participating actively, observing, and interacting with others. Therefore, by including real objects and realistic toys, young children can select the appropriate tools that meet their needs in symbolic play. Include open-ended materials in each center for the young children who are ready to introduce more abstract representations and thinking into their play and increase their opportunities for creative problem solving. You can include scraps of wood, small boxes, and pieces of fabric to inspire a child's use of imaginative play.

Establishing Boundaries of Centers

Establish centers with clearly defined spaces. The children must be able to identify the center and determine where it begins and ends. A clear visual identification of the center helps children know where to go, what the boundaries of the space are, and that the activities go on within the center.

When determining the boundaries, look at the space from a child's eye level. Sit on the floor or crawl around the space to see what children will see. Construct boundaries that are appropriate for the children's size. Young children, who are 2 1/2"–3" tall, do not need walls that touch the ceiling to separate the center space. Folding screens, bookcases, or other dividers only need to be slightly above the children's line of vision to communicate where the center stops. Another advantage of low boundaries is that the teacher can easily observe what is happening in all the centers. This will assist in determining where to provide support or what observations teachers can accomplish in a given day.

Cardboard Screens

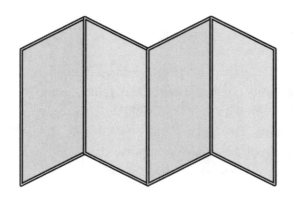

Cut large refrigerator or appliance box at one corner. Open to produce a screen. Staple the base to four pieces of wood to make the screen more substantial. Cardboard screens can be painted, covered with fabric, or left plain. Also, large cardboard boxes can be glued or stapled together to produce a three-dimensional divider or display area.

Plastic Screens

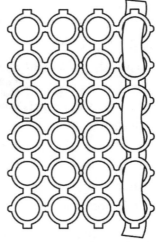

Staple plastic drink holders together. Weave strips of fabric or crepe paper through the openings to add texture and color. Suspend from the ceiling or between two pieces of furniture.

Cable Spool

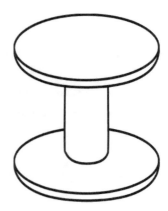

Use a cable spool as a low table to display books or provide work space. Be sure to sand the tube to reduce splintering and cover its top with contact paper for additional smoothness.

Wooden Frames

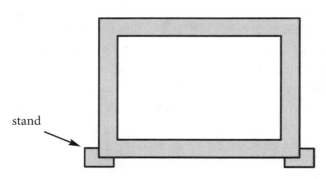

stand

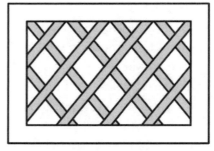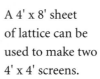

A 4' x 8' sheet of lattice can be used to make two 4' x 4' screens.

Use a wooden frame as a base for many different dividers.

The frame with lattice or fabric creates an attractive divider.

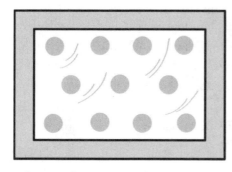

Fabric can be stapled to frame.

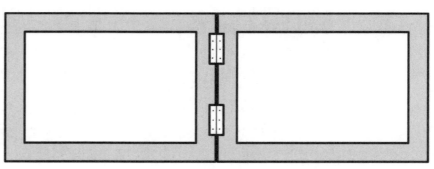

Attach two frames with two hinges to produce a screen. These dividers can also serve as display area.

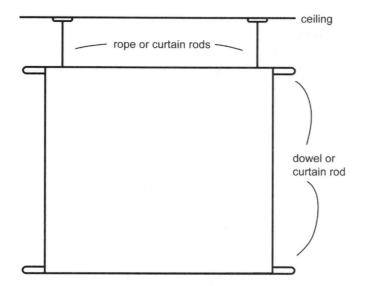

ceiling

rope or curtain rods

dowel or curtain rod

Join PVC pipe together to make a divider. Fabric can be hemmed and gathered around the pipe.

Staple a long piece of fabric to a 1" dowel rod placed at the top and bottom of the hanging. Use inexpensive fabric such as gauze, netting, cotton, or burlap. Also, hang a clothesline between centers. Drape a sheet or old blanket over the clothesline. Display artwork or pictures related to the center on the sheet or blanket.

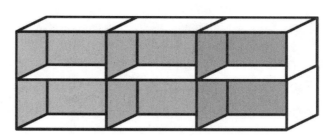

Glue or tape empty shoe boxes together to provide low storage dividers for centers. Cover the outside of the unit with contact paper to make the divider more durable. Store materials for the center inside the boxes.

Space definition can be as simple as an area rug, a lattice screen, or an appliance box that is cut open and stapled to a piece of lumber. The cost or complexity of the dividers is not important. The critical factor is that each center has a boundary the children can clearly understand. When using bookcases as dividers, the front and back can provide display space for two different centers. Draping fabric fastened to dowel rods, attaching the fabric to the ceiling, or connecting it to a wood frame adds interest and helps the children identify the center spaces. Add visual appeal by selecting textured fabric that comes in attractive colors. Use inexpensive fabric, such as netting or muslin, to separate areas. Using plants as a living divider between two areas is an excellent idea for the Nature Center. The illustrated ideas for establishing boundaries are inexpensive and simple for a teacher to make.

If boundaries do not exist, children wander in and out or run aimlessly between the centers. By establishing clear borders, children learn to manage their own behavior and focus on the task in the center. Dividers can also help eliminate visual distractions that can cause children to lose their concentration as they see others moving around the room.

Planning Centers

Effective centers require planning. Design your centers to provide specific learning opportunities for the children using them. The objectives for a center provide the framework for planning. It is important, however, to remember that these objectives reflect only a small part of the learning that occurs in each center. Additional learning opportunities happen spontaneously when the children select and control the direction of their play. Centers provide time for children to construct their own learning and grow and learn based on their interests. This important match provides a powerful tool for helping young children reach their potential.

Time Frame for Center Play

Children need sufficient time in a center. It is better for young children to be very involved in one center than simply to "visit" several centers. Children need time to select materials, determine roles, discuss activities, and implement play sequences. Provide a minimum of 30 minutes for sustained play to occur. Longer periods, from 45 minutes to one hour, encourage more involvement in play. If the teacher observes a child who is having difficulty participating for this length of time, let the child make another choice. Teachers should do this, however, on an individual basis, because, typically, the longer the child is in a center, the more involved the child's play will become.

Planning for Children's Choices

One of the strengths of centers is that they let young children make choices. Children who have an array of centers to choose from become more involved in the play and maintain their interest in the activity for longer periods. Each day, children should have an opportunity to choose the center where they will work.

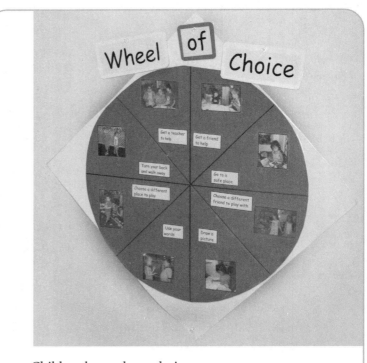

Children learn about choices.

Early childhood teachers use various approaches to manage centers and children's choices. Some teachers use a self-managing system for operating centers. In this approach, the teacher designs the centers to accommodate four to six children. The physical setup of the center helps to control the number of children using it. For example, putting two easels and one table with four chairs in the Art Center communicates to young children that six children can work in this center at a time. In this management system, children choose a center and work in that area until they are finished. They move to another center when they determine that space is available in the new area.

Some teachers design more elaborate systems with which to manage their centers. They find that planning boards help children understand the selection system and identify specific ways to choose another center. The planning board includes a logo, picture, and/or words that represent the centers that are available on a specific day. Teachers use the board during large-group time to help children see which centers are available. The board includes some centers that are available for selection every day, such as the Library, Home Living, Art, and Block Centers. Other centers are available on a

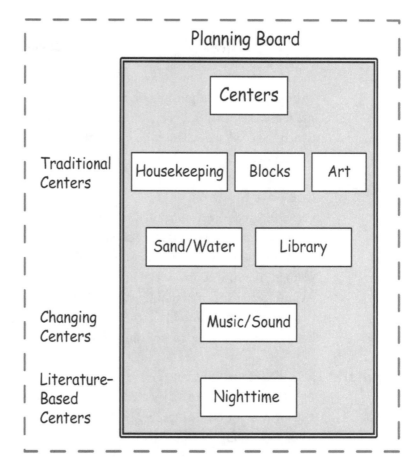

rotating basis at different times during the year. If a center is not open on a specific day, place a red "stop" sign to communicate that the center is not available and that the child needs to choose another center.

The planning board may contain either library pockets or Velcro or hook pieces indicating the number of spaces available for children in the center. Children make their choices and place their names on their center selections on the board. This provides a visual record of the centers that the children choose and of the remaining spaces for other children. A variation of this idea is to provide pockets, clothespins, necklaces, or hooks on a board at the entrance of the centers. Using this technique, the children take their nametags to the centers and place them in pockets. When each child leaves the center, he removes his nametag and takes it to the new center, placing it in that center's pocket. Other children view the empty pockets outside the centers and can easily determine when spaces are available for them. When using this system it is not necessary for the children to return to a centrally located planning board to make another center choice. This reduces the traffic in the classroom and assists the "wandering child" who is trying to make a decision about where to go.

Which system works best? Each teacher must select the approach that works best for the children who will be using the centers. For the management system to work effectively, use it consistently, ensuring the children understand the steps they must follow. Taking the time early in the year to explain and demonstrate to the children the procedures for using centers the children will help reduce confusion and ensure that the system works smoothly.

ROTATING THROUGH ALL CENTERS

Some early childhood teachers think that it is important for children to experience all centers in addition to the "child's choice" time. If this is a concern, let children choose the center during the morning. At another time during the day, pick specific centers for the children to visit. Use a chart, written plan, or rotation system to determine which children should be at particular centers. No matter what management system, establish a time each day for the children to choose the center in which they will work. This is an essential part of how centers provide opportunity for individual development.

CLEAN-UP TIME

Cleaning up the area is the final step in center play. As children learn how to make choices and participate in role-playing, they should also experience putting materials away. Facilitate the process by providing organized storage in each center. Clearly label the storage containers with pictures, logos, and/or words that are easy for young children to use. A toy box or art box does not encourage sorting or organized storage for future use. Labels, clear bins, and storage containers turn clean-up time into in another learning opportunity. Caring for the center and its materials helps children develop responsible behavior.

Teachers' Role During Center Time

TEACHERS AS OBSERVERS OF CHILDREN

During center time, the teacher becomes a "child watcher," observing a child, noticing children who are working together, recording the language children use, or evaluating a child's use of a specific skill. Use this recorded information in the children's portfolios and as an evaluation tool to determine children's development in specific areas. These documented observations help during discussions with family members and other teaching team members. This information is also useful when planning new centers and selecting developmentally appropriate activities to include in the classroom.

TEACHERS AS A RESOURCE

As teachers move around the centers, they serve as a resource for children who need help on a project. In this role, teachers listen and ask questions that help children develop problem-solving skills. If the children are having difficulty, teachers can move into the play and participate as a co-player for a short time, modeling involvement in the center. As a co-player, teachers participate in the play by taking on a minor role or posing questions that will encourage the children to become more involved in the activity. It is important that teachers not dominate the play or direct the activity, but rather become a member of the playgroup. If the children are participating and involved in play in the center, teachers should not interfere but rather allow their activity to develop. The goal is for teachers to move out of the play, as children develop interest and participate in activities.

TEACHERS AS EVALUATORS OF CENTERS

When centers are in operation, teachers can observe how the centers are functioning and children's use of the areas. Are the centers providing safe, predictable activity? Are there places children can work alone, with a partner, and with a small group? Are centers providing opportunities for children to use all areas of the curriculum? Do children need new centers or props to capture their interest? Are there meaningful literacy opportunities in each center? Are there areas that are intriguing and challenging? Are there opportunities for all children to use the centers? Observation during center time can lead to improvements in centers and adjustments to suit the children's needs.

Recording Children's Use of Centers

Use a large chart to keep a record of the centers that the children use. After center time each day, show the children how to mark off the centers he used, making a graph of the children's participation. Alternatively, design an individual record sheet that is appropriate for the developmental level of the children in the classroom. For a beginning level, draw logos and pictures on the sheet. The child can then simply mark the centers he visited that day. With older children, record the centers they used each day or keep a record of their participation over a week.

Keep these records in the individual child's folder and review them to identify patterns of center use. Provide space for children to "write" about play in the center, if they choose.

Some early childhood teachers provide a journal for children to "write" about their experiences in centers. This allows children to draw pictures of their activities or use invented spelling as they describe their play. Do not evaluate or criticize the children's work in the journals; value it as a step on the road to writing. These beginning scribbles, random letters, and creative spellings are important steps in the developing writing process. These attempts to communicate clearly demonstrate the children's increased understanding of letters and words.

Center Learning					
Child's Name				Week	
Center Name	Mon	Tues	Wed	Thur	Fri
Housekeeping Library Blocks Art Science/Nature Grocery					
This is what I did:	Place to write				

USING CENTERS

If children have never used centers, regardless of how old they are, they need to learn how centers work. An effective method for learning about centers is to bring the children around to visit each center during the first weeks the children are in the classroom and to talk about the props and play possibilities that exist in each center. These opportunities for exploration and discussion help children understand the centers and provide beginning ideas for how they may interact within the area. After introducing the centers, collect various items from each center and bring them to circle or group time. The children will enjoy guessing where the props belong while increasing their understanding of the existing centers.

Next, the children learn how to select a center, record their choices, and move to the appropriate spaces in the centers. They understand how to make another choice when they finish in one area. Children who lack experience in making choices may have difficulty with the decision-making process. Assist these children by providing limited choices until they feel more confident with a large number of center options. For instance, ask, "Would you like to go to the Block Area or Art Center?" After the child has more experience choosing, give him more options.

Children construct buildings, paint pictures, compose songs, make puppets, create hats, write books, and develop many other products when they work in centers. It is important to find ways that the children can display their creations and to provide them with ways of keeping their projects. Valuing children's work helps them understand that what they create in the centers is very important. Have a camera available for the builder to take a picture of his block construction, or the repairperson can photograph the toy he repaired in the Toy Workshop Center, or the camper can take pictures of people in a tent. Use low bulletin boards to display artwork, written compositions, or projects for the children and families to enjoy. Make a big book of things that happened in a specific center. Include photographs, drawings, or written descriptions of activities that occurred in the center. Including the children's names as well as labels for the pictures provides another literacy opportunity as well as a way to record the work that the children complete.

Changing and Rearranging Centers, and Storage in Centers

Centers need changes, rearrangements, and new and different materials in order to maintain the children's focus. Children will lose interest in a Home Living Center set up in September and not updated until June. Often, children will stop choosing a center or will simply use the materials in inappropriate ways when they start to lose interest in the center. Rotating materials in and out of the centers will renew interest in play. The addition of new materials also stimulates new play ideas. Because these changes are important for effective center operation, this book includes ideas in each center plan for adding new materials to an "ailing" center.

It is not necessary to reinvent centers every year. Collect items to expand traditional centers or build collections for new centers. Prop boxes that have center names and the dates during which the children used the center on the outside help the teacher have a place to keep old and new materials. When you find an item during the year, add it to the box for future use. Labels for prop boxes may include a place to record additional materials that the center needs. When storing props, remember to identify items what would be appropriate to add to the center in the future. A storage system with prop boxes makes sharing and collecting center materials easy.

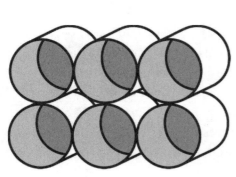

Attach moving storage tubes or cardboard ice cream tubes with screws and nuts to make a storage unit. This unit is very durable and can be used for years. The tubes can be spray painted or covered with colorful contact paper.

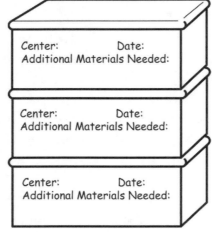

Center: Date:
Additional Materials Needed:

Center: Date:
Additional Materials Needed:

Center: Date:
Additional Materials Needed:

Stored and labeled prop boxes

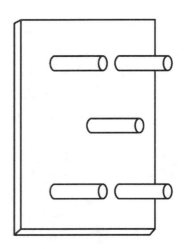

Children need to see the dress-up clothes that are in the center. Wooden pegs provide a secure hanger and increase visual appeal.

Resources for Teachers

A scrounge list includes sources where teachers can find free and inexpensive materials for centers.

Scrounge List

Free Materials	Source
bubble wrap	furniture stores and shipping companies
carpet pieces and squares	carpet stores and decorating shops
catalogs	stores with catalog ordering
colored paper	copy companies
computer paper	businesses or industries
display racks	card shops, grocery stores, bookstores, and department stores
exposed X-ray films	doctors or dentists offices and hospitals
fruit crates and trays	grocery stores
large cable spools	telephone companies, cable TV companies, and electrical supply companies
large cardboard boxes	furniture and appliance stores
large plastic food containers	restaurants and cafeterias
newsprint	newspaper publishers
round shipping boxes	shipping companies and manufacturers
scraps of wood	lumber companies and do-it-yourself stores
small boxes	department stores, shoe stores, and discount stores
Styrofoam packing pieces	packages mailed or received

Nature Items	Source
nuts, rocks, leaves, and branches	woodlands and parks

Inexpensive Materials	Source
contact paper	building supply and discount stores
dowel rods	building supply stores
dress-up clothes	flea market or garage sales
fabric	remnants, fabric shops, and scraps from those who sew or quilt
lattice and peg boards	building supply stores
masking tape and white glue	discount stores and school supply stores
nails, bolts, and screws	building supply stores
tent and parachute	military surplus stores
wallpaper	discount or salvage wallpaper stores
yarn, macramé rope, and string	craft shops and discount stores

Scrounge List (continued)

Items from Families

baby food jars

birthday and holiday cards or postcards

clothespins

coffee cans, frozen food dinner trays, empty thread spools, plastic jars, and bottles

detergent scoops

discarded pots, pans, utensils

flowers, plants, or seeds

gift wrap

lids and plastic jars of different sizes

old books, magazines, and newspapers

old hats, gloves, and dance costumes

old woodworking or kitchen tools

plastic pieces from packages and chocolate boxes

Popsicle sticks

scraps of fabric, trim, or decorations

Note: The attached CD contains a sample letter to family members and guardians introducing them to the concept of centers in the classroom.

Conclusion

Play is an important vehicle for optimal development of all young children. It is increasingly becoming clear that the developing brain needs play. New reports by outstanding professionals, educators, and pediatricians emphasize that play is essential for young children to develop appropriately. Learning centers provide a place that encourages sociodramatic play and where amazing learning can and will occur.

Planning, organization, and management are essential to the successful use of centers in the early childhood classroom. Spending time and effort in the development phase will ensure that centers function effectively and that young children receive the maximum benefit from their play in centers both indoors and outdoors.

References

American Academy of Pediatrics, Ginsburg, K. R., & the Committee on Communications and the Committee on Psychosocial Aspects of Child and Family Health. 2007, January. Clinical report: The importance of play in promoting healthy child development and maintaining strong parent-child bonds. *Pediatrics*, 119(1), 182–191. Retrieved from www.pediatrics.org/cgi/content/full/119/1/182.

Bergen, D. 2002. The role of pretend play in children's cognitive development. *Early Childhood Research & Practice*, 4(1), 2–15.

Christie, J. 2003, February. The story behind play and literacy. Paper presented at the Annual Conference of The Association for the Study of Play, Charleston, SC.

Christie, J. F. 1998. Play as a medium for literacy development. In D. Fromberg & D. Bergen (Eds.), *Play from birth to twelve and beyond: Contexts, perspectives, and meanings* (pp. 50–55). New York: Garland.

Dettore, E. Jr. 2007. The value and contribution of play to preschoolers' development. In C. J. Ferguson & E. Dettore, Jr. (Eds.), *To play or not to play: Is it really a question?* (pp. 33–42). Olney, MD: Association for Childhood Education International.

Dickinson, D., & Tabors, P. 2001. *Beginning literacy with language: Young children learning at home and school.* Baltimore, MD: Paul H. Brookes.

Ferguson, C. 1999. Building literacy with child-constructed sociodramatic play centers. *Dimensions of Early Childhood*, 27(3), 23–29.

Frost, J., Wortham, S., & Reifel, S. 2001. *Play and child development.* Upper Saddle River, NJ: Merrill/Prentice-Hall.

Jensen, E. 2000. Moving with the brain in mind. *Educational Leadership*, 58(3), 34–37.

Roskos, K. 2001, Summer. A synthesis of literacy in play research. *National Association for the Education of Young Children: Play, Policy, & Practice Connections Newsletter, VI*(1).

Shore, R. 1997. *Rethinking the brain: New insights into early development.* New York: Families and Work Institute.

Smilansky, S. 1968. *The effects of sociodramatic play on disadvantaged preschool children.* New York: John Wiley & Sons.

Vygotsky, L. 1967. Play and the role of mental development in the child. *Soviet Psychology*, 5, 6–18.

ADDITIONAL READING

Alliance for Childhood. 2003. *Time for play everyday: It's fun and fundamental.* College Park, MD: Alliance for Childhood. Available online at www.turnthepage.com/upload/403.pdf.

Bergen, D. 2007. Play and the brain. In C. J. Ferguson & E. Dettore, Jr. (Eds.), *To play or not to play: Is it really a question?* (pp. 11–22). Olney, MD: Association for Childhood Education International.

Dodge, D. T., & Colker, L. J. 1992. *The creative curriculum for early childhood (3rd ed.).* Washington, DC: Teaching Strategies, Inc.

Elkind, D. 2007. *The power of play: How spontaneous, imaginative activities lead to happier, healthier children.* Cambridge, MA: Da Capo Press.

Ferguson, C. J., & Dettore, E. Jr. (Eds.). 2007. *To play or not to play: Is it really a question?* Olney, MD: Association for Childhood Education International.

Ferguson, C. J., & McNulty, C. P. 2006, Spring. Learning through sciodramatic play. *Kappa Delta Pi Record*. Available online at www.kdp.org/pdf/publications/ferguson.pdf.

Fromberg, D. 2002. *Play and meaning in early childhood education*. Boston: Allyn & Bacon.

Isbenberg, J. P., & Quisenberry, N. 2002. Play: Essential for all children. A position paper of the Association for Childhood Education International. *Childhood Education*, 79, 33–39. Retrieved from www.acei.org/playpaper.htm.

Johnson, J., Christie, J., & Yawkey, T. 1999. *Play and early development (2nd ed.)*. New York: Longman.

Perlmutter, J., & Laminack, L. 1993. Sociodramatic play: A stage for practicing literacy. *Dimensions of Early Childhood*, 4(21), 13–16, 31.

Piaget, J. 1963. *The origins of intelligence in children*. New York: W.W. Norton & Company.

Singer, D. G., Golinkoff, R., & Hirsh-Pasek, K. (Eds.). 2006. *Play = learning: How play motivates and enhances children's cognitive and socio-emotional growth*. New York: Oxford University Press.

Smilansky, S., & Shefatya, L. 1990. *Facilitating play: A medium for promoting cognitive, socio-emotional and academic development in young children*. Gaithersburg, MD: Psychosocial and Educational Publications.

Wilmes, L., & Wilmes, D. 1991. *Learning centers: Open-ended activities*. Elgin, IL: Building Blocks.

Zigler, E. F., Singer, D. G., & Bishop-Josef, S. J. (Eds.). 2004. *Children's play: The roots of reading*. Washington, DC: Zero to Three Press.

WEBSITES TO VISIT

Playing for Keeps—Play ideas for families and educators: www.playingforkeeps.org

International Association for the Child's Rights to Play: www.ipausa.org

CHAPTER 2

Traditional Centers:
The Same but Different

This first group of Traditional Centers has a long history of use in early childhood programs. These are often set up in the classroom for extended periods. Some, such as the Block and Home Living Centers, you can use for the entire year, with new props and materials added regularly to keep the children interested and to extend their play. In classrooms with limited space, consider transforming these Traditional Centers for two to three weeks into Sociodramatic or Unique Centers. For example, for a brief time, the Block Center could become the Construction Center, or the Art Center could become the Author/Illustrator Center. After the appropriate time frame, based on the children's interest and involvement, change the center back to the Traditional Center that was there before the transformation.

The traditional centers in this chapter have been included in early childhood programs for many years. These centers encourage children's active participation and encourage their learning, including the development of intellectual, social-emotional, and physical abilities.

Each center plan includes the following:
- an introduction,
- learning objectives for the center,
- a time frame for the center,
- a letter to families about the center (found on the attached CD),
- an illustrated layout of the center,
- a list of related vocabulary,
- a list of Family- or Teacher-Collected Props,
- a web showing the integrated learning occurring in the center,
- child-created props,
- center activities,
- ideas on how to add spark to a center, and
- ways to evaluate the center.

An important addition in each center plan is the inclusion of literacy components, books, and writing. The combination of traditional centers and literacy materials provides new opportunities for young children to develop literacy in meaningful ways.

Art Studio Center

Author/Illustrator Center

Block Center

Home Living Center

Library Center

Music and Sound Center

Sand and Water Center

Science and Nature Center

Small Motor Center

Summary

Young children are very creative and enjoy using art materials to express their ideas. By experimenting with different media, children can begin to understand both their world and how to use the tools in their world to communicate. In the early childhood years, the creative process is more important than the products children develop. The Art Studio Center should be a place to enjoy artistic creations while providing support for the children's beginning efforts.

Introducing the Center

The Art Studio Center should include a wide variety of materials and choices that are easily accessible for the children. For example, consider including in the center a junk box that provides a unique collection of materials, such as scraps of colorful paper, foil pieces, lace, yarn, tissue paper, buttons, wire, and so on. To introduce the Art Studio Center, choose a time early in the year to bring the junk box to circle or group time. Pull an item out of the box and ask the children to tell you what it is. Then, lead a brainstorming session, encouraging the children to think of possible uses for the item. For example, for a piece of foil, you may ask, "How could you use this? Could you bend or wrinkle it? How could you put several pieces together? What could you add to it?" After this discussion, show the children where you put these materials in the Art Studio Center, so they can easily find them.

Learning Objectives for Children in the Art Studio Center

1. To become more creative as they participate in art activities.
2. To understand their world as they experiment with many different materials and tools.
3. To learn about artists and illustrators.
4. To build self-confidence, as they make decisions and implement ideas.
5. To develop their skill with scissors, glue, markers, and other tools.

Time Frame for the Art Studio Center

The Art Studio Center should be available throughout the year. Include open-ended art materials that the children can select and use in their own way. During circle or group time, describe a planned art activity you will include in the center for children who want to participate in a more directed art project. Encourage the children in the Art Studio Center to be creative and to experiment with different materials and techniques.

 Note: The attached CD contains a sample letter to send to families, introducing them to the Art Studio Center.

A dry-erase board provides another surface for drawing.

Vocabulary Enrichment

artist
attach
clay
color
construct
create
creative
decorate
design
display
easel
frame
illustrator
individual
mural
original
paint
sculpture
shape
texture
three-dimensional
unique

Web of Integrated Learning

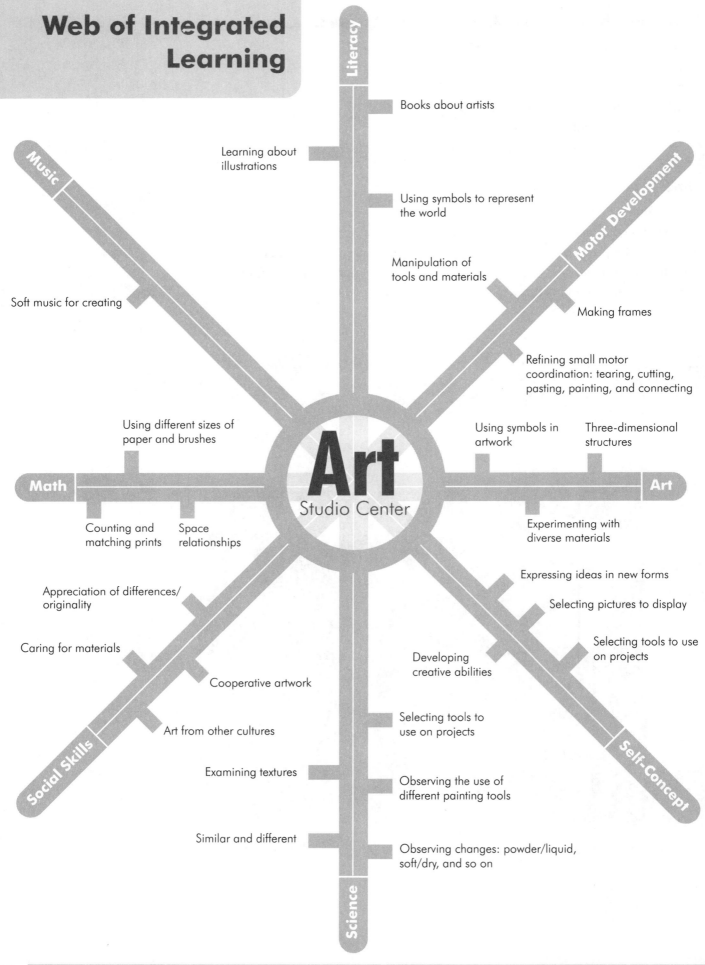

Art Studio Center

Literacy
- Books about artists
- Learning about illustrations
- Using symbols to represent the world
- Manipulation of tools and materials

Music
- Soft music for creating

Motor Development
- Making frames
- Refining small motor coordination: tearing, cutting, pasting, painting, and connecting

Math
- Using different sizes of paper and brushes
- Counting and matching prints
- Space relationships

Art
- Using symbols in artwork
- Three-dimensional structures
- Experimenting with diverse materials
- Expressing ideas in new forms
- Selecting pictures to display
- Selecting tools to use on projects

Social Skills
- Appreciation of differences/ originality
- Caring for materials
- Cooperative artwork
- Art from other cultures

Self-Concept
- Developing creative abilities
- Selecting tools to use on projects

Science
- Examining textures
- Similar and different
- Observing the use of different painting tools
- Observing changes: powder/liquid, soft/dry, and so on

- ❏ chalk
- ❏ clay
- ❏ crayons
- ❏ easel
- ❏ feathers
- ❏ glue
- ❏ large sheets of plastic, newspaper, or shower curtain liners (to cover tables and floor)
- ❏ markers
- ❏ paint rollers
- ❏ paintbrushes
- ❏ painting smocks or old shirts
- ❏ paper (in a variety of colors, sizes, and textures):
  - ❏ cardboard
  - ❏ coffee filters
  - ❏ computer paper
  - ❏ construction
  - ❏ finger paint paper
  - ❏ foil
  - ❏ manila folders
- ❏ newspapers
- ❏ newsprint
- ❏ paper towels
- ❏ tissue paper
- ❏ wallpaper
- ❏ wax paper
- ❏ playdough (made from different recipes)
- ❏ scissors
- ❏ sponges
- ❏ three-dimensional materials:
  - ❏ bubble wrap
  - ❏ cotton
  - ❏ electrical wire pieces
  - ❏ pie plates
  - ❏ pipe cleaners
  - ❏ small boxes
  - ❏ straws
  - ❏ toothpicks
- ❏ water source (sink or tub of water)

Craft sticks and clay were used to create a castle.

Art Museum   SELF-CONCEPT

       medium-sized boxes or large appliance box
       paint and brushes
       tape and glue
       wallpaper, contact paper, or fabric

- Build a display area for the children's artwork by gluing several medium-sized boxes together or by attaching their artwork to an appliance box.
- Paint these structures with black or bright colors.
- Cover some boxes with wallpaper, contact paper, or fabric.
- The children select a picture or creation they would like to display in the Art Museum.

Hanging Art   ART

       artwork
       beautiful objects:
           beads
           clay pieces
           feathers
           jewelry
           nature items
           pieces of colored plastic
           small bottles of colored water
       clothes hangers
       dowel rods (thin)
       fishing line
       small three-dimensional objects
       tape
       yarn

- With the help of the children, attach yarn or fishing line to a clothes hanger or dowel rod. It may be easier to use tape to hold the line rather than tying it up. Make sure to place the tape around the entire rod to hold the line securely.
- Ask the children to select the artwork to hang at various lengths, and to add small objects related to the picture or selected by the children because of their beauty.
- The children hang these pieces in the Art Studio Center or in the classroom. Offer help as needed.
- Vary the length and height of the displays to add visual interest.

paint, crayons, or foil

pizza boxes

scissors

- Make frames by cutting pizza boxes to fit the dimensions of sheets of art paper.
- Paint the pizza boxes or decorate them with foil to provide a shadow-box frame for the children's pictures.
- After completing the frames, the children select which pictures they want to display. This allows them to evaluate their own artwork and decide what they want others to enjoy.

Styrofoam Block Holders   MOTOR DEVELOPMENT

markers

scissors or knife (for use by an adult)

Styrofoam packing material

tempera paint and paintbrushes

- Make a storage container for scissors and markers using solid Styrofoam packing material.
- Cut the Styrofoam into thick blocks and make deep holes in the surface.
- Paint the Styrofoam blocks with tempera paint or decorate them with markers.
- Place these holders on the art table so the children have easy access to scissors and markers.

Activities for the Art Studio Center

A House Like Me   ART

The Big Orange Splot by Daniel M. Pinkwater

crayons and markers

paint and brushes

paper

- Read _The Big Orange Splot_ to the children.
- Set out crayons, markers, paint, brushes, and paper, for the children to draw or paint a mural of their neighborhood.
- Challenge each child makes a house that looks like her.

Collage

cardboard or brown paper (large pieces)
glue
nature items

- With the children, collect nature items common to the season and place them in the Art Studio Center.
- The children glue the natural seasonal items to a large piece of cardboard or sheet of brown paper. Write the children's names beside the items they found and mounted to the board, and display this group collage in the classroom.

Cutting Practice

materials to cut:
    card inserts from magazines
    inexpensive wallpaper pieces
    newspaper advertisements
    stiff paper
    stiff ribbon
plastic container
several pairs of child-safe scissors

- Set several pairs of scissors and easy-to-cut materials out in a plastic container.
- This activity provides an opportunity for children to practice cutting the materials, and, in doing so, develop a skill they will need in many future art projects.

Illustrators

several books illustrated by the same illustrator, such as Eric Carle or Ezra Jack Keats
stapler
tools and materials used by the illustrator you choose

- Display books illustrated by a particular artist. Feature this illustrator for a week, discussing with the children the artist's techniques.
- In the Art Studio Center, place materials and tools like those the illustrator uses, and invite the children to experiment with creating their own pictures using these materials.
- Collect several of each child's pictures together, and help the child staple them together to make a book.
- If necessary, help the children write their names on the covers of their books, identifying them as the illustrators of the books.

clay or playdough

household objects, sponge pieces, or newspaper

paper, cardboard, fabric, or wallpaper

shallow containers

tempera paint

- Pour different colors of tempera paint in shallow containers.
- Set the containers out and invite the children to make prints by dipping household objects, sponge pieces, or crumpled newspaper in tempera paint, then using them to print on paper, cardboard, fabric, or wallpaper.
- To make this a three-dimensional activity, set out several pieces of clay or playdough and for the children to make impressions of the objects with which they made prints.

Texture Box   SCIENCE

blindfold

glue

materials (a variety with different textures):

  bark

  burlap

  corduroy

  cork pieces

  cotton balls

  foil

  sandpaper

  screen

  silk

  yarn

shoeboxes

- Collect a variety of materials that have different textures.
- Ask the children to select and glue the textured materials onto shoeboxes.
- Help the children blindfold each other, and then challenge them to touch and identify the various textures.

Tissue Paper Creations   ART/MOTOR DEVELOPMENT

cardboard pieces with openings

floor lamp or table lamp

large paintbrushes

poster board or heavy paper

thinned white glue

tissue paper (sheets of various colors)

- Provide cardboard or poster board pieces with large openings in their centers. Invite each child to select a piece she will use as her frame, along with several strips of tissue paper.
- Show each child how to brush glue onto pieces of tissue paper and then set the tissue paper on her frame so it overlaps along the edges and covers its opening.
- While adding the layers, encourage the child to hold her papered frame in front of the light, so she can observe the changes in color and design that occur as she adds more and more layers of paper.
- When the children finish, display their tissue paper creations in the window or hanging below a light.

Adding Spark to the Art Studio Center

Add a new painting tool, such as a toothbrush, bottle brush, dishwashing liquid "wand," spray bottle, paint roller, pine branch, sponge, or medicine dropper to the center, and invite the children to use it with the tempera paint. These unusual tools give children the freedom to paint in a new way. Try cutting some sponges into various shapes so the children can use them to make print patterns. Include a variety of papers on which the children can test the new tools, discover how they respond, and discover ways to combine the various materials.

The Essential Literacy Connection

Reading/Writing Opportunities

- Create signs and labels for the Art Museum displays.
- Display labels and descriptions of artwork that the children dictate to the teacher or "write" themselves.

Other Printed Materials

- Display books or magazines that include creative craft ideas appropriate for young children.
- Show the children posters of artwork that display an artist's name and work.

Books for the Art Studio Center

Beaumont, K. 2005. *I Ain't Gonna Paint No More!* San Diego, CA: Harcourt. *One creative child floods his world with color, first painting the walls, then the ceiling, then himself!*

dePaola, T. 2007. *Mr. Satie and the Great Art Contest.* London, UK: Puffin. *Mr. Satie comes to visit his niece and nephew Rosalie and Conrad. They love his visits because he always has exciting stories to tell about his adventures Abroad. During this particular visit, Mr. Satie tells of two artists in Paris who he helped become friends.*

Johnson, C. 1958. *Harold and the Purple Crayon.* New York: HarperCollins. *This story describes a boy's excursion with a purple crayon. The crayon draws him through many adventures while meeting new friends along the way.*

Lionni, L. 1968. *The Biggest House in the World.* New York: Pantheon. *A little snail wants to have the biggest house in the world, until one day his wise father tells him an intriguing story. The moral of the story is that sometimes things are better small.*

Pinkwater, D. M. 1992. *The Big Orange Splot.* New York: Hastings House. *Mr. Plumbean lived on a street where all the houses were the same. One day, paint falls on his roof by accident and his house becomes different. Mr. Plumbean creates a house that suits "him" like no other house.*

Walsh, E. S. 1989. *Mouse Paint.* San Diego, CA: Harcourt. *Three white mice find three paint jars containing the colors red, blue, and yellow. They discover new colors as they scamper about the book, mixing and creating artful blends of paint.*

An easel gives the artist a good view of the painting.

Evaluation of the Art Studio Center

(This form is on the CD that comes with this book.)
Ask yourself the following questions to evaluate the Art Studio Center in your classroom:
- Are children experimenting with different types of materials and tools?
- Are children creating different types of pictures and sculptures?
- Are children demonstrating their understanding of different ways to use the materials available in the center?
- Are children proud of their artwork and interested in displaying their creations?

Observation of the Individual Child

(This form is on the CD that comes with this book. Always date observations of each child.)
- Does the child enjoy participating in the Art Studio Center? How can you tell?
- Is the child using art materials to represent her world (pictures of family, pets, children, and so on)?
- How is the child's small motor coordination when using tools, paper, scissors, glue, overlapping, and tearing?
- Have you observed the child creating something unusual? What is she creating and how?
- Does the child display examples of creative problem solving when, for instance, something doesn't work, when a material the child wants is not available, or when another child is using the item?

Summary

The Author/Illustrator Center nurtures children's literacy and includes many opportunities to "write" and draw. Here, each child will be able to work at her level because all the materials are open-ended and allow for many different ways of creating. The variety of writing and drawing materials, matched with a range of easily accessible tools, makes this a wonderful place for young children to "write." Here, they can communicate their ideas, record their thoughts, and display the work they want to share. Part of this experience is learning about what authors and illustrators do by providing some examples of various authors' and illustrators' works.

Introducing the Center

This center connects closely with other literacy activities that occur in the classroom. Circle or group time book readings should include discussions of the authors of the books, as well as their illustrators. Place some of these books in the Author/Illustrator Center, so the children can take a closer look at the both the text and drawings. These can inspire the children to "write" or draw in a similar or uniquely different way. When the children create books or illustrations in the Author/Illustrator Center, engage them in discussions about their creations and encourage them to share their work with the other children.

Learning Objectives for Children in the Author/Illustrator Center

1. To encourage communication in a symbolic form through writing and/or illustrating.
2. To recognize the importance of writing as a way to express ideas.
3. To value illustrations as a way to communicate.
4. To experience a variety of tools that they can use in writing and illustrating.
5. To appreciate the writing and illustrating of others.

Time Frame for the Author/Illustrator Center

Because the Author/Illustrator Center provides an important connection to literacy, be sure it stays set up in the classroom throughout the year. Rotate papers, books, and tools into the center so that interest and involvement will remain high during this extended period. If there is space, set up the center in the Art Studio Center. Be sure, however, that each center has a clearly defined space so the young children can understand which activities to do in each space.

 Note: The attached CD contains a sample letter to send to families, introducing them to the Author/Illustrator Center.

Sometimes a child needs a teacher's support.

Web of Integrated Learning

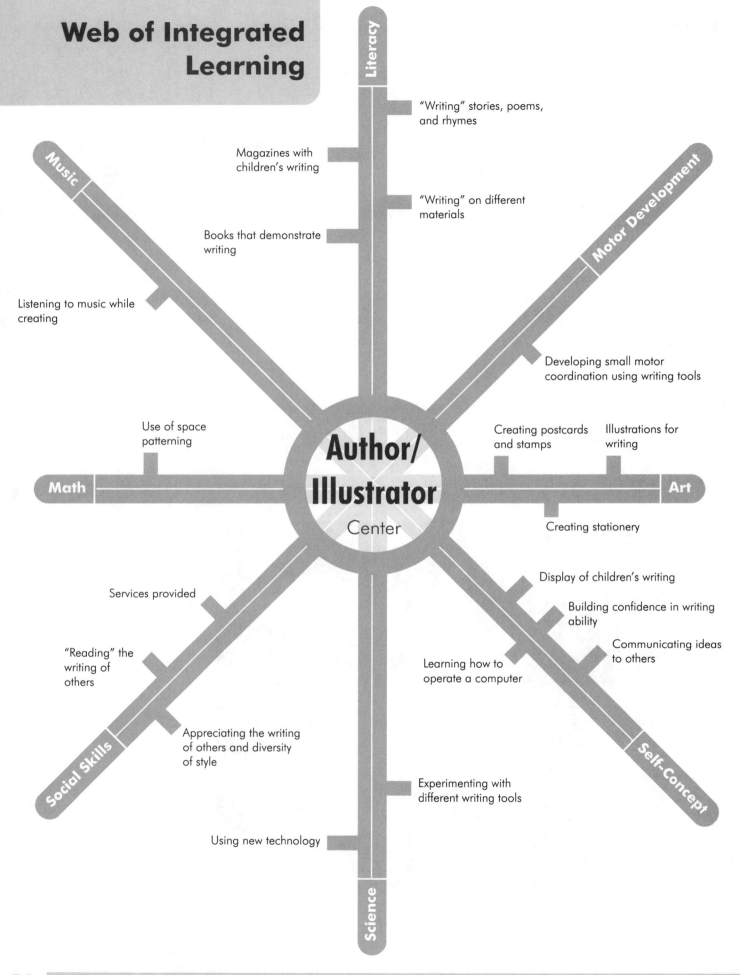

Author/Illustrator Center

Literacy
- "Writing" stories, poems, and rhymes
- Magazines with children's writing
- "Writing" on different materials
- Books that demonstrate writing

Music
- Listening to music while creating

Math
- Use of space patterning

Motor Development
- Developing small motor coordination using writing tools

Art
- Creating postcards and stamps
- Illustrations for writing
- Creating stationery

Self-Concept
- Display of children's writing
- Building confidence in writing ability
- Communicating ideas to others

Science
- Learning how to operate a computer
- Experimenting with different writing tools
- Using new technology

Social Skills
- Services provided
- "Reading" the writing of others
- Appreciating the writing of others and diversity of style

Family- or Teacher-Collected Props for the Author/Illustrator Center

- ❏ books illustrated by Eric Carle, Ezra Jack Keats, Leo Lionni, Audrey Wood, Tomie dePaola, and others
- ❏ contact paper
- ❏ craft sticks
- ❏ magazines
- ❏ neon glue
- ❏ paint: tempera and watercolor
- ❏ paper:
  - ❏ butcher paper
  - ❏ computer paper
  - ❏ construction paper
  - ❏ graph paper
  - ❏ lined and unlined paper in varied sizes
  - ❏ newsprint
  - ❏ old greeting cards
  - ❏ wrapping paper
  - ❏ scraps of fabric
  - ❏ stamp pad and letters

- ❏ tools:
  - ❏ hole punch
  - ❏ scissors
  - ❏ stapler
  - ❏ typewriter
  - ❏ wipe-off cards/small slate board
- ❏ writing tools:
  - ❏ chalk
  - ❏ colored pencils
  - ❏ markers
  - ❏ pencils

Keeping a personal journal encourages writing and drawing

Postcards
ART

blank paper
markers and crayons
old greeting cards or postcards
paper
scissors
tape

- The children make postcards for the Author/Illustrator Center by cutting paper to postcard size and drawing pictures of stamps on the cards.
- Help the children write messages on the opposite sides of the pictures.
- The children can also reuse old greeting cards or postcards by pasting blank paper over a postcard's old address and message, and then "write" new messages in the blank area.

Post Office with Mailboxes
SOCIAL SKILLS

glue or tape
markers or crayons
shoeboxes or cardboard tubes

- Set out shoeboxes and cardboard tubes and help each child to use the shoeboxes and cardboard tubes to make a mailbox to receive letters. Glue or tape these mailboxes together, so they will stay together as the children deliver mail to their classmates.
- Help display each child's name and picture on the front of her mailbox, for easy letter delivery.

Premade Books
LITERACY

colorful paper/wrapping paper
paper
hole punch
plastic container
yarn, shoestrings, ribbon

- Set out several pieces of paper for the children to attach together to make books of various sizes, shapes, and designs. Include blank pages to write in them later. Offer help as needed.
- When each child has her collection of paper together, she punches holes along one edge and then thread yarn or ribbon through the holes to form the book's spine.
- Store the books in a container in the Author/Illustrator Center.

Stationery

markers, rubber stamps, stencils, or prints
paper

- Set out the various materials for the children to use to design their own stationery, using markers, rubber stamps, stencils, or prints.
- These personal letterheads encourage children to "write" to each other.

Activities for the Author/Illustrator Center

Children's Writings

tape
writings by children

- Encourage the children to share their writings with one another during circle or group time or in the Author/Illustrator Center.
- After "reading" their work, designate a space where the children can display their "writings" for other children to see.
- Collect "writings" from children in other classrooms, or from magazines that include children's work, such as *Stone Soup: The Magazine by Children*.

Famous Illustrators

several books that have the same illustrator
materials that are similar to the ones used by the illustrator, such as torn paper for Ezra Jack Keats or texture collage for Jeannie Baker

- Place the books and materials in the Author/Illustrator Center.
- After the children examine the books, encourage them to experiment with the materials and create their own illustrations.
- Write each child's name on the creations she makes.

Guest Writers

no materials needed

- Encourage older children from other classes to visit your classroom and serve as guest writers in the Author/Illustrator Center.
- The visiting children can read and discuss their own writing with the younger children.

letters, packages, and other junk mail

cut or torn paper

markers, color pencils, or tempera paint

- Set out various letters, packages, and junk mail in the center for the children to use as inspiration to make their own postage stamps.
- Help the children make stamps from pieces of cut or torn paper, decorating them with markers, color pencils, or tempera paint.

Writing Wall   MOTOR DEVELOPMENT

markers and pencils

newsprint

push pins

string

- Cover one wall of the Author/Illustrator Center with newsprint, so the children can "write" big messages that would not fit on small paper.
- Put strings on markers and pencils, and, with push pins, attach them to the wall beside the newsprint so there will always be markers or pencils available for the children to use to "write" on the wall.
- Wall writing helps develop motor coordination and serves as another way to display and value children's writing.

Adding Spark to the Author/Illustrator Center

The children can select a few of their "writings" to include in a book. Bind together and place this work in the Author/Illustrator Center so the other children can check out the work of their classmates. This collection of children's "writings" may inspire others to make up and "write" their own stories.

The Essential Literacy Connection

Reading/Writing Opportunities

- Set out several books illustrated by the same individuals for the children to study.
- Help the children discriminate materials and patterns.
- Encourage the children to use writing and drawing tools.
- Help the children make a book of writings/illustrations.

Other Printed Materials

- Set out art catalogs for the children to explore.
- Explain the color wheel to the children.

Books for the Author/Illustrator Center

Carle, E. 1996. *Little Cloud*. New York: Philomel. *In this familiar storyline, which involves the whimsical world of ever-changing shapes in the sky, Little Cloud drifts away from his wispy friends and entertains himself by changing into different shapes.*

Caseley, J. 1994. *Dear Annie*. New York: HarperCollins. *Annie and her grandfather communicate over the years by writing letters to one another. They write of their lives and their visits. When Annie brings her letters for show-and-tell at school, the letters motivate her classmates to seek their own pen pals.*

dePaola, T. 2001. *Bill and Pete to the Rescue*. New York: Putnam. *Bill and Pete swim from the banks of the Nile to New Orleans. Readers find this adventure both enjoyable and exciting.*

Juster, Norton. 2005. *The Hello, Goodbye Window*. Illustrated by Chris Raschka. New York: Hyperion. *The kitchen window at Nana's house is a magical gateway for one little girl.*

Williams, V. B. 1988. *Stringbean's Trip to the Shining Sea*. Illustrated by Jennifer & Vera B. Williams. New York: Greenwillow. *A young boy, named Stringbean Coe, recounts the events of his trip out West with his brother, Fred, through a collection of picture postcards and photographs mailed back home. As each new postcard arrives, the family gets an update on the boys' latest adventures.*

Wood, A., & Wood, D. 2000. *The Napping House*. San Diego, CA: Red Wagon. *The sleepy household congregates on Granny's bed, slowly building a very relaxed pile of bodies in shifting positions.*

Evaluation of the Author/Illustrator Center

(This form is on the CD that comes with this book.)

Ask yourself the following questions to evaluate the Author/Illustrator Center in your classroom:

- Are the children "writing" and/or illustrating in the center?
- Are children interested in sharing their "writings" with their friends?
- Are children using a variety of tools for "writing" in the center?
- Are the children appreciating others' "writings" in the Author/Illustrator Center?

Observation of the Individual Child

(This form is on the CD that comes with this book. Always date observations of each child.)

- Is the child choosing to "write" or illustrate in this center? What work is she doing?
- Does the child want to share her work with others or put it away? Why?
- Have you seen the child using different tools? Which ones, and how is she manipulating them?
- Is the child beginning to use the vocabulary terms *author* and *illustrator* in appropriate ways?
- Describe the child's "writing" and "illustrating."

Summary

For over 150 years, blocks have been an essential material in classrooms for young children. Block play enhances all areas of a child's development, including the physical, social, and intellectual domains. The Block Center includes many types of building materials for children to use in their constructions and combinations. The design of this center encourages children to be active builders as they think about their constructions, discuss the possibilities, and dramatize the functions of their projects. Because the Block Center provides opened-ended materials with many possibilities, it is a wonderful place for children of differing developmental levels and abilities. Here, they will be able to build at their own levels and experience success at construction.

Introducing the Center

Visit the Block Center with the children and together examine the blocks. Discuss the similarities and differences of the blocks, as well as their uses. This is also an appropriate time to talk about the responsibilities of block play, including cleanup and respect for one another's work. By adding new materials and props, this center can stay fresh throughout the year. When you add new materials to the Block Center, support new and more complex block play by encouraging the children to discuss the new possibilities these materials present.

Learning Objectives for Children in the Block Center

1. To problem solve as they construct with blocks.
2. To expand their expressive language as they talk about building and constructing.
3. To learn to cooperate as they share and collaborate on building.
4. To recognize and appreciate the works of others.
5. To organize their world using symbolic representations in block play.

Time Frame for the Block Center

The Block Center should be available for children to use throughout the year. Occasionally adding materials and props to the Block Center enriches children's play and helps introduce new themes into the play. This will ensure that the center remains interesting and challenging all year long. Periodically adding new building materials inspires children to think and create with blocks in different ways.

 Note: The attached CD contains a sample letter to send to families, introducing them to the Block Center.

This sign communicates: "Don't touch the structure."

Vocabulary Enrichment

apartments
architect
balance
bridge
builders
complex
connector
construct
cooperate
design
foundation
garage
ground level
housing
incline
interstate
model
park
plan
pulley
shapes:
    circle
    curve
    cylinder
    rectangle
    square
    triangle
skyscraper
stable
transport
vehicle

Web of Integrated Learning

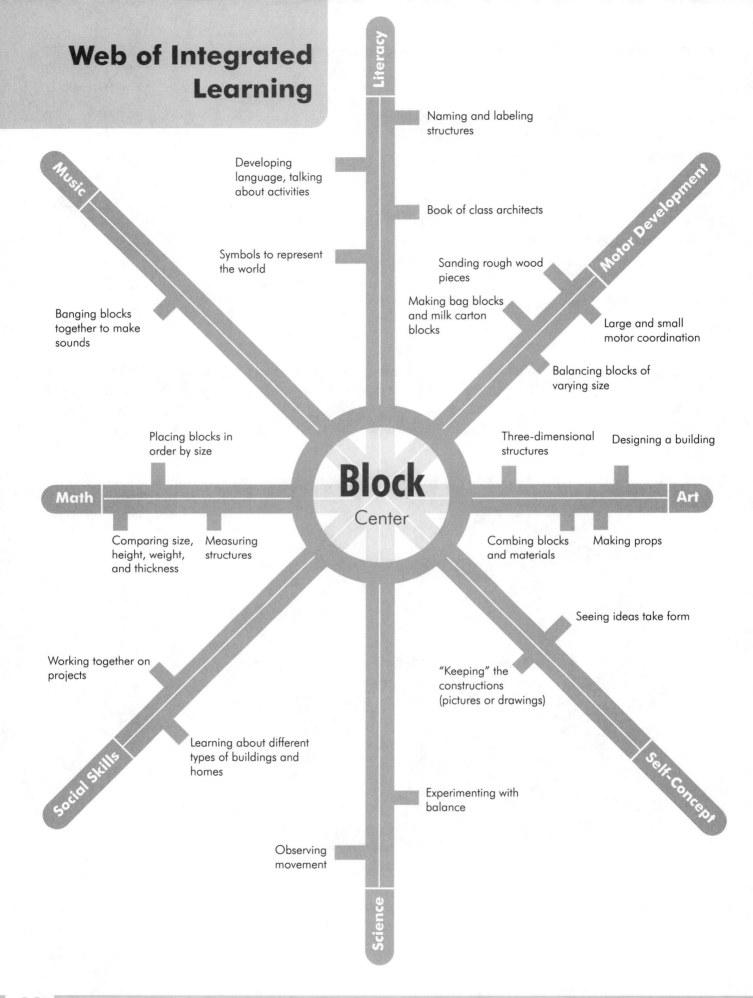

Block Center

Literacy
- Naming and labeling structures
- Developing language, talking about activities
- Book of class architects
- Symbols to represent the world

Music
- Banging blocks together to make sounds

Motor Development
- Sanding rough wood pieces
- Making bag blocks and milk carton blocks
- Large and small motor coordination
- Balancing blocks of varying size

Math
- Placing blocks in order by size
- Comparing size, height, weight, and thickness
- Measuring structures

Art
- Three-dimensional structures
- Designing a building
- Combing blocks and materials
- Making props

Social Skills
- Working together on projects
- Learning about different types of buildings and homes

Self-Concept
- Seeing ideas take form
- "Keeping" the constructions (pictures or drawings)

Science
- Experimenting with balance
- Observing movement

- ❏ foam blocks or waffle blocks
- ❏ large piece of carpet (to cover the block center floor, to absorb the sounds of the building process, and to absorb sounds from demolition of the structures)
- ❏ large hollow wood blocks
- ❏ materials that encourage dramatic play
- ❏ mechanical devices:
  - ❏ incline
  - ❏ pulley
  - ❏ wheels
- ❏ miniature animals from farms, zoo, and forest
- ❏ miniature multicultural people (men, women, and children)
- ❏ miniature transportation vehicles (cars, trucks, boats, airplanes, and buses)
- ❏ set of unit blocks (include ramps, cylinders, curves, and intersections)
- ❏ sturdy floor lamp or clip-on light
- ❏ traffic signs
- ❏ wheelbarrow, large toy truck, wagon

Blocks can be anything you want them to be.

Bag Blocks

MOTOR DEVELOPMENT

brown paper grocery bags
newspaper
stapler
tape

- Make large blocks from brown paper grocery bags to add to the Block Center.
- Crunch newspaper and pack it inside the bags until they are full.
- Staple and tape the tops closed so they are durable for block play.
- These big, lightweight blocks add variety to building materials available for use in the Block Center.

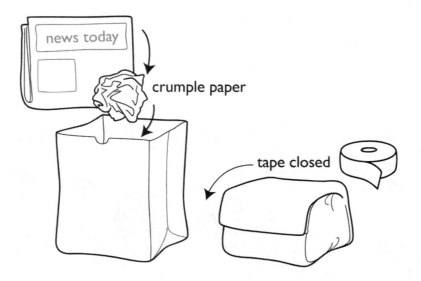

news today

crumple paper

tape closed

Inexpensive Wooden Blocks

MOTOR DEVELOPMENT

wood pieces from lumber yards
sandpaper

- Lumber companies will often donate wooden pieces that the children can use in the Block Center.
- The children prepare these blocks for the center by sanding the rough edges with sandpaper. This helps develop the children's small motor coordination.

Milk Carton Blocks

milk containers (pint and half-pint size)
sand, rice, and other similar
  granular items
tape
contact paper

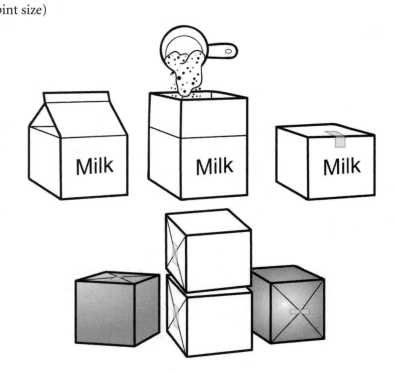

- Empty and wash several pint
  and half-pint cardboard
  milk containers.
- Set the containers out for
  the children to fill with sand,
  rice, or another material.
- Tape containers closed and
  decorate with contact paper.
- These blocks provide
  building materials for new
  projects in the center.

Stick People

stiff paper or lightweight poster board
markers
scissors
tape or glue
craft sticks or tongue depressors

- The children draw people, animals, or trees on stiff paper or lightweight poster board.
- Cut out the drawings. (Adult-only step.)
- Help the children tape or glue the drawings to the ends of craft stick or tongue depressors.
- The children use the Stick People for dramatic play in the Block Center.

Moving Blocks Outside

MOTOR DEVELOPMENT

blocks
props

- Move sets of blocks and props outside so the children can build in a different environment.
- Building with blocks in a new site can encourage the children to create in original ways. The expanded space and uneven ground present challenges that require the children to problem solve as they adjust to the natural building terrain.

Prop Boxes

SOCIAL SKILLS

(see list of specific materials for various prop boxes below)
large box
clear plastic containers
marker

- There are a number of prop boxes that you can develop to inspire new or expanded play in the Block Center.
- Collect and store these miniature materials in clear plastic containers, and label the containers with both a picture of the item and its name.
- Store the prop box materials so the children can access them easily if they have a construction idea, or keep them somewhere close to the Block Center so the teacher can put the container on the floor if the children want to use the materials in it.

Building Site Prop Box
blank paper and pencils (for creating plans)
blueprints
construction signs (keep out, caution, hard hat required, construction site)
dump trucks, crane, building machines
four-wheel dolly (like those used to move large plants)
3–4 hard hats
materials for pulley: 2 block pulleys (1 single and 1 double) and heavy twine/cord
2 measuring tapes
wheelbarrow

Farm Prop Box
fence and string/ribbon
miniature equipment: tractor, hoes, wagon, wheelbarrow
miniature people
small farm animals

Racetrack Prop Box
caution flag (yellow), finish flag/finish line
helmets
miniature cars, trucks, and wreckers
pictures of racetrack, cars, and so on
race banners (checkered flag design)
race fan t-shirts
tool box for working on cars
vinyl fabric with road track design

Safari Prop Box
binoculars
cans/packages of snack foods
fabric for tents
miniature Jeeps
miniature wild animals

Recording the Constructions

markers
paper
pictures of structures
scrapbook or paper stapled together (if desired)
tape

- It is important to help the children find ways to "keep" their block constructions. Children who invest a great deal of time and thought in a structure often do not want to take it apart when it is time to clean up.
- To preserve the children's structures, take pictures of the architects standing or sitting near their buildings.
- Post these pictures with the names of the children who contributed to building the structures on the bulletin board in the Block Center for everyone to admire long after the children dismantle the structures.
- As the photos of the structures begin to accumulate, consider collecting them into a book of "award-winning" designs. This book may also stimulate new block building ideas as the children observe other children's work.

Adding Spark to the Block Center

A unique building material encourages children to use flexible thinking while combining blocks in a new way. Consider adding a piece of plastic, linoleum, lattice, or plywood to the center. These materials challenge children to connect their structures in original ways.

Reading/Writing Opportunities

- Provide paper and charts for listing the names of the children involved in building projects.
- Provide strips of paper on which the children can "write" the names of their structures and names of the builders.

Other Printed Materials

- Use telephone books to place orders for building supplies.
- Look at newspaper flyers advertising home and building supply sales.

Books for the Block Center

Anderson, J. 2004. *How It Happens at the Building Site.* Minneapolis, MN: Clara House. *This book describes how things happen at a construction site.*

Barton, B. 1990. *Building a House.* New York: William Morrow. *This book begins with a simple blueprint of a house. It depicts the steps involved in the construction of a house from digging the foundation to the completion of the project.*

Bridges, S. 2007. *I Drive a Bulldozer.* Minneapolis, MN: Picture Window Books. *This is the story of driving a bulldozer at a construction site.*

Bridges, S. 2007. *I Drive a Dump Truck.* Minneapolis, MN: Picture Window Books. *This is the story of driving a dump truck at a construction site.*

Dahl, M. 2004. *One Big Building.* Minneapolis, MN: Picture Window Books. *This counting book follows the construction of a building from the first plans to the last of its 12 stories. Readers can find hidden numbers on an activity page.*

Hutchins, P. 1987. *Changes, Changes.* New York: Aladdin. *This wordless picture book follows two block-made characters through the building of block structures. The characters transform blocks into functional objects, such as a house, boat, train, and water hose.*

This teacher is reading a story that inspires the children's building.

Evaluation of the Block Center

(This form is on the CD that comes with this book.)

Ask yourself the following questions to evaluate the Block Center in your classroom:

- Are children working on block constructions for a focused period?
- Do children value their constructions?
- Is the children's coordination improving as they build block structures?
- Are the children discussing their ideas and creations during the building process?
- Are block constructions becoming more complex, and does the activity involve dramatic play?

Observation of the Individual Child

(This form is on the CD that comes with this book. Always date observations of each child.)

- What is the child building? How complex is the structure?
- What building-related vocabulary and language is the child using?
- Do you see evidence of cooperation? What did you observe?
- Is the child using dramatic play related to the construction? What roles, sequences, or themes is she using?
- How is the child dealing with success and failure? Provide examples.

Summary

The Home Living Center is an essential element in an early childhood classroom. This area is the perfect transition from home to school. Young children are familiar with the roles and materials available in the Home Living Center. They can be adults, children, or the family's crying baby as they dramatize familiar roles. In this safe environment, children can act out their ideas and experiment with props. Often, children who are unsure about classroom happenings will return to the predictable environment of the Home Living Center to build their self-confidence.

Introducing the Center

Introduce the Home Living Center during the first week of school. Visit the center with small groups of children and discuss the materials that are in the area. During this visit to the center, and during subsequent play in this center, remember that families today vary in composition. Children will dramatize the activities of the family and their roles as they have experienced them.

Learning Objectives for Children in the Home Living Center

1. To expand the children's oral language skills as they talk about the activities taking place.
2. To develop a positive view of their capabilities as they dramatize familiar happenings.
3. To begin to understand other people, and learn about their needs and responsibilities.
4. To use literacy materials in meaningful ways as they play in the home environment.
5. To participate in collaborative experiences related to home living.

Time Frame for the Home Living Center

Keep the Home Living Center set up during the entire year. Periodically change the props to help maintain the children's interest in it over a long period. If the materials are appropriate and change from time to time, children of varying ages and in multiage groups will enjoy participating in the Home Living Center. Be sure to include clothing for both men and women. Items from the culture of the children in the classroom will also help them make personal connections to the center. For example, food and clothing that children may see in their homes will make them feel more comfortable and inspire more play.

 Note: The attached CD contains a sample letter to send to families, introducing them to the Home Living Center.

Children collaborate in the kitchen.

Vocabulary Enrichment

baby
cleanup
clock
cooperate
cradle
dress-up
family
groceries
home
iron/ironing board
kitchen
organize
parent
photograph
prepare
refrigerator
relative
responsibilities
storage
stove
toaster
toddler
vacuum
visit

Web of Integrated Learning

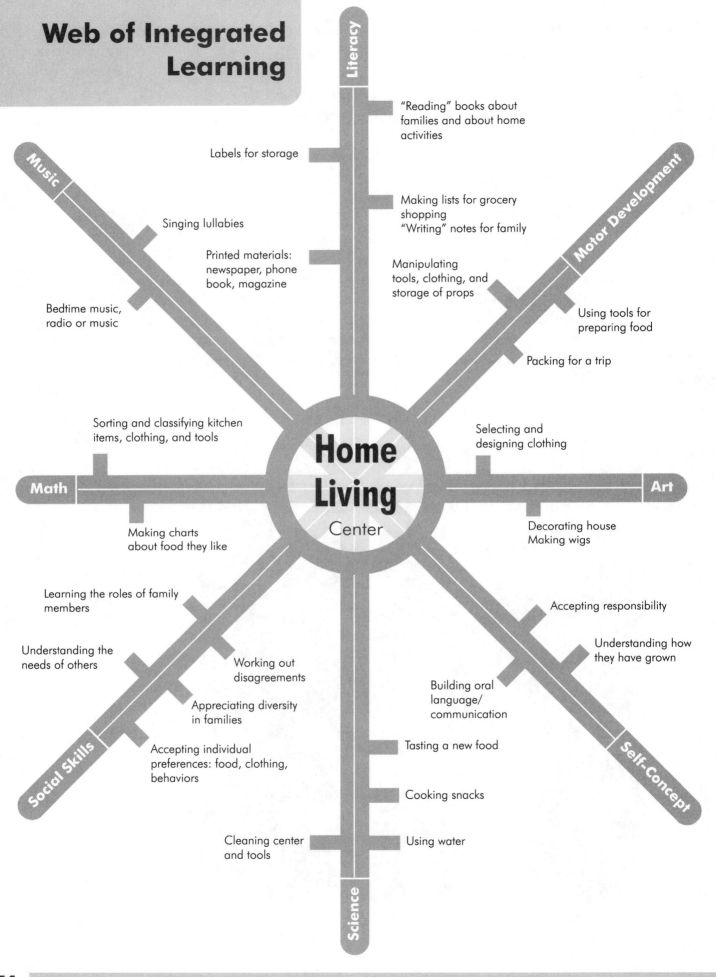

Home Living Center

Literacy
- "Reading" books about families and about home activities
- Making lists for grocery shopping "Writing" notes for family
- Manipulating tools, clothing, and storage of props

Music
- Singing lullabies
- Printed materials: newspaper, phone book, magazine
- Bedtime music, radio or music
- Labels for storage

Motor Development
- Using tools for preparing food
- Packing for a trip

Math
- Sorting and classifying kitchen items, clothing, and tools
- Making charts about food they like

Art
- Selecting and designing clothing
- Decorating house Making wigs

Social Skills
- Learning the roles of family members
- Understanding the needs of others
- Working out disagreements
- Appreciating diversity in families
- Accepting individual preferences: food, clothing, behaviors

Self-Concept
- Accepting responsibility
- Understanding how they have grown

Science
- Building oral language/ communication
- Tasting a new food
- Cooking snacks
- Using water
- Cleaning center and tools

- ❏ baby items:
  - ❏ baby bed
  - ❏ bottles
  - ❏ doll
  - ❏ high chair
- ❏ cleaning tools and materials:
  - ❏ broom
  - ❏ bucket
  - ❏ dustpan
  - ❏ mop
  - ❏ sponges
  - ❏ vacuum cleaner
- ❏ collection of dress-up clothes (clothing should be available for different genders, ages, sizes, and seasons):
  - ❏ baby clothes
  - ❏ boots (winter season)
  - ❏ clothes for adults
  - ❏ flip-flops (summer season)
  - ❏ hats
  - ❏ heavy coats (winter season)
  - ❏ mittens (winter season)
  - ❏ swimsuits (summer season)
- ❏ collection of empty containers:
  - ❏ boxes of pasta
  - ❏ cans of soup
  - ❏ cereal boxes
  - ❏ frozen vegetables
  - ❏ laundry detergent
  - ❏ spices
- ❏ communication tools:
  - ❏ cell phone
  - ❏ intercom/walkie talkie, radio
  - ❏ telephone

- ❏ cooking utensils:
  - ❏ cookie sheet
  - ❏ egg beater
  - ❏ muffin pan
  - ❏ pans
  - ❏ pots
  - ❏ rolling pin
  - ❏ skillets
- ❏ full-length unbreakable mirror
- ❏ kitchen appliances (can be made out of cardboard boxes):
  - ❏ refrigerator
  - ❏ sink
  - ❏ stove
- ❏ photographs of children and their families
- ❏ sink with cabinet for washing and storing dishes
- ❏ small table with chairs
- ❏ "sticky" notes
- ❏ white board and markers

Designer Clothes

ART

basket
belts or clothespins
pieces of fabric or scarves

- Collect pieces of scrap fabric or scarves and place them in a basket.
- Set out the basket and invite the children to tie pieces together, push fabric inside belts, or attach the pieces of cloth together with clothespins to create clothes to wear while in the Home Living Center.
- Be sure to include a floor-length unbreakable mirror in the Home Living Center, so the children can admire their creations.

Food I Like to Eat

MATH

chart paper
markers or crayons

- Make a large chart with pictures of food that children in the classroom eat.
- Invite each child to make a mark on the chart, indicating the food she likes best, or the food she would prefer to imagine cooking in the center.
- This graph visually represents the different taste preferences of the children.

Making Wigs

ART

pantyhose or sock
glue
yarn, strips of paper, or cloth

- The children will love to make wigs they can wear in the Home Living Center.
- Use pantyhose or socks to form the base. Add yarn, strips of paper, or cloth to the base to represent different hairstyles. Use old tights or socks of different colors to create pigtails, ponytails, or fancy topknots.
- These creative wigs allow the children to try out new roles and situations while they control the play.

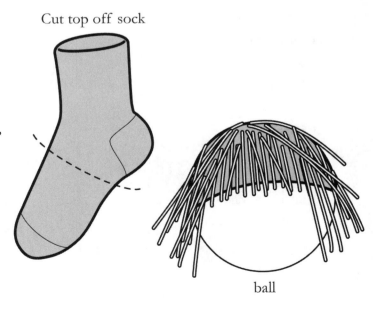

Cut top off sock

ball

markers or crayons
paper
tape

- Set out the materials for the children to use to make labels for storage in the Home Living Center.
- Help the children make outlines on sheets of paper of the smaller objects you want stored in the Home Living Center and attach them to the appropriate places on the Home Living Center's cabinets, closets, and shelves. Ask the children to make drawings of larger items, and then display the drawings in the appropriate storage areas of the Home Living Center.
- These child-made labels help the children select materials and make clean-up time easier.

Activities for the Home Living Center

A Repair Box   MOTOR DEVELOPMENT

old repair and owner's manuals
tools: bolts, fuses, pliers, screwdriver, screws, wires, wrenches, and so on
tool bag or box
receipt book and pen

- Collect tools to repair appliances in the Home Living Center. Place tools in a plastic tool bag or fishing tackle box.
  Safety note: Teach children proper use of tools and closely supervise the children's use of tools.
- Place old manuals for appliances in the tool bag/box so the children can look at the diagrams of machine parts and directions for maintenance.
- After the children finish "repairing" various items, they use a receipt book and pen to "write" bills for the work they have done.

Cleaning   LITERACY

Mouse Cleaning by Rose-Marie Provencher
cleaning materials such as sponges, mops, empty spray bottle, broom, dustpan, and so on

- After sharing *Mouse Cleaning* in circle time add new cleaning items, such as sponges, mop, empty spray bottle, broom, dustpan, and so on, to the center.

Baby Place SOCIAL SKILLS

baby bottles
baby crib
baby dolls (at least two)
baby toys
blankets
books
diapers and baby clothes
lamp
rocking chair

- Set up a baby space in the
  Home Living Center.
  Include a floor lamp or
  lighting in the space to
  encourage reading to
  babies, as well as a place for
  changing and dressing
  babies. A soft blanket is also
  helpful for rocking and
  soothing a crying baby.
- The children pretend to
  care for the baby dolls.

"Daddy" is changing a dirty diaper.

Cooking a New Food SCIENCE

ingredients for a new recipe

- Set out the ingredients for a new recipe.
- The children prepare the recipe in the center and, later, serve it to the other children during
  snack time.

cardboard pieces for the front and back covers

copies of photographs of families of children in the classroom (these will not be returned)

hole punch

lace, string, or a stapler

markers or crayons

scrapbook pages

stickers

- Set out markers, crayons, and sheets of paper. Each child can create a page for the phone book. Each page may include photos of family members or pictures cut from magazines, names of family members written on the page, a phone number (real or imagined), and any other items or decorations the child would like on the page.
- After the children finish making their pages for the phone book, collect them and set them between the two pieces of cardboard that will serve as its back and front covers.
- Use the hole punch and string or lace to tie the phone book together, or simply staple the pages along one edge. Place the phone book near the phone in the Home Living Center.

Adding Spark to the Home Living Center

A new prop often inspires different play themes in the Home Living Center. Some successful additions include a piece of hose and a firefighter's hat; a new pet (stuffed animal) with pet supplies; or a sewing box with buttons, yarn, scissors, and a large plastic needle.

Reading/Writing Opportunities

- Provide newspapers, magazines, cookbooks, books for bedtime reading, and "sticky" notepads.
- Include markers and paper for "writing" notes to family members, making out grocery lists, or "writing" recipes.

Other Printed Materials

- Bring in a phone book and catalogs.
- Provide photo albums and scrapbooks.
- Identify food labels.

Books for the Home Living Center

Baker, Jeannie. 2004. *Home.* New York: Greenwillow. *A wordless picture book that observes the changes in a neighborhood from before a girl is born until she is an adult, as it first decays and then is renewed by the efforts of the residents.*

Himes, A. G. 1988. *Daddy Makes the Best Spaghetti.* New York: Houghton Mifflin. *Not only does Corey's father make the best spaghetti, but he also dresses up as Bathman and acts like a barking dog.*

Keats, E. J. 1998. *Peter's Chair.* New York: Penguin. *When Peter discovers his blue furniture is being painted pink for a new baby sister, he rescues the last unpainted item, a chair, and runs away.*

Masurel, C. 2003. *Two Homes.* New York: Candlewick. *A young boy named Alex enjoys the homes of both of his parents who live apart but love Alex very much.*

Provencher, Rose-Marie. 2001. *Mouse Cleaning.* Illustrated by Bruno Pons. New York. Henry Holt. *Grandma Twilly is a squirrel whose house is in dire need of a thorough cleaning. Despite her overflowing laundry pile and unwashed stack of dishes, she cannot get motivated and only wants to rock in her rocking chair. However, the discovery of a mouse in her house sparks a cleaning frenzy.*

Rylant, C. 1985. *The Relatives Came.* Illustrated by Stephen Gammel. New York: Bradbury Press. *One very small house is big enough to make room for many relatives. This story describes the joys and humor of having relatives visit.*

Spinelli, E. 2002. *When Mama Comes Home Tonight.* New York: Aladdin. *When Mama arrives home, she and her child enjoy a series of activities together before bedtime.*

Evaluation of the Home Living Center

(This form is on the CD that comes with this book.)

Ask yourself the following questions to evaluate the Home Living Center in your classroom:

- Are children playing different roles in the center?
- Are children expanding their oral language as they talk with others in the center?
- Are children using the Home Living Center materials in dramatic play?
- Are children choosing to return to the Home Living Center throughout the year?
- Are the children using writing tools and books during center play?

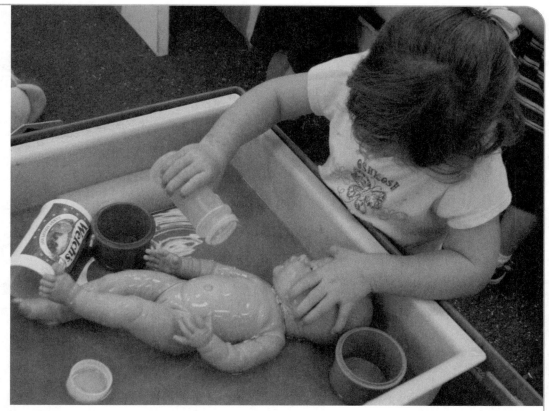

This baby doll gets a bath.

Observation of the Individual Child

(This form is on the CD that comes with this book. Always date observations of each child.)

- What language is the child using in the center? Record specific words, phrases, and ideas.
- How is the child dramatizing the different roles?
- Is the child organizing, grouping, or arranging the props? Which ones, and in what ways?
- Have you heard the child interacting with others in the center? What was the specific observation?
- Is the child able to sustain play in this safe place? How long and in what way?

Summary

The Library Center is an important area in the early childhood classroom. Its design should draw children to the area and capture their interest in books and related materials. For the center to appeal to young children, it must match their active approach to learning. The suggestions that follow help turn the Library Center into the hub of classroom activity—a place where children choose to go to "read."

A special feature, such as a tent or canopy, can help children recognize the Library Center as an interesting place. Display picture books so that the children can see the covers and select among them. Include a variety of reading materials, magazines, and children's newspaper pages to expand the possibilities and choices available to emergent readers. Soft pillows, stuffed toys, and area rugs can make the space warm and inviting. Good lighting is essential for reading and easy to achieve with the inclusion of a substantial floor lamp, clip-on lights, or a table lamp.

Introducing the Center

Take the children to visit a public library or the school library. Invite them to observe as you check out a book that you will read to them in the Library Center. Let the children know that the Library Center is a special place for enjoying books and stories in the classroom.

Learning Objectives for Children in the Library Center

1. To develop an interest in reading materials, such as books, magazines, reference materials, and recorded books.
2. To enjoy stories in different forms: recordings, flannel boards, shared reading, and storytelling.
3. To participate actively in interactions with books, turning pages, looking at pictures, "reading" books, retelling stories, and listening to stories.
4. To learn the elements of books: content (beginning, middle, end), authors, and illustrators.

Time Frame for the Library Center

A Library Center is an invaluable part of every early childhood classroom. Change the collection of books in the Library Center monthly, and include various interesting materials in the center to help maintain the children's enthusiasm throughout the year. The Library Center shows children how books are important and becomes a special place where children can enjoy books.

 Note: The attached CD contains a sample letter to send to families, introducing them to the Library Center.

The library provides a place to "read" a book independently.

Vocabulary Enrichment

author
binding
book pocket
borrow
card file
cassette tape
checkout
children's magazine
date
dictionary
flannel board
humor
illustrator
informational book
librarian
library
listening
magnet/magnetic
   board
manipulative book
picture book
read aloud
realistic story
repetition
return
storytelling

Web of Integrated Learning

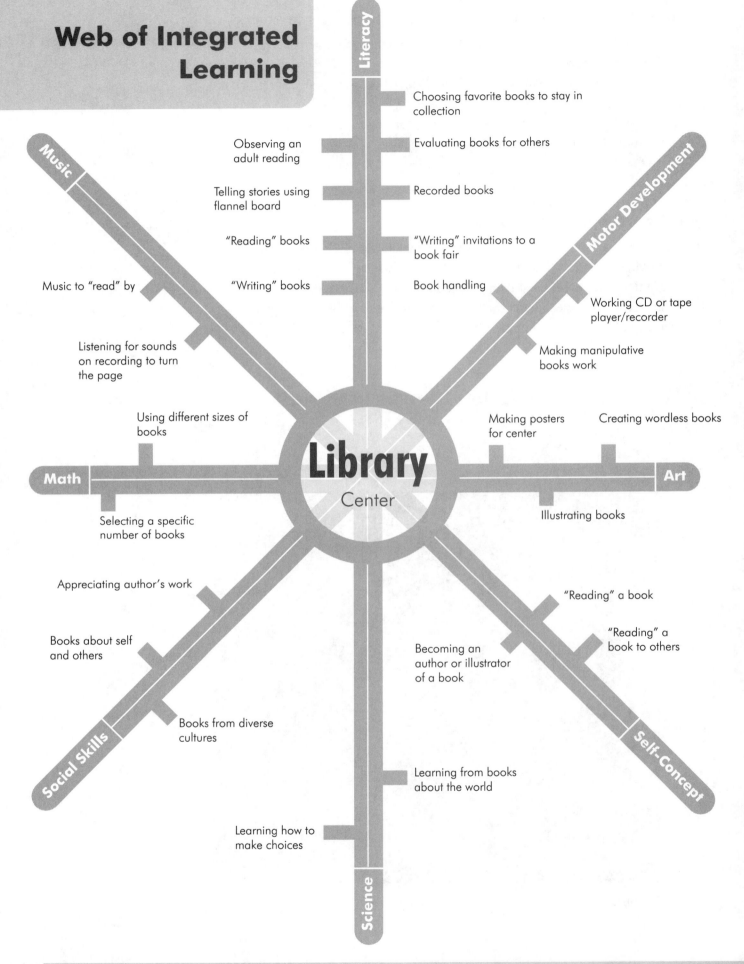

Library Center

Literacy
- Choosing favorite books to stay in collection
- Observing an adult reading
- Evaluating books for others
- Telling stories using flannel board
- Recorded books
- "Reading" books
- "Writing" invitations to a book fair
- "Writing" books
- Book handling

Music
- Music to "read" by
- Listening for sounds on recording to turn the page

Motor Development
- Working CD or tape player/recorder
- Making manipulative books work
- Making posters for center

Art
- Creating wordless books
- Illustrating books

Math
- Using different sizes of books
- Selecting a specific number of books

Self-Concept
- "Reading" a book
- "Reading" a book to others
- Becoming an author or illustrator of a book

Social Skills
- Appreciating author's work
- Books about self and others
- Books from diverse cultures

Science
- Learning from books about the world
- Learning how to make choices

- ❏ CD or tape player (one that is easy for young children to use)
- ❏ books (minimum of five) for each child who will be in the center at one time (five children in the center with five books each equals 25 books)
- ❏ children's magazines (*Ranger Rick, Ladybug, Big Backyard*, and *Sesame Street*)
- ❏ collection of children's books appropriate for the interest and developmental level of the children in the classroom
- ❏ earphones (provide private listening opportunities)
- ❏ flannel board with story pieces in zipper-close bags (used by children in retelling stories)
- ❏ lamp or clip-on light (provides a well-lighted area for better reading)
- ❏ large cardboard box (can be opened on one side to create a private reading space; a flashlight inside the box adds to the enticement of the area)
- ❏ newspapers and "Mini Page" (children's newspaper section)
- ❏ pillows that are soft and movable (such as lawn chair cushions)
- ❏ posters of book characters or pictures of children reading
- ❏ recorded books (book and recording kept together in zipper-close bags)
- ❏ rocking chair
- ❏ small table and chair (used when stamping books and signing names)
- ❏ soft area rugs
- ❏ soft cuddly animals or teddy bears for snuggling while reading
- ❏ stamp, ink pad, and cards (to check out books)
- ❏ unusual item that draws interest to the area (dome tent, bathtub, couch with legs cut off, suspended parachute, raised platform, or air mattress)

This attractive Library Center invites children to enjoy books.

Big Book LITERACY

paper
pictures of the children "reading"
stapler
tape or glue

- Take photographs of the children "reading" in the Library Center.
- Set the photographs out with several sheets of paper and tape or glue.
- A group of children can make a big book together by pasting or taping the photos of themselves to different pieces of paper.
- Once the children finish attaching the photos to paper, collect their sheets of paper and staple them together into a book.
- Label the photographs of the children with their names and the names of the books they are "reading."

Book Posters ART

markers and crayons
paint and brushes
paper, poster board, wallpaper, or cardboard (large pieces)
tape

- Set out the various materials for the children to create posters advertising a favorite book or character.
- Display these large pictures on the wall in the Library Center.

Child-Made Books ART

crayons and markers
envelopes cut in half (for library pocket)
paper
stapler
tape or glue
wallpaper samples

- The children can become authors and illustrators by making their own books for the Library Center.
- Set out paper, crayons, and markers for the children to make several drawings. They can follow a narrative that the children can dictate to you so they can include it in their books, or the books can simply contain their drawings.
- Once the children finish making their books, they can use wallpaper samples as covers of their books so they look like "the real thing."

- Help the children staple the pages together inside the wallpaper covers, so they begin to look like books.
- Write the title and name of the author and illustrator on the covers of the books.
- Help the children glue or tape cut halves of envelopes inside the back cover. These will hold library cards that the children can use to check the books out of the Library Center.

Children "Reading"   LITERACY

CD or tape recorder
books

- Make recordings of children "reading" some of the books in the Library Center.
- Include a sound, such as a handclap or beep, to let the listener know when to turn the page.
- Children love these recordings and will often choose to listen to them.

Activities for the Library Center

A Story Collection   LITERACY

construction paper, wallpaper samples, foil, and so on
paper
stapler and/or tape

- Make a book that includes stories told by children in the class.
- Ask each child to dictate a story to you.
- Once you finish recording the children's stories, the children can make an attractive cover using various materials, and then staple it to their story pages.
- This story collection may inspire the children to create new stories and retell old favorites.

Book Fair   LITERACY

books—new, used, and child-created
crayons
markers
paper

- Write a note to children's families asking them to donate books to the class for a book fair.
- Include new books, used books, books the children's families donate, and books made by the children. Help the children make and send invitations to the book fair to children in other classrooms and to their families.
- Use the money you and the children raise through the book fair to purchase additional books and story recordings for the classroom Library Center.

no materials needed

- Whenever you add a new collection of books to the Library Center, ask the children to choose which of the books already in the center should remain. This ensures that the children's old favorites will remain in the Library Center. Children enjoy "reading" these favorites repeatedly.

Flannel Board Stories   LITERACY

children's favorite books
crayons
flannel and cardboard
flannel board
glue
markers
sandpaper or felt
scissors
stiff paper or thin Pellon
zipper-close bags with labels

- Ask the children to choose their favorite books in the Library Center. Use these stories to make flannel board presentations.
- Set out stiff paper or Pellon, crayons, and markers for the children to draw the characters, scenery, and props that they will need to tell the story (they can work in small groups or individually).
- Help the children paste small pieces of coarse sandpaper or felt to the backs of the characters and scenery they have created, so they will stick to the flannel board.
- Help the children construct small, portable flannel boards by taping inexpensive flannel to cardboard.
- Place the characters and scenery along with other flannel stories in labeled, zipper-close bags and store them in the Library Center.
- Encourage the children to take a story home to share with friends and family members.
- These retelling experiences increase the child's comprehension of the story while building confidence in their language abilities.
- Invite the children to make recordings of themselves telling their stories. Others can use the recordings to act out the stories using the flannel boards and materials.

Guest Reader/Storyteller   SOCIAL SKILLS

family member or retired adult

- Ask a family member or retired adult to come to the classroom during center time.
- Ask the visitor to sit in a rocking chair in the Library Center and read a book of her choice, or to be available to read different books that the children request. Observing an adult reading helps demonstrate to the young children what happens in the Library Center.

Carlo and the Really Nice Librarian by J. Spanyol

- Read *Carlo and the Really Nice Librarian* to the children, and then engage them in a discussion about the responsibilities of workers in the library.
- This book includes pictures of a librarian working and interacting with young children.
- Sharing this book helps children understand the role of the librarian and use that information as they "pretend" in the Library Center.

Wordless Books   ART

crayons
markers
paper
plastic bags
stapler

- The children create wordless books.
- Set out crayons, markers, and paper for the children to use to draw illustrations.
- Once the children finish their drawings, help them place them inside plastic bags, then challenge the children to put the pictures in an order so that a narrative begins to form, and staple the bags into book form so that they can still remove the pictures from the bags.
- If the children want to change a picture or event in a story, show them how they can remove or reorder an illustration by taking it from its bag and inserting another version or putting the picture in a new place. Wordless books, such as those by Mercer Mayer, will inspire the children's stories.

Adding Spark to the Library Center

Observe the children as they explore the Library Center. When they begin to lose interest in the available materials, add an unusual book or new prop to the area. For example, include both large and small book versions of *Chicken Soup with Rice: A Book of Months* or *The Very Quiet Cricket* to add interest to the Library Center.

The Essential Literacy Connection

Reading/Writing Opportunities

- Ideas for signs to put up in the Library Center include a sign showing hours of operation, "no smoking," "book returns," "quiet please," and so on.
- Set out inkpads and stamps for the children to use when they check out books. Children can "sign" their names on unlined cards.
- Make a chart of favorite books by listing some books on a sheet of paper and putting it on the wall in the Library Center. Invite the children to give their reviews by drawing smiley faces beside those books they most enjoy.

Books for the Library Center

Brown, M. 2003. *D.W.'s Library Card*. Boston, MA: Little Brown. *D.W. can't wait to get a library card, but first she must learn to write her own name. She practices and practices, and finally gets a library card of her very own.*

Cousins, L. 2005. *Maisy Goes to the Library*. Cambridge, MA: Candlewick. *Maisy likes going to the library to read books in a quiet place. She and her friends soon find out that there are many things to do in the library and some of them aren't very quiet!*

Mayer, M. 1992. *A Boy, a Dog, and a Frog*. New York: Dial. *Creative drawings describe an adventurous day shared by a boy, a dog, and a frog. The three characters develop a secure and lasting relationship.*

Meister, C., & Davis, R. 2000. *Tiny Goes to the Library*. London: Puffin. *Tiny, the dog, likes to go places with his best friend. When they go to the library, Tiny has to stay outside. When they bring books home from the library, Tiny isn't much help.*

Spanyol, J. 2004. *Carlo and the Really Nice Librarian*. Cambridge, MA: Candlewick Press. *Carlo the giraffe and his friends explore the library and realize that the library is a really neat place, even if the librarian is a crocodile!*

Terry, S. 2006. *"L" Is for Library*. Illustrated by Nicole Wong. Fort Atkinson, WI: Upstart Books. *This ABC book uses the letters of the alphabet to describe everything to do with libraries.*

Books are displayed so the children can see the covers.

Evaluation of the Library Center

(This form is on the CD that comes with this book.)

Ask yourself the following questions to evaluate the Library Center in your classroom:

- Are children "reading" books in the Library Center?
- Are children choosing to go to the Library Center during free choice time?
- Are children using the props and materials in the Library Center to "read" or tell stories to others?
- Are children remaining in the area for a reasonable amount of time? Have they spent enough time to examine a book and its contents?
- Are children talking about the books or props they work with in the Library Center?

Observation of the Individual Child

(This form is on the CD that comes with this book. Always date observations of each child.)

- Is the child choosing to go to the Library Center during center time or other times during the day?
- Is the child looking at and manipulating books in the Library Center?
- How long is the child staying in the Library Center? How is she using the time?
- Is the child using any props that relate to the stories? Which ones?
- Is the child talking about any books or props in the Library Center? What language is she using?
- Are there indications that the child is enjoying the Library Center and the books in the area?

Summary

Music is an essential element in the development of the "whole child" and should be an integral part of an early childhood classroom. This Music and Sound Center provides a meaningful way for young children to develop an interest in music as they select instruments, recordings, and activities. They also have the opportunity to return to favorites that will allow for both experimentation and expansion of their musical ideas.

Introducing the Center

Music and sounds captivate young children. Beginning in infancy and continuing into childhood, music inspires joyful responses to sounds and rhythms. A Music and Sound Center is an environment where children experience sounds and create their own music. In this center, young children are the musicians, composing and often sharing their music with others. Share a ukulele, an Autoharp, a triangle, or other musical instrument that children may not have seen during circle or group time. Let children strum the strings and listen to the sounds the "new" instrument produces. Place this instrument in the Music and Sound Center at the conclusion of circle or group time.

Learning Objectives for Children in the Music and Sound Center

1. To enjoy making music and participating in musical activities.
2. To explore sounds produced by many different objects and instruments.
3. To listen to a variety of music: vocal, band, orchestra, instrumental, and group.
4. To experiment with new ways to produce music and sounds.
5. To build confidence as they gain musical experience.

Time Frame for the Music and Sound Center

Rotate the Music and Sound Center in and out of the early childhood program throughout the year, keeping it set up for approximately two to three weeks at a time. Each time the center returns to the classroom, it should renew the children's interest in making music. Sometimes, the Music and Sound Center remains in the classroom throughout the year. This generally occurs when children express continued interest in the area if the teacher has a special reason to keep it set up longer. If the center is in the classroom for an extended period, it is essential to add new elements to it frequently and to rotate different recordings in and out of the space.

 Note: The attached CD contains a sample letter to send to families, introducing them to the Music and Sound Center.

Various instruments provide a way to experiment with rhythm.

Web of Integrated Learning

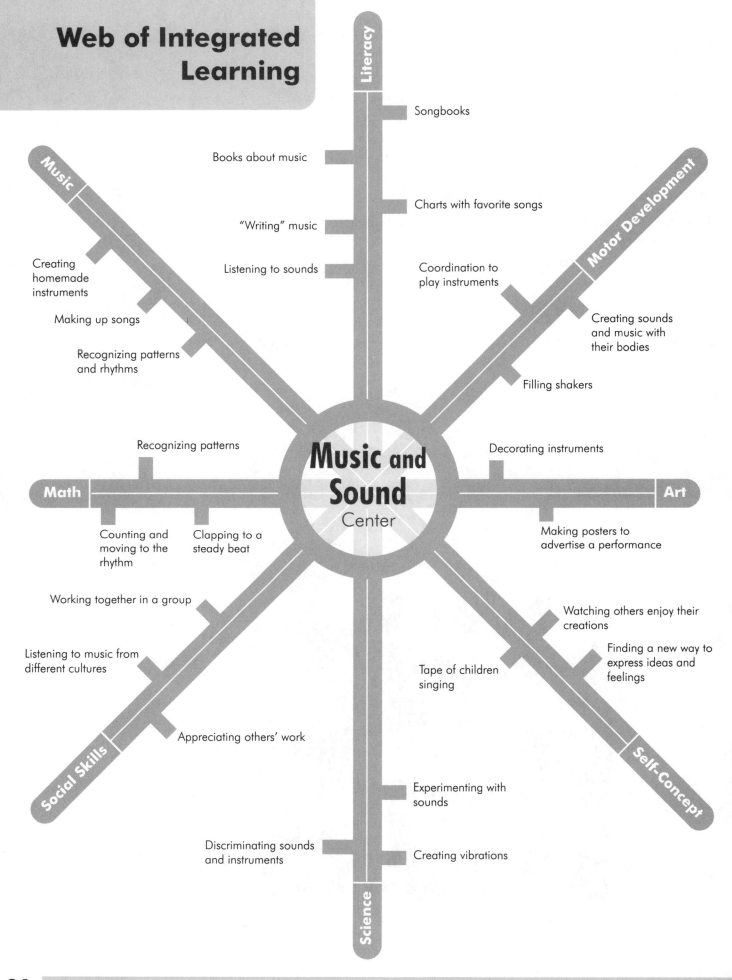

Music and Sound Center

Literacy
- Songbooks
- Books about music
- Charts with favorite songs
- "Writing" music
- Listening to sounds

Music
- Creating homemade instruments
- Making up songs
- Recognizing patterns and rhythms

Motor Development
- Coordination to play instruments
- Creating sounds and music with their bodies
- Filling shakers

Math
- Recognizing patterns
- Counting and moving to the rhythm
- Clapping to a steady beat

Art
- Decorating instruments
- Making posters to advertise a performance

Social Skills
- Working together in a group
- Listening to music from different cultures
- Appreciating others' work

Self-Concept
- Watching others enjoy their creations
- Finding a new way to express ideas and feelings

Science
- Tape of children singing
- Experimenting with sounds
- Discriminating sounds and instruments
- Creating vibrations

Family- or Teacher-Collected Props for the Music and Sound Center

❏ During the early years, it is important to expose children to a variety of music as they begin to develop preferences.

❏ CD or tape player and media (Include a variety of performers on recordings: children singing, professional performers, orchestras, and bands.)

❏ recordings of different types of music (folk, classical, bluegrass, rap, or rock)

❏ recordings of music from different cultures with appropriate instruments

❏ rhythm instruments:
   ❏ bells
   ❏ cymbals
   ❏ drums
   ❏ rhythm sticks
   ❏ sand blocks
   ❏ shakers
   ❏ triangles
   ❏ xylophone

These girls are creating rhythm patterns on the drums.

Sing a Song! SELF-CONCEPT

CD or tape recorder
crayons or markers
homemade instruments, or other small instruments
paper
pictures of children
glue or tape
cardboard rolls (from paper towels or wrapping paper)
small rubber ball

- During circle or group time, make recordings of the children singing their favorite songs.
- Set out various homemade and other small instruments for the children to use as they record their songs or replay the recordings.
- Set out paper, markers, and crayons for the children to use to make covers for their album. Add pictures of the children to the covers, as well as their names.
- Set out the recordings for the children to listen to their singing or to solos by their classmates.
- Make a microphone by gluing a small rubber ball to a cardboard roll and setting it out in the Music Center for the children to use when singing. This prop often motivates the young singers to give amazing performances.

Musical Body Sounds MOTOR DEVELOPMENT

chart tablet paper
markers

- Ask the children to find ways to make music with their bodies (clapping, tapping feet, patting chest, popping lips, and so on).
- Use these sounds to create a song.
- Set out paper and markers for the children to use to draw pictures or symbols on chart paper to make a written record of the music and to repeat the composition.
- Place these charts on the walls in the Music and Sound Center for other children to use.

Shakers MOTOR DEVELOPMENT

aluminum cans
beans, rice, bells, nuts, pennies, rocks
masking tape or contact paper

- Create shakers that vary in the sound they produce.
- Set out the various materials for the children use to fill the aluminum cans with varying amounts of beans, rice, bells, nuts, pennies, nails, or rocks.

- Help the children cover the openings on their cans with masking tape or pieces of contact paper.
- Invite the children to decorate the outsides of their can with small pieces of contact paper.
- The children shake their new instruments together, learning how each shaker produces a different sound.
- The children use the shakers to make music or accompany their singing.

Activities for the Music and Sound Center

Combo

SOCIAL SKILLS

recording device

- Ask the children to work together to create the accompaniment for a favorite song. Record their creation and place the recording in the center.

Swinging and Playing

MUSIC & MOTOR DEVELOPMENT

clear plastic containers
large screws, bells, pieces of wood, forks, spoons, plastic measuring cups, plastic bottles, and so on
rhythm sticks
twine or rope
wooden dowel

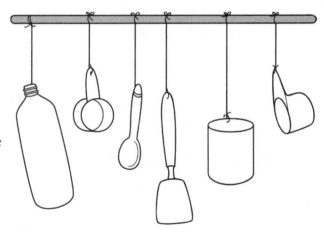

- Suspend a wooden dowel rod from the ceiling in the classroom, or hang it between two bookcases.
- The children select some of the following items: large screws, bells, pieces of wood, forks, spoons, plastic measuring cups, plastic bottles, and so on. The children use twine or rope to attach their items to the dowel rod.
- The children select the items they want to hear and then tap them with a rhythm stick or drum mallet to create a sound.
- Children can create songs by arranging a group of items on a string and playing them in sequence.

cotton
discarded pantyhose, rubber ball, or thick yarn
dowel rods (6" x ¼"–½")
glue
plastic bottles, drums, or a xylophone

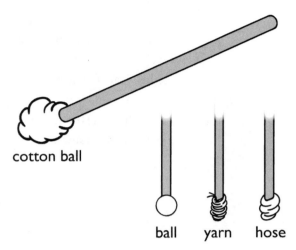

cotton ball

ball   yarn   hose

- Use a dowel rod, ¼"–½" in diameter, as the handle for the mallet.
- Make the head of the mallet by gluing a rubber ball to the base, gluing cotton to the end, wrapping pantyhose around the end, or wrapping thick yarn around the end of the dowel rod.
- Let the children experiment with the different sounds the various mallets produce when they strike plastic bottles, drums, or a xylophone.

Adding Spark to the Music and Sound Center

Invite a middle school or high school musician who plays in the band or orchestra to the Music and Sound Center. Ask this musician to play her instrument for the children to enjoy. This also encourages developing musicians.

The Essential Literacy Connection

Reading/Writing Opportunities
- Children "write" songs with pictures or symbols.
- Children "write" invitations or flyers for a concert or special performance.

Other Printed Materials
- Bring in music books of children's songs. Display catalogs of musical instruments.
- Write words of the children's favorite songs on chart paper and display them in the center.
- Provide programs from musical performances and advertisements of coming events in the newspaper.

Books for the Music and Sound Center
Brown, M. 1993. *Hand Rhymes*. New York: Puffin. *This book consists of various nursery rhymes. It includes diagrams, which allow children to reproduce fingerplays.*

Cox, J. 2003. *My Family Plays Music*. New York: Holiday House. *A musical family with talents for playing a variety of instruments enjoys getting together to celebrate.*

Isadora, R. 1979. *Ben's Trumpet*. Illustrated by David Antsey. New York: Greenwillow. *Ben pretends to play the trumpet in this story. His dream comes true when the trumpeter from the Zig Zag Jazzy Club lets Ben play his trumpet.*

Johnson, A. 2004. *Violet's Music.* Illustrated by Laura Huliska-Beith. New York: Dial. *From the days she banged her rattle in the crib, Violet has been looking for friends to share her love of music.*

Pinkney, B. 1997. *Max Found Two Sticks.* New York: Simon & Schuster. *The peace and quiet following Max's decision to put his instruments away drives the neighbors just as crazy as his constant practicing.*

Thaler, M. 2000. *Music Teacher from the Black Lagoon.* New York: Cartwheel. *A boy contemplates all the horrible stories he has heard about the music teacher, Miss LaNote, and the ordeals she forces her students to endure.*

Evaluation of the Music and Sound Center

(This form is on the CD that comes with this book.)

Ask yourself the following questions to evaluate the Music and Sound Center in your classroom:

- Are children using the musical instruments included in the center?
- Are children experimenting with different sounds the instruments and everyday objects produce?
- Are children making instruments and combining materials to create music?
- Are children enjoying different kinds of music?
- Are children gaining confidence in their musical abilities?

A keyboard provides another way to compose music.

Observation of the Individual Child

(This form is on the CD that comes with this book. Always date observations of each child.)

- Is the child choosing to go the Music and Sound Center? What is she doing in the area?
- Have you observed the child experimenting with different sounds and instruments? In what ways?
- Is the child listening to different types of music? Is there a specific type of music in which she indicates a special interest?
- Is the child performing individually or with others? In what way?
- Is this an area of special interest for this child? How was this determined?

How is sand used?

Sand Art

funnels

shovels and cups

blocks

animals

cars and trucks

Summary

Sand and Water play is important for young children. These natural materials encourage them to explore and experiment as they learn about their world. As children interact with the materials, they refine their coordination and develop new approaches for successful use of tools. Children's interest in sand and water makes this center an effective place to increase their attention span while involving them in meaningful activities. It is possible to separate these two natural materials into individual centers: Sand Center or Water Center. The children can use many of the same tools and activities with either or both of the centers.

Manipulating sand and water is a sensory experience that involves seeing, touching, hearing, and moving. Young children need these real materials to explore their senses and provide appropriate opportunities for enriching this area of development. Sand and water are also very responsive materials to young children's manipulations and provide immediate feedback when they are pouring, digging, dipping, and measuring. This responsiveness helps children understand how to influence the environment and make changes.

Introducing the Center

Because sand and water fascinate young children, simply discuss with the children the properties of the two materials. Pose questions such as, "Have you ever touched sand or water? How does it feel? Can you hold it in your hands? How could you move it from place to place?" Share a plastic measuring cup. Ask, "How could you use this cup in the center?" Let them manipulate a clear piece of plastic tubing. Ask, "What could you do with this in the center?" Focus on involving the children in interactive conversations about the natural materials.

Learning Objectives for Children in the Sand and Water Center

1. To learn about natural elements in the environment.
2. To develop small motor coordination as they manipulate the materials and tools.
3. To experiment with material that is immediately responsive to their actions.
4. To use problem solving as they explore the properties of sand and water.
5. To develop their senses of sight, touch, and movement.
6. To use language to describe the properties of sand and water.

Time Frame for the Sand and Water Center

This center can include either sand or water, or both. This will determine the amount of time that this center should be set up in the classroom. Different combinations of natural materials and tools will make this an effective center to rotate in and out of the classroom throughout the year. Consider moving the center outside when the weather permits.

 Note: The attached CD contains a sample letter to send to families, introducing them to the Sand and Water Center.

Dirt responds in new ways when children are using spoons and cups.

Vocabulary Enrichment

change

clean up

dip

examine

experiment

float/sink

funnel

height/depth

measure

miniature

mold

more/less

pattern

pour

respond

scientific

scoop

sift

smooth/rough

storage

texture

tool

track

tunnel

wet/dry

wheel

Web of Integrated Learning

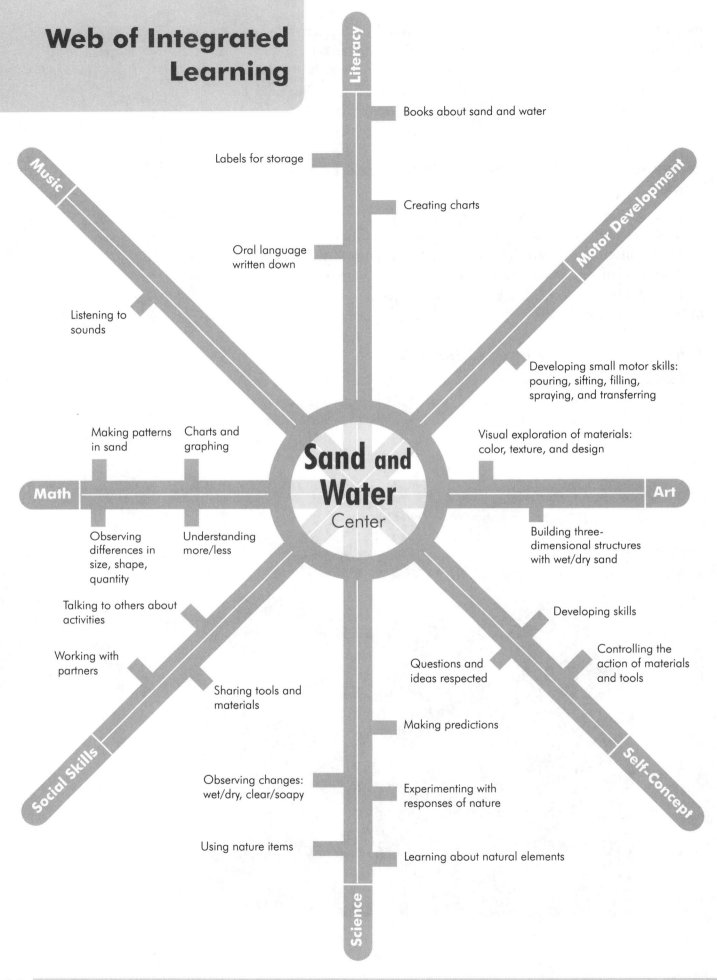

Literacy
- Books about sand and water
- Labels for storage
- Creating charts
- Oral language written down

Music
- Listening to sounds

Motor Development
- Developing small motor skills: pouring, sifting, filling, spraying, and transferring

Math
- Making patterns in sand
- Charts and graphing
- Observing differences in size, shape, quantity
- Understanding more/less

Art
- Visual exploration of materials: color, texture, and design
- Building three-dimensional structures with wet/dry sand

Sand and Water Center

Social Skills
- Talking to others about activities
- Working with partners
- Sharing tools and materials

Self-Concept
- Developing skills
- Controlling the action of materials and tools
- Questions and ideas respected

Science
- Making predictions
- Observing changes: wet/dry, clear/soapy
- Experimenting with responses of nature
- Using nature items
- Learning about natural elements

Family- or Teacher-Collected Props for the Sand and Water Center

- ❏ bag of sterilized play sand
- ❏ balance scale
- ❏ broom and dustpan
- ❏ clear plastic boxes (to store and organize props)
- ❏ funnels
- ❏ hand vacuum cleaner
- ❏ kitchen tools:
  - ❏ egg beaters
  - ❏ ladles
  - ❏ large spoons (with and without strainer holes)
  - ❏ margarine tubs
  - ❏ plastic salt shakers
  - ❏ tongs
  - ❏ medicine droppers
  - ❏ plastic eggs
  - ❏ plastic measuring spoons
  - ❏ plastic nested measuring cups
- ❏ plastic or shower curtain liners (Place on the tabletop and on the floor under the sand and water sites.)
- ❏ plastic tubing
- ❏ plastic turkey basting syringes
- ❏ rocks, pebbles, pieces of wood, shells
- ❏ rubber animals
- ❏ sand and/or water table (Make economical tables, by using plastic baby tubs on low tables.)
- ❏ small broom and dustpan or small hand-held vacuum
- ❏ small buckets and shovels
- ❏ small plastic wheeled toys
- ❏ sponges
- ❏ spray bottles containing water (to dampen sand and keep dust down)
- ❏ strainer
- ❏ straws
- ❏ toy people
- ❏ various sizes of plastic bottles (including squirt and spray containers)
- ❏ whisks

Children discover that wet sand and dry sand respond differently.

Building Boats
SCIENCE

corks
glue
small scraps of paper
Styrofoam or wood pieces
toothpicks

- Children design and build boats or other items for water activities.
- After the children create their boats, invite them to test them in the water to see if they will float.

Child-Made Sifters
MOTOR DEVELOPMENT

disposable pie pans or cooking pans of various sizes
pencil or other writing tool

- Set out the disposable pie pans and pencils.
- Help the children use the pencils to poke holes through the bottoms of the pans, making basic sifters. Some may have a few holes and others may have many.
- The children experiment with their sifters in the Sand and Water Center. They will discover that the number of holes they poked in the sifters will affect the flow of the sand or water.

Funnels for Pouring
MOTOR DEVELOPMENT

heavy paper, foil, plastic-covered shelf liner (consider using plastic cups with younger children)
tape or stapler
scissors

- The children how to roll the paper into a cone. (Offer help as needed.)
- The children staple or tape their cones together and cut a hole in the bottom of each cone.
- The children experiment with pouring sand and water through the funnel.
- They may find ways of improving their designs.

Hole in the Cup
SCIENCE

collection of paper and Styrofoam cups in a variety of sizes
pencil or small paintbrush
sand, water, small pebbles

- Each child punches a hole (or multiple holes) in the bottom of a cup. (Offer help as needed.)
- The children pour or dip water, sand, or small pebbles into the cup.
- The children describe the amounts of water, sand, or small pebbles that flow through the holes in their cups.

box (plastic)
nature items: acorns, feathers, pieces of bark, leaves, pinecones, rocks, and so on

- Bring the children on a walk or field trip to collect items from nature.
- After they finish collecting several items, return to the classroom.
- Place the materials in a plastic box and encourage the children to use the materials in play activities in the Sand and Water Center.

Activities for the Sand and Water Center

Dramatic Play SOCIAL SKILLS

fish/sea creatures (plastic)
small plastic people

- Add small plastic toy people to inspire dramatic play in the sand area.
- The toys encourage children to take on roles, discuss happenings, and dramatize activities as they participate in the center.

Mud Play MOTOR DEVELOPMENT

Amazing Mud by Jean Anderson
mud at water table

- Read *Amazing Mud* to the children or talk with them about mud.
- Set out a muddy mixture of dirt and water on the water table.
- Allow the children to experience the unique experience of mud in the water table by exploring it and experimenting with it.

New Materials SCIENCE

- Change the children's sand and water play experience by adding a different material in the table or tub. Some examples that have worked effectively with young children include the following:

confetti (small strips of colorful paper)
dirt/mud
ice cubes
pebbles added to sand
sawdust or large wood shavings
shells
snow
Styrofoam pieces

mild dishwashing detergent

baby doll clothes or plastic dishes

drying rack

large sheet of paper

marker

● Add a mild dishwashing detergent to the water table to produce bubbles and promote washing activities.

● The children can wash baby doll clothes and place them on a folding drying rack or to wash plastic dishes from different activities.

● Let the children discover that that soapy water cleans items that clear water alone cannot clean.

● After using soapy water, use a large sheet of paper to make a chart of the children's discussions of the similarities and differences of the two types of water.

Clear and Soapy Water

Differences	Similarities
1. Soapy water gets things cleaner.	2. Both are wet.

Wet and Dry (Sand)

We Use Water by Robin Nelson

cookie cutters

gelatin molds

ice cubes

marker

measuring spoons

paper

plastic measuring cup

small plastic bucket

small water sprayer/mister

● Read a book about the opposites of wet and dry, or discuss the concepts of wet and dry with the children.

● During circle or group time or in the Sand and Water Center, discuss with the children the similarities and differences in wet and dry sand. Help them explore the various textures by pouring, dipping, and using objects to make imprints in the sand.

● Use a large sheet of paper to create a chart about the children's observations of the differences between wet and dry sand.

● Display the chart in the center.

Adding Spark to the Sand and Water Center

- Colored water—If children are losing interest in water play, add food coloring to the water. Colored water provides a new incentive to play in the center and sparks imagination.

Children exploring water and its properties

The Essential Literacy Connection

Reading/Writing Opportunities

- Read books to the children about sand, water, mud, and wet/dry.
- Help the children create a chart from their descriptions of sand and water.
- Create charts that record the children's predictions about whether objects will float or sink.
- Make a book illustrating the tools the children used in sand and water play. Include the names of the children who used the tools.
- Provide water colors, paintbrushes, and paper (than can be wetted) for the children to experiment with creating pictures and symbols.

Books for the Sand and Water Center

Anderson, J. 2006. *Amazing Mud*. Reading essentials. Logan, IA: Perfection Learning. *This book introduces mud to young children, and it includes an experiment to show which type of soil makes the best mud pies. The author also includes a description on how to make a miniature mud house.*

Asch, F. 2000. *Water*. San Diego, CA: Voyager Books. *This picture book illustrates the importance of water. Asch identifies the many places that water is found.*

London, J. 2001. *Sun Dance, Water Dance*. Illustrated by Greg Couch. New York: Penguin. *London's flowing text takes an energetic group of kids through a hot, sunny day to a cool, starry night.*

Nelson, R. 2003. *We Use Water*. Minneapolis, MN: Lerner. *Children explore the many uses of water in daily life.*

Peters, L. W. 1988. *The Sun, the Wind and the Rain*. Illustrated by Ted Rand. New York: Henry Holt. *This is the story of two mountains, the earth's foundation, and Elizabeth's mountain made of sand. The illustrations demonstrate how the earth began and how small streams grow into rivers.*

Prager, E. 2000. *Jump into Science: Sand*. Illustrated by Nancy Woodman. Washington, DC: National Geographic Society. *This book gives a description of how sand forms, what it is made of, and how it moves from place to place.*

Evaluation of the Sand and Water Center

(This form is on the CD that comes with this book.)
Ask yourself the following questions to evaluate the Sand and Water Center in your classroom:

- Are the children exploring the properties of sand/water?
- Do children choose a variety of props to experiment in the Sand and Water Center?
- Are children improving their small motor coordination as they use tools to pour, sift, and fill?
- Are the children using the materials responsibly and cleaning up when they finish playing in the center?
- Are the children discussing their activities as they participate in the center?

What can you do with water?

(This form is on the CD that comes with this book. Always date observations of each child.)

- How does the child react to the sand and water? Does she enjoy or avoid it?
- How is the child using her hands and fingers when sifting, pouring, feeling, or moving the natural materials (small motor coordination)?
- Is the child aware and noticing the movement and response of the sand and water? How?
- Is there evidence that the child is using problem-solving skills while experimenting with materials? What did you observe?

Water is always fascinating to young children.

- Is the child using her senses to explore sand/water? How?
- Have you seen the child participating in the care and cleanup of the center? In what ways?
- If a child is seeking or avoiding contact with sand and/or water, refer to *Sensory Integration* by Christy Isbell and Rebecca Isbell, available from Gryphon House.

Summary

Young children are curious about the things in their world. Encourage their exploration in the Science and Nature Center, where children become scientists, learning about materials they have seen, or exploring new items that capture their interest. This area allows children to examine things closely, compare and contrast, and draw conclusions about their observations. In this center, nature and young children combine to produce a stimulating environment that provides a positive base for the beginnings of scientific inquiry.

Introducing the Center

Bring in a nature item that will be of interest to the children during circle or group time. For example, in the fall you could share acorns, pinecones, various nuts, bird nests, and so on. In the spring use a flower bulb, such as narcissus or crocus, to stimulate interest, talk about planting, and make predictions about the blooms. Then, place the bulbs and materials needed for planting in the Science and Nature Center where children can plan, observe, and record the changes that take place. Also, set up a chart where children can document the plants' growth and changes.

Learning Objectives for Children in the Science and Nature Center

1. To learn about the natural environment.
2. To encourage experimentation with materials and tools.
3. To gain an appreciation for the use of scientific methods of inquiry.
4. To follow a systematic method for observing and recording information.
5. To nurture an interest in nature and the environment in which they live.

Time Frame for the Science and Nature Center

Use the Science and Nature Center throughout the year—adding items that are part of seasonal changes as those changes occur. Basic science items, such as a magnifying glass, clear plastic containers, and so on, can remain the same while the new natural, seasonal items will help renew interest in the center over time.

Note: The attached CD contains a sample letter to send to families, introducing them to the Science and Nature Center.

A Science and Nature Center invites children to examine objects.

Vocabulary Enrichment

arrange

chart

collect

compare

conclusion

curious

discover

display

environment

estimate

examine

guess

label

measure

nature

observe

order

predict

protect

question

same/different

select

sort/classify

time

Web of Integrated Learning

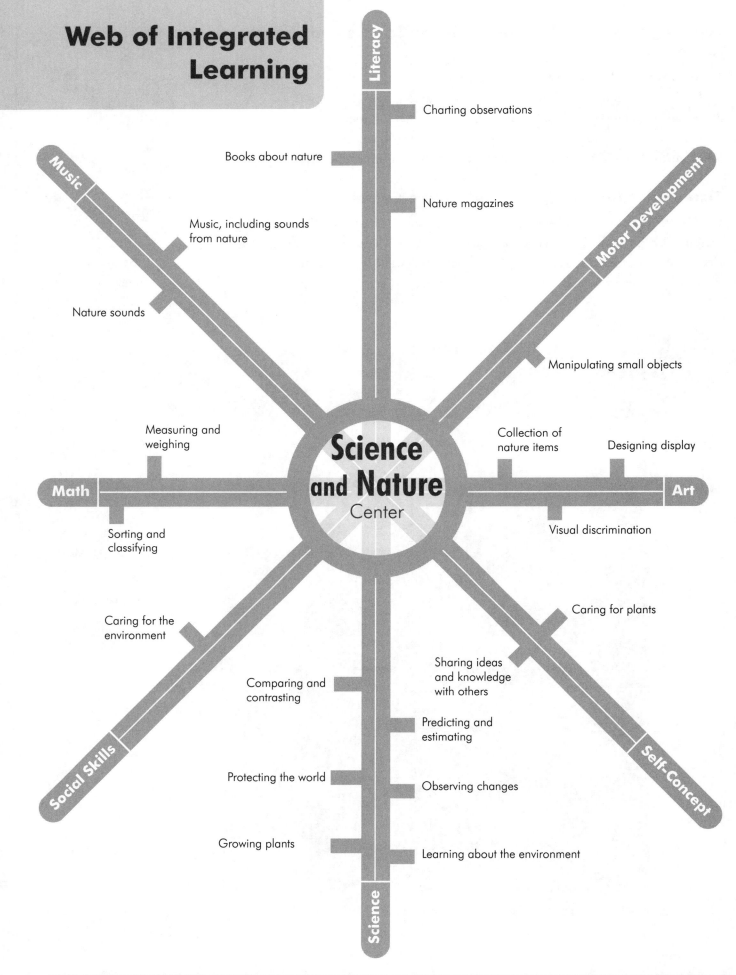

Science and Nature Center

Literacy
- Charting observations
- Books about nature
- Nature magazines

Music
- Music, including sounds from nature
- Nature sounds

Motor Development
- Manipulating small objects

Math
- Measuring and weighing
- Sorting and classifying

Art
- Collection of nature items
- Designing display
- Visual discrimination

Social Skills
- Caring for the environment
- Comparing and contrasting

Self-Concept
- Caring for plants
- Sharing ideas and knowledge with others

Science
- Predicting and estimating
- Protecting the world
- Observing changes
- Growing plants
- Learning about the environment

Family- or Teacher-Collected Props for the Science and Nature Center

- ❏ aquarium (for fish or for growing plants)
- ❏ balance scale
- ❏ boxes for display
- ❏ chart paper and markers
- ❏ class pet (guinea pig, white mouse, hermit crab, or hamster)
- ❏ clear plastic jars with lids
- ❏ eyedroppers
- ❏ funnels
- ❏ gloves
- ❏ large colander
- ❏ large magnifying glass
- ❏ measuring tools, cups, spoons
- ❏ plastic tubing
- ❏ plastic tubs
- ❏ sponges
- ❏ tweezers
- ❏ unbreakable mirror

How does a frog feel?

Collections

collection of nature items:

acorns	leaves
birdseed	moss
butterflies	pinecones
feathers	plants
flowers	rocks
insects	shells
plastic containers	twigs

- Bring the children on a nature walk and collect various nature items.
- Set out several plastic containers that the children can use to collect, sort, and store their natural items.
- The children can examine, compare, and contrast the items in their collections.

Tunneling Worm Farm

bag of potting soil

clear plastic 1-liter bottles (soda bottles work well)

duct tape

piece of black construction paper

scissors

spray bottle filled with water, or access to a sink

tape

vegetable or fruit scraps or honey with cornmeal

worms dug from flower beds (spring through fall) or purchased from
   bait store/fishing shop or pet shop

- Cut the top portions off of several clear plastic bottles. Cover any sharp edges with duct tape. Make a few small holes in their bottoms to drain excess water (adult-only step).
- Set out the containers for the children to wash and clean.
- The children measure and dip potting soil into the plastic containers, filling them so the soil stands 2"–3" from the top.
- The children use the spray bottle or sink to spray the dirt with water.
- Set out the container of worms. The children place a few on the tops of their containers. The worms will dig their way into the soil.
- Help the children cover the outsides of their bottles with black construction paper. This will encourage the worms to build tunnels next to the bottles' clear walls.
- Later, the children remove the construction paper for a view of the tunnels. Place the paper back on the bottle after viewing, so the worms will continue to have a good environment for living and sleeping.
- Feed worms with vegetable/fruit scraps or honey with cornmeal by placing the food on the top of the soil.

Growing Plants

SCIENCE

pot with soil, cup and toothpicks, or rooting compound   markers
seeds, a potato, or plant   paper

- With the children, grow plants from seeds, from a potato, or from plants propagated from another plant.
- Observe and record the changes that occur as the plant grows.

Litter Collection

SOCIAL SKILLS

garbage bags   latex gloves

- During outdoor time, provide the children with several bags for them to use to collect litter. Be sure to remind the children only to collect litter that is free of contaminants (no food wrappers or obviously germ-ridden items).
  Note: Give the children gloves to wear as they collect the litter.
- Place the litter in the Science and Nature Center and engage the children in a comparison of these items to nature items.

Nature Walk

LITERACY

Lost in the Woods by Carl R. Sams   chart table paper and markers

- Read *Lost in the Woods* to the children.
- Take the children on a nature walk.
- After the walk, ask the children to draw the things they saw on their trip or help them make a chart of what they saw.
- If the children make drawings, attach the drawings to a large piece of paper in the order in which the children observed them.

Predicting and Estimating

SCIENCE

chart
markers
materials from nature

- Pose questions to the children, such as: "How many acorns are in this jar?" or "Which is heavier, a container of leaves or a container of pine needles?"
- Encourage the children to find answers by experimenting with materials in the center.
- Record the results on a chart in the Science and Nature Center.

Print in Playdough   ART

nature items   playdough

- Show the children how to create impressions of natural items by pressing them into playdough.
- Examine the impressions with the children, looking for and identifying details.
- The children can let the playdough harden so it keeps its impression, or they can return it to its container to use it again later.

Rocks   MATH

collection of rocks   measuring tape or ruler
scale

- Add a collection of rocks to the Science and Nature Center.
- Invite the children to pick up and compare and contrast the rocks.
- The children can weigh, measure, and classify the rocks in their collection.

Rubbings   ART

crayons with paper removed   paper

- Show the children how to make rubbings of nature items by placing paper over the items and rubbing the paper with a dark, peeled crayon.
- Once the children finish their rubbings, ask them to bring all the rubbings to the Science and Nature Center.
- Engage the children in a discussion of the differences and similarities between the various rubbings.

Adding Spark to the Science and Nature Center

Place straws next to a plastic bowl containing a mixture of dishwashing liquid and warm water about 2"–3" deep. Encourage children in the center to investigate the mixture to see how they can use straws to manipulate and change the liquid. Let children record their experiences by drawing pictures of their observations.

The Essential Literacy Connection

Reading/Writing Opportunities

- Make pamphlets and reference books about nature, science, and experiments available to the children.
- Create charts the children can use for observation and study, and help them record information on charts.
- Label items so the children can experience the spelling of the items' names.
- Graph, chart, and record information the children collect in the center.
- Keep a journal of what the children see and experience on a nature walk or field trip.

Other Printed Materials

- Bring in a book about the care of the class pet.
- Provide science magazines, such as *Your Big Backyard* and *Ranger Rick*.

Books for the Science and Nature Center

Carle, E. 2004. *A House for Hermit Crab.* New York: Little Simon. *Hermit Crab moves out of his small home on the sea floor in search of a new residence. He meets many friends along the way in his quest for finding the perfect home.*

Fleming, D. 1995. *In the Tall, Tall Grass.* New York: Henry Holt. *Bold, bright, stylized collage illustrations capture the eye and imagination while the simple, rhyming text tells this outstanding nature tale.*

Hawes, J. 1991. *Fireflies in the Night.* Illustrated by Ellen Alexander. New York: HarperCollins. *A favorite grandfather shares the magic of nature with a little girl.*

Hoban, T. 1990. *Shadows and Reflections.* New York: Greenwillow. *Photographs without text illustrate shadows and reflections of various objects, animals, and people.*

Sams, Carl R., & Stoick, Jean. 2004. *Lost in the Woods: A Photographic Fantasy.* Milford, MI: Carl R. Sams Photography. *The forest is abuzz over a newborn fawn. Various creatures have spotted him and all are worried that he may be lost. Despite his assurance that he is just waiting for his mother, the animals chime in with comments and offers of help. She returns, time passes, and the fawn grows stronger. He sees other young animals maturing, and by the end of the story, he is big enough to go exploring with his mother.*

Wick, W. 2004. *Can You See What I See? Cool collections: picture puzzles to search and solve.* New York: Scholastic, Inc. *Readers search for hidden objects in photographs of buttons, dinosaurs, robots, shells, cars, animals, leaves, beads, game pieces, and the contents of a junk drawer.*

Evaluation of the Science and Nature Center

(This form is on the CD that comes with this book.)

Ask yourself the following questions to evaluate the Science and Nature Center in your classroom:

- Are children interested in the items included in the Science and Nature Center?
- Are children talking to each other about the nature items?
- Are children examining and exploring materials with the tools available in a systematic way?
- Are the children using charting and/or other methods to record information?
- Are the children finding new ways to learn about nature?

Observation of the Individual Child

(This form is on the CD that comes with this book. Always date observations of each child.)

- What interests the child the most in the Science and Nature Center?
- Is the child using new vocabulary in communication or play? What is an example?
- Is this child studying items in a systematic way? How?
- Have you seen the child enter records on a chart or in a book? Explain.
- Is the child using books, brochures, and charts in the center? Which is she using, and how?

Summary

Young children are in a period of rapid development in many areas. In motor development, there are major changes in large or gross movement, walking, running, and throwing. However, less visible changes also occur as young children gain skills in using their small motor abilities. The Small Motor Center focuses on small- or fine-motor activities and provides interesting possibilities that allow each young child to work on a level that is appropriate for her. The open-ended, challenging experiences provide opportunities for children to experiment, practice, and extend their small motor coordination. They will increasingly refine their skills as they use them when dressing, drawing, cutting, writing, and lacing.

Introducing the Center

Collect a number of toys or materials for the children to use in the Small Motor Center. Place these inside a wrapped cardboard box, complete with lid. During circle or group time, encourage the children to reach inside the box and pull out an item. With the children, discuss what the item is and how they might use it. Some items that may capture their interest include golf tees, small plastic cups, small nuts, small blocks, and miniature figures.

Learning Objectives for Children in the Small Motor Center

1. To develop small motor coordination by participating in activities.
2. To improve children's skills in dressing, drawing, and cutting.
3. To experiment with a variety of tools that the children can use with their hands.
4. To gain confidence in the ability to use small motor skills.
5. To cooperate with others in projects and activities.
6. To use oral communication.

Time Frame for the Small Motor Center

This center can be set up in the classroom many times during the year. Most young children will need a variety of opportunities to explore, use, and refine their small motor skills. Because this center provides meaningful activities that the child is able to select, it is especially helpful in encouraging small motor development. Consider placing some of the materials from this center in other areas of the classroom when the Small Motor Center is not available. Reintroduce this center throughout the year and observe the children's growing competencies.

 Note: The attached CD contains a sample letter to send to families, introducing them to the Small Motor Center.

Vocabulary Enrichment

assembly
attach
base
build
clothespin
connect
coordination
fit
follow
glue
lace
miniature
nuts
puzzle
same/different
scissors
small/large
sort
steady beat
store
trace
tread
trim

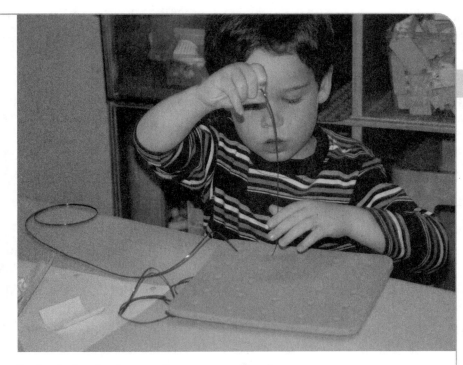

Lacing helps develop small motor coordination.

Web of Integrated Learning

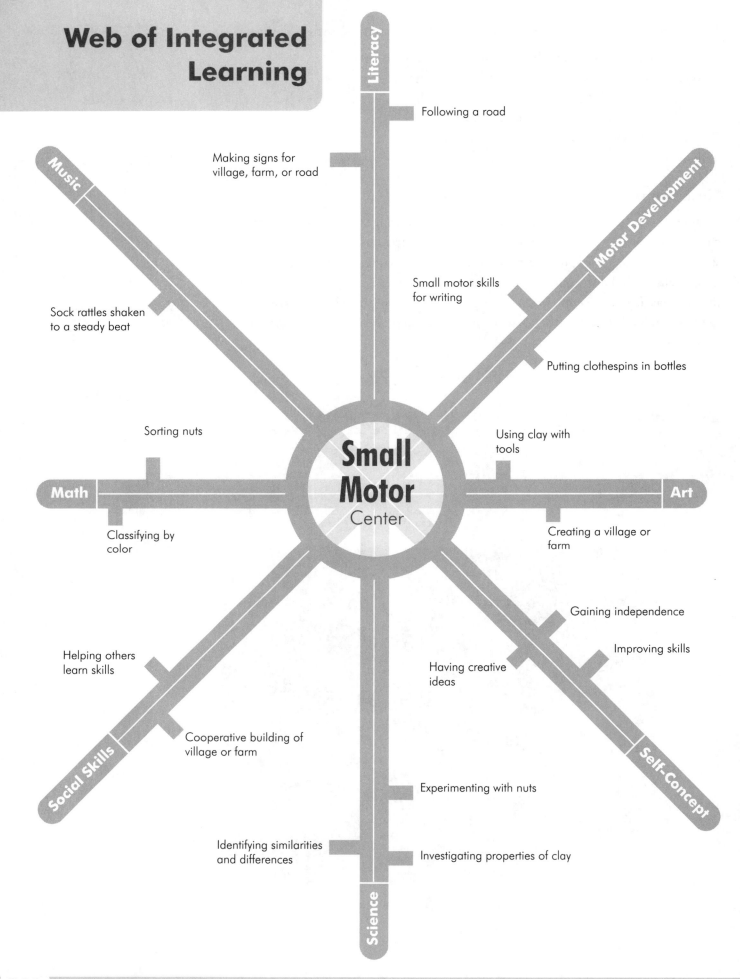

Small Motor Center

Literacy
- Following a road
- Making signs for village, farm, or road
- Small motor skills for writing

Motor Development
- Putting clothespins in bottles
- Using clay with tools

Art
- Creating a village or farm

Self-Concept
- Gaining independence
- Improving skills
- Having creative ideas

Science
- Experimenting with nuts
- Investigating properties of clay
- Identifying similarities and differences

Social Skills
- Cooperative building of village or farm
- Helping others learn skills

Math
- Classifying by color
- Sorting nuts

Music
- Sock rattles shaken to a steady beat

Family- or Teacher-Collected Props for the Small Motor Center

- ❏ brushes and paint
- ❏ cardboard, plywood, or foam board pieces
- ❏ chalk, markers, color pencils
- ❏ clay
- ❏ clear plastic zipper-closure bags
- ❏ golf tees, toothpicks, small dowel rods
- ❏ miniature blocks
- ❏ peg boards
- ❏ puzzles
- ❏ Q-tips, medicine droppers, small spoons, tongs

- ❏ sandpaper block
- ❏ scraps of contact paper
- ❏ scissors and clippers
- ❏ small beads
- ❏ small cardboard boxes
- ❏ small people, animals, cars/trucks
- ❏ small scraps of wood
- ❏ small sheets of colored paper
- ❏ thick yarn or shoestrings
- ❏ variety of clear plastic bottles and containers

Styrofoam is easy to hammer and connect with pegs.

Collecting and Sorting

MATH

items that can the children use to build a model village or farm

plastic containers

- Ask the children to go on a hunt through the classroom to find small items that they can use to build a miniature village or farm.
- Once the children identify and collect these items, ask the children to group them in plastic containers.
- They can draw or "write" labels for the containers.
- Store the containers in the Small Motor Center.

Sock Rattle

MUSIC

boom box

CD of marching or steady-beat music

old clean white adult athletic socks

small pebbles or nuts

small plastic container or tub for butter or cream cheese

- Set out the small containers and socks. Ask each child to put one container inside the bottom of a sock.
- Next, help the children put small pebbles or nuts into the plastic container inside the sock, then twist the top of the sock and pull it down over the container. This will secure the pebbles or nuts inside the sock.
- Invite the children to select the music they will play as they keep time using their sock rattles.
- Place the sock rattles in the Small Motor Center.

Sorting Game

MATH

box to hold bags and nut collections

collection of a variety of nuts (five or six of each kind):

    acorns

    almonds

    Brazil nuts

    chestnuts

    pecans

    walnuts

small plastic zipper-closure bags

- Place all the nuts in a box, along with several small, clear plastic bags.
- First, invite the children to explore the different types of nuts: how they feel, look, move, and so on.

- Next, ask the children to look for similar and matching nuts, and place the similar nuts in bags together.
- After sorting, ask the children to place the plastic bags filled with nuts in the Small Motor Center.

Activities for the Small Motor Center

Clay and Tools

A R T

artist clay
clear plastic container containing the following tools:
    forks
    pebbles
    pencils
    plastic knives
    plastic ruler
    small rolling pin
plastic shower curtain
small tub of water

- Cover a low table with the plastic shower curtain.
- Place the containers of tools and water on the table.
- Set out the artist clay. The children can experiment with the clay by rolling it into balls or making "snakes."
- They may also roll out the clay and use the tools to make patterns or cut the clay.

Fill the Bottle

MOTOR DEVELOPMENT

variety of clear plastic bottles: 1-liter and 12-ounce sizes
plastic colored clothespins
colored stickers consistent with colors of clothespins
plastic container to hold items

- Set out the bottles and clothespins for the children to explore.
- After a period of exploration, they can begin to deposit the clothespins into the bottles. At first, the children will simply put the clothespins in and take them out of the bottles.
- Later, place a different-colored sticker on the outside of each bottle, and several matching dots on the clothespins inside those bottles.
- Some children will want to sort the pins by color and placing them in the appropriate bottle.
- When finished, empty and store all the bottles in a container in the Small Motor Center.

cardboard rolls (from paper towels, wrapping paper, and so on)
colored construction paper
glue
large sheet of butcher paper
large Styrofoam piece
markers
masking tape
miniature people or animals
sand
scissors
small cardboard boxes
small plastic cups
stones
toothpicks
twigs
yarn or string

- Engage the children in a discussion about parts of the village or farm they want to create. The children may what they want to create and draw a plan on the butcher paper. During this process, the children can experiment with making houses, trees, roads, rivers, fences, and so on.
- Set out the various materials the children can use to create their model village or farm.
- Using their plans, they can try out their ideas and re-plan, if adjustments are needed.
- Consider placing the butcher paper plan on top of a Styrofoam base and attaching it with toothpicks or tape.
- Leave the village or farm on the table so other children can add to the plot over the entire period you have the Small Motor Center set up in the classroom.

Nutty Stringing   MOTOR DEVELOPMENT

collection of metal/iron nuts in various sizes, thicknesses, and shapes (these are available
   at building supply stores)
containers to hold nuts
5 or 6 heavy-duty shoestrings

- Set out the containers of various nuts for the children to explore.
- Once the children are familiar with the nuts, they can use the shoestrings for creating necklaces, bracelets, or other items. The children will likely need assistance in making a knot in the end of the shoestring, so the nuts will not fall off.

collection of small cars and trucks

colored electrical tape

large piece of vinyl, cardboard, or white-erase board (preferably a light color)

washable markers

- Place the piece of board on the ground, and set out washable markers so the children can draw the outline of a track for their cars and trucks. Help the children use the colorful electrical tape to create starting and finishing lines on the board.
- Once the children complete the track, encourage them to drive their cars and trucks around the track, starting and finishing where appropriate.

Adding Spark to the Small Motor Center

Ask a family member or carpenter to visit the center and bring wood scraps. Have sandpaper or sandpaper blocks available for the visitor and children to use. Cover the floor with a plastic tablecloth or shower curtain. Invite the children to sit on the floor and sand the rough edges of the wood scraps. Add these to the Small Motor Center or the Block Center when they are smooth to the touch. Also, consider painting or decorating the blocks.

The Essential Literacy Connection

Reading/Writing Opportunities

- Make signs for the village, farm, or roadways.
- All small motor activities help children develop the coordination necessary for writing.

Other Printed Materials

- Engage the children in a discussion about typical road signs. Set out examples for them to see.
- Attach labels to bottles and containers to help the children identify what the containers hold.

Books for the Small Motor Center

Pluckrose, H. 1995. *Sorting.* San Francisco, CA: Children's Press. *Children can work at solving math problems with this fun and colorful book. The photographs and simple text encourage children to talk about mathematical topics.*

Steiner, J. 1999. *Look-Alikes, Jr.: The More You Look, the More You See!* Boston, MA: Little Brown. *Simple verses challenge readers to identify the everyday objects that make up 11 three-dimensional scenes, including a house, kitchen, bedroom, school bus, train, farm, and rocket.*

Wick, W. 2002. *Can You See What I See?* New York: Scholastic Inc. *This search-and-find puzzle book is wonderfully designed and illustrated to catch the attention of young readers.*

Evaluation of the Small Motor Center

(This form is on the CD that comes with this book.)

Ask yourself the following questions to evaluate the Small Motor Center in your classroom:

- Are the children choosing to work in this center?
- What materials and toys are they finding interesting?
- Are there adequate possibilities for small motor development?
- Do you see children working together on any of the activities?
- Are children persistent and focused on activities? Which ones?
- What new vocabulary and language are the children using during the experiences in the Small Motor Center?

Observation of the Individual Child

(This form is on the CD that comes with this book. Always date observations of each child.)

- How is this child using small motor skills? Give an example that demonstrates your conclusion.
- Is the child working on any activity for an extended period? Which one, and for how long?
- Has this child assisted another child in the center? Who, and in what way?
- Have you observed any improvement in the child's small motor skills? What have you observed specifically and using what material?
- Does the child choose to go to this center? What if you suggest it to her?
- What seems to be the most difficult task for this child? What follow-up activities might help the child master this task?

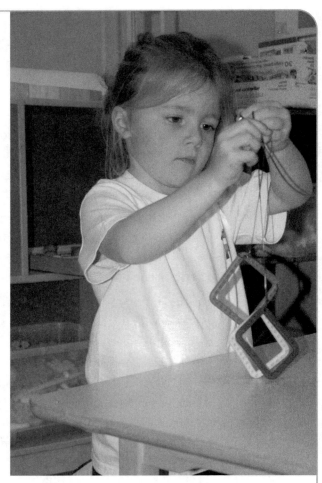

Stringing objects is difficult for many young children.

Sociodramatic Centers:

Encouraging Role-Playing and Cooperative Play

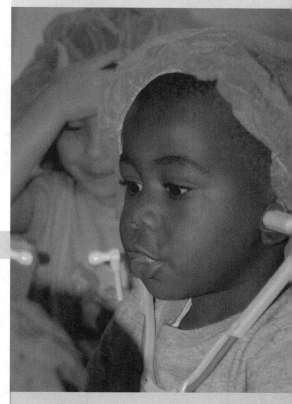

This chapter focuses on centers that encourage sociodramatic play. This type of play includes role-playing, cooperation, talking with each other, and developing a sequence of events during play. Although many centers provide opportunities for this type of play, the sociodramatic centers in this section are especially effective for nurturing children's growing capabilities related to play that is more complex. Because these centers relate to places and people that many young children have experienced, they provide the setting and props for being a doctor, salesperson, or restaurant server.

Select the sociodramatic centers your children have experienced, or take the children on a field trip so you can develop their understanding of what happens in particular workplaces, stimulate their thinking, and provide the content for their role-playing. Sociodramatic center encourages children to develop language skills as they talk to other children, enhance communication skills as they role-play and set up play activities in the center, learn about their world as they recreate realistic situations, and develop problem-solving skills.

Bakery and Cooking Center

Construction Center

Doctor's Office Center

Garage Sale or Flea Market Center

Grocery Store Center

Long Ago Center

Mall Center

Pet Store Center

Repair Shop Center

Restaurant Center

Sign Shop Center

Toy Workshop Center

Summary

Young children enjoy cooking activities. They can talk, read, follow directions, and conclude with a delicious creation they can eat. The Bakery and Cooking Center captures young children's interest and extends the cooking experience into dramatic play. It also encourages children to select specific roles, play in sequence, and discuss their cooking experiences. This stimulating theme environment provides young children with many opportunities to expand their understanding through meaningful activities.

Introducing the Center

Introduce the children to the Bakery and Cooking Center by collecting cooking utensils that people typically use in bakeries or kitchens. At circle or group time, present these utensils (hidden inside a cake box or large box) to the children. Interesting cooking items include a large wooden spoon, an egg beater, a pastry cutter, and a frosting tube. Identify the tools and discuss with the children the proper ways to use these tools. After circle or group time, place these items in the Bakery and Cooking Center for the children to explore and use.

Learning Objectives for Children in the Bakery and Cooking Center

1. To work cooperatively to make a product.
2. To use reading and writing in functional ways.
3. To develop their language skills by discussing the cooking experience.
4. To learn about the work people in the community do and the services they provide.
5. To observe the ways ingredients change through dipping, stirring, cooking, or freezing.

Time Frame for the Bakery and Cooking Center

The Bakery and Cooking Center provides interesting activities for approximately two to three weeks. Observe the children in the center. If play is becoming repetitive, change or close the Bakery and Cooking Center.

 Note: The attached CD contains a sample letter to send to families, introducing them to the Bakery and Cooking Center.

Realistic props help these boys role-play.

Vocabulary Enrichment

apron
baker's dozen
blending
chef
cook
cooling rack
customer
decorate
filling
hot plate
icing/frosting
ingredient
measuring cup
measuring spoon
mixer
muffin tin
oven
preheat
recipe
rise
sale
sample
sifting
spice
stir
temperature
utensil

Web of Integrated Learning

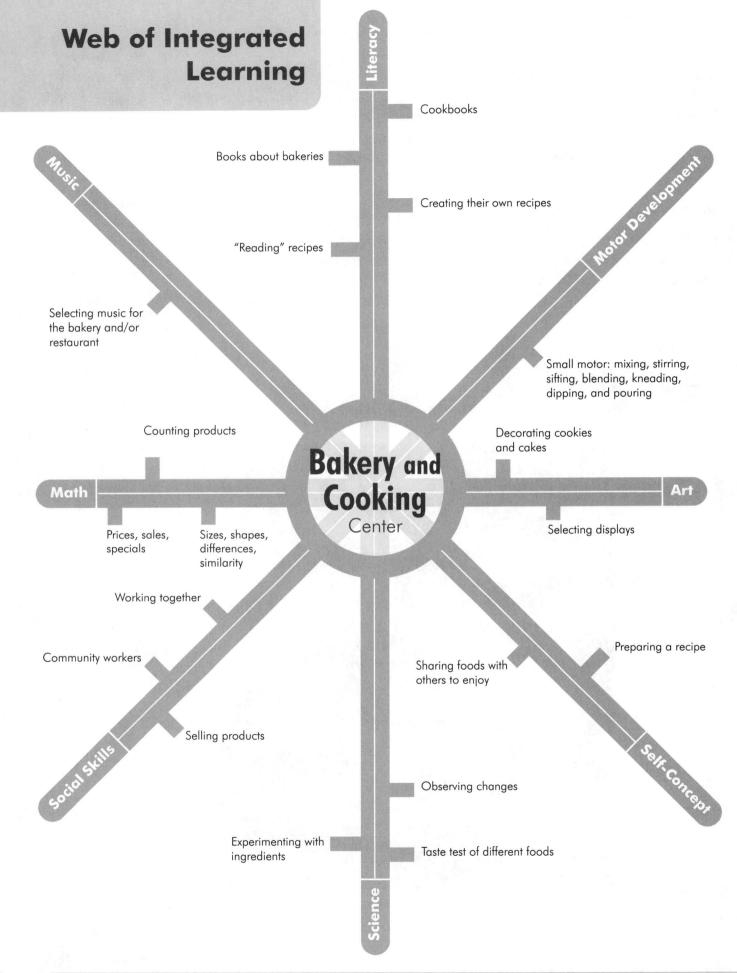

Bakery and Cooking Center

Literacy
- Cookbooks
- Books about bakeries
- Creating their own recipes
- "Reading" recipes

Music
- Selecting music for the bakery and/or restaurant

Motor Development
- Small motor: mixing, stirring, sifting, blending, kneading, dipping, and pouring

Math
- Counting products
- Prices, sales, specials
- Sizes, shapes, differences, similarity

Art
- Decorating cookies and cakes
- Selecting displays
- Preparing a recipe

Social Skills
- Working together
- Community workers
- Selling products

Self-Concept
- Sharing foods with others to enjoy

Science
- Observing changes
- Experimenting with ingredients
- Taste test of different foods

- ❏ bakery boxes and bags
- ❏ cash register
- ❏ cooking utensils:
  - ❏ cookie sheets
  - ❏ cooling rack
  - ❏ crock pot
  - ❏ hand-turned mixer
  - ❏ large bowl
  - ❏ large spoons
  - ❏ measuring tools
  - ❏ pie pans
  - ❏ rolling pin
- ❏ display items:
  - ❏ clear cake storage
  - ❏ clear containers
  - ❏ plastic jars
  - ❏ electric skillet
  - ❏ hot pads

An oven mitt protects his hands while he bakes.

Advertisements for the Bakery
LITERACY

    markers and crayons
    newspaper advertisements
    old magazines
    paper
    scissors
    tape

- The children think of a name for the bakery. Once they decide on a name, they use paper, markers, and crayons to design signs for the bakery as well as lists of the items they want to make available. Show the children old newspaper and magazine advertisements to give them ideas about how to design their signs.
- The children create a menu that includes items and prices.
- Make signs that display names and prices of items and put the signs on the wall.
- Display these signs and the menu at the entrance to the center as well as inside the bakery.

Bakery Oven
MOTOR DEVELOPMENT

    large appliance box
    scissors
    spools and metal lids
    tape and glue

- Bakers prepare many items at the same time, so they need a large industrial-size oven.
- With the children, build an enormous oven using a large cardboard appliance box.
- The children make the oven more interesting by attaching spools and metal lids for the controls so the children can adjust the temperature from broil to bake.
- The children will love to use this oven to prepare large numbers of cookies, muffins, or loaves of bread.

Chef's Hats and Aprons
MOTOR DEVELOPMENT

    old sheets or white paper bags
    poster board
    stapler
    scissors
    markers
    glue

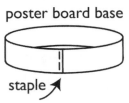

poster board base

staple

- Construct a chef's hat out of old sheets or white paper bags and poster board by wrapping the material into a large tube and stapling it so the form will hold.
- Staple a headband made of poster board around the inside of each chef's hat.
- The children write their names or the name of the bakery on their hats.
- Make simple aprons out of sheets and decorate them with markers or attach trim to them by gluing material to the fabric.

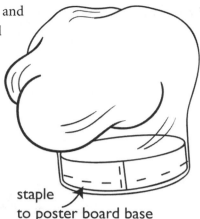

staple
to poster board base

Class Cookbook

LITERACY

cookbooks
copies of recipes from home
stapler
recipe cards

- Set out cookbooks and recipe cards in the Bakery and Cooking Center for the children to explore.
- At the end of the day, the children ask their parents or family members to share copies of recipes that their children like to eat at home.
- When the children come in the next day, collect the recipes their family members copied for them, and engage the children in a discussion about the recipes.
- After discussing the recipes, the children to select their favorites and place them in a large cookbook.
- Set this cookbook of the class's favorite recipes in the Bakery and Cooking Center for the children to "read" and try preparing.

Food Mural

MATH

child-safe scissors
glue
large sheet of paper
magazines
tape

- Set out several magazines that contain pictures of food.
- The children look through the magazines and cut out pictures of food that they might buy at a bakery, and then glue these pictures on a large sheet of paper to display in the Bakery and Cooking Center.
- The children discuss the items in the bakery and determine which foods they would like to cook in the center.

alum (1 rounded teaspoon)

bowl and spoon

flour (1 cup)

paint, if desired

salt (1 cup)

trays

water

- The children create cookies and pastries for the bakery using playdough that hardens.
- The children paint these "pretend" pastries and then place them on trays for display in the Bakery and Cooking Center. One successful recipe is below:

Salt and Alum Modeling Dough (From *Mudworks: Creative Clay, Dough, and Modeling Experiences*, by MaryAnn Kohl. Reprinted with permission from Bright Ring Publishing.)
- Add water slowly to the alum, flour, and salt in a bowl.
- Knead until clay-like.
- Model, as with any clay.
- Dry to extreme hardness and paint, if desired.

Activities for the Bakery and Cooking Center

A Busy Day at the Bakery   SOCIAL SKILLS

Out and About at the Bakery by Jennifer A. Ericsson

- Read *Out and About at the Bakery* to the children during circle or group time.
- Follow this with a discussion of what it would be like to work in a bakery on a busy day.
- Ask the children to dramatize what it would be like to have several orders that the children need to prepare in a hurry.
- Extend this play into the Bakery and Cooking Center.

Cake Decorating   SOCIAL SKILLS

cupcakes (one for each child)

frosting

family member or professional cake decorator

plastic bags

scissors

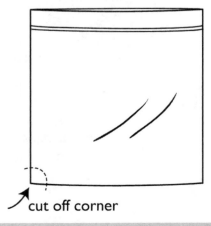
cut off corner

- Before the activity, cut small holes in the corners of several plastic bags. The children fill the plastic bags with various colors of frosting.

- Ask a family member or professional cake decorator to come demonstrate his or her decorating skills for the children.
- After the demonstration, set out several cupcakes and the plastic bags full of frosting and invite each child to decorate one cupcake.
- It is important for each child to have the opportunity to create his own design and give it a personal taste test.

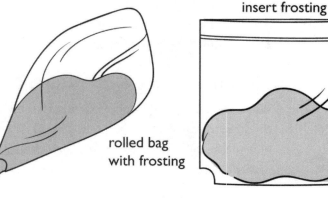

insert frosting

rolled bag with frosting

Create Your Own Snack

SELF-CONCEPT

ingredients (in bowls): chow mein noodles, different dry cereals, pretzels, raisins, small crackers, small marshmallows
markers
paper
plastic bags
tape

- Set out the out bowls of ingredients for the children to combine in several different ways, and then put their mixtures into plastic bags.
- Help the children write out the various ingredients in their mixtures on sheets of paper and attach these lists to their packages, dictate some of the ingredients in their mixture, or draw pictures that represent the items. These can be attached to the snack they have created.

New Product

SOCIAL SKILLS

new recipe or bakery product

- Display a new recipe or set out a new bakery product for the young bakers to taste.
- The children discuss the new product and decide whether they want to add this item to their menu.
- This provides the children with an opportunity to learn that individuals have different taste preferences.

Visit the Kitchen

SOCIAL SKILLS

chart tablet
markers

- Visit the center kitchen, or take the children on a field trip to a local bakery.
- Many centers and schools have large stoves, ovens, refrigerators, mixers, and cooking utensils. Ask the kitchen staff to describe them to the children.

- After the children return to the classroom, set out paper and markers for the children to "write" notes or draw pictures for the staff of the kitchen they visited.
- Copy down the notes that children dictate to you and add them to the thank-you notes.

Adding Spark to the Bakery and Cooking Center

When the Bakery and Cooking Center is losing momentum, have a "real" bake sale. Help the children prepare cookies, party mix, bread, or cupcakes to sell to other children in the program or to family members as they pick up their children. This helps children make the connection between the real world of work and customers and their pretend play.

The Essential Literacy Connection

Reading/Writing Opportunities

- Set out reference books and cookbooks for the children to explore.
- Make signs for items in the center. Be sure to include their prices.
- Create a class cookbook, containing several of the children's favorite recipes.
- Make recipe cards that can be copied and given to families.
- Include a pad and pencil in the center so the children can take "customers'" orders. This order form helps children to start to understand the usefulness of writing and keeping records of transactions.
- Paper and markers are useful for creating advertising specials or announcing new products.
- Write thank-you notes to the kitchen staff.
- Write or dictate the ingredients in their trail mix.

Other Printed Materials

- Pick up some price lists from local bakeries.
- Bring in recipe files and cookbooks.
- Look at magazines that include pictures and recipes of food preparation.
- Display newspaper advertisements for bakery items.

Books for the Bakery and Cooking Center

Cousins, L. 1999. *Maisy Makes Gingerbread.* Cambridge, MA: Candlewick Press. *Maisy and her friends mix, roll, cut, and bake gingerbread.*

Ericsson, Jennifer. 2003. *Out and About at the Bakery.* Illustrated by Anne McMullen. Minneapolis, MN: Picture Window Books. *Children in the story take a field trip to the bakery.*

Freeman, D. 2004. *Corduroy Writes a Letter.* London, UK: Puffin. *Lisa notices that her favorite cookies have fewer sprinkles, so her mother suggests that Lisa write a letter to the bakery. Lisa is too afraid to write a letter, but Corduroy isn't. He writes the letter for her. Will the baker listen to advice from a bear?*

Hutchins, P. 1986. *The Doorbell Rang.* New York: Greenwillow Books. *Each time the doorbell rings, more friends come to taste Ma's delicious cookies. When the cookies are gone, Grandma appears with a fresh batch, just in time!*

Lillegard, D. 1986. *I Can Be a Baker.* Chicago: Children's Press. *This book describes the variety of equipment that a bakery uses. It shows how to prepare different pastries and breads.*

Numeroff, L. 1985. *If You Give a Mouse a Cookie.* Illustrated by Felicia Bond. New York: HarperCollins. *Bright illustrations and repetitive language in this book convey a sequence of events that results from giving an energetic mouse a cookie.*

Evaluation of the Bakery and Cooking Center

(This form is on the CD that comes with this book.)

Ask yourself the following questions to evaluate the Bakery and Cooking Center in your classroom:

- Are the children talking about the bakery activities as they participate in them?
- Are children using cookbooks, recipe cards, or other printed materials as they work in the Bakery and Cooking Center?
- Are children cooperating as they prepare and sell bakery products?
- Are children participating in "reading" and "writing" activities in the bakery?
- Are children demonstrating an increased understanding of the functions and roles of workers and customers in a bakery?

Observation of the Individual Child

(This form is on the CD that comes with this book. Always date observations of each child.)

- Is the child involved in the cooking in the Bakery and Cooking Center? In what way?
- What vocabulary does the child use as he participates in the center?
- Do you observe the child using "reading" and "writing" in appropriate and meaningful ways? Explain.
- Is the child working with other children to create a recipe or cooking experience?
- Is the child role-playing? What role is he playing, and how does he depict it?

Summary

The Construction Center encourages young children to plan, problem solve, and build. In this center, children will design and create buildings and structures that challenge their thinking. In the Construction Center, children draw, nail, glue, and combine materials in more permanent ways than are available in the Block Center. The center also encourages the children to expand and embellish their structures over the period that it is in operation. Be sure to display the final products, making the names of their designers and builders visible so all can see and appreciate their work. The different building techniques, longer work period, and the complex products the children create make the Construction Center an important addition to the early childhood classroom.

Introducing the Center

Introduce the children to the Construction Center at circle or group time by setting out a collection of materials that will be in the center. Include Styrofoam pieces, corrugated cardboard, metal and plastic containers, bubble wrap, and scraps of lumber. Invite the children to examine, feel, and discuss the materials. Demonstrate ways to attach the materials and ask the children for suggestions of other ways to combine pieces. Return these materials to the Construction Center for the children to use.

Learning Objectives for Children in the Construction Center

1. To design and construct three-dimensional products.
2. To use creative thinking as they solve problems while building.
3. To increase their self-confidence as they complete the constructions and display their work.
4. To develop flexible thinking as they use new and unique materials.
5. To develop collaborative skills while working with others on design and building.

Time Frame for the Construction Center

Include the Construction Center in the early childhood classroom at different times during the year. Located nearby, it can serve as an extension of the Block Center. If working in a small classroom, consider transforming the Block Center into the Construction Center for several weeks. Usually, a two- to three-week period is an appropriate period to have the Construction Center in operation. After the second week, observe children in the center to determine if it needs a new spark to keep the center functioning effectively. If there is construction going on around the school, revive the Construction Center in the classroom by visiting the worksite. Return to the building site over several days or weeks so children can observe and discuss the changes that occur in the construction process.

 Note: The attached CD contains a sample letter to send to families, introducing them to the Construction Center.

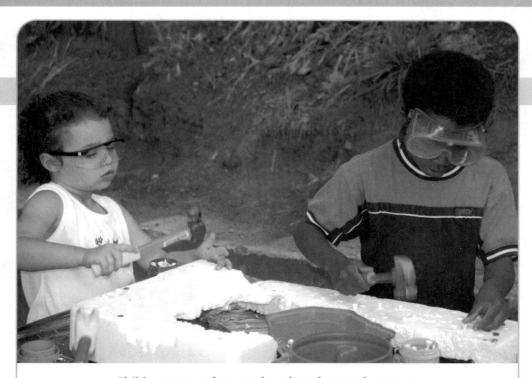
Children wear safety goggles when they use hammers.

Vocabulary Enrichment

attach
blueprint
carpenter
clamp
combine
construction worker
contract
design
drill
frame
glue
golf tee
hammer
hardhat
lumber
nail
project director
saw
screwdriver
secure
site
Styrofoam
tool box
tool
woodworking

Web of Integrated Learning

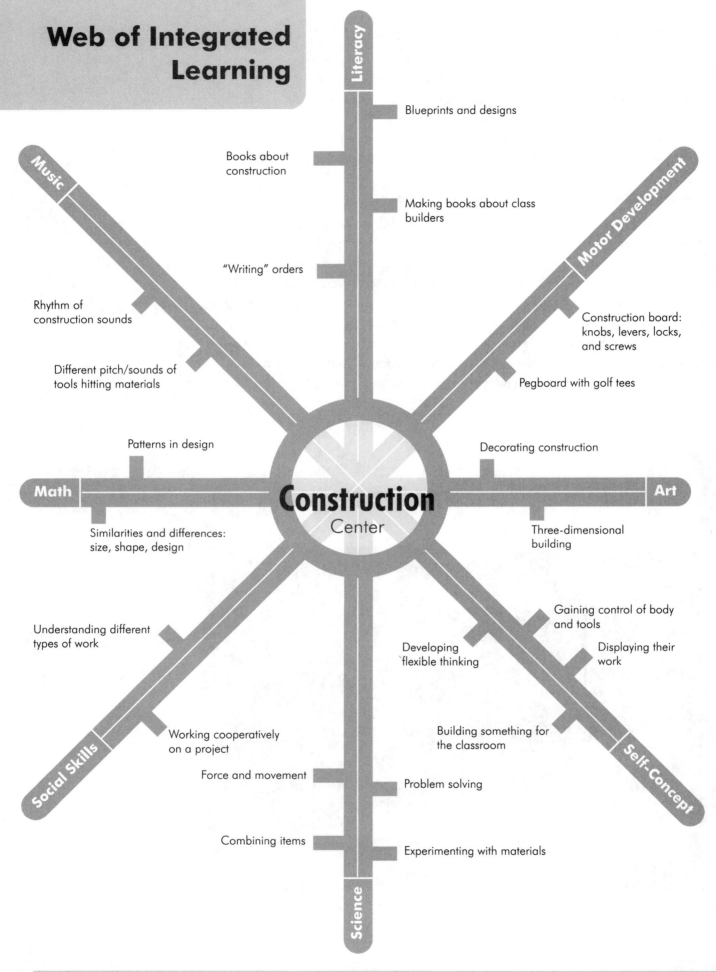

Construction Center

Literacy
- Blueprints and designs
- Books about construction
- Making books about class builders
- "Writing" orders

Music
- Rhythm of construction sounds
- Different pitch/sounds of tools hitting materials

Motor Development
- Construction board: knobs, levers, locks, and screws
- Pegboard with golf tees

Art
- Decorating construction
- Three-dimensional building

Math
- Patterns in design
- Similarities and differences: size, shape, design

Self-Concept
- Gaining control of body and tools
- Displaying their work
- Developing flexible thinking
- Building something for the classroom

Social Skills
- Understanding different types of work
- Working cooperatively on a project

Science
- Force and movement
- Problem solving
- Combining items
- Experimenting with materials

- ❏ cardboard boxes and pieces of corrugated board
- ❏ construction tools (**Safety Note:** Demonstrate the proper use of tools and supervise activities.):
  - ❏ hammer
  - ❏ level
  - ❏ manual screwdriver
  - ❏ measuring tapes
  - ❏ pliers
  - ❏ wrench
  - ❏ fabric—pieces of sheer fabrics in ½-yard to 1-yard sizes
- ❏ items to connect and combine materials:
  - ❏ golf tees
  - ❏ masking tape
  - ❏ nails
  - ❏ screws
  - ❏ toothpicks
  - ❏ wire

- ❏ materials to decorate construction:
  - ❏ bark
  - ❏ contact paper
  - ❏ foil
  - ❏ markers
  - ❏ newspaper comic pages
  - ❏ plastic strips
  - ❏ plastic wrap
  - ❏ wallpaper scraps
- ❏ plastic interlocking blocks and other building blocks (for building small structures or creating a model)
- ❏ safety goggles and yellow plastic hardhats (Use the goggles and hardhats as a way to limit the number of children using the center. All children must wear hardhats and goggles when working in the Construction Center.)
- ❏ scrap pieces of white pine or other soft wood
- ❏ Styrofoam pieces and sheets
- ❏ table with clamp

Long tubes are challenging to use in construction.

Carpenter's Belt

MOTOR DEVELOPMENT

scissors (adult only)   scraps of brown vinyl

- Cut scraps of brown vinyl into strips that will fit around the children's waists (adult step).
- The children use these to hold tools, golf tees, and other items that people might use in construction.

Container for Construction Pieces

ART

box, wood-grain contact paper, paint and brushes, or markers

- Set out a box. The children cover it with wood-grain contact paper strips, paint it with tempera paint, or decorate it with markers.
- Use the box to store loose materials that children use as they build.

A Construction Book

LITERACY

blank book or paper stapled together   wood-grain contact paper
pictures of children with their constructions

- Take pictures of the children with their constructions.
- Put the pictures in a book.
- Cover the book with pieces of wood-grain contact paper.
- Inside, encourage the children to write or dictate to you descriptions of the objects in each picture (drawing or photograph).
- This book values children's work while inspiring the children to think of and make other designs in the Construction Center.

Activities for the Construction Center

Styrofoam Structure

MOTOR DEVELOPMENT

clamps (variety of sizes)
colored electrical tape
golf tees
large sheets of white paper
markers
plywood piece (serves as base of structure)
scissors/clippers
Styrofoam packing material (variety of sizes)
wood glue

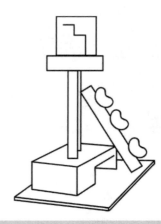

- Set out several building materials and challenge the children to imagine, plan, and build structures out of them.
- Help the children connect the various parts of their structures using a variety of options: golf tees, electrical tape, glue, clamps, or cutting.
- Encourage the children to think of different possibilities and to determine cooperatively what to construct.
- Keep the structures in the Construction Center so the children can work on adding and attaching new elements over the two- to three-week period.
- Take pictures throughout the process, so that later the children can see themselves designing, working together, and expanding their projects. Also take pictures of the final products. Display these photographs and engage the children in a discussion about them during circle or group time or reflection time.

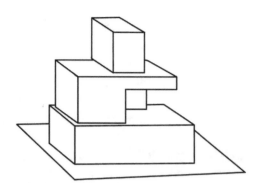

A Carpenter

SELF-CONCEPT

carpenter or retired woodworker

- Invite a carpenter or retired woodworker to visit the Construction Center to discuss woodworking and group participation with the children.
- Prior to the visit, ask if the carpenter is willing to build a bookcase or storage unit for the classroom while visiting in the center. If the carpenter is willing to do so, let the children assist the carpenter during the building process.
- The children will take great pride in helping construct a bookcase that they can then use in their classroom.

Construction Boards

MOTOR DEVELOPMENT

knobs
levers
locks
nails
piece of wood
screws

- Help the children design and build a busy board with knobs, levers, locks, nails, and screws.
- After the children finish building the board, set it out in the Construction Center so they

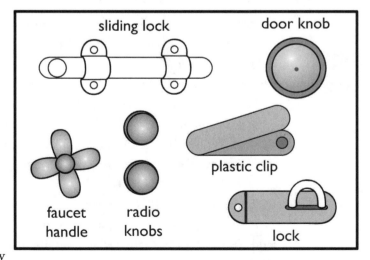

can use it to develop the small motor skills they need for building. The items on the board items can be removed, rescrewed, or added to many times.

large golf tees   piece of pegboard

- Build a pegboard in which the children can insert golf tees. Larger golf tees are easy for small hands to manipulate while developing eye-hand coordination.
- Allow the children to explore ways to create designs by inserting the golf tees into the board.

Adding Spark to the Construction Center

Take the children on a nature walk to collect items that they can use in their construction. Generate new interest in the center by collecting twigs, limbs, or pieces of natural materials that exist in the world. These natural construction materials will inspire the children to imagine new ways of building, attaching, and expanding. This structure will also look very different from the ones they have been working on in the Construction Center previously. Talking with the children about their creations encourages them to compare and discuss their work between each other.

The Essential Literacy Connection

Reading/Writing Opportunities

- Include architectural books and magazines that show interesting constructions.
- Include or make order forms for builders to fill out to indicate the materials they need.
- Make signs to explain the construction that is occurring on the site.
- Provide large sheets of paper, rulers, tracing shapes, and pencils to draw and label designs for possible construction.

Other Printed Materials

- Bring in building supply books and advertisements from newspapers.
- Find blueprints and other drawings by architects for the children to look through.

Books for the Construction Center

Barton, B. 1987. *Machines at Work.* New York: HarperCollins. *This story portrays a day at a construction site. The workers use various machines and tools to knock down a building and build a new one in its place.*

Chronicle Books LLC Staff. 2003. *C Is for Construction: Big Trucks and Diggers from A to Z.* San Francisco: Chronicle Books. *Kids love trucks and diggers. This alphabet book has all their favorites, from the speedy skid steer loader to the giant 797 off-highway truck.*

Crosbie, M. J., & Rosenthal, S. 1993. *Architecture Shapes.* Washington, DC: The Preservation Press. *This book allows young readers to match various geometric shapes with full-color photographs of architectural constructions.*

Gibbons, G. 1982. *Tool Book.* New York: Holiday House. *The tool book contains simple drawings of common tools and shows how they work.*

Hudson, C. W. 2006. *Construction Zone.* Photos by Richard Sobol. Cambridge, MA: Candlewick Press. *This book shows and explains construction-zone activities, equipment, and jargon.*

Olson, K. C. 2004. *Construction Countdown.* New York: Henry Holt. *This book introduces various construction vehicles at work, from dump trucks and earthmovers to bulldozers and pay-loaders, counting them down from 10 to 1.*

Roth, S. L. 2004. *Hard Hat Area*. New York: Bloomsbury USA Children's Books. *Kristen, an apprentice at a big building site, is responsible for checking with the ironworkers and bringing them snacks and tools. The illustrations clearly show the organized chaos of a building site.*

Evaluation of the Construction Center

(This form is on the CD that comes with this book.)

Ask yourself the following questions to evaluate the Construction Center in your classroom:

- Are the children constructing with materials that they have not used before?
- Are children working together to determine how to design and build projects?
- Are children using problem solving and creative thinking as they construct buildings?
- Are children becoming more confident in their abilities to use the materials and tools available in the Construction Center?
- Are the books and writing materials you put in the Construction Center encouraging literacy?

Observation of the Individual Child

(This form is on the CD that comes with this book. Always date observations of each child.)

- What materials does the child to use? How does he use them?
- Record the different vocabulary words the child uses while working in the Construction Center.
- What kinds of small motor skills is the child using? How would you evaluate his abilities? Give specific examples to demonstrate this conclusion.
- Have you observed the child engaging in cooperative behavior while building? Give an example.
- Has the child come up with some creative or unique ideas for construction? Explain.

Hammering pegs into Styrofoam is a new experience for these girls.

Summary

The Doctor's Office Center includes many possibilities for developing literacy. During medical exams, the children (as doctor or patient) talk about the illness and discuss treatment. In this center, children have opportunities to write: making appointments, creating charts, and giving prescriptions. This literacy is very meaningful for the children because it relates to their experiences, lets them continue to develop their reading and writing skills, and gives them the opportunity to work at their own level. In this play, children are putting their literacy learning to use.

Introducing the Center

Introduce the children to the Doctor's Office Center by discussing their past visits to the doctor's office. During these conversations, focus on the benefits of these visits and the help that health professionals provide to children. Bring some interesting props to the center to expand the children's oral language and build their vocabulary. For example, a stethoscope, X-rays, or scales can extend the conversation and provide new words/phrases that relate to the Doctor's Office Center and the play that occurs in that area.

Learning Objectives for Children in the Doctor's Office Center

1. Learn about the services that health care professionals provide.
2. Use new vocabulary that relates to the doctor's office.
3. Play different roles to appreciate the assistance these community helpers provide.
4. Use sociodramatic play to alleviate some of their concerns and fears about visiting the doctor.
5. Use "reading" and "writing" in activities where they serve an essential function.

Time Frame for the Doctor's Office Center

Keep the Doctor's Office Center set up for at least two weeks. This is adequate time for children to examine the materials and move into role-playing that relates to health care. As with any center, keep it in operation for a longer period if the children's interest remains high.

 Note: The attached CD contains a sample letter to send to families, introducing them to the Doctor's Office Center.

Can he hear his patient's heartbeat?

Vocabulary Enrichment

ambulance
appointment
bandage
blood pressure
check-up
doctor
emergency
examination table
height/weight
hospital bed
medicine
nurse
record
reflex
scale
shot/vaccination
smock
splint
stethoscope
thermometer
tongue depressor
X-ray

Web of Integrated Learning

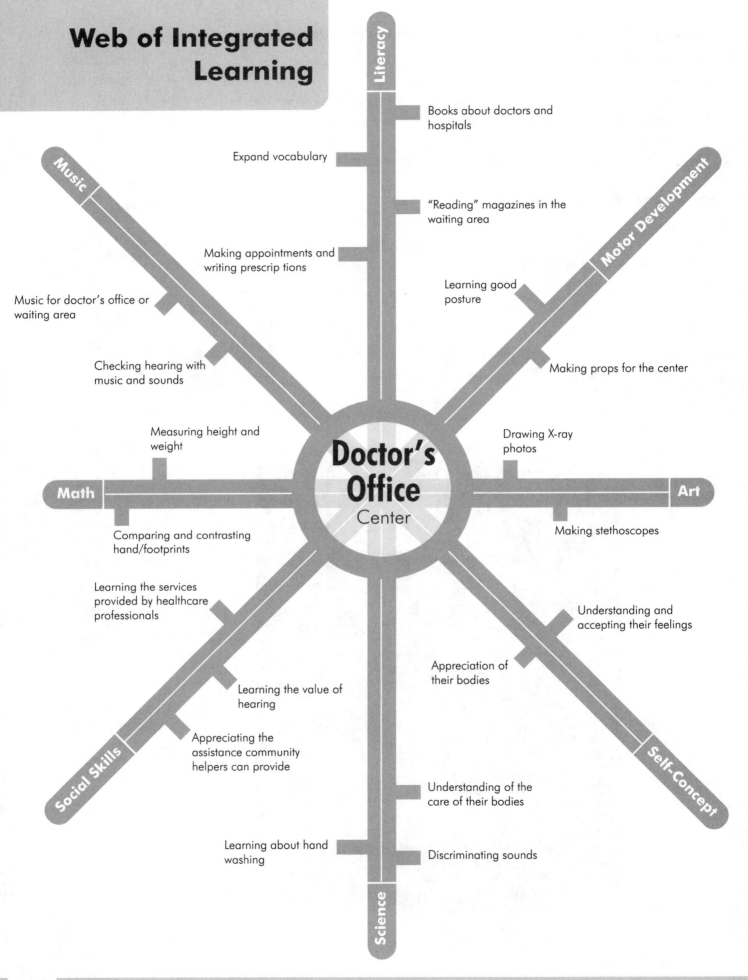

Literacy
- Books about doctors and hospitals
- Expand vocabulary
- "Reading" magazines in the waiting area
- Making appointments and writing prescriptions

Motor Development
- Learning good posture
- Making props for the center

Music
- Music for doctor's office or waiting area
- Checking hearing with music and sounds

Art
- Drawing X-ray photos
- Making stethoscopes

Math
- Measuring height and weight
- Comparing and contrasting hand/footprints

Doctor's Office Center

Self-Concept
- Understanding and accepting their feelings
- Appreciation of their bodies

Social Skills
- Learning the services provided by healthcare professionals
- Learning the value of hearing
- Appreciating the assistance community helpers can provide

Science
- Understanding of the care of their bodies
- Learning about hand washing
- Discriminating sounds

- ❏ clipboards
- ❏ computer/typewriter for office
- ❏ first aid supplies:
    - ❏ bandages
    - ❏ cotton balls
    - ❏ empty alcohol bottle
    - ❏ empty antiseptic tubes
    - ❏ gauze
- ❏ child-safe scissors
  (blunt, if possible)
- ❏ soap
- ❏ tape
- ❏ gloves
- ❏ lab jackets
- ❏ masks
- ❏ old glasses
- ❏ old X-ray photos
- ❏ prescription pads
- ❏ stethoscope
- ❏ telephone
- ❏ wagon for moving hospital
  patients

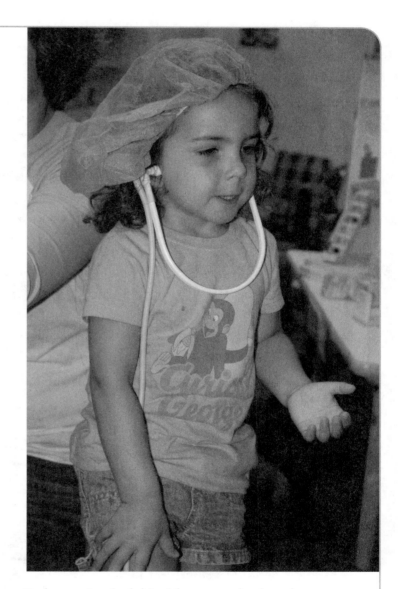

Real props inspired this girl to pretend to be a doctor.

Ambulance for Emergency Care

child's wagon
markers
paper
pillows
plastic container or cup
tape

- Use a child's wagon as the frame for the ambulance. Tape paper around the outside of the wagon and set out markers for the children to use decorate the wagon so it resembles the images of ambulances and the toy ambulances available in the Doctor's Office Center.
- Place pillows inside the wagon.
- The children make a siren from a plastic container or cup. They can paint it red or blue and attach it to the top of side of the wagon.
- As the children work, they can discuss the design and sound of ambulances the children have seen.

These Foods Are Good for You!

chart paper or poster board
health magazines and newspaper advertisements with images of various foods
child-safe scissors
glue

- Create a large mural by attaching a long sheet of paper to the center's wall.
- Label the mural "These Foods Are Good for Us" along the top of the paper.
- The children look through the old magazines and newspaper advertisements for pictures of healthy foods to cut or tear out and glue to the mural.
- The children add to the mural during the entire time that the center is in operation.
- Later, discuss with the children the choices they made about what to display on the mural.

Records of Shots

poster board
markers
pencils
ruler
small photographs of each child
stickers

- Create a chart that lists all the children's names or small photos of the children along its left side and the names of various shots and immunizations the children should receive over time along the top.
- When each child receives a shot or immunization, invite that child to put a sticker or mark in the correct box beside his name to indicate that he has received that shot.

Stethoscope

small cups
straws
yarn

- Let each child use yarn, straws, and small cups to make a stethoscope to use in the center.
- The children use their finished stethoscopes to pretend to listen to one another's let's use their heartbeats.

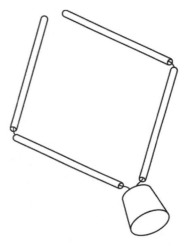

Activities for the Doctor's Office Center

Hand Washing

chart describing steps of hand washing
liquid soap
paper towels
water

- New medical information about the transmission of colds emphasizes the importance of hand washing for both children and adults in classrooms.
- Post a chart in the center that describes the steps of hand washing.
- Remind the children to follow the steps on the chart as they wash their hands.

CD player
earphones
recording of sounds from the environment

- Set up an area for hearing tests. Include a CD player and earphones.
- On the recording, instruct the child to clap his hands when he hears a sound. Suggested sounds on the recording include a door closing, a whistle, a buzzer, an ambulance siren, a telephone ringing, an elevator door closing, or a doctor or nurse speaking.

Large Eye Chart with Pictures   LITERACY

brochure about need for eye exam
chair for patient
eye chart
eye patch
old glasses
pointer
referral pad for additional testing

- Tape an eye chart to the wall in the Doctor's Office Center.
- The children in the center use the eye chart to test the vision of the other children.
- Explain to the children that to give a vision test, they should cover one eye with a patch, test that eye by trying to read the letters on the eye chart, and then do the same with the other eye.
- The doctor can use a pointer to indicate which lines the child she is testing should identify.
- After the test, the doctor determines if everything is okay or if she needs to refer the "patient" for additional testing, or give the patient a pair of old glasses.

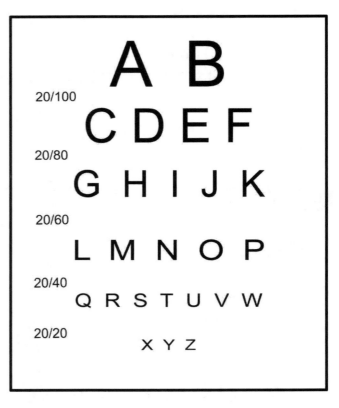

construction paper
markers
paper (large sheet)
tape

- Make outlines of the children's handprints and footprints on small pieces of paper.
- Tape a large piece of paper on the wall in the Doctor's Office Center.
- Two children work together: one child stands and the other marks the height of the child with the paper pieces.
- Compare, contrast, and group the handprints and footprints.

X-rays   ART

old X-ray photos
black construction paper
chalk

- In a window by the center, display X-ray photos of hands, spines, skulls, legs, and feet.
- As the children examine the X-ray photos, challenge them to name the parts of the body they represent.
- Set out black construction paper and white chalk and encourage the children to make drawings that look similar to the X-ray photos.

Adding Spark to the Doctor's Office Center

Add a nursery to the Doctor's Office Center. To set up the nursery, include baby dolls, scales, a rocking chair, baby bottles, diapers, and soft music. This area lets children care for a baby and talk about their experiences. Many young children have babies in their families and should therefore enjoy this experience.

Reading/Writing Opportunities

- Create health charts.
- Set out pads of paper so the children can "write" prescriptions. "Writing" a prescription allows children to suggest, in a written form, medicine that is needed for a sick child.
- Set out a clipboard in the center where the children can "sign in." A clipboard, with paper and attached pencil, encourages children to write the information that needs to stay on record in a doctor's office or hospital.
- An appointment book with a telephone gives children the tools they need to make doctor's appointments.

Other Printed Materials

- Find and display magazines for the office and waiting area. Look through pamphlets and brochures about health care issues.
- Put up eye charts and body charts in the center.
- The poster of hand washing steps gives the children the opportunity to follow a set of directions.
- Children can track their medical history with the file of shot records.
- Nutrition chart and magazines are available for children to explore.
- Place an office-hours chart at the entrance to the center.
- Set out several "no smoking" signs and symbols.

Books for the Doctor's Office Center

Cousins, L. 2001. *Doctor Maisy.* Cambridge, MA: Candlewick. *Doctor Maisy and Nurse Tallulah play hospital.*

Dealey, E. 2005. *Goldie Locks Has Chicken Pox.* New York: Aladdin. *When Goldie Locks comes down with chicken pox, her brother teases her and she is unable to visit with Bo Peep, Little Red, and other friends.*

Flanagan, A. 1997. *Ask Nurse Pfaff, She'll Help You!* New York: Children's Press. *Simple text and photos describe the work of a nurse taking care of patients at a hospital.*

Fluet, C. 2005. *A Day in the Life of a Nurse.* Mankato, MN: Capstone. *Explains how nurses work during their shift, what they wear, how they help doctors, and what tools they use.*

Freeman, D. 2005. *Corduroy Goes to the Doctor.* Illustrated by Lisa McCue. New York: Viking. *The story follows Corduroy on a visit to the doctor, from beginning to end.*

Maisner, H. 2004. *Time to See the Doctor.* Illustrated by Kristina Stephenson. Boston, MA: Kingfisher. *This story presents a positive message about visiting the doctor.*

Ross, T. 2000. *Wash Your Hands!* Brooklyn, NY: Kane/Miller. *When the little princess hears about germs and nasty things living all around her, she understands why she needs to wash her hands frequently.*

Evaluation of the Doctor's Office Center

(This form is on the CD that comes with this book.)

Ask yourself the following questions to evaluate the Doctor's Office Center in your classroom:

- Are children using new vocabulary in their play?
- Are children demonstrating their understanding of the services provided in a doctor's office?
- Are children treating their "patients" in appropriate ways?
- Do children seem to be addressing some of their fears and concerns about doctors' offices?
- Are children developing an awareness of the benefits of proper health care?

Observation of the Individual Child

(This form is on the CD that comes with this book. Always date observations of each child.)

- What role is the child playing in the Doctor's Office Center? Is he demonstrating an understanding of this role? How?
- Is the child using new vocabulary while involved in the play activity? Explain.
- Did you observe the child describing or expressing any fear or concerns about the Doctor's Office Center? Describe.
- Is the child gaining new understanding of health issues, such as nutrition, hand washing, exams, and so on? Give specific examples.

*Is the child "reading" and "writing" in the appropriate play situations? Keep examples of the child's work in a portfolio or file.

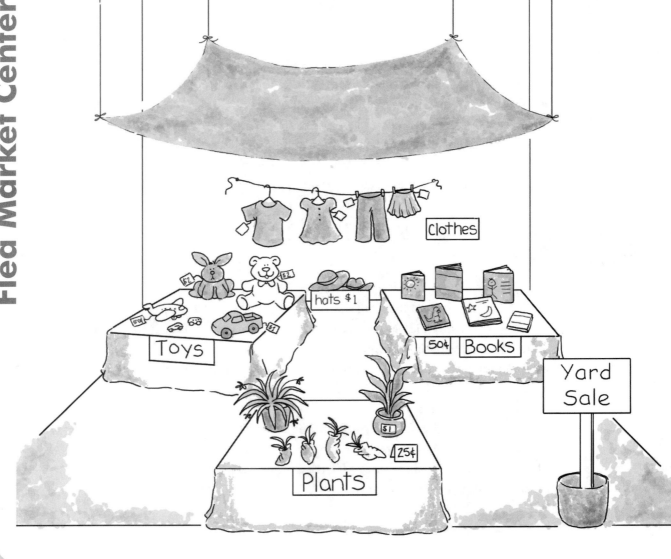

Summary

What do you do with things that are no longer useful? Many people sell the items in a garage sale or at a flea market. The Garage Sale or Flea Market Center is a place where sellers can display their wares. Here, they try to persuade potential customers to buy their products. What the children sell can range from clothes they've outgrown to crafts or plants. As the teacher and children plan the center together, they can determine the items they will sell at the class Garage Sale or Flea Market. They can collect items, make art projects, prepare food, or grow plants to sell or with which they can barter.

Introducing the Center

Bring in some old common household items from your home that you are going to discard or sell. Some interesting possibilities could be baby clothing, old hats, unusual toys, or an old chair or stool. Talk with the children about what they can do with these items. Explain the concept of reselling, and then introduce the concept of a Garage Sale or Flea Market.

Learning Objectives for Children in the Garage Sale or Flea Market Center

1. To collect and produce items that the children sell or exchange with one another.
2. To experience buying and selling items.
3. To enhance literacy skills by creating signs, posters, and sales slips.
4. To expand their language as they learn new vocabulary and practice communicating with others.
5. To learn to reuse items rather than throwing them away.

Time Frame for the Garage Sale or Flea Market Center

Keep the Garage Sale or Flea Market Center open for two to three weeks. Observe children's interest and participation to determine what amount of time works best.

 Note: The attached CD contains a sample letter to send to families, introducing them to the Garage Sale or Flea Market Center.

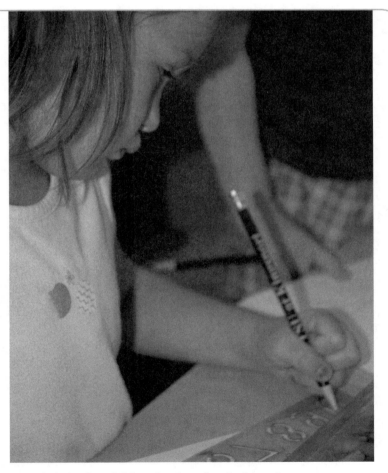

Stencils help this child make signs for the big sale.

Vocabulary Enrichment

appliance
auto part
barter
booth
change
check
display
exchange
garden tool
haggle
mark down
market
money: dollar, quarter, dime, nickel, penny
names of specific items that will be sold in the Garage Sale or Flea Market Center
price
product
recycle
reduce
tool
treasure
useful

Web of Integrated Learning

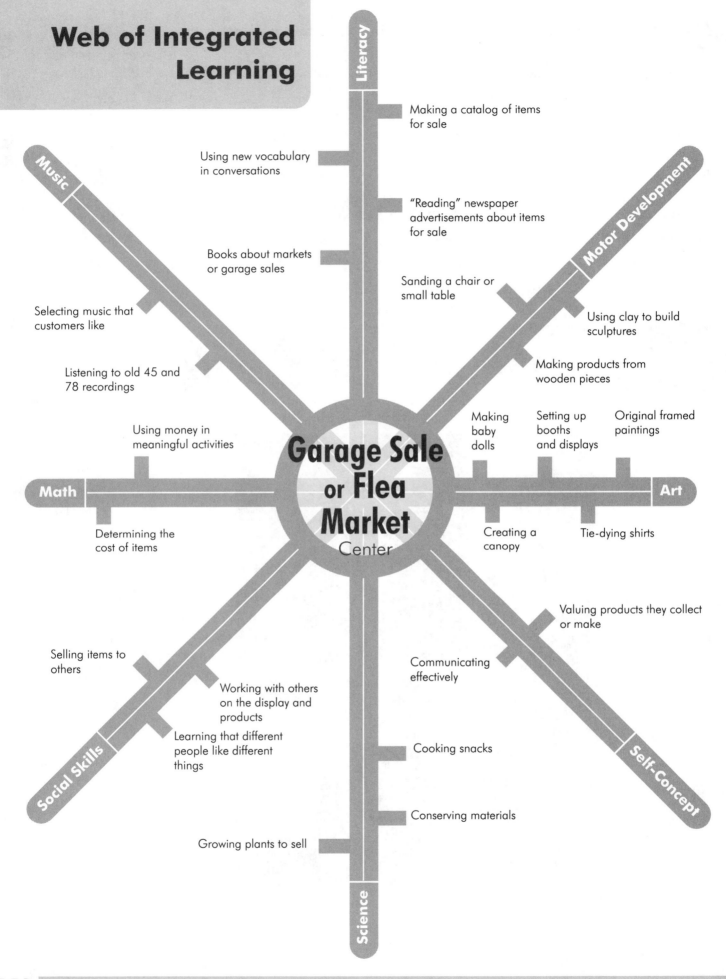

Literacy
- Making a catalog of items for sale
- Using new vocabulary in conversations
- "Reading" newspaper advertisements about items for sale
- Books about markets or garage sales

Music
- Selecting music that customers like
- Listening to old 45 and 78 recordings

Motor Development
- Sanding a chair or small table
- Using clay to build sculptures
- Making products from wooden pieces

Math
- Using money in meaningful activities
- Determining the cost of items

Art
- Making baby dolls
- Setting up booths and displays
- Original framed paintings
- Creating a canopy
- Tie-dying shirts

Garage Sale or Flea Market Center

Self-Concept
- Valuing products they collect or make
- Communicating effectively

Social Skills
- Selling items to others
- Working with others on the display and products
- Learning that different people like different things

Science
- Cooking snacks
- Conserving materials
- Growing plants to sell

Family- or Teacher-Collected Props for the Garage Sale or Flea Market Center

- ❏ clothesline
- ❏ clothespins
- ❏ clear trays for display
- ❏ items for sale:
    - ❏ car accessories
    - ❏ kitchen tools
    - ❏ old children's toys
    - ❏ old clothing
    - ❏ small appliances
    - ❏ used books
- ❏ several low tables
- ❏ sheets, fabric, or canopies to cover some displays

The newspapers have advertisements for garage sales.

Child-Created Props for the Garage Sale or Flea Market Center

(The children can make a variety of products to sell in the Garage Sale or Flea Market Center)

Canopy for the Market   ART

old sheets
markers
paint
paintbrushes

- Make an attractive and colorful canopy for the Garage Sale or Flea Market Center.
- Set out old sheets for the children to decorate with tempera paint or markers, creating big colorful designs and patterns.
- Suspend the canopy above the displays in the market.

Collecting Items from Other Centers   MOTOR DEVELOPMENT

items from other centers in the class
tape and markers

- The children collect some items from the Home Living Center, Library Center, or other centers to use in the Garage Sale or Flea Market Center.
- Use the tape to label the items with the names of the centers from which the children take them so they know where to return the items when the sale ends.

Grow Plants   SCIENCE

discarded flower pots
ribbon
rooting compound (optional)
spider plants, piggy back plants, and ferns
wrapping paper or wallpaper

- Help the children propagate plants to sell at the Garage Sale or Flea Market Center. Plants that are easy to grow include spider plants, piggyback plants, and ferns. Speed up the process by using a rooting compound on the stems of the plants the children grow.
- When the children are ready to set out their plants for the Garage Sale or Flea Market, set out discarded flowerpots from a greenhouse or nursery and encourage the children to cover the pots with wrapping paper or wallpaper, and then to put the plants in the flowerpots.
- Tie a ribbon around the top of the pot to make the plant more attractive.

glue   paper

markers   scissors

paint   small boxes

paintbrushes

- With the children, construct a money box for each display and sales area. Let children work together in pairs to make the container.
- The children cover their small boxes with paper or paint and decorate them in a way that indicates they belong in the sales area.
- Next, set out several sheets of paper cut to approximate the size of dollar bills and invite the children to make play money to keep in the money box so they can make change when they sell various items.

Original Paintings   ART

cardboard, wallpaper, foil, or Styrofoam trays   paintbrushes

glue   paper

paint   scissors

- Set out various art materials for the children to make paintings in the Art Center.
- When the children complete their masterpieces, they can frame them using cardboard, wallpaper, foil, or Styrofoam trays to make them more appealing to customers.
- Set up a gallery of paintings displayed on a clothesline in the Garage Sale or Flea Market Center. Be sure to label the art with the name of the work, its artist's name, and its price.

Activities for the Garage Sale or Flea Market Center

Book Sale and Repair   MOTOR DEVELOPMENT

old children's books and reference books

markers

scissors

tape

- Children can repair tears, battered covers, and pictures in used books. For example, invisible tape can be used to fix torn pages, and colored electrical tape could be used on covers or spine to make them stronger.
- After repairing the books, ask the children to price them and add them to the Garage Sale or Flea Market Center.
- Encourage the children to buy and return various books from the Garage Sale or Flea Market Center.

block of wood	sandpaper
glue	spool
old wooden chair	stapler

- Set out an old wooden chair in an area of the Garage Sale or Flea Market Center for the children to sand, reviving a discarded item and preparing it for resale.
- Coarse sandpaper stapled to a block of wood with a spool handle is a simple tool for young children to use.

Tie-Dying Old T-Shirts ART

buckets or bowls	rubber bands or string
clean T-shirts	small spray mist bottles
fabric dyes	sponges or brushes

- There are many techniques available today to prepare tie-dyed shirts. All methods begin with a clean shirt.
- Pull a section of the shirt into a point and secure at several intervals with tightly twisted rubber bands or tightly tied string. Dip the shirt into bowls of dye. Untie the shirt and allow it to dry.
- Some dyes come prepared for direct application, while others require dissolving the dye in hot water.
- The children can also paint the dyes onto shirts with sponges or brushes.
- Another method is to immerse sections of the shirt into pans of heated dye.
- An additional variation is to fill small spray bottles with dye and invite the children to spray the dye onto the shirts.
- Any of these techniques will produce individually creative results.
- Consider combining two or more techniques to encourage additional creativity.

Clay Sculptures MOTOR DEVELOPMENT

clay	toothpicks or pieces of straws

- Set out a large amount of modeling clay with which the children can create unusual sculptures to display in the Garage Sale or Flea Market Center. Also, make several toothpicks or pieces of straw available for the children to use to cut, mark, and manipulate the clay.
- Children can also use pieces of clay and toothpicks or straws to make sculptures.

Wooden Toys or Products MOTOR DEVELOPMENT

glue	scraps of lumber

- Visit local lumber yards and woodworking shops to collect their discarded turnings, spools, and scraps of lumber.
- The children glue the pieces together to create toys, tables, or other items.
- Help the children label and price their creations for sale in the Garage Sale or Flea Market Center.

cotton or Polyfil
discarded pantyhose
fabric scraps
glue
markers
pieces of fabric
rubber band or piece
  of twine

- Help each child make an
  inexpensive baby doll from
  fabric scraps and discarded
  pantyhose.
- To make each doll, follow the steps below:
  - Form the head of the baby by stuffing a piece of
    pantyhose with cotton or Polyfil.
  - Use a rubber band or piece of twine to form the neck.
  - Give the children markers and ask each to draw the face
    of his doll.
  - Make the baby's dress by gluing a piece of fabric around
    the neck.
- When the children complete their dolls, each should look
  different.
- Sell them in the Garage Sale or Flea Market Center.

Golden Oldies   MUSIC

low table
old 45 and 78 records and recordings of radio programs from before television
record player, tape player, or CD player
two or more boxes or plastic containers to hold recordings

- Set up a record player with a collection of old 45 and 78 records.
- Let the children select, listen to, and compare the music on these records.
- The children can help others learn to play the machines.
- After the children listen to the records, they can discuss which recordings they want to keep and
  the ones they want to sell.
- Label two boxes, one with "Keep" and the other with "Sell." The children organize the records
  into the two categories.

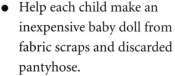

marker
popcorn
poster board
small plastic bags
various spices and flavors, such as Italian seasoning, cheese, cinnamon, lemon pepper, or onion

- Set out several containers of popcorn, several possible spices and things that will add flavor to the popcorn, as well as the small plastic bags.
- Place a handful of popcorn in a bag for each child, and challenge the children to experiment with adding seasonings to the popcorn, sealing and shaking the bags, then tasting their new popcorn flavor.
- Discuss the flavors with the children, and set up a piece of poster board where they can record their personal preferences and determine the flavor to sell in the Garage Sale or Flea Market Center.

Adding Spark to the Garage Sale or Flea Market Center

When interest is fading, have a big markdown sale. The children can sell all the items that remain at reduced prices, and make new signs advertising the lower costs. Children can also change the display to indicate these changes.

The Essential Literacy Connection

Reading/Writing Opportunities

- Include several children's books in this center.
- Keep a record of the sales in a notebook.
- Encourage the children to make a chart with a map of the booths and write down what each booth offers for sale.
- The children make signs, advertisements, and "sale" signs.
- In this center, the children can use pens, markers, paintbrushes, and stamps.

Other Printed Materials

- Make a catalog of sale items that local stores advertise in magazines or newspapers.
- Offer old books for sale in the Garage Sale or Flea Market Center.
- Make signs for items, directions to sale, and prices.

Books for the Garage Sale or Flea Market Center

Berenstain, S. and J. 1999. *The Berenstain Bears Think of Those in Need*. New York: Random House. *Mama Bear decides that the family has too many things-toys, books, games, and more. They sort through their stuff and take the extra to the children's hospital, the Old Bears Home, and the Bears-Who-Care store.*

Brown, M. T. 1999. *Arthur, Clean Your Room!* Step into reading. New York: Random House. *His sister D.W. convinces Arthur to have a garage sale after his mother tells him to get rid of the junk in his room, but things do not work out exactly as he had planned.*

Kerns, T. 1985. *Flea Market Fleas from A to Z.* Johnson City, TN: Overmountain Press. *Sam looks for fleas at his local flea market but finds other treasures instead.*

Lobel, A. 1989. *On Market Street.* Illustrated by Anita Lobel. New York: HarperCollins. *The creative illustrations show all the items—from A to Z—that are available for purchase on Market Street.*

Riley, K. 1999. *The Big Sale.* Brookfield, CT: Millbrook. *Jeff and Jenna take some old toys to sell at Grandpa's tag sale, but they bring home much more than they sell.*

Evaluation of the Garage Sale or Flea Market Center

(This form is on the CD that comes with this book.)

Ask yourself the following questions to evaluate the Garage Sale or Flea Market Center in your classroom:

- Are children making items to sell in the Garage Sale or Flea Market Center?
- Are children talking about reusing items, creating products, and setting up appealing displays?
- Are children using money as they buy and sell in the center?
- Does thinking of new ideas for products and displays enhance the children's creativity?
- Are children working cooperatively to set up and maintain the Garage Sale or Flea Market Center?

Observation of the Individual Child

(This form is on the CD that comes with this book. Always date observations of each child.)

- Is this child familiar with the idea of reselling? What can you observe to help you reach this conclusion?
- What vocabulary and language is the child using in the center? Record specific language.
- Is the child using the signs in meaningful ways? How?
- What role is the child playing in the center? How is the child demonstrating these responsibilities?
- Do you see this child talking, working, and collaborating with other children in the center? In what ways?

Summary

Most young children are familiar with visiting the grocery store. At the grocery store, they see food, select items, and watch adults pay for the groceries. These experiences are the basis for children's participation in the Grocery Store Center. Using the Grocery Store Center theme encourages children to play roles and participate actively as they learn about their world.

Introducing the Center

If possible, before opening the Grocery Store Center, take the children on a field trip to a local grocery store. Discuss some of the foods and products they see in the store. Also, talk about some of the people who work in a grocery store and what their responsibilities are. In the store, let the children select vegetables in the produce section, and then purchase them. Back in the classroom, make soup using the vegetables the children picked at the grocery store. While the children prepare the soup, list the vegetables on a chart. Encourage the children to draw pictures on the chart next to the names of the vegetables. Place this chart in the produce section of the Grocery Store Center.

Learning Objectives for Children in the Grocery Store Center

1. To learn about the world in which they live.
2. To relate real-world experiences play.
3. To expand their language as they use new vocabulary that relates to the grocery store.
4. To learn how a grocery store operates and the work that the employees do.

Time Frame for the Grocery Store Center

This center is effective in the classroom for two to three weeks, although many children will enjoy it for a longer period. Let the experiences and interests of the children in the classroom influence how long you keep the center operating.

 Note: The attached CD contains a sample letter to send to families, introducing them to the Grocery Store Center.

Groceries are scanned at the checkout.

Vocabulary Enrichment

aisle

bagger

bakery

bar code

bill

bread

buggy

canned item

cereal

check out

cleaning supplies

customer

dairy product

display

frozen food

fruit

magazine

manager

meat

pasta

poultry

price

produce

purchase

Web of Integrated Learning

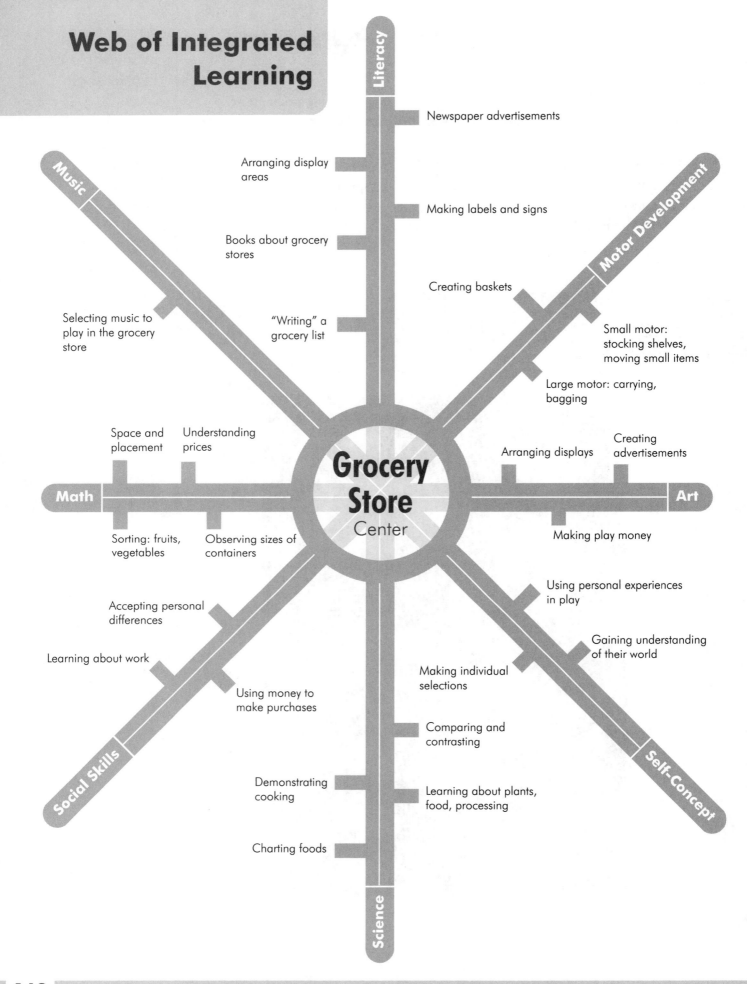

Music
- Selecting music to play in the grocery store

Literacy
- Newspaper advertisements
- Arranging display areas
- Making labels and signs
- Books about grocery stores
- "Writing" a grocery list

Motor Development
- Creating baskets
- Small motor: stocking shelves, moving small items
- Large motor: carrying, bagging

Math
- Space and placement
- Understanding prices
- Sorting: fruits, vegetables
- Observing sizes of containers

Grocery Store Center

Art
- Arranging displays
- Creating advertisements
- Making play money

Self-Concept
- Using personal experiences in play
- Gaining understanding of their world
- Making individual selections
- Comparing and contrasting

Social Skills
- Accepting personal differences
- Learning about work
- Using money to make purchases

Science
- Demonstrating cooking
- Learning about plants, food, processing
- Charting foods

- ❏ cash register
- ❏ empty food containers (Be sure to include food items that are frequently eaten by the children in the classroom.):
    - ❏ boxes of pasta
    - ❏ canned food
    - ❏ frozen food containers
    - ❏ jugs
    - ❏ milk cartons
    - ❏ plastic jars
- ❏ paper bags and plastic bags
- ❏ plastic baskets
- ❏ plastic fruit and vegetables
- ❏ signs and displays from a grocery store

Baskets for Groceries

MOTOR DEVELOPMENT

cardboard boxes, such as shoeboxes
chenille stems
markers and crayons

- Show the children how to construct grocery baskets using cardboard boxes.
- Ask the children to decorate the boxes and attach chenille stems for handles.
- Use these child-size baskets when the children make purchases and check out of the grocery store.

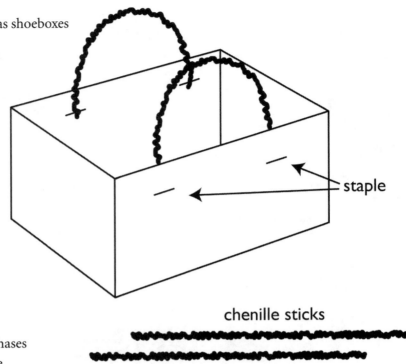

staple

chenille sticks

Display Areas

LITERACY

boxes, shelves, and bookcases
crayons
markers
paper
scissors
tape
cans and boxes of food

- Ask the children to combine boxes, shelves, and bookcases to make areas to display different types of food.
- Set out paper, markers, and crayons for the children to make signs that display and identify the items.
- The children stack the cans or boxes, displaying items at different heights and in interesting ways that will capture the "customer's" attention.

Play Money

crayons   scissors
green, brown, and silver paper   markers

- Make play money to use in the grocery store.
- Cut sheets of green, brown, and silver paper into pieces to use as dollars and coins.
- Display a dollar, quarter, dime, nickel, and penny in the center for children to examine as they make their money.
  Note: It is important to remember that the children are making representations of money and are not ready to copy the details of the coins or dollars.
- This activity provides opportunities for the children to recognize the similarities and differences of money and to use it in play activities.

Activities for the Grocery Store Center

Cooking Demonstrations

SCIENCE

ingredients to prepare pizza, hot chocolate, and so on
napkins
small plates, bowls, spoons, and so on
table

- Set up a table in the grocery store where an individual child or partners can prepare a food in the grocery store. Examples of foods the children can prepare are frozen pizza, hot chocolate, vegetable pieces, crackers with peanut butter, and pudding.
- After the children finish preparing the food, they give out samples to the shoppers in the grocery store.

Sorting

MATH

empty food containers   laminated chart
plastic grocery cart or basket   markers

- Place various kinds of empty food containers in a plastic grocery cart or basket.
- Encourage the children to classify the items by placing the foods that are alike into a grocery cart or basket together.
- A variation of this activity is for children to sort the foods based on their own food preferences: foods they like and foods they do not like.
- Place a laminated chart on a table for the children to use as they determine their food preferences.

crayons
food items from the center
markers
paper

- Let the children in the Grocery Store Center determine a product they want to have on special for the week.
- After they select the item and decide the special price, they build a display and make signs advertising the sale.
- Include samples of the "real" item available for purchase at the booth.

Adding Spark to the Grocery Store Center

Transform the Grocery Store Center into a "Super Store." Let the children decide what new things to sell in the expanded store. Ideas for new departments include adding a florist station, a bakery, a cosmetics station, a toys department, sections for books and tapes, a bank, and a restaurant. These additions will add new products and services while extending the learning opportunities for the children using the "Super Store."

The Essential Literacy Connection

Reading/Writing Opportunities

- Keep paper, pads, and pencils in the grocery store to encourage children to write lists, note prices, or create a grocery bill.
- Have the children make labels and signs to organize the store or advertise weekly specials.
- List the items the children might want to sell in the grocery store if they owned it.
- Draw or write a newspaper ad for the grocery store. Use pictures or prices from old newspaper ads.

This boy decides which items to put on his grocery list.

Other Printed Materials

- Provide newspaper advertisements from local grocery stores.
- Display seed catalogs that contain pictures of fruits and vegetables.

Books for the Grocery Store Center

Ehlert, L. 1994. *Eating the Alphabet: Fruits & Vegetables from A to Z.* San Diego, CA: Harcourt. *This book contains an alphabetical tour of the world of fruits and vegetables, from apricot and artichoke to yam and zucchini.*

Krull, K. 2001. *Supermarket.* New York: Holiday House. *Explains modern supermarkets and how they work, how they are organized, how they display items, and how they keep track of the items they sell.*

Mayer, M. 1998. *Just Shopping with Mom.* New York: Random House. *Mayer's colorful illustrations and simple text tell of an adventurous shopping trip. Mayer's critter and his mom shop in various stores, including the grocery store, pet store, and clothing store.*

Evaluation of the Grocery Store Center

(This form is on the CD that comes with this book.)

Ask yourself the following questions to evaluate the Grocery Store Center in your classroom:

- Are children using their experiences in the Grocery Store Center in their play?
- Are children using new vocabulary as they describe their activities in the center?
- Do you observe sequential play in the Grocery Store Center (in which the children go to the grocery store, make selections, pay for their groceries, bag the groceries, and so on)?
- Are children incorporating the roles of grocery store workers into their play?
- Are children beginning to gain an understanding of economics as they use money, run specials, determine prices, and pay bills?

Observation of the Individual Child

(This form is on the CD that comes with this book. Always date observations of each child.)

- Is the child showing interest in the grocery store and its operation?
- Is the child identifying labels, foods, or money? Describe your observations.
- Is the child playing any roles in the Grocery Store Center? Which roles and how?
- Is the child using words and language in the center? Give specific examples.
- Is there any indication that the child is developing a basic understanding of the economics of a grocery store, such as selling, buying, paying for items, recognizing the cost of items, and so on?

Summary

Young children often categorize time into two periods: now and long ago. For young children, long ago often means when their great grandparents or grandparents were young, before television, or before they were born. As children learn about "long ago," they may begin to formulate a basic understanding of time, depending on their developmental level. In the Long Ago Center they will have the opportunity to investigate what life was like many years ago. They will begin to value and appreciate another time and the special people who were part of that world.

Introducing the Center

During circle or group time, show the children some old hats and other clothing, such as aprons, shawls, ankle-high lace-up shoes, and overalls. Ask the children questions about the items. For example, "Who do you think wore this long ago? Why did they wear it? Have you ever worn anything like this? Do you think your grandparents might have worn these?" Explain to the children that you will put these pieces of clothing in the Long Ago Center. There the children can try on clothes worn a long time ago and experiment with activities done in the past, such as writing with chalk and preparing butter.

Learning Objectives for Children in the Long Ago Center

1. To begin to understand time through experiences that help demonstrate the concept of "long ago."
2. To learn about activities that occurred when their grandparents were young.
3. To enjoy books and stories that relate to "long ago."
4. To develop oral language as they listen and talk to older people.
5. To gain an appreciation for this special time and the people who lived "long ago."

Time Frame for the Long Ago Center

This center will interest young children for about two weeks. Fall is an excellent time to set up this center, because many communities have festivals in the fall that include some of the activities that occurred "long ago." If interest is high, keep the Long Ago Center open for an additional period. When the children are no longer playing in the Long Ago Center, close the center.

 Note: The attached CD contains a sample letter to send to families, introducing them to the Long Ago Center.

Boots help this child play the role of a cowboy.

Vocabulary Enrichment

barter
beehive
candle making
canning
carriage
cellar
chalk
churning butter
community
crop
dried
farming
fiddling
garden
grandparent
horse
horseback
milking
overalls
rail fence
schoolhouse
senior citizen
slate board
stable
storytelling
washboard
weave, warp, and
    weft
well

Web of Integrated Learning

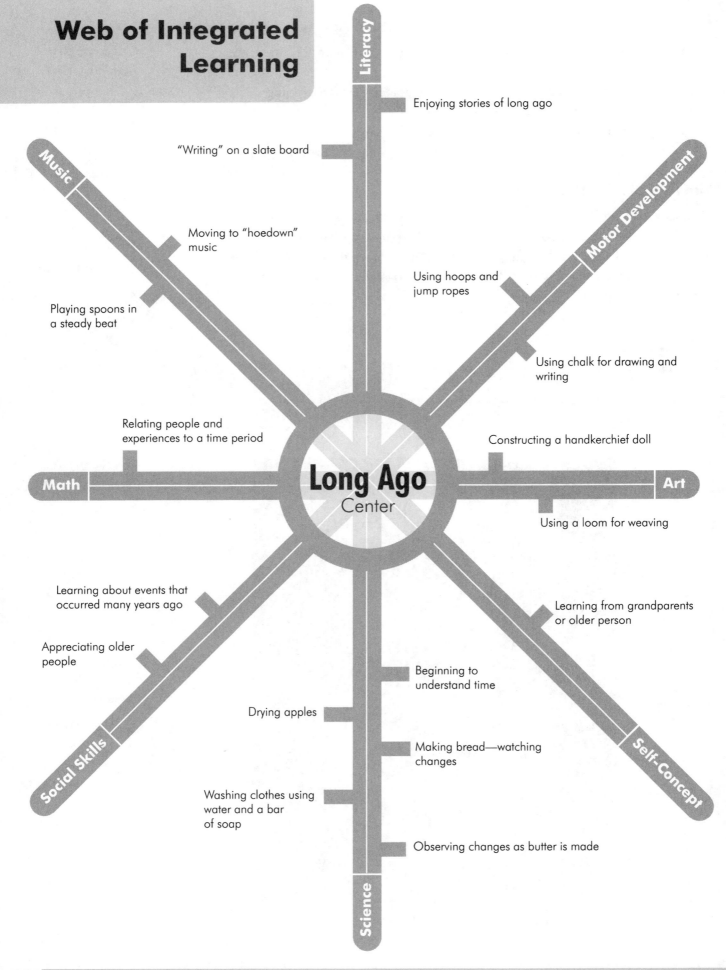

Literacy
- Enjoying stories of long ago
- "Writing" on a slate board

Music
- Moving to "hoedown" music
- Playing spoons in a steady beat

Motor Development
- Using hoops and jump ropes
- Using chalk for drawing and writing

Art
- Constructing a handkerchief doll
- Using a loom for weaving

Math
- Relating people and experiences to a time period

Long Ago Center

Social Skills
- Learning about events that occurred many years ago
- Appreciating older people

Self-Concept
- Learning from grandparents or older person

Science
- Beginning to understand time
- Drying apples
- Making bread—watching changes
- Washing clothes using water and a bar of soap
- Observing changes as butter is made

- ❏ dress-up clothes:
    - ❏ aprons
    - ❏ bonnets
    - ❏ long skirts
    - ❏ overalls
    - ❏ shawls
    - ❏ straw hats
    - ❏ work gloves
- ❏ individual slate boards or blackboard
- ❏ large blocks (from the Block Center)
- ❏ old items that can be examined:
    - ❏ books
    - ❏ candle molds
    - ❏ churn
    - ❏ cooking utensils
    - ❏ dolls
    - ❏ hand-turned drill
    - ❏ tools
    - ❏ toys
    - ❏ wooden bowl and spoon

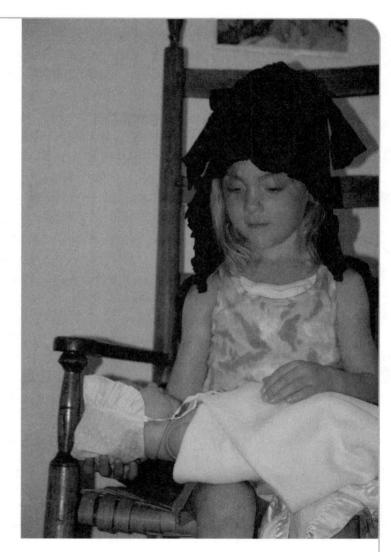

"Mommy" is taking care of a sick baby.

House-Raising

blocks or giant interlocking blocks (large)
brown paper grocery bags or large piece of cardboard
large appliance box
paint
paintbrushes
pictures of log or frame houses
scissors

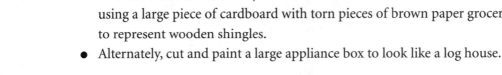

- The children look at pictures of log or frame houses to help them get ideas for their construction.
- The children build a house using the various large blocks or giant interlocking blocks.
- The house should be large enough for several children to fit inside it, so they can play in it after they finish construction.
- The children make a roof by using a large piece of cardboard with torn pieces of brown paper grocery bags glued to the base to represent wooden shingles.
- Alternately, cut and paint a large appliance box to look like a log house.

Old Time Schoolhouse

large appliance box
old books
paint
paintbrushes
slate board and chalk
wooden children's chairs

- Turn the house (from the previous House Raising activity) into a one-room schoolhouse, or use a large appliance box to make another building that will serve as a one-room school.
- Set out paint so the children can decorate the interior and exterior of the schoolhouse.
- Encourage the children to add other props, including child-sized old wooden chairs, old books, and a blackboard/slate board with chalk for children to use.

Drying Apples

apples
cheesecloth
cookie sheet
cutting board
dull, child-safe table knife
sharp knife (adult only)
tray

- Use a sharp knife to cut several fresh apples into slices and place them on a tray in the Long Ago Center (adult step).
- Give each child a piece of apple to taste and examine the texture of the apple.
- After tasting a piece, each child takes another piece of apple and uses the dull table knife to cut it into smaller pieces.
- Place the small pieces on a cookie sheet and cover with cheesecloth.
- Set the sheet beside a window and let the apple pieces dry. Allow to dry beside a window.
- As the apple pieces dry, the children observe the changes and taste the dried apples during the process, as well as when the experiment is complete.
- After the children discuss the differences between fresh and dried apples, chart their findings.

Handkerchief Doll

white tissue, handkerchief, or white fabric squares (12" x 12")
cotton or Polyfil
glue and additional yarn (optional)
markers
yarn

- The children create baby dolls, using white tissues, handkerchiefs, or white fabric squares to make the bodies, by following these steps:
  - Place each "body" flat on a table.
  - Place a cotton ball or small amount of Polyfil on the center of the body.
  - Gather up the center area to form the doll's head.
  - Stuff the head with additional cotton or Polyfil (if necessary) and secure with a piece of yarn.
  - Use a marker to draw a face on the doll's head.
  - If desired, glue on yarn to give the doll hair.

chart paper
grandparents or senior citizens
markers

● Because young children do not have experiences with "long ago," they need to collect information about this time.
● Brainstorm with the children to come up with ways to find out what life was like long ago. If no children mention this possibility, suggest that one way to collect information is to talk with their grandparents or senior citizens.
● It is helpful to send information home about the interview, so parents and family members understand the process and the kind of information the children want to collect.
● If personal interviews are not possible, invite a retired teacher or other senior citizen into the classroom to talk about what life was like long ago.
● After the interview, develop an experience chart that includes some of the important information the senior citizen shared with the children.

Making Butter   SCIENCE

baby food jars
crackers or bread
cream or whole milk
dull, child-safe table knives

● Pour cream or whole milk into baby food jars.
● Set the jars out. Each child picks up one jar.
● Invite the children to shake the jars until butter begins to form inside them.
● The children spread the butter on crackers or bread for a snack similar to what people ate a long time ago.

Making Pretzels   SCIENCE

baking sheet
bowl
ingredients for recipe:
   dry yeast
   egg
   flour
   honey
   salt
   shortening
   warm water

measuring cups
measuring spoons
oven
oven mitts
spoon
towel

- This simple bread recipe rises quickly, maintaining young children's interest in the process:

Ingredients:

"Edible Sculpting Dough" (from *Preschool Art* by MaryAnn Kohl. Reprinted with permission.)

1 package (2 ¼ teaspoon) dry yeast

1 ¼ cups (345 ml) very warm water

1 egg

¼ cup (60 ml) honey

1 teaspoon salt

¼ cup (50 g) shortening

5 cups (1000 g) flour

Recipe:
- Mix the yeast and very warm water in a bowl.
- Add the egg, honey, salt, and shortening.
- Slowly mix in the flour until a ball of dough forms.
- Add a little more flour if the dough is too sticky.
- Knead the dough by hand on a floured board.
- Begin sculpting, making only flat figures, because the dough will rise.
- Cover the sculptures with a towel and place in a warm place to rise for about 30 minutes. For very puffy sculptures, let the dough rise longer.
- Bake at 350° for 20 minutes, or until golden brown.
- Eat the sculptures or save them as they are.

Old Photo Album

LITERACY

glue

old black and white pictures and photographs

scrapbook or sheets of paper stapled together

- Collect old black and white pictures and photographs from long ago. If families have some, consider asking to make photocopies of them for the children to use in the classroom.
- Set out a scrapbook or album in which the children can place the pictures of families, horses, pets, houses, schools, and other interesting things.
- Encourage the children to look at the photographs and discuss what is happening in each.

bluegrass or country music recordings
spoons

- Music was an important part of life long ago. Banjo or fiddle playing often provided the evening's entertainment for families. Spoons were an inexpensive and readily available instrument people used to add rhythm to the music.
- The children can experiment playing with playing spoons.
- Although the position necessary for playing the spoons properly may be too difficult for young hands, the children can simply tap the spoons together in a steady beat to accompany bluegrass or country music.

Senior Visitors   SOCIAL SKILLS

senior citizen group or retired teachers

- Invite a group of senior citizens or retired teachers to volunteer in the classroom.
- These special people can provide stories or the individual attention that young children love to receive.

Washing Clothes   SCIENCE

bar of soap
clothesline
clothespins
spare articles of clothing
tub of water
washboard

- Set up a place where the children can wash clothes by hand.
- Include a tub, a bar of soap, and a washboard.
- Help the children hang the clothes on a line to dry after they finish washing them.

10" and 12" lightweight pieces of wood (2 each)

hammer

heavy yarn or macramé cord

nails

strips of coarse fabric, ribbons, rope, natural materials, and so on

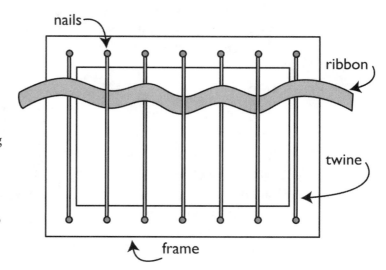

- Make a loom that is large enough (10" x 12") for young children to use by following the steps below:
- Use nails to attach two 12" pieces of lightweight wood to the ends of two 10" pieces of lightweight wood, so they form a rectangle.
- Hammer in approximately eight nails with large heads at 1" intervals along both the top and bottom of the frame. To make a simpler loom, hammer only four nails at the top and bottom at a greater interval.
- Tie heavy yarn or macramé cord from each nail at the top to the corresponding nail at the bottom to create the foundation (the warp of a loom).
- Once you have several looms prepared, set them out along with strips of coarse fabric, ribbons, rope, other natural materials, and so on. If necessary, demonstrate how to weave the materials over and under through the cords of the loom.
- The children weave heavy yarn, strips of coarse fabric, or other materials over and under the warp pieces to form the weave (weft).

Writing and Drawing on Slate Boards   L I T E R A C Y

chalk

small individual slate boards

- Purchase small individual slate boards for use in the Old Time Schoolhouse mentioned in the Child-Created Props section of the Long Ago Center.
- Because the schoolhouse is small, you will only need two or three boards at a time for the children.
- The chalk and slate boards allow children to experiment with a new, different writing tool and observe the results.

Adding Spark to the Long Ago Center

A barn dance or hoedown adds excitement to the Long Ago Center. Play a bluegrass recording or Copland's "Hoe Down" to entice the children to move with the music and add new interest to the Long Ago Center.

Reading/Writing Opportunities

- Write thank-you notes to volunteers who worked in the center or special visitors who came to describe what life was like long ago or demonstrate a skill that was once done only by hand.
- Write stories that describe what life was like long ago.

Other Printed Materials

- Display magazines for senior citizens that include pictures of older persons involved in various activities.
- Find and set out various brochures from historical reenactment parks or historical sights.

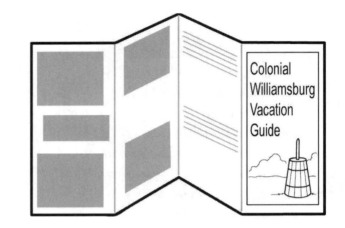

Books for the Long Ago Center

England, K. 2007. *Grandfather's Wrinkles*. Illustrated by Richard McFarland. New York: Flashlight Press. *Lucy asks her grandfather why his "skin does not fit him." He describes his memories to Lucy and shares the cause of each line on his face.*

Hoberman, M. A. 2007. *I'm Going to Grandma's*. Illustrated by Tiphanie Beeke. Florida: Harcourt. *Why is this visit to Grandma's different from all other visits? Because this time, the little girl gets to spend the night. She dresses up in an old wedding gown, hears Grandpa play 'Three Blind Mice' on his musical saw, and listens to Grandma tell stories connected to the patchwork quilt covering the bed.*

Johnston, T. 1996. *The Quilt Story*. Illustrated by Tomie dePaola. New York: Penguin. *Long ago, a young girl put her patchwork quilt in the attic. Years later, another young girl finds it and discovers how it helps her feel secure.*

Katz, K. 2004. *Grandpa and Me*. New York: Little Simon. *Let's make pizza with Grandpa! A board book that allows children to lift flaps to find everything you need to make pizza.*

Pinkney, G. J. 1999. *Back Home*. Illustrated by Jerry Pinkney. New York: Penguin. *A young girl returns to visit relatives on the farm where she was born.*

Wilder, L. I. 1996. *Going West*. New York: HarperCollins. *A young pioneer girl and her family prepare to leave the big woods of Wisconsin and travel west in their covered wagon.*

Ziefert, H. 2006. *Grandma, It's for You!* Illustrated by Lauren Browne. Maplewood, NJ: Blue Apple Books. *Lulu wants to make an extra-special present for her grandmother, so she decides to create the most beautiful hat she can imagine. She puts the hat together with things that Grandma loves: flowers, feathers, necklaces, and ribbon. Grandma loves it!*

Evaluation of the Long Ago Center

(This form is on the CD that comes with this book.)

Ask yourself the following questions to evaluate the Long Ago Center in your classroom:

- Are children beginning to understand that some things were different long ago?
- Are children listening to and questioning senior citizens about their lives and using that information in their Long Ago Center play?
- Are children participating in the activities of the Long Ago Center?
- Are the children enjoying and retelling the stories they hear and read about long ago?
- Are children demonstrating an appreciation for long ago and the people who lived during that time?

Observation of the Individual Child

(This form is on the CD that comes with this book. Always date observations of each child.)

- What items interest the child in the Long Ago Center? Describe the items and the child's interest.
- Is the child dressing up in old-time clothing? What is he selecting to wear?
- Is he playing with other children or independently? Is the child using language and making collaborative decisions?
- Is the child using books or writing materials? Which ones is he using and in what ways?
- Is the child using vocabulary that relates to long ago? What is he saying?

Summary

In today's society, the mall has become the center of community activity. In the mall, we can buy clothes, purchase food in "food courts," and be entertained. Friends meet at the mall and are involved in special activities in these places. Most children have visited a mall and have seen the different types of shops that are inside. The design of the Mall Center works to capitalize on children's interest in these large shopping areas. There is a greater amount of flexibility built into the Mall Center plan, primarily to allow teachers to custom design a Mall Center reflective of the mall located in their community. The center describes a number of possible stores and entertainment activities so the teacher can easily duplicate a setting that is likely to be familiar to the children.

Introducing the Center

If possible, introduce the Mall Center by visiting a local mall or shopping center "strip mall." If possible, choose a time when there is a special event or performance. These additional activities will provide more opportunities to incorporate a variety of activities in play. Before you visit, talk about the shops they will see and some of the roles people play in these areas. Be sure to include the cleaning crew that works to keep the mall free of trash.

Learning Objectives for Children in the Mall Center

1. To learn about the world in which they live.
2. To make their personal, real-world experiences relate to their play in the Mall Center.
3. To observe how a business operates and how it sells products.
4. To experience environmental print in meaningful situations.
5. To experiment with different professions and experience the work that people in these positions do.

Time Frame for the Mall Center

This center includes stores and services of interest to young children, with various stores rotating into the mall as they are necessary. With these changes to the stores, the Mall Center can be in operation for two to three weeks. Periodically adding new stores to the center will stimulate interest and expand play opportunities.

 Note: The attached CD contains a sample letter to send to families, introducing them to the Mall Center.

Toy cell phones encourage conversations and language development.

Vocabulary Enrichment

advertisement
bargain
book store
clerk
customer
department store
display
drug store
food court
home accessory
mall
manager
men's wear
movie theater
photography
purchase
receipt
record/cassette
    tape/CD
register
sale
salon
shoe store
shopping
window display
women's clothing

Web of Integrated Learning

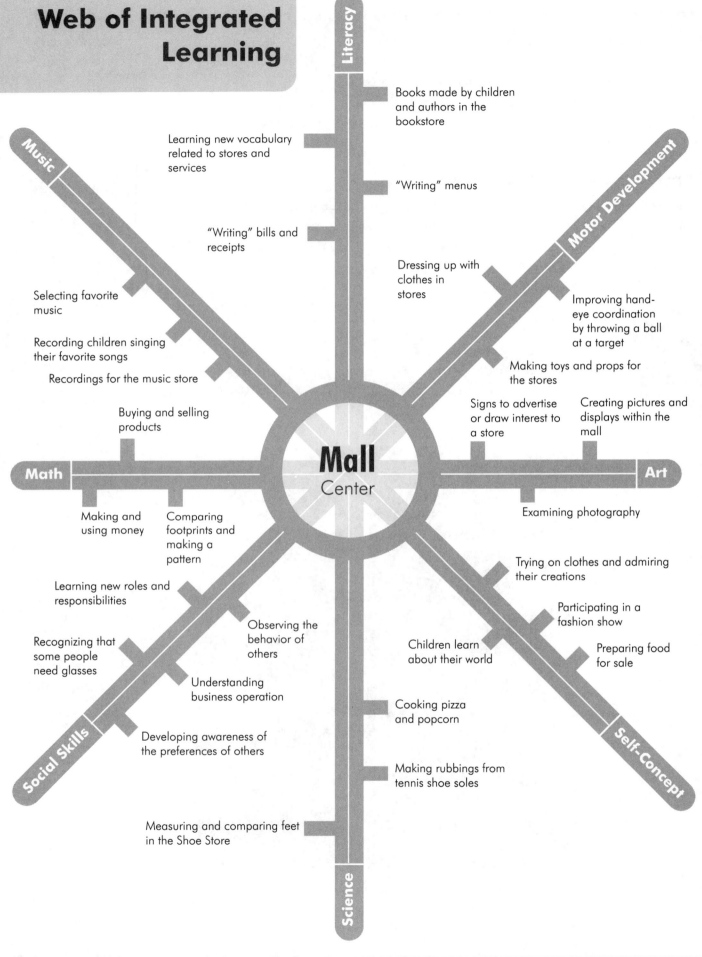

Literacy
- Books made by children and authors in the bookstore
- "Writing" menus
- Learning new vocabulary related to stores and services
- "Writing" bills and receipts

Music
- Selecting favorite music
- Recording children singing their favorite songs
- Recordings for the music store

Motor Development
- Dressing up with clothes in stores
- Improving hand-eye coordination by throwing a ball at a target
- Making toys and props for the stores

Art
- Signs to advertise or draw interest to a store
- Creating pictures and displays within the mall
- Examining photography
- Trying on clothes and admiring their creations
- Participating in a fashion show
- Preparing food for sale

Math
- Buying and selling products
- Making and using money
- Comparing footprints and making a pattern

Mall Center

Self-Concept
- Children learn about their world

Social Skills
- Learning new roles and responsibilities
- Recognizing that some people need glasses
- Observing the behavior of others
- Understanding business operation
- Developing awareness of the preferences of others

Science
- Cooking pizza and popcorn
- Making rubbings from tennis shoe soles
- Measuring and comparing feet in the Shoe Store

- ❑ shoe store:
  - ❑ chairs
  - ❑ handbags
  - ❑ measuring ruler
  - ❑ old shoes (baby, men, women, cowboy boots, and so on)
  - ❑ shoeboxes
  - ❑ unbreakable mirror
- ❑ women's clothing store:
  - ❑ advertisements from newspapers
  - ❑ floor-length unbreakable mirror
  - ❑ gloves
  - ❑ hat
  - ❑ jewelry
  - ❑ mannequin
  - ❑ sale signs
  - ❑ variety of dresses, shirts, skirts, scarves, earrings, bracelets, and so on
- ❑ book store:
  - ❑ CD player
  - ❑ collection of children's books, including paperback and hardcover books on a variety of topics
  - ❑ featured children's book
  - ❑ magazines
  - ❑ pillows and a seating area for examining the books
  - ❑ recorded books
- ❑ toy store:
  - ❑ boxes and bags for packing
  - ❑ low table for experimenting with table toys

- ❑ musical toys
- ❑ puzzles, balls, dolls, blocks, and manipulatives
- ❑ toy catalogs
- ❑ salon:
  - ❑ appointment book
  - ❑ blow dryer
  - ❑ chairs
  - ❑ combs/brushes
  - ❑ empty spray bottles and styling product containers
  - ❑ hairstyle books and magazines
  - ❑ hand mirror
  - ❑ Styrofoam wig heads with wigs
  - ❑ telephone
- ❑ food court or restaurant:
  - ❑ cooking utensils
  - ❑ cups
  - ❑ grill
  - ❑ paper plates
  - ❑ plastic forks and spoons
  - ❑ signs for foods/menu
  - ❑ tables and chairs
- ❑ pet store:
  - ❑ books about pets
  - ❑ cages
  - ❑ fish tank
  - ❑ pet supplies
  - ❑ stuffed animals
- ❑ men's clothing store:
  - ❑ advertisements from newspaper
  - ❑ floor-length unbreakable mirror
  - ❑ mannequin

- ❑ sale signs
- ❑ variety of shirts, pants, jackets, hats, belts, gloves, coats
- ❑ music store:
  - ❑ CD player
  - ❑ keyboard
  - ❑ music books
  - ❑ musical instruments
  - ❑ recordings
- ❑ movie theater:
  - ❑ snack stand
  - ❑ video player
  - ❑ videos
- ❑ photography/camera store:
  - ❑ cameras
  - ❑ film
  - ❑ frames
  - ❑ lights
  - ❑ negatives
  - ❑ old photographs
  - ❑ photographs
  - ❑ scissors
  - ❑ scrapbooks/pages
- ❑ optical store:
  - ❑ chairs
  - ❑ children's glasses
  - ❑ exam room sign
  - ❑ eye chart
  - ❑ glasses cases
  - ❑ mirrors
  - ❑ sunglasses
  - ❑ *Two-for-one* sign

Sale!

Bookstore
SELF-CONCEPT

books made by the children
pictures of book characters made by the children
pictures of favorite books

- Display books the children make, pictures of favorite books, and pictures of interesting characters drawn by the children.
  Note: One method for making books: the children cut paper to the size of book they want, glue pictures or drawings on the pages, punch holes in the pages, and then lace the pages together with yarn, thick string, or shoelaces.

Food Court
SOCIAL SKILLS

crayons
ingredients for simple recipes
markers
paper

- Ask the children to select foods they want to sell in the food court.
- The children make signs and menus for the food they will be selling.
- Prepare simple recipes, such as English muffin pizza, rice, tacos, or stuffed potatoes.

Men's Store
MOTOR DEVELOPMENT

scraps of fabric
thick yarn or cord

- Set out the various materials for the children to make belts, hats, or scarves for display and sale.
- The children can drape the fabric, use belts to hold the pieces, and use paper to create hats and scarves to try on in the Men's Store.

Music Store
MUSIC

tape or CD recorder
recording media

- Make recordings for the Music Store.
- Record songs sung by the children
- Set out a tape player or other media player on which the children can listen to these recordings or recordings of songs the children played at another time, such as in the Music and Sound Center.

Optical Store

crayons
large or medium boxes
markers
old socks
pantyhose
yarn

- For this store, the children make games that require hand-eye coordination.
- Decorate large or medium boxes to use as targets.
- Set out socks, pantyhose, and yarn for the children to make into balls they can throw into the boxes.

Pet Store

tape
thick yarn or cord

- Make tape, yarn, and cords available for the children to make collars and leashes out of the materials, and then sell them in the Pet Store.

Photography Shop

crayons
instant-print camera
large sheet of butcher paper
markers
tape

- Set up an area where the children can take pictures.
- The children make a backdrop by decorating large sheets of butcher paper with markers and crayons and then attach it to the wall.
- Consider making an instant-print camera available to the children, to add to the realism of the Photography Shop.
  Note: The children can use a toy camera if they don't have a real one.

Sale!

Shoe Store

crayons
markers
paper
shoeboxes
shoes from the Dramatic Play Center

- Set out crayons, markers, and paper for the children to make signs to advertise a shoe sale.
- Set up display racks on which the children can arrange the shoes. (Display racks can be made from shoeboxes, stacked, and glue together to show the items that are available to buy.)

Toy Store

junk box with assorted materials:
    chenille stems
    contact paper
    electrical wire
    masking tape
    plastic pieces
    poster board
    small boxes of various shapes
    Styrofoam pieces
    wallpaper scraps
    wood scraps
    tape and glue

- Add a junk box with some of the materials listed above and for the children to make toys they would like to sell.
- Help the children design, build, and price the toys they make for the toy store.

Women's Clothing Store

fabric or old sheets
old socks
trim

- The children use pieces of fabric or old sheets to make women's clothes and hats out of old socks.
- Set out the trim so that children can use it to decorate the clothes they make.

A Special Event

decorations
markers
paper
schedule of events at the local mall

- Organize this activity to coordinate with local happenings at the mall, such as flower shows, car shows, band or orchestral performances, or art shows.
- Designate a section of the center where this event can occur, and let the children design, prepare, and carry out the event. Include decorations in the space.
- Help the children "write" flyers to distribute to shoppers in the Mall Center announcing the time and activities for this special event.

Men's and Women's Clothing Store: A Fashion Show

clothing from stores in the Mall Center

- The children select and wear clothing from the Mall Center stores.
- They model these outfits in the "Commons" of the Mall Center.
- The children take turns being the announcer introducing and describing the clothing the models are wearing.

Optical Store: Target Practice

markers
paper
soft balls or yarn balls

- Draw a large bull's eye target and place it on the wall in the Optical Store.
- The children throw soft balls or yarn balls at the target.
- Use this activity to improve hand–eye coordination.

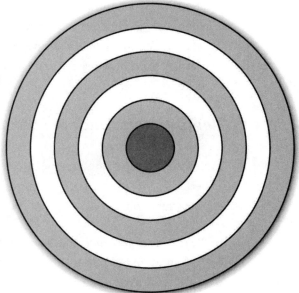

Shoe Store: Footprints

paper
markers
rulers
scissors
tape

- Set several sheets of paper on the ground. The children use markers to draw outlines around the other children's feet.
- Measure the footprints, cut them out, and use rulers to measure them and group the outlines by size.
- Use these prints to make paths around the Shoe Store.

Shoe Store: Rubbings

children's tennis shoes
large sheet of paper
black crayons with paper removed
scissors

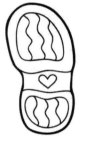

- Children's tennis shoes have interesting designs on the soles. Use these three-dimensional designs to produce rubbings by placing white paper over the soles of the shoes and then rubbing black crayons over the paper that covers the shoe soles, recreating the patterns.
- After the children make rubbings on single sheets of paper, the children can make several rubbings on one sheet of paper, and then cut a large shoe shape out of the paper. Attach to a larger sheet of paper to create a mural for the Shoe Store.

Children's Clothing Store: Back to School

Five Little Monkeys Go Shopping by Eileen Christelow
paper
crayons, markers

- Read *Five Little Monkeys Go Shopping* to the children.
- The children create signs that announce a "back to school" sale.
- Children use clothing and materials that relate to returning to school in the store in the Mall Center.

Photography: Exhibit

colorful paper or simple frames
photographs
pictures drawn by the children
tape

- The children take photographs and/or draw pictures to exhibit in the Mall Center.
- Mount these photographs on colored paper or in simple frames.

Bookstore: Author's Signing

"authors'" table
books made by the children
markers

- The children make wordless picture books to display and "sell" in the Bookstore.
  Note: These wordless books are made from drawings and paintings created by the children and do not include any print. The pictures are combined into book form. A title and author's page can be added if children are interested.
- When the books are complete, invite the children to go to the author's table to sign or autograph the books.
- The children tell the other children about their books and "sign" the book-covers with their names.

Music Store: Select Your Favorite

CD player
chart
recordings of different kinds of music

- Play recordings of different types of music in the music store.
- The children discuss the various kinds of music.
- Ask the children to vote for their favorite recording on a large chart displayed in the Mall Center.

Adding Spark to the Mall Center

Having a big "sale" in the Mall Center such as "After-Christmas Sale," "Presidents' Day Sale," or "Back-to-School Sale" can add many activities to the Mall Center. For the big mall sale, ask the children to mark down prices, rearrange the items, and make advertisements for the big price reductions.

Sale!

Reading/Writing Opportunities

- For the many different stores and operations in the Mall Center, paper and pencils encourage taking orders, writing bills, and giving receipts.
- Cash registers, phone books, phone, and paper inspire taking phone orders.
- Charts, menus, and sale signs provide opportunities for children to write meaningful messages and observe the results.

Other Printed Materials

- Advertisements from the newspaper or magazines, and catalogs that relate to stores.
- Make signs for stores and sales (open/closed and hours of operation), and label various items.

Books for the Mall Center (Select books to match the stores included in the Mall Center)

Brown, M. 2007. *Arthur's Pet Business.* New York: Little Brown. *Arthur finds a job working with pets to prove to his parents that he is responsible enough to have his own puppy.*

Christelow, E. 2007. *Five Little Monkeys Go Shopping.* New York: Clarion. *The day before school starts, Mama takes her five little monkeys shopping for clothes. The five little monkeys wander off and get separated from Mama. Will Mama ever find her five little monkeys?*

Day, A. 1989. *Carl Goes Shopping.* New York: Farrar Straus Giroux. *A dog named Carl accompanies his owner to the mall and is left in charge of watching the family baby. Carl and the baby take an adventurous trip through the mall.*

Klein, A. F., 2006. *Max Goes Shopping.* Illustrated by Mernie Gallagher-Cole. Minneapolis, MN: Picture Window Books. *Max enjoys shopping at a variety of stores.*

Murphy, S.. 2006. *Mall Mania.* Illustrated by Renee Andriani. New York: HarperCollins. *Shopping, counting, and a birthday present all add up to a surprise ending on Mall Mania Day!*

Stair, K. S. 2004. *Glasses, Glasses, Oh What Do I See?* Illustrated by Joyce Sandness. Washington, DC: Book Publishers Network. *A trip to the eye doctor can be a life-changing experience for a child with vision problems. This book provides a child-friendly look at eye-exams as the author tells the journey of her own son when he went from blurriness to a bright new day.*

Waber, B. 2001. *Fast Food! Gulp! Gulp!* Boston, MA: Houghton Mifflin. *These fast-food patrons want their food fast, and the pace of the story quickens into a maddening dash of orders and consumption until Colonel Mane's cook quits.*

(This form is on the CD that comes with this book.) Ask yourself the following questions to evaluate the Mall Center in your classroom:

- Are children participating in different activities in the stores?
- Are children using vocabulary that relates to specific stores and their products?
- Are children trying out different roles as they participate in the different stores and special events?
- Are children working cooperatively to set up displays, arrange merchandise, and prepare for sales?
- Are the children using and creating printed materials in their play?

This firefighter is wearing heels and carrying a purse.

Observation of the Individual Child

(This form is on the CD that comes with this book. Always date observations of each child.)

- Which stores does the child prefer to play in? What is the child doing in the store?
- Is the child role-playing? What role and how?
- What vocabulary is the child using in stores? Does it relate to a specific store and products?
- Is the child using play money and cash registers or sorting items? Describe.
- Is there evidence of collaboration in play? Explain.

Summary

Animals fascinate most young children, and children would often like to have a pet. Today, across the country, there are huge stores that focus on pets, their care, and grooming. In these places, animals are on display, food and supplies are for sale, and books are available to learn about specific pets. Set up the Pet Store Center as a superstore for animal lovers. Children will be able to see pets, select leashes and collars, and assume the roles of veterinarians working on the site.

In this center, children can pretend they have a wonderful pet, and learn to be responsible for the care, feeding, and nurturing of these treasured animals. The center also gives children the opportunity to talk, write, and read about pets. This center provides a wonderful environment in which the children can learn and develop.

Introducing the Center

If possible, visit a pet store with the children. If you are not able to visit, bring in pictures of different pets that children typically have. Consider asking those children with pets to bring in pictures of them. Talk with the children about what pets they have or might like to have. If you or a family in your classroom has a pet that is tame and child-friendly, bring it in for a short visit with the children. Before bringing in the pet, discuss with the children how they must be gentle with pets. Also consider placing stuffed animals in the Pet Store Center to inspire interest in animals among the children.

Learning Objectives for Children in the Pet Store Center

1. To develop their understanding of responsibility by caring for and nurturing pets (and pretend pets).
2. To enhance an interest in books, as children listen and "read" stories about pets.
3. To expand oral language skills by discussing pets.
4. To experience positive social interaction by engaging in cooperative activities.
5. To learn about pet grooming and general care.

Time Frame for the Pet Store Center

Set up the Pet Store Center early in the year, while the children are learning about the care of their classroom pets. Leave the center up for at least two weeks; reintroduce the Pet Store Center later in the school year.

 Note: The attached CD contains a sample letter to send to families, introducing them to the Pet Store Center.

Hamsters are interesting to observe in the Pet Store Center.

Vocabulary Enrichment

bed
bedding
brush
care
carrier
clippers
collar
comb
feeding
flea powder
gentle
gerbil
goldfish
grooming
guinea pig
hamster
kennel
kitten
leash
medicine
mice
obedience
puppy
hermit crab
tag
tank
train
trimmer
treat
vaccine
vet/veterinarian
walk
wash
water

Web of Integrated Learning

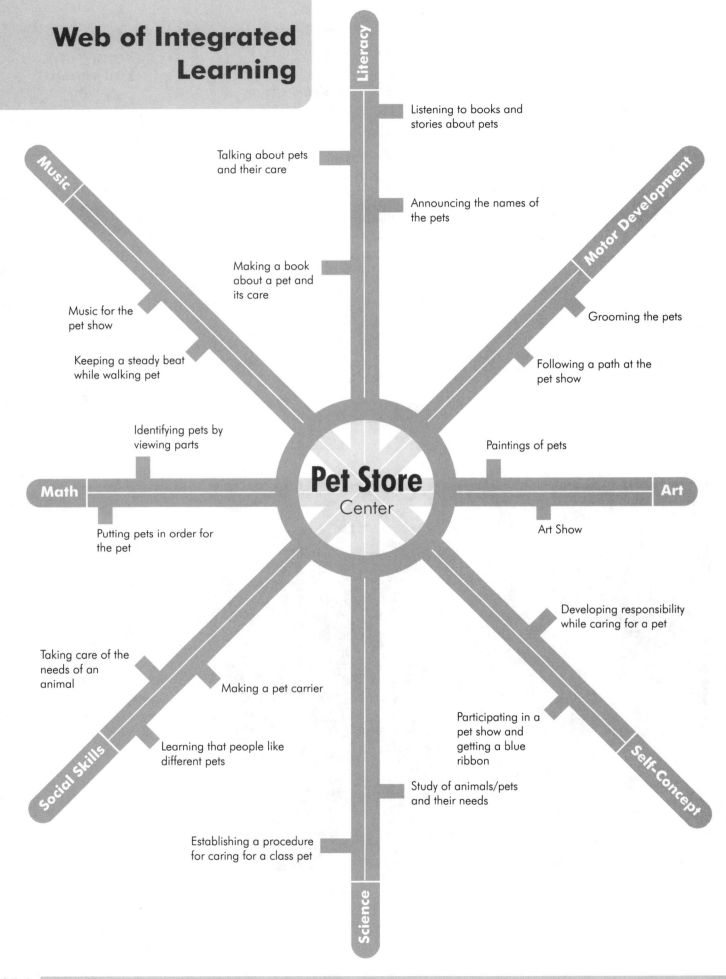

Pet Store Center

Literacy
- Listening to books and stories about pets
- Talking about pets and their care
- Announcing the names of the pets
- Making a book about a pet and its care

Music
- Music for the pet show
- Keeping a steady beat while walking pet

Motor Development
- Grooming the pets
- Following a path at the pet show

Math
- Identifying pets by viewing parts
- Putting pets in order for the pet

Art
- Paintings of pets
- Art Show

Self-Concept
- Developing responsibility while caring for a pet
- Participating in a pet show and getting a blue ribbon

Social Skills
- Taking care of the needs of an animal
- Making a pet carrier
- Learning that people like different pets

Science
- Study of animals/pets and their needs
- Establishing a procedure for caring for a class pet

- ❏ aquarium with fish
- ❏ baby bottles (small plastic)
- ❏ bird cage
- ❏ cardboard boxes (medium size—can be found at grocery stores or discount stores)
- ❏ carrier for small animal
- ❏ class pet (hamster, guinea pig, white mice, and so on)
- ❏ containers (empty, labeled as listed below):
  - ❏ bird food
  - ❏ cat food
  - ❏ dog food
  - ❏ fish food
  - ❏ flea powder
  - ❏ hair conditioner
  - ❏ pet shampoo
  - ❏ newspaper
- ❏ pet supplies:
  - ❏ blow dryer
  - ❏ brush
  - ❏ comb
- ❏ scales for weighing
- ❏ stuffed animals that can be used at "pets" in the Pet Store Center

A visiting puppy is a great temporary addition to the Pet Store Center.

Child-Created Props for the Pet Store Center

Carriers for Pets

SOCIAL SKILLS

cardboard boxes — scissors
fabric — tape
markers — books about pets

- The children make carriers out of cardboard boxes, using lengths of fabric to make their handles to use with their pets for when they travel with their animals or take them to the vet. **Note:** One way to make carriers is to attach pieces of fabric to the side of the box for handles. The pet (stuffed animal) can be placed in the box and carried around the store.
- Help the children write their pet's name on the carriers and decorate their exteriors.
- If possible, attach a book to the side of each carrier that includes the instructions for caring for the pet when they are away.

Collars and Leashes

MOTOR DEVELOPMENT

buttons — markers — rope — scraps of colorful fabric
fabric paint — ribbons — scissors — trim

- Set out the materials listed above for the children to make and decorate collars and leashes for the pets. Also, use these in a pet show.
- The collars will be used to decorate the pets, and the leashes will be used to "walk" the pet in the show.

Paintings of Pets

ART

paper, paint and paintbrushes

- Set out paints, paintbrushes, and paper for the children to use to make paintings of their pets or of pets they would like to have.
- Use one wall in the Pet Store Center to display each child's painting of his pet or a pet he would like to have.
- Label the paintings with the artists' names and the names of the pets they depict.

Pet Show Path

MOTOR DEVELOPMENT

fabric — sheets of dark plastic
rope — tape

- With the children, designate an area in the center to hold a pet show.
- Make a circular path from dark plastic taped to the floor or use tape to mark a route for the display.
- Use the path when the children are "showing" their pets.
- If desired, make collars and leashes from fabric or rope and use them to lead pets around the path.

Grooming

SOCIAL SKILLS

grooming supplies: low table
   blow dryer   comb
   bowl of water   soft brush

pictures of ways to groom pets
plastic toy pets and other animals

- Groom the pets in the Pet Show Center.
- On a low table, set out several toy animals as well as various grooming supplies.
- The children wash, blow dry, brush, comb, and/or dress the pets.

Mystery Pet

MATH

large brown envelopes or file folders
pictures of pets and other animals
scissors

- Cut a hole in the front of several large brown envelopes or file folders.
- Place various pictures of pets in the envelopes so only portions of their bodies are visible through the holes in the envelopes.
- Set out the envelopes and challenge the children to look at a part of the animal through the hole, working individually or with a partner to identify the mystery creature.
- Alternately, the children can place pictures inside an envelope and challenge a friend to name the mystery pet.

Pet Book

LITERACY

blank book or several sheets of paper stapled together
glue
magazines
pictures of pets

- The children bring pictures of their pets to include in a pet book. Make several magazines with images of animals available so those children who do not bring in photos can still include images of animals in the book.
- The children attach their photos and cutouts to the pet book. The children write or dictate interesting facts about their pets.

blue construction paper   scissors
markers   toy animals and pets
paper

- Help the children plan and make flyers to advertise a pet show. Encourage them to think of a name for the pet show, and include it on all their flyers and promotional materials.
- The children groom and train their pets in preparation for the big show.
- Select an announcer to call the names of the pets as their owners walk around the path with their pets. (Use the path the children selected earlier as the walkway for the pet show.)
- Award blue ribbons to all the pets (and owners) participating in the show.

Vet Visit   SCIENCE

appointment book   markers
eyedropper   pamphlets about care of animals
gloves   paper
large apron   small empty bottles
low table

- Open a veterinary office in the Pet Store Center.
- Set out materials so the children can make signs for the office as well as those that read, "Doctor is in." Set them out in the veterinary office. Make several toy medical supplies available for the office.
- Among the various doctor's materials, set out a book where the children can make appointments for their pets, as well as a pad and pencil available so the children pretending to be veterinarians can write prescriptions.
- Include brochures and pamphlets about the care of pets in the center.

Adding Spark to the Pet Store Center

Bring a real pet in to provide renewed interest in the Pet Store Center. The visiting pet could be a rabbit, lizard, sand crab, kitten, or any other animal that young children can handle safely. Talk with the person bringing the pet to the classroom before the visit, so he understands the educational benefit of the visit and so he can anticipate any questions that young children may ask during the visit.

The Essential Literacy Connection

Reading/Writing Opportunities

- Set out books about pet care.
- The children can write appointments and prescription and medicine orders on writing tablets.
- Create labels on food, toys, and supplies.
- Each child can develop a book of instructions for caring for his "pet."
- Make labels for pet supplies and cages.

Other Printed Materials

- Find books about the care of dogs, cats, birds, fish, or other pets that the children in the class may have at home.

Books for the Pet Store Center

Grogan, J. 2007. *Bad Dog Marley.* Illustrated by Richard Cowdrey. New York: HarperCollins. *Mommy, Daddy, Cassie, and Baby Louie welcome Marley, their new Labrador pup, into their family. But Marley does not stay a tiny puppy for long. He grows and grows, and the bigger Marley gets, the bigger trouble he gets into. Will this family have to find a new home for their big, crazy, pure-hearted dog?*

Keats, E. J. 2001. *Pet Show!* New York: Puffin. *Everyone is talking about the neighborhood pet show, and Archie can't wait. His friends are bringing dogs and birds, and he is going to enter the cat that lives nearby. But when it's time to go, the cat is nowhere to be found. The contest is about to start. What can Archie do?*

Leonard, M. 1999. *The Pet Vet.* Illustrated by Dorothy Handelman. Minneapolis, MN: Lerner. *A child pretends to be a veterinarian who heals sick pets.*

Mayer, M. 1998. *Just Me and My Puppy.* New York: Random House. *Mayer's comical illustrations and text tell the story of a little boy who wants a puppy. He shows how he cares for the puppy, as well as the fun times they are able to share.*

Namm, D. 2004. *Pick a Pet.* Illustrated by Maribel Suarez. New York: Scholastic, Inc. *Choosing a pet is difficult, so this young girl visits a zoo, a petting farm, and a pet store in search of the best pet.*

Evaluation of the Pet Store Center

(This form is on the CD that comes with this book.)

Ask yourself the following questions to evaluate the Pet Store Center in your classroom:

- Are children participating in the activities in the Pet Store Center?
- Are children interested in children's books that relate to the Pet Store Center?
- Are the children demonstrating responsible behavior as they care for and nurture pets?
- Are children helping to set up the pet show and do they take turns using the grooming area?
- Are children becoming more responsible for the care of the classroom pet?

Observation of the Individual Child

(This form is on the CD that comes with this book. Always date observations of each child.)

- Is the child interested in pets? How is he responding to real and pretend animals?
- Does the child have a pet? Can he tell you about it?
- Describe the play of the child in the Pet Store Center. Is he role-playing? Is he demonstrating use of his imagination?
- Does the child express interest in any of the books or pamphlets? Which one(s)?
- Did the child participate in the pet show? What animal did he use?

Summary

Young children are very curious about their world and everything in it. They ask millions of questions: "Why?" "What's that?" and "What makes it do that?" In the Repair Shop Center, they will be able to indulge this curiosity and examine items that are part of their experiences. In this center, they will be able to play with items, take them apart, and investigate their internal workings. Matching the child's curiosity with a carefully planned Repair Shop Center will produce a wonderful learning environment where the children can make important connections.

Stock the Repair Shop Center with a collection of tools as well as old and broken small appliances that the children will have the opportunity to take apart and sometimes even put back together again. During their participation in the Repair Shop Center, young children will be talking about their work, thinking creatively, solving problems, using small motor skills, and "reading" manuals. This type of integrated learning in a high-interest center will certainly invite their active participation and sustained work on a repair project.

Introducing the Center

Bring a collection of tools appropriate for work with household items to circle or group time. A small set of screwdrivers or wrenches will be of interest and useful in the Repair Shop Center. Discuss their names, sizes, and uses. A simple demonstration of how to use a screwdriver to remove a screw will be sufficient to interest the children in the center and make them want to use that item to explore the appliances in the Repair Shop Center.

Learning Objectives for Children in the Repair Shop Center

1. To use their curiosity in meaningful ways as they examine materials.
2. To develop small motor skills as they work on the items in the Repair Shop Center.
3. To use their problem-solving abilities as they attempt to understand the workings of small machines.
4. To enhance their language skills by discussing with one another the various materials in the center.
5. To learn that other children can contribute helpful and important suggestions, and to discover the benefits of working together.

Time Frame for the Repair Shop Center

Rotate the Repair Shop Center in and out of the classroom several times each year. Use the shop for about two weeks, and bring it back a few months later with new items for the children to examine.

 Note: The attached CD contains a sample letter to send to families, introducing them to the Repair Shop Center.

These children are working together to repair a mixer.

Glue

Web of Integrated Learning

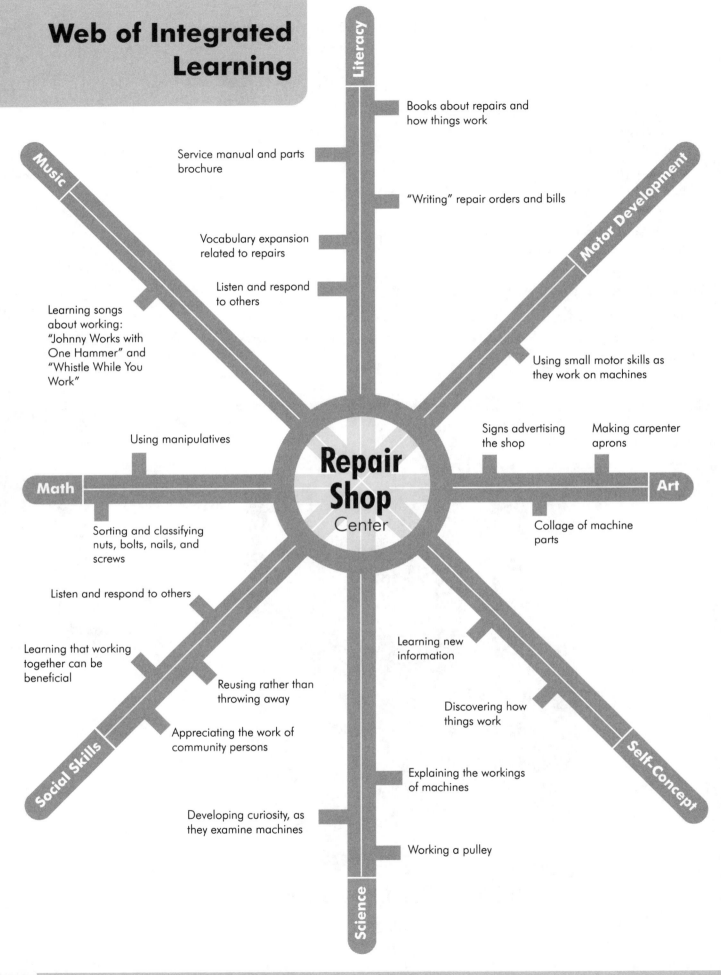

Literacy
- Books about repairs and how things work
- Service manual and parts brochure
- "Writing" repair orders and bills
- Vocabulary expansion related to repairs
- Listen and respond to others

Music
- Learning songs about working: "Johnny Works with One Hammer" and "Whistle While You Work"

Motor Development
- Using small motor skills as they work on machines

Math
- Using manipulatives
- Sorting and classifying nuts, bolts, nails, and screws

Art
- Signs advertising the shop
- Making carpenter aprons
- Collage of machine parts

Social Skills
- Listen and respond to others
- Learning that working together can be beneficial
- Reusing rather than throwing away
- Appreciating the work of community persons

Self-Concept
- Learning new information
- Discovering how things work

Science
- Explaining the workings of machines
- Developing curiosity, as they examine machines
- Working a pulley

Repair Shop Center

Family- or Teacher-Collected Props for the Repair Shop Center

Safety Note: Demonstrate for the children the proper ways to use the tools. Limit the number of children in this shop to three or four, and be sure an adult is always there to supervise and help. Remove sharp or dangerous parts of appliances, including plugs. Check items to be sure they are safe before placing them in the Repair Shop Center.

- ❏ clip-on light
- ❏ low table covered with plastic
- ❏ manipulatives that relate to the shop and develop
  - ❏ small motor coordination:
  - ❏ busy boards
  - ❏ cash register
  - ❏ gears that can be assembled and turned
  - ❏ puzzles of carpenter tools
  - ❏ small interlocking plastic pieces
- ❏ old and broken appliances that can be taken apart by the children (Ask for donations or buy at garage sales.):
  - ❏ clocks
  - ❏ electric shaver
  - ❏ hairdryer
  - ❏ iron
  - ❏ mixer
  - ❏ record player/CD player/VCR
  - ❏ sweeper
  - ❏ timer
  - ❏ toaster

- ❏ tool assortment:
  - ❏ bolts
  - ❏ C-clamp
  - ❏ clothespins
  - ❏ electrical tape
  - ❏ glue
  - ❏ masking tape
  - ❏ measuring tape
  - ❏ nuts
  - ❏ pliers
  - ❏ ruler
  - ❏ screwdrivers (Phillips and standard)
  - ❏ screws
  - ❏ washers
  - ❏ wrench (small adjustable)
- ❏ tool box or fishing tackle box

Name the Shop

crayons
markers
paper
tape

- Invite the children to name the Repair Shop Center, as well as decide upon its operating hours and the services available.
- Set out the markers, crayons, paper, and tape, and then help the children make signs advertising the shop, making sure they include all the repair shop's information.
- Also, remind the children to make "open" and "closed" signs.

Storage Area

glue
labels for "repaired" and "needs work"
labels for tools
paint and brushes (if desired)
shoeboxes and other small and large boxes

- Set out shoeboxes and other small boxes for the children to use to make containers for the machines they repair.
- Glue shoeboxes or other small boxes together for an organized storage area.
- The children paint the boxes different colors or paint patterns on them.
- Talk with the children about the benefits of having a single storage area, explaining that when a customer returns to collect an item, they can go to the storage area and find it easily.

Work Apron

fabric glue
old sheets
scissors
stiff fabric

- Cut a carpenter's apron from old sheets.
- Cut out pockets from stiff fabric and glue them to the apron with fabric glue.
- When the glue is dry, these new pockets can hold tools the children frequently use for repair work in the Repair Shop Center.

Broken Toys

MOTOR DEVELOPMENT

basket, broken toys, family member or carpenter

- Place the broken toys in a basket in the classroom in the Repair Shop Center.
- Ask family members or a carpenter to come to the Repair Shop Center and help repair these broken toys.
- Encourage the children to observe the repairs, talk about them with the carpenter, and to help when possible.

Collage of Parts

ART

large piece of cardboard, glue or tape
small parts from appliances such as bolts, nuts, screws, small gears, washers, and wood pieces

- Set out a large piece of cardboard from an appliance box for the children to use the base for their collage in the Repair Shop Center.
- The children can take several small parts taken from various appliances and glue or tape the parts to the cardboard.
- Display this collage in the customer area of the Repair Shop Center.

Making Patterns for Storage

MATH

black marker or crayon
heavy paper or poster board
tools (unusual shapes)

- Each child can place a tool on a sheet of paper, and then use a marker or crayon to draw the outline of the tool.
- Once the children finish drawing the outline of their tools, collect the sheets of paper, mix them up, and the children can match the tools to their patterns.
- Keep the tool outlines, and use them to organize the tools in the work area.

Pulley

SCIENCE

clothesline hook, plastic basket, pulley

- Thread a clothesline through a pulley and run the clothesline along one corner of the center to construct a repair assembly line like those repair people use to move an appliance from one workstation to another.
- Hook a plastic basket to the pulley.
- The children place an item in need of repair into the basket and then pull the cord to move the item from one area of the Repair Shop Center to another.

coffee can

marker

paper (large pieces)

plastic bowls or muffin tins

screws, nuts, bolts

- Store a collection of screws, nuts, and bolts in a coffee can.
- The children take items from the coffee can and sort similar items into plastic bowls or muffin tins.
- On a large sheet of paper, make a chart on which the children can tally the results of the sorting.
- Use this collection to make a chart with the outline of some of the items in the can.
- The children match the item in the can to the appropriate outline.
- Also the children can count and compare the number of items they are sorting.

Work Chart   MATH

chart paper

marker

pictures of appliances

- Before the activity, create the chart by drawing a grid and writing the names of the items the children will "repair." Include various possible steps involved in repairing, such as "Broken," "In Repair," and "Fixed."
- Show the chart to the children.
- The children can keep track of the items they are repairing by marking the chart.
- This graph provides the children with a visual representation of the work they are doing.

Adding Spark to the Repair Shop Center

Inspire new interest in the Repair Shop Center by setting out paint so the children can decorate the items in the center. Include tempera paint, brushes, rollers, sponges, contact paper, colored tape, and stickers for painting and decorating the machines. With this new addition of materials, children will be able to make the items "look better" when they are in the Repair Shop Center.

The Essential Literacy Connection

Reading/Writing Opportunities

- When a "customer" brings in a broken appliance, the "repair person" records information on a form attached with drawings of parts.
- With the children, prepare a chart of working hours. The children mark the chart when they work in the Repair Shop Center. This provides a visual record of their work schedules.

Other Printed Materials

- Bring in mechanics' magazines, catalogs of tools, parts, and appliances, or service manuals with drawings of parts.

Books for the Repair Shop Center

Auerbach, A. 2001. *Bob's Busy World.* Illustrated by Mel Grant. New York: Simon & Schuster. *Join Bob and Wendy and all the machines as they fix and repair all sorts of stuff!*

MacKeen, L. A. 1989. *Who Can Fix It?* Kansas City, MO: Landmark Editions. *This book is loaded with fun and puns! When Jeremiah T. Fitz's car stops running, several animals offer suggestions for fixing it and Mr. Fitz takes everything they say literally. The results are hilarious. The illustrations are bright and clever.*

Mazer, A. 1999. *The Fixits.* Illustrated by Paul Meisel. New York: Hyperion. *After Michael and Augusta break their mother's favorite plate, they call the Fixits, who shatter more than the china.*

McPhail, D. 1999. *Fix-It.* Minneapolis, MN: Tandem Library. *One morning, baby Emma wakes up and the television will not work. Her mom, dad, and even the repairman cannot fix it. Emma's mother reads her a book and she soon forgets about the television, even though her dad figured out the problem: it was unplugged.*

Thomas, M. 2000. *A Day with a Plumber.* New York: Children's Press. *This book describes what plumbers do on an average day and the many kinds of work they do.*

Evaluation of the Repair Shop Center

(This form is on the CD that comes with this book.)

Ask yourself the following questions to evaluate the Repair Shop Center in your classroom:

- Are the children curious about the tools and appliances in the Repair Shop Center?
- Are children beginning to use the names of tools, machine parts, and appliances?
- Is the small motor coordination of the children improving as they work in the Repair Shop Center?
- Are children discussing problems and ideas with other children as they work together?
- Are the children's attention spans growing as they participate in the activities that are of interest to them?

Observation of the Individual Child

(This form is on the CD that comes with this book. Always date observations of each child.)

- Which items and tools in the Repair Shop Center interest the child? Describe how the child demonstrates this interest.
- Is the child using new vocabulary and expanded language in the Repair Shop Center? What are some examples?
- How is the child's small motor coordination improving while using tools and exploring items in the Repair Shop Center? Give a specific observation.
- Is the child exhibiting curiosity in various parts of the Repair Shop Center? In what situation?
- Has the child participated in collaborative work in the Repair Shop Center?

Summary

One of the most interesting centers for young children is the Restaurant Center. Most young children have eaten in a restaurant, either full-service or fast food. If the children decide to recreate a restaurant that most are familiar with and want to visit, their play will be more complex and satisfying. In this Restaurant Center, children can prepare the food, take orders, be the customer, or be part of the clean-up crew. The Restaurant Center directly relates to their experiences and helps them better understand the world in which they live.

In the Restaurant Center, the children are learning many things: new vocabulary, roles, procedures, responsibilities, and teamwork. They can also "read" menus, "write" orders, and discuss choices. This active center provides many opportunities for integrated and meaningful learning.

Introducing the Center

A trip to a local full-service restaurant or fast-food restaurant helps children observe closely and talk with the staff about their work. Often, restaurants allow children to visit the food preparation area and offer them samples of the food they serve. This field trip will give the children additional ideas about restaurants and activities they can replicate in the Restaurant Center.

Learning Objectives for Children in the Restaurant Center

1. To learn about how food service providers operate.
2. To learn about nutrition as it relates to their lives.
3. To participate in functional literacy activities.
4. To develop their oral language as they participate in role-playing activities.
5. To extend meaningful experiences.

Time Frame for the Restaurant Center

Take a week to set up the Restaurant Center. Involve the children in selecting the restaurant they want to recreate and encourage them to create signs, advertisements, decorations, and set up workstations for the restaurant. The actual operation of the restaurant can go on for two to three weeks. However, if the interest and participation is high, continue to keep the center open.

Note: The attached CD contains a sample letter to send to families, introducing them to the Restaurant Center.

A real menu from a restaurant adds interest in the Restaurant Center.

Vocabulary Enrichment

beverage
bill
buffet
cashier
chef
cleanup
course
customer
dessert
dinner music
dishwasher
host/hostess
kitchen
manager
menu
order
reservation
salad bar
selection
server
service
setup
silverware
special
takeout
tip
waiter/waitress

Web of Integrated Learning

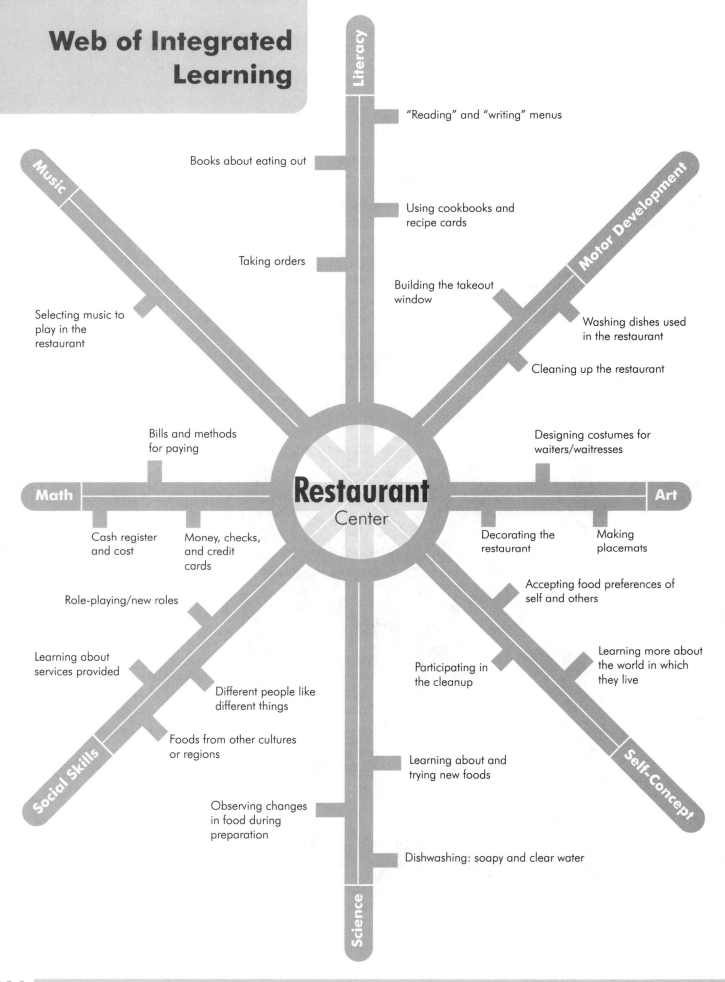

Restaurant Center

Literacy
- "Reading" and "writing" menus
- Books about eating out
- Using cookbooks and recipe cards
- Taking orders
- Building the takeout window

Music
- Selecting music to play in the restaurant

Motor Development
- Washing dishes used in the restaurant
- Cleaning up the restaurant

Math
- Bills and methods for paying
- Cash register and cost
- Money, checks, and credit cards

Art
- Designing costumes for waiters/waitresses
- Decorating the restaurant
- Making placemats

Social Skills
- Role-playing/new roles
- Learning about services provided
- Different people like different things
- Foods from other cultures or regions

Self-Concept
- Accepting food preferences of self and others
- Learning more about the world in which they live

Science
- Participating in the cleanup
- Learning about and trying new foods
- Observing changes in food during preparation
- Dishwashing: soapy and clear water

- ❏ bowls
- ❏ cash register
- ❏ cooking utensils
- ❏ cups
- ❏ dishes (unbreakable)
- ❏ forks
- ❏ knives
- ❏ paper tablecloths
- ❏ pitcher
- ❏ plates
- ❏ props related to the specific type of restaurant
- ❏ sink, refrigerator, and stove from the Home Living Center
- ❏ small tables and chairs
- ❏ spoons
- ❏ unbreakable child-safe utensils

This waiter is "writing" the order on the pad.

Check, Money, or Credit Card

MATH

cardboard credit cards (if available, dummy cards from credit card offers)
crayons
markers
paper
scissors

- The children make play money, checks, and credit cards. The children cut out pieces of paper in the correct sizes, and then decorate the money or checks however they like.
- The children role-play with these items, pretending to pay for their orders or take payments from customers.

Costumes for Servers

ART

scissors
scraps of paper and fabric
stapler and tape

- Let the children determine the type of restaurant they want to establish, as well as the types of outfits the wait staff will wear.
- Help the children design and make their wait staff outfits out of scraps of paper and fabric.
- Outfits could include aprons, hats, belts, and any other decorations they think will make them stand out.

Decorating the Restaurant

ART

fabric
paint
paintbrushes
pictures
scissors
tape

- The children use the materials to decorate the restaurant by painting the walls (made from cardboard boxes), hanging pictures, or making draperies for the windows.

crayons
markers
poster board or photo album pages

● After the children determine the food they want to serve at their restaurant, set out markers and crayons so they can make menus from poster board or photo album pages.
● The "wait staff" can then give these menus to the "customers" when they are waiting to order.

Activities for the Restaurant Center

Clean-up Crew
SOCIAL SKILLS

paper towels
plastic carrier for cleaning supplies
sponges
spray bottles
keys

● The children determine how the clean-up crew will clean up the restaurant after closing. This includes cleaning tables, windows, and doors, as well as putting items back in appropriate places for business the next day.
● The children to clean the Restaurant Center.
● Finally, they close up the restaurant, including locking it up.

Dishwashing
MOTOR DEVELOPMENT

plastic dishes, utensils, and small pots and pans
2 plastic tubs
sponges
dishwashing detergent

● The children wash plastic dishes, utensils, and small pots and pans, as they work in the restaurant.
● Fill two small plastic tubs—one with soapy water for washing, and one with clear water for rinsing.
● This experience often leads to a discussion of the differences between water in the two tubs.

family member or other adult
food from another country or culture

- Invite a family member or other adult to the Restaurant Center to prepare a food that many of the children have not experienced. This food may be from another culture or a different region of the country, thereby helping the children appreciate different cultures.
- Let the children observe the preparation, taste the results, and appreciate the cook's talent.

Music for Eating   MUSIC

recordings of different kinds of music:
    big band
    classical
    country
    folk
    jazz
    new age

- Let the children listen to a number of recordings of different types of music for the children, discussing their differences and what about the music the children enjoy.
- They decide which recording they want to play in the Restaurant Center.

Nutrition   SELF-CONCEPT

advertisements from newspaper or flyers
child-safe scissors
crayons
glue
large sheet of white/color paper
markers
menus
old magazines

- Talk about foods that are healthy.
- Take a vote among the children to determine which nutritious foods they want to include on their restaurant's menu.
- The children decide how to identify the items on the menu so other children will know that these are healthy foods, such as developing a logo to put beside each healthy item on the menu.
- Set out markers, crayons, and other materials so the children can make a mural of the foods that are available and healthy. Encourage the children to cut out pictures of healthy foods from magazines and paste them to the mural. Help them put the healthy food logo on the chart beside each picture of healthy food.

clear contact paper or laminating machine
colored paper
markers
stick-on decorations
knife, fork, and spoon

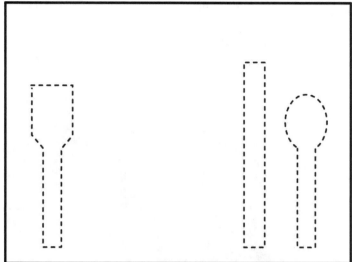

- The children use colored paper and markers to make placemats. The children may draw pictures on the paper or put stick on decorations on the paper.
- The children trace around a fork, knife, and spoon, on the paper to provide a pattern for setting the table in the Restaurant Center.
- To make the placemats more durable, laminate them, or cover them with clear contact paper.

Take-Out Window   MOTOR DEVELOPMENT

cardboard box
chenille stems
paint
paintbrushes
scissors
Styrofoam cups (small)

- Set out a cardboard box for the children to paint and decorate so that it resembles a drive-up or pick-up window.
- The children make toy headsets out of chenille stems and small Styrofoam cups to wear when taking orders.

Adding Spark to the Restaurant Center

When interest is declining in the Restaurant Center, transform the area into a Pizza Restaurant. The menu and atmosphere of the new restaurant will change, as well as the manner of serving food. This change will draw children back to the center for new cooking and eating. An interesting book related to the Pizza Restaurant is Claire St-Onge's *Caillou at a Fancy Restaurant*. Add fancy items to the Restaurant Center, such as a tablecloth, candle (unlit), cloth napkins, and soft music.

Reading/Writing Opportunities

- Children can draw and "write" items on a menu.
- Children can create signs that advertise the restaurant, its specials, or new items.
- Children can pay their bills with "checks" or "credit cards" requiring them to "sign" their names.
- The child who works as the server "writes" down customer orders.
- The children create "open" and "closed" signs.

Taking an order is a meaningful writing experience.

Other Printed Materials

- Find advertisements from the newspaper for restaurants or food items.
- Bring in cooking magazines that include pictures of prepared food and recipes.
- Collect menus from this and other restaurants.
- Set out cookbook recipe collections for the children to review.

Books for the Restaurant Center

Barron, R. 2004. *Showdown at the Food Pyramid.* New York: Putnam. *When snack foods take over the food pyramid and make it collapse, members of the various food groups have to work together and use the Great Food Guide to rebuild it.*

Calmenson, S. 1995. *Dinner at the Panda Palace.* New York: HarperCollins. *Mr. Panda, owner of the Panda Palace restaurant, manages to find seating for all of his animal patrons on a very busy night.*

London, J. 2003. *Froggy Eats Out.* New York: Puffin. *After Froggy misbehaves at a fancy restaurant, his parents take him to a "fast flies" restaurant to celebrate their anniversary.*

Mayer, M. 2003. *Frog Goes to Dinner.* New York: Dial. *Having stowed away in a pocket, Frog wreaks havoc and creates disgrace for the family at the posh restaurant where they are having dinner.*

Shaw, N. 1995. *Sheep Out to Eat.* New York: Houghton Mifflin. *Five hungry sheep discover that a tea shop may not be the best place for them to eat.*

St-Onge, C. 2005. *Caillou at a Fancy Restaurant.* Montreal, Canada: Chouette Publishing. *Mommy and Daddy take Caillou to a fancy restaurant for the very first time while Rosie stays home with the babysitter.*

Evaluation of the Restaurant Center

(This form is on the CD that comes with this book.)

Ask yourself the following questions to evaluate the Restaurant Center in your classroom:

- Are the children talking about the menu, food preparation, and orders they are taking?
- Are the children acting out different roles in the Restaurant Center?
- Are the children reading and writing in meaningful situations?
- Are the children discussing the nutritional values of foods?
- Are the children making appropriate choices for the menus, decorations, and services for the Restaurant Center?

Observation of the Individual Child

(This form is on the CD that comes with this book. Always date observations of each child.)

- Did the child participate in the discussion and selection of the Restaurant Center? What did he say?
- What role is this child enacting? Describe.
- Is there evidence of literacy understanding with books, printed materials, or writing?
- Is the child playing and acting out the various positions in the appropriate sequences? Explain.
- Is the child collaborating on certain work? On which task? In what ways are you seeing evidence of collaboration?

Summary

The Sign Shop Center provides an interesting environment where young children can make signs, write, and use print. They can select from a wide range of possibilities what tools they want to use to create their signs. In this center, the children are able to use print in meaningful ways, such as creating "open," "closed," and "exit" signs. After making the signs, the children can place them in appropriate places in the classroom, work areas, or other special places. The Sign Shop Center also inspires children to work together and collaborate on the signs, determining what to write, how to write it, and where to display the signs. The Sign Shop Center also gives the children the opportunity to explore various aspects of the business world, as the children decide what to charge, create a portfolio, write bills, and conduct sales.

Introducing the Center

Begin by touring the building and classroom with the children. Encourage the children to focus on the signs that are in their space and what they tell them. (If there are only a few signs on display in the building, consider adding some before the tour.) Later in the week, set up the Sign Shop Center and encourage the children to help decide what tools they might use in the shop. After selecting the tools, help the children set up a workroom for printing and an area for sales. In some instances, you may need to demonstrate for the children various ways of printing, painting, or using new tools.

Learning Objectives for Children in the Sign Shop Center

1. To recognize print in the classroom, building, and environment.
2. To discover that printed signs communicate messages.
3. To improve problem-solving skills while making choices relating to tools, materials, and sign use.
4. To work with peers to create and display signs.
5. To enhance their creative abilities by designing and decorating signs.
6. To learn about how small businesses operate.

Time Frame for the Sign Shop Center

The Sign Shop Center should be in operation for two to three weeks. After this time, label the sign-making materials and store them in the Art or Author/Illustrator Center. The children will understand how and when to use the materials from the Sign Shop Center.

Note: The attached CD contains a sample letter to send to families, introducing them to the Sign Shop Center.

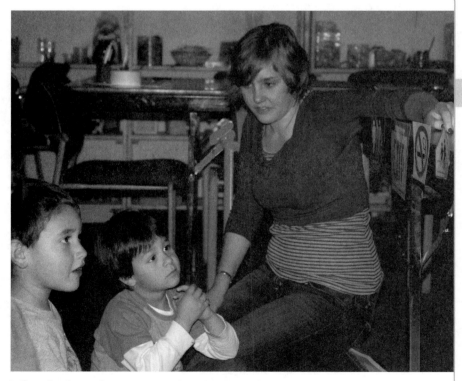

What do these signs communicate?

Vocabulary Enrichment

business
buy/purchase
clock in/out
communicate
customer
decorate
design
display
exit
letter
measuring
no smoking
office
open/closed
portfolio
print
restroom (men's and
   women's)
select
sell
spacing
stop
team
thick/thin

Web of Integrated Learning

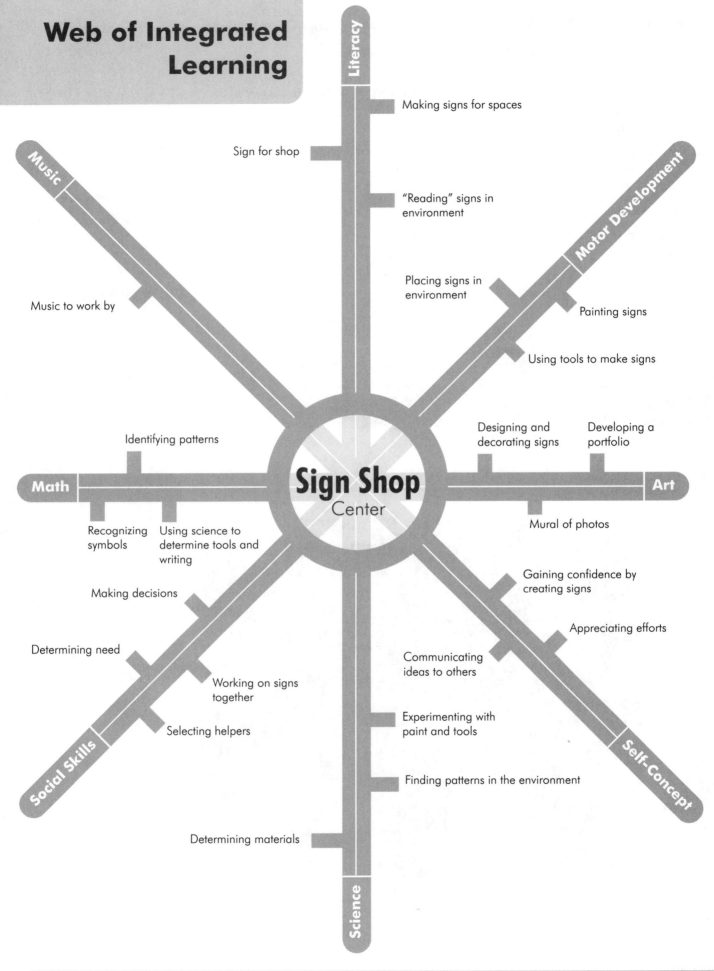

Music
- Music to work by

Literacy
- Making signs for spaces
- Sign for shop
- "Reading" signs in environment
- Placing signs in environment

Motor Development
- Painting signs
- Using tools to make signs

Math
- Identifying patterns
- Recognizing symbols
- Using science to determine tools and writing

Art
- Designing and decorating signs
- Developing a portfolio
- Mural of photos

Sign Shop Center

Social Skills
- Making decisions
- Determining need
- Working on signs together
- Selecting helpers

Self-Concept
- Gaining confidence by creating signs
- Appreciating efforts
- Communicating ideas to others
- Experimenting with paint and tools
- Finding patterns in the environment

Science
- Determining materials

- ❏ cake pans or small roasting pans
- ❏ cash register
- ❏ clipboards with pens
- ❏ large clock
- ❏ old shower curtains
- ❏ old signs: "for sale," "garage sale," "exit," and so on
- ❏ paintbrushes of various sizes
- ❏ paint trays
- ❏ play money: bills and coins
- ❏ ruler

Printing with letters can help a young child make signs.

Name of the Shop   LITERACY

large sheets or a roll of butcher paper   paintbrushes
low table   tempera paint
plastic sheets or shower curtain   markers

- Cover the area under the table with plastic.
- The children can decide on a name for the Sign Shop, and create/display the selected name at the entrance to the shop.

Pattern Hunt   MATH

plastic basket or bag   various items from the classroom

- Set out a plastic basket or bag and invite the children to look through the classroom for items that might create interesting prints when the children are decorating their signs. Possibilities include plastic blocks, small car/truck wheels, golf tees, spoons, forks, bottle lids, and so on.
- The found items can be used to create patterns to decorate the signs, posters, or books.

Taking Pictures   ART

butcher paper (large sheet)   printer and printer paper
digital camera   markers
poster board

- Demonstrate for the children how to use a digital camera, and then bring them on a walk, looking for signs in the school and the surrounding area.
- When a child sees a sign, the child takes a picture of it.
- Bring the children back into the classroom and print their photographs. After printing, the children use the images to create a photomural, and call it "Signs in Our School."

Decorating Signs   ART

items with interesting shapes that will create designs or patterns when used to make prints:
lids   plastic forks
pastry brush   potato masher
pastry cutter   sponge
plastic cups

paper
stamps
paint roller
paint tray, small cake pan,
  or small roasting pan
  with edge (at least 1")
scissors
sponge brushes
thick tempera paint:
  several colors

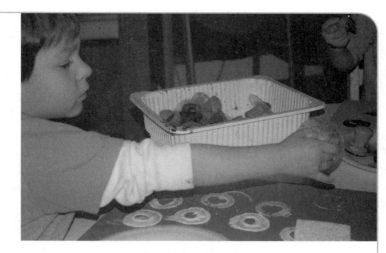

Signs can be decorated with attractive artwork.

- The children will need time to experiment with the tools and the paint.
- They will determine the designs they can produce.
- After this period of exploration, they will begin to elaborate on the basic signs.
- Display some of the decorated signs on the wall in the work area of the Sign Shop Center.
- Some children will replicate the work of others, whereas others will create original signs. Each of these approaches is acceptable and demonstrates different levels of development and self-confidence.

Portfolio of Signs

ART

digital camera	printer
glue	scissors
large scrapbook	signs that demonstrate what can be purchased by the customer

- After the children design, print, and decorate various signs, ask them to look at their creations and select the ones they want to include in the portfolio.
- Take and print photographs of each child with his favorite sign.
- After printing the signs, set them out so the children can arrange them in a scrapbook.
- The children may want to add their names and the prices they want to charge for their signs to the scrapbook. This portfolio becomes the catalog the "customers" can use to decide which signs they want to order.

Sign in, Please

LITERACY

clipboard	pens
large clock	sheets of paper with lines spaced at least 2" apart
low table or small desk	

- Place a clipboard with paper near the entrance of the Sign Shop Center. Attach a label to it that reads "sign in/sign out."

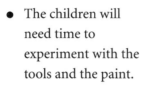

- When they arrive, the children working in the Sign Shop Center sign in by making a scribble, putting down letters, or writing their names (whatever they are capable of at their current level of writing) on the clipboard.
- The clock is in the center to develop children's awareness of time, not for the children to write down or tell a specific time.
- When the children leave the center, they will "Sign out."

Signs for Our Classroom MOTOR DEVELOPMENT

markers
paint
paintbrushes
paper (several large sheets)
plastic letters for printing
tape and other adhesive materials

- Engage the children in a discussion about the different signs they think might be necessary to put up in the classroom. Possibilities include an "exit" sign (for going outside), restroom signs, signs with the children's names beside their cubbies, signs indicating places to wash hands, signs of school hours, a "caution" sign for the steps, labels of materials in work areas, and so on.
- Creative young children will come up with many additional ideas for signs and where they are needed.
- Set out markers, paintbrushes, paint, paper, and plastic letters so the children can begin to create some of the signs they discussed. Talk with the children as they work, and help them with spelling and writing various information on the signs.
- After they finish making their signs, the children can attach them in the appropriate places.

Adding Spark to the Sign Shop Center

Bring in miniature road signs to help stimulate the children to come up with new possibilities for signs to make. Designing "stop," speed limit, "caution," construction work, and other related signs will help the children identify them and understand what the signs mean when they encounter them in the world.

The Essential Literacy Connection

Reading/Writing Opportunities

- This center helps children develop an awareness of environmental print.
- Children print signs and use paintbrushes, rollers, and stamps.
- The children create a portfolio.
- The children sign in and out of the Sign Shop Center.
- Children examine books and advertisements that include signs.

Other Printed Materials

- The children experiment with using catalogs, "sticky" notes, and order forms.
- Children take and then observe and discuss photos of signs inside the school.

Books for the Sign Shop Center

D. K. Publishing. 2006. *Signs in Our World*. New York: Author. *This informative book introduces children to many of the signs visible in today's world.*

Hill, M. 2003. *Signs at the Store*. New York: Children's Press. *On a trip to the grocery store with her father, Carly notices the various signs that help them, including those that show where to find certain items, what they cost, and which checkout line is open.*

Hoban, T. 1983. *I Read Signs*. New York: Greenwillow. *This book introduces signs children frequently see along the highway.*

Searcy, J. 2006. *Signs in Our World*. London, UK: DK Publishing. *This brightly illustrated guide offers information and plenty of color photos of signs. Most of the signs in the book are those that American children will see along the highway or in their towns and cities.*

Evaluation of the Sign Shop Center

(This form is on the CD that comes with this book.)

Ask yourself the following questions to evaluate the Sign Shop Center in your classroom:

- Do the children display interest in working in the Sign Shop Center?
- What tools do the children use as they make signs? Which tools do they not use?
- Are the children demonstrating a growing awareness of the signs in their environment?
- What kinds of signs are the children producing: drawings, scribbles, random letters, or beginnings of words?
- Are the children placing the signs in appropriate places in the classroom, building, or playground?
- Are the children working together to create and design the signs?

Observation of the Individual Child

(This form is on the CD that comes with this book. Always date observations of each child.)

- Is this child choosing to work in the Sign Shop Center? Describe what he does in the area.
- Which signs has the child identified in the classroom, building, or outside? Does the child recognize the sign and is he able to determine what the sign communicates?
- How would you describe the skill level of the child when printing with objects or letters? Give an example that helps in coming to this conclusion.
- Is the child using new vocabulary that relates to the sign shop? What new words is he using?
- Have you seen this child working alone, beside others, or collaborating to design a sign?
- Is the child signing in and out of the Sign Shop Center? How is he writing his name?

Summary

In today's world, people frequently throw things away rather than repair them. The Toy Workshop Center provides a place where young children can experience repairing items, rather than just throwing them away. Repairing and reusing toys provides the children with an introduction to the concept of recycling. Either distribute the toys the children "repair" throughout the classroom, or give them to another childcare facility or group of children. This will help the children develop an interest in helping and caring for others.

Because toys are the tools of children's play, this Toy Workshop Center provides meaningful experiences with items that are an important part of the children's lives.

There are also many books that focus on toys that you can use to expand the children's language skills, both through listening to their content and discussing them afterward. Also, the children will develop their small motor skills in this center by using use glue, tape, clamps, and other tools.

Introducing the Center

During circle or group time, read the children a book about toys. Possibilities include *Corduroy's Christmas Surprise* or *Alexander and the Wind-Up Mouse*. Talk with the children about their favorite toys. On chart paper, write down the toys they name. Then, ask the children to discuss times they lost or broke a toy. What did they do? How did they feel? Could they repair it or replace it?

Place the book read during circle or group time in the Toy Workshop Center.

Learning Objectives for Children in the Toy Workshop Center

1. To incorporate the content of the stories into their play.
2. To learn that they can repair and reuse toys.
3. To work cooperatively on projects that relate to the toy theme.
4. To improve their small motor coordination as they construct and repair toys.
5. To enjoy new books that relate to a specific theme.

Time Frame for the Toy Workshop Center

This center can function effectively for two to three weeks. During this time, add old or broken toys to the center to expand the workshop. It will also be helpful to add the books you read too the children during circle or group time, along with a related toy, to the Toy Workshop Center.

 Note: The attached CD contains a sample letter to send to families, introducing them to the Toy Workshop Center.

Vocabulary Enrichment

attach

classify

construct

cooperate

decorate

design

different/unique

dressing

durable

favorite

float

homemade

inexpensive

packing

parade

parts

pretend

repair

rhyming

toy

wind-up

workshop

Connecting plastic pipes can improve children's small motor skills.

Web of Integrated Learning

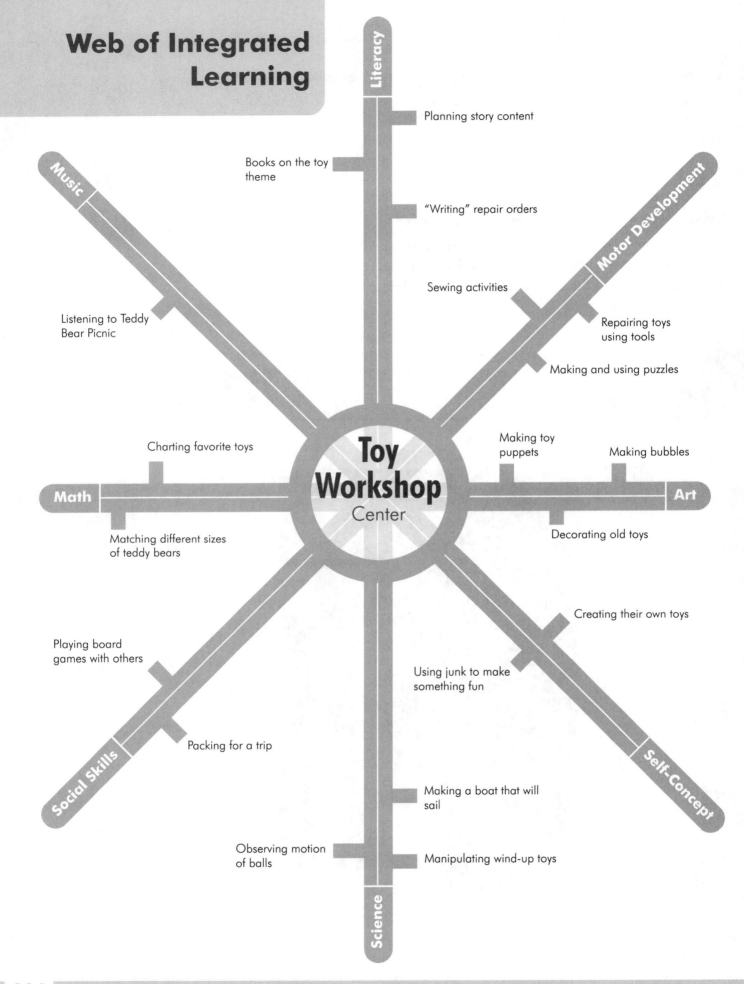

Literacy
- Planning story content
- Books on the toy theme
- "Writing" repair orders

Motor Development
- Sewing activities
- Repairing toys using tools
- Making and using puzzles

Music
- Listening to Teddy Bear Picnic

Math
- Charting favorite toys
- Matching different sizes of teddy bears

Art
- Making toy puppets
- Making bubbles
- Decorating old toys

Toy Workshop Center

Self-Concept
- Creating their own toys
- Using junk to make something fun

Social Skills
- Playing board games with others
- Packing for a trip

Science
- Making a boat that will sail
- Manipulating wind-up toys
- Observing motion of balls

- ❑ baby bath tub
- ❑ collection of balls:
  - ❑ beach ball
  - ❑ Nerf ball
  - ❑ ping pong ball
  - ❑ rubber ball
  - ❑ tennis ball
  - ❑ Velcro ball
  - ❑ other balls
- ❑ junk items:
  - ❑ buttons
  - ❑ chenille stems
  - ❑ foil
  - ❑ lids
  - ❑ pieces of fabric
  - ❑ plastic trays
  - ❑ plastic wheels
  - ❑ refrigerator dishes
  - ❑ small bars of soap
  - ❑ straws
  - ❑ Styrofoam boxes
  - ❑ tin cans
  - ❑ toy catalogs
- ❑ old toys that can be repaired or decorated
- ❑ plastic dishwashing tub with one box of corn starch, food coloring, and spray bottle filled with water
- ❑ plastic squeeze bottles, the type that contained salad dressing

- ❑ poster board and cardboard pieces
- ❑ repair box for fixing broken toys:
  - ❑ clamp
  - ❑ contact paper
  - ❑ electrical tape
  - ❑ glue
  - ❑ hammer
  - ❑ nails
  - ❑ screwdriver
  - ❑ screws
- ❑ sewing materials:
  - ❑ cloth tape
  - ❑ fabric glue
  - ❑ hole punch
  - ❑ large buttons
  - ❑ large plastic needles
  - ❑ netting
  - ❑ pieces of contact paper
  - ❑ ribbons
  - ❑ thick yarn
  - ❑ trim
  - ❑ variety of fabrics that are easy to sew
- ❑ stickers and contact paper
- ❑ stuffed animals, including a teddy bear
- ❑ tempera paint and a variety of sizes of brushes

Bear Cover

old sheet
paint
shallow trays
toy- or teddy bear-shaped cookie cutters

- The children use shallow trays of paint and toy- or teddy bear-shaped cookie cutters to print designs on an old sheet.
- When the children finish making their prints on the sheet, they hang it between boxes so it create a private reading space.

Free Toys

chenille stems
clay
glue
junk items
materials for making low-cost toys
tape

- The children use junk items to create interesting and low-cost toys. Possible materials include craft sticks, Styrofoam peanuts, string, yarn, clothespins, spools, small dowel rods, plastic wheels, cardboard pieces, wood scraps, rubber bands, plastic pieces, nails, pinecones, twigs, plastic bottles, and other available items.
- Provide glue, clay, tape, chenille stems, or electrical wire for the children to use to hold the toys together.
- Set up a display in the center of "free toys" the children have created. Be sure to include each child's name and the name of the toy he constructed.

Toy Puzzles

glue
scissors
Styrofoam trays
toy catalogs

- Set out several toy catalogs, child-safe scissors, and containers of glue. Invite the children to cut out pictures of toys from the catalogs and then glue them on a Styrofoam tray.
- After the glue on the pictures dries, help the children cut their tray into pieces, making puzzles.
- Challenge the children to put the pictures back together or share their puzzles with friends.

Toy Repair

old or broken toys
several decorative items such
as plastic pieces, contact
paper, foil, and so on
tools

- Set out various old or broken toys in one area of the Toy Workshop Center, making a toy repair shop.
- Invite the children to work on fixing and decorating old or broken toys.
- Provide a collection of tools and decorative items for this toy repair area.

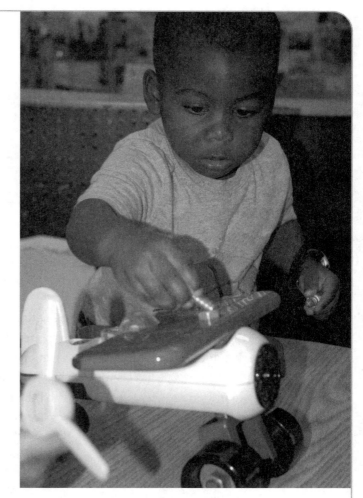

What tools are needed to fix a toy airplane?

Activities for the Toy Workshop Center

Ball Play

large plastic laundry basket
assortment of balls

- Use a large plastic laundry basket for target practice.
- The children toss different balls into the basket and observe the various ways each respond. Balls that move differently include beach balls, large rubber balls, tennis balls, ping pong balls, plastic practice golf balls, Wiffle balls, cloth balls, yarn balls, and so on.
- The children stand at different distances from the basket, as they try to be successful with various balls.

bubble solution ingredients:
  dishwashing detergent
  water
  white corn syrup
measuring cup
large jar
squeeze bottles
funnels
large plastic tray, dishpan, or length
  of plastic

2 cups dish soap   6 cups water

- The children make their own
  bubble solution following the
  directions on a rebus card.
  Note: The rebus of the steps to
  make a bubble solution is on the CD that is part of this book.
- Cover the solution and store it in the refrigerator to extend suds'
  shelf life. Allow the mixture to warm up before using it.
- Once the recipe has been made, help the children use funnels to
  pour it into squeeze bottles. (Do all mixing and squeezing on a
  plastic tray, dishpan, or on a table covered with plastic.)
- After the children finish filling their bottles, help them reattach
  the squeeze tops. With the spouts open, the children squeeze
  bubbles from their bottles.
- For older children, consider challenging them to compare the
  cost of making homemade bubbles with that of commercial
  bubble mix.

3/4 cup white corn syrup

1. Mix!   2. Shake!

3. Wait 4 hours.

cardboard or pieces of linoleum
colored poster board
contact paper pieces
markers

miniature toys
shapes of construction paper
stickers

- Young children enjoy playing simple board games. Because of their level of development, however, the children often find the games' specific rules constraining and frustrating. In the Workshop Center, the children have the opportunity to create their own board games and make up simple rules to guide and accompany their play.
- Provide colored poster board, shapes of construction paper, stickers, markers, and contact paper pieces for the children to use in making their games.
- The children use cardboard or pieces of linoleum as bases for their boards.
- Include several miniature toys for the players to use on their boards.
- In the games the children design, all players can be winners.

Gooey Goo   SCIENCE

cornstarch
plastic dishpan
powdered tempera paint
spray bottle filled with water

- To create strange and interesting goo, follow the steps below:
  - Pour half of a box of cornstarch into the bottom of a plastic dishpan.
  - Ask the children to choose a color of dry tempera paint, add it to the mixture, and then wet the mixture with water from the spray bottle.
- When the mixture is moist, the children put their hands into the container and feel and squeeze the unusual goo.

  Note: Be sure to put a shower curtain or plastic under the table where the children will be working.

What Should Eddie Pack? by Matt Mitter

markers

paper

small suitcase or overnight bag

toys

- Read the children *What Should Eddie Pack?* which tells the story of a little boy who must decide what to take on a trip.
- After finishing the book, set out a small suitcase or overnight bag and several toys. The children pick which toys they want to use to fill the bag.
- This prop may lead children to discuss which of their toys they would take with them on a trip.
- Set out paper and markers so the children can write, dictate, or draw lists of the toys they would like to take with them.

Sailing a Toy Boat   SCIENCE

paper

plastic tub of water

scissors

Styrofoam trays or bars of Ivory™ soap

toothpicks or straws

water with blue food coloring

- Young children can build and use a toy boat in the Toy Workshop Center.
- Use Styrofoam trays or bars of soap for the hull of a boat.
- The children cut paper into the shapes of sails and attach them to straws or toothpicks, and then poke them into the hulls.
- The children try out their boats in a plastic baby tub containing a small amount of water.

Sewing on a Button   MOTOR DEVELOPMENT

Corduroy by Don Freeman

cardboard pieces

huge buttons or buttons made out of cardboard

pieces of heavy fabric

sewing materials: large plastic needles with big eyes, yarn

- Read *Corduroy* to the children. It will inspire them for this sewing activity.
- Place large plastic needles with big eyes with yarn thread in a plastic storage box.
  Safety Note: Be sure the needles are safe for the children to use.
- Set out several large buttons or make several buttons out of cardboard. Demonstrate for the children how to sew them onto pieces of heavy fabric.
- Children who are unable to sew can glue buttons and cardboard button shapes on a cardboard piece.

Unique Center: Box Center
Boxes inspire creative play.

Traditional Center: Art Studio Center
Clay provides a three-dimensional art experience.

Outdoor Center: Adventure Center
Add trucks to outdoor adventure play.

Outdoor Center:
Car Wash Center
A water hose can help rinse riding toys.

Sociodramatic Center: Repair Shop Center
Children can use flexible wire to repair toys.

Outdoor Center: Car Wash Center
Soapy water is used to clean a toy truck.

Traditional Center:
Block Center
Use plastic crates to move
block play outside.

Traditional Center:
Science and Nature Center
It is fascinating to observe
living things!

Sociodramatic Center: Construction Center
A variety of materials encourages creative
thinking.

Traditional Center: Home Living Center
"Daddy" is changing a dirty diaper.

Outdoor Center:
Adventure Center
This large tube provides a quiet retreat outside.

Outdoor Center: Adventure Center
Use existing play equipment to create an obstacle course.

Traditional Center: Music and Sound Center
These firefighters enjoy listening to music.

Outdoor Center:
Farm Center
Even farmers take a break from work!

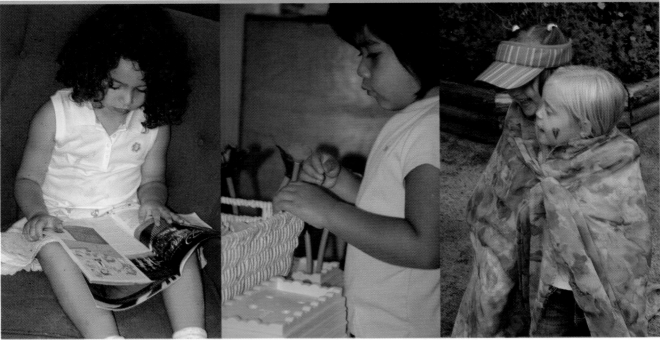

Traditional Center: Library Center
Include books and magazines in many
centers for children to "read."

Traditional Center:
Small Motor Center
Small items can be stored and displayed
in woven baskets.

Outdoor Center:
Outdoor Drama Center
Actors can create costumes from
beautiful fabric.

Traditional Center:
Library Center
These children in dress-up clothes are selecting books to "read."

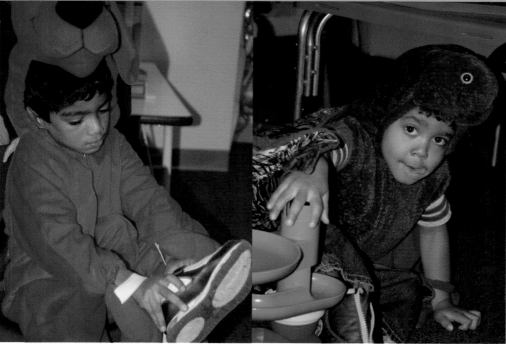

Sociodramatic Center: Mall Center
Trying on shoes in the mall store can be quite interesting.

Sociodramatic Center: Construction Center
Construction and dress-up can happen in the same center.

Unique Center: Project Center
This area encourages children to follow their interests.

Traditional Center: Small Motor Center
Playing with miniature dolls and furniture develops small motor skills.

Traditional Center: Author/Illustrator Center
This illustrator is creating pictures for her book.

Sociodramatic Center:
Restaurant Center
These chefs are selecting
items for the menu.

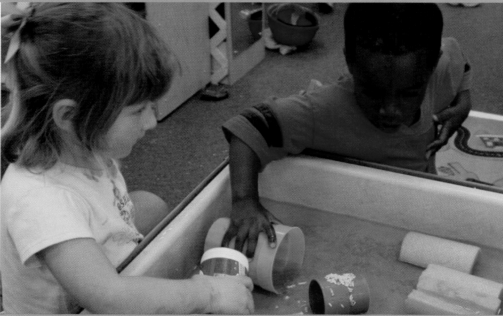

Traditional Center:
Sand and Water Center
Young scientists are
exploring the properties of
sand and water.

Unique Center: Laughing Center
Trying on funny glasses makes her laugh.

Unique Center: Storytelling Center
This child is taking a picture of the storyteller.

CD player

crumpled paper

hole punch

large-eye needle and yarn

picnic basket

recording of "The Teddy Bears' Picnic"

various sizes of teddy bears cut out of brown wrapping paper

- Place a CD player and a recording of "The Teddy Bears' Picnic" in a picnic basket. Include several brown wrapping paper cutout pairs of teddy bears in various sizes.
- The children use a hole-punch to make holes around the edges of the paired teddy bear cutouts.
- The children sew the two matching sides together and stuff them with crumpled paper to produce their own teddy bears.

Toy Puppets

ART

decorative materials: yarn, contact paper, buttons, trim, and so on

glue

plastic baskets

puppet materials: Styrofoam cups, straws, chenille stems, old mittens, and so on

- The children create puppets using simple designs using Styrofoam cups, straws, chenille stems, old mittens, construction paper, craft sticks, felt shapes, and so on.
- Each child keeps his materials in a separate plastic basket.
- The children use glue to decorate their puppets with yarn, contact paper, buttons, trim, and so on.
- Make cardboard keys for a wind-up toy that relates to Alexander and the Wind-Up Mouse.

Wind-up Toys

SCIENCE

wind-up toys

- A collection of wind-up toys provides an interesting discovery opportunity for young children.
- As the children work with the toys, ask them questions about what generates the toys' actions, ways to make the toys move differently, how long they move, and so on.

Adding Spark to the Toy Workshop Center

Collect teddy bears of different sizes and add them to the Toy Workshop Center. Include several pieces of clothing that the children can use to dress the teddy bears. Be sure to place *Jesse Bear, What Will You Wear?* with the clothing in the center to extend the play of the book.

The Essential Literacy Connection

Reading/Writing Opportunities

- Include toy repair forms for workers in the toy repair shop.
- Include carbon paper or paper that makes a copy of the writing to capture their interest.
- Make a chart of toys the children like. Children can draw their favorite toys on the chart.
- The sewing and repairing activities in this center develop the children's small motor coordination.
- Read the children books about toys.
- The children develop and play board games.
- Use puppets to dramatize communication.
- Small motor coordination: sewing and repairing.

Other Printed Materials

- Bring in toy catalogs.
- Display magazines that describe how to make simple toys.
- Bring in newspaper flyers from toy stores.
- Help the children follow directions to make puppets.
- Help the children follow the recipe to make bubble mix.

Books for the Toy Workshop Center

Carlstrom, N. 2005. *Jesse Bear, What Will You Wear?* Illustrated by Bruce Degen. New York: Aladdin. *Jesse Bear must decide what to wear for the day. Throughout the story, Jesse Bear talks in a rhyming pattern about each item of clothing he will wear. At the end of the story, Jesse Bear decides what to wear to bed.*

Cunliffe, J. 1998. *The Forgotten Toys: Hospital Toys.* New York: Scholastic, Inc. *The toys, Annie and Teddy, go to the hospital in search of a doctor to fix Teddy's arm.*

Falconer, I. 2006. *Olivia and the Missing Toy.* New York: Simon & Schuster. *A young pig named Olivia finds that her favorite toy is missing. After searching the entire house, Olivia finds the family dog ripping up her toy. Her parents suggest buying a new toy to replace it, but Olivia decides to sew the toy back together and realizes it is more special than ever.*

Freeman, D. 2000. *Corduroy's Christmas Surprise.* Illustrated by Lisa McCue. New York: Penguin. *Corduroy requests Christmas gifts for his friends and finds a surprise for himself, too.*

Freeman, D. 2007. *Corduroy.* New York: Puffin. *Corduroy, a stuffed bear in the toy department of a large store, is waiting for a child to take him home. His one problem is that he is missing one of the buttons on his overalls. This story follows his search for his button and describes how he finds a home.*

Lionni, L. 2006. *Alexander and the Wind-Up Mouse.* New York: Knopf. *Alexander, a live mouse, meets Willy, a wind-up mouse. A magic lizard and a purple pebble help them develop their friendship.*

Marzollo, J. 2006. *I Spy Mystery: A Book of Picture Riddles.* Photos by Walter Wick. New York: Scholastic, Inc. *Large colorful pictures show various toys grouped by themes. The rhyming text asks readers to identify different items they see in the pictures.*

Scott-Waters, M. 2004. *The Toymaker: Paper Toys You Can Make Yourself.* Costa Mesa, CA: Scott-Waters Design. *This book contains easy instructions on how to make toys such as Spinners, Marble Mice, and a Sun Box. These are easy for young children to make and older children will be intrigued by them as well.*

Evaluation of the Toy Workshop Center

(This form is on the CD that comes with this book.)

Ask yourself the following questions to evaluate the Toy Workshop Center in your classroom:

- Are children being creative as they make their toys?
- Are children relating the focus books to their play in the Toy Workshop Center?
- Are the children cooperating as they participate in group projects?
- Are children expanding their language skills as they interact in the center?
- Are the children "reading" and "writing" in the Toy Workshop Center?
- Are children participating in small motor activities?

Observation of the Individual Child

(This form is on the CD that comes with this book. Always date observations of each child.)

- Is the child watching or participating in the repair of the toys? Explain.
- Is the child playing with recycled toys?
- Has the child come up with ideas and/or methods to repair any of the toys? Which ones and how?
- Does the child talk about repairing or recycling toys? What language is he using? What is his attitude about recycling?
- Is the child working with others on projects in the Toy Workshop Center? In what way?

Unique Centers:

Creative Additions to the Classroom

The unique centers in this chapter provide creative play areas that will challenge young children to think in new ways and venture into different settings. These centers encourage both the children and teacher to think creatively, as they determine which props they need, which activities to include, and which play situations can occur. It is important to select the Unique Center that provides the "right match," within the children's range of understanding, while extending their possibilities.

In these Unique Centers, children will learn new vocabulary, experiment with different materials, think about varied situations, and adjust to others in their play. Although learning can occur in all centers, the Unique Centers will especially promote creative thinking and problem solving—skills that will be essential in the future.

CHAPTER 4

Fitness Center

Box Center

Dance Studio Center

Hat Center

Laughing Center

Nighttime Center

Party Center

Recycling Center

Sensory Center

Space Center

Storytelling Center

Project Center

We walked 1 mile!

Sue Mike Jane Mia Jose Paul

Kid Exercise

games P.E.

Eat Healthy

toss

50 50 25 25

Summary

Many children have seen exercise programs on television or have visited aerobics classes with their families. Some have heard discussions of healthy practices and physical fitness. The Fitness Center allows children to participate in fitness activities while developing motor coordination and learning about health and nutrition. These fitness experiences can have a positive influence on the children's lifestyles both today and in the future.

Introducing the Center

Open the Fitness Center by introducing a children's movement recording. After children participate with the recording, discuss the benefits of "working out." Introduce some of the activities that will be available in the Fitness Center. Discuss how exercise is good for the body and makes us stronger.

Learning Objectives for Children in the Fitness Center

1. To participate in physical activities that will positively influence large motor coordination.
2. To learn about their bodies' physical capabilities.
3. To recognize the importance of exercise as a healthy practice.
4. To enjoy the physical activities included in the center.
5. To establish a pattern of exercise and participation in fitness activities that will continue throughout their lives.

Time Frame for the Fitness Center

This center will interest most young children for approximately two to three weeks. The activities and materials in the fitness center relate to the study of health and nutrition that is included in the curriculum through out the year.

 Note: The attached CD contains a sample letter to send to families, introducing them to the Fitness Center.

These children have figured out how to reach the bars—use buckets!

Vocabulary Enrichment

aerobics
balance beam
bar bells
cool-down
exercise
exercise bike
exercise mat
gym
hand weight
hoop
instructor
jog
jumping jacks
leotard
locker room
muscles
pulse rate
punching bag
scale
schedule
stretching
tempo: fast or slow
timer
warm-up
weights
workout

Web of Integrated Learning

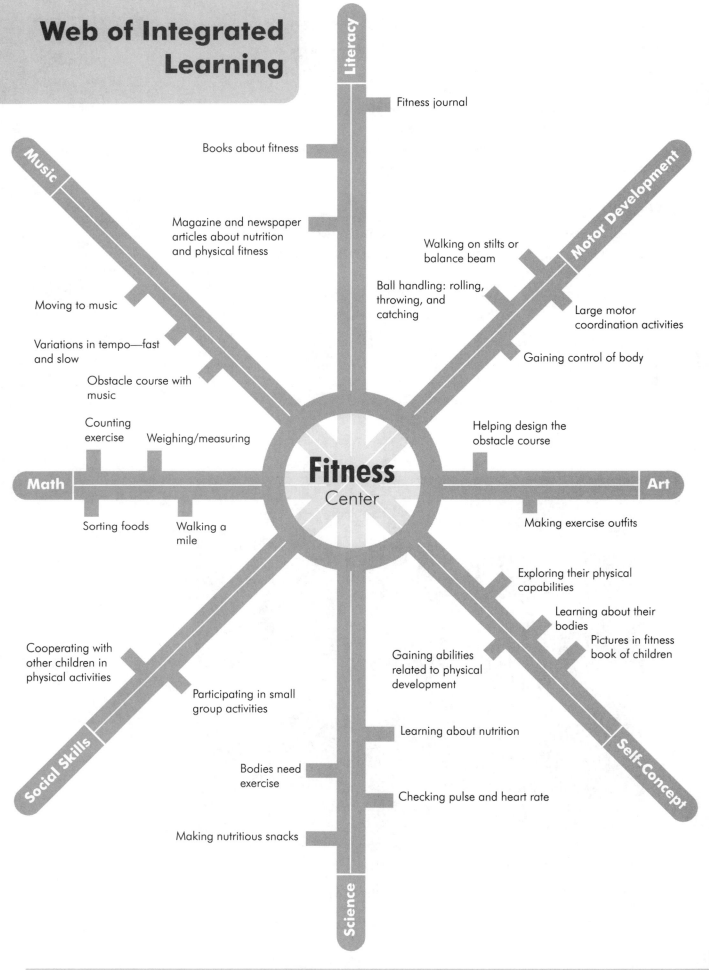

Literacy
- Fitness journal
- Books about fitness
- Magazine and newspaper articles about nutrition and physical fitness

Music
- Moving to music
- Variations in tempo—fast and slow
- Obstacle course with music

Motor Development
- Walking on stilts or balance beam
- Ball handling: rolling, throwing, and catching
- Large motor coordination activities
- Gaining control of body

Math
- Counting exercise
- Weighing/measuring
- Sorting foods
- Walking a mile

Fitness Center

Art
- Helping design the obstacle course
- Making exercise outfits

Self-Concept
- Exploring their physical capabilities
- Learning about their bodies
- Pictures in fitness book of children
- Gaining abilities related to physical development

Social Skills
- Cooperating with other children in physical activities
- Participating in small group activities

Science
- Learning about nutrition
- Bodies need exercise
- Checking pulse and heart rate
- Making nutritious snacks

- ❑ CD or tape player and music recordings
- ❑ balance beam
- ❑ clipboard
- ❑ different types of balls:
    - ❑ beach ball
    - ❑ foam ball
    - ❑ kickball
    - ❑ ping pong ball
- ❑ dress-up clothes:
    - ❑ exercise shorts
    - ❑ leotards
    - ❑ T-shirts
    - ❑ warm-up suits
- ❑ exercise bike (Attach an old tricycle to a large piece of plywood with bolts. The children will enjoy using a stationary bike that is just the right size)
- ❑ exercise mats
- ❑ jump ropes
- ❑ large mirror
- ❑ scales for weighing
- ❑ small blocks for step exercise (These can be borrowed from the Block Center)
- ❑ small trampoline
- ❑ therapy ball
- ❑ timer
- ❑ video exercise tapes/DVDs and recordings for children

This boy is demonstrating his strength by lifting the weights over his head.

Barbells
MOTOR DEVELOPMENT

balloons or paper bags stuffed with paper
large tinker toys or dowel rods

- The children can attach balloons or paper bags stuffed with paper to the ends of tinker toys or dowel rods in order to make "barbells" and "weights."
- The children use these "weights" when participating in exercise classes or when lifting weights to build strength.

Exercise Props
ART

child-safe scissors
markers
old tube socks
pieces of fabric and glue

- The children make sweatbands and wristbands by cutting off the tops of old tube socks.
- The children decorate their bands with markers or by gluing on pieces of fabric.
- The children can wear the exercise bands on their heads, wrists, or ankles.

Pantyhose Balls
MOTOR DEVELOPMENT

bucket
old pantyhose
Polyfil fiber
scissors (adult only)

- Set out old sets of pantyhose for the children to use to make balls of various sizes to use in the Fitness Center.
- Cut off pieces of the pantyhose legs and tie knots in one end of each (adult-only step).
- Next, set out Polyfil fiber so the children can stuff their piece of hose with it.
- When the children finish filling their pieces of hose, they tie the loose ends together, making a ball.
- The children can throw these soft balls into a large plastic bucket, toss them to a partner, or squeeze them and describe the sensation.

Stilts
MOTOR DEVELOPMENT

duct tape
empty tin cans with tops removed
ice pick or sharp scissors (adult use only)
rope

- The children make stilts by using tin cans and rope.
- Help each child attach duct tape to the open edges of two matching cans.
- Turn each child's two cans over and use an ice pick or sharp scissors to punch a hole on the bottom of each can (adult-only step).

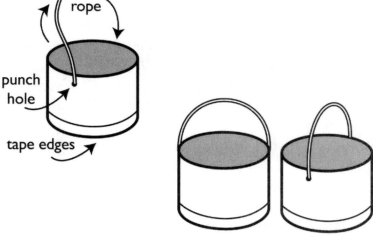

- Show the children how to thread a rope through the holes. There should be enough rope looped through the hole that each child can fit her foot inside it snugly.
- Provide a variety of sizes of cans, so the children can experiment with walking at different heights and experience various degrees of difficulty.

Activities for the Fitness Center

Fitness Book

LITERACY

camera
picture album
pictures of the children

- Take pictures of the children exercising and using the health club equipment.
- Develop or print the pictures, label them with the children's names, and place them in an album.
- Set the book out in the Fitness Center for other children to "read."

Fitness Journal

LITERACY

crayons
markers
paper
stapler

- Staple a few pieces of paper together.
- Make a Fitness Journal for each child.
- Write the child's name on the cover of her journal.

- The children can describe their exercise by drawing pictures or "writing" in their journals each day.
- Accept all levels of beginning writing efforts in the journals.
- Keep the journals in the Fitness Center, so the children can record their exercises immediately after they finish each activity.
- The children can take the journal home over the weekend, so they can record fitness activities they do while away from their classroom.

Fitness Obstacle Course   MOTOR DEVELOPMENT

balance beam
box
hula hoop
large wooden block
tape
tennis shoe prints made from construction paper

- Set up an obstacle course in the center that requires the children to use their large muscles. Suggested obstacles include:
  - a box to climb through
  - a hula hoop on the floor to jump into and out of
  - a beam to walk along
  - a mat to roll over on
  - a large wooden block to carry from one spot to another
  - stepping stones to walk along
- Set the various obstacles at different places in the classroom, and use cutouts of tennis shoeprints to establish a path to follow through the course.
- Each week, rearrange the obstacle course to provide new challenges.
- Create signs that can provide directions and warnings, such as "stop" or "slow."

Good for You   MATH

chart paper
empty food packages (both nutritious and junk foods)
markers or crayons

- Collect empty packages of nutritious and junk foods.
- Engage the children in discussions about the different foods and encourage them to indicate which foods they prefer.
- Set out chart paper, and make two columns on it, one labeled "Good for You" and the other "Junk Food." The children identify which foods belong in the two categories, then "write" the names of each in the appropriate categories.

CD or tape player
selection of recorded music

- Place a CD or tape player and music that varies significantly in tempo in the Fitness Center for the children to play.
- The children listen carefully to the music and move to its beat.
- The children move in their own ways, so the activity is creative.

A floor-length mirror encourages moving and dancing.

Passing the Ball   M O T O R   D E V E L O P M E N T

large rubber balls
large plastic baskets

- Set out large rubber balls for the children to use in a variety of activities, such as the following:
  - Toss the balls into large plastic baskets
  - Roll the balls between partners
- Ball activities provide important motor development experiences because they require young children to coordinate the use of their eyes and hands.
- Begin with simple experiences, so the children can build their confidence, then move on to more involved activities.

clock or watch with second hand display

- Demonstrate to the children how to check your pulse rate.
- Let each child take her own pulse, experimenting with taking the pulse at the wrist and under the jaw, just below the ear.
- Encourage children to participate in activities that will vary their pulse rates, such as sitting or running.
- As they check their pulse rates, children will begin to understand the relationship between pulse rates and their level of exertion.

Racetrack   MOTOR DEVELOPMENT

Bicycle Race by Donald Crews
markers
paper
tape or chalk
flag or streamer
riding toys, such as tricycles and big wheels
scissors

- Introduce the racetrack activity by reading *Bicycle Race* to the children.
- Set up a track outside on the playground on which the children can ride their wheel toys. Use tape or chalk to draw the boundaries of the track. A flag or streamer can be placed at the end of the track to identify the finish line.
- Let the children ride at their own speed. When each child crosses the finish line, that child is declared a winner.

Recipes   SELF-CONCEPT

paper
recipes and ingredients for healthy snacks
stapler

- During group time, the children can suggest some healthy and quick snacks that they enjoy. Help them find recipes for these snacks, or ask them to bring recipes from home.
- Collect the children's recipes into a book of healthy snacks that the children can prepare in class.
- Set out some ingredients for various no-cook recipes in the Fitness Center so the children can make nutritious snacks to eat after they finish exercising.

family member or fitness center employee

- Invite a family member who teaches or participates in exercise classes to visit the Fitness Center to demonstrate different fitness training exercises for the children.
- Encourage the children to participate in the demonstration.

Walk a Mile   MOTOR DEVELOPMENT

rope or tape for start and finish lines
ribbons cut from colored paper
chart paper
markers

- Before the children arrive, measure a mile walk around the school, playground, or park.
- Ask the children to bring athletic clothes to class this day, or set out athletic clothes for the children to dress in, then take the children outside and walk the mile with them.
- Decorate specific start and finish lines outside. At the finish line, distribute ribbons to each child who participates in the walk.
- If possible, take pictures of the children at the finish line and display them in the Fitness Center.
- Create a chart in the Fitness Center where the children can keep a record of each time they walk a mile. Depending on the children's writing skills, one child might make a check mark on the chart by her name and another child might draw a picture on the chart. The checks or pictures could be counted to see how many times each child had walked.

Adding Spark to the Fitness Center

Set up a snack stand in the Fitness Center. Have a tasting party with nutritious foods with which the children may not be familiar. Examples include sunflower seeds, alfalfa sprouts, unique pastas, trail mix, drinks, and so on.

Reading/Writing Opportunities

- Include a sign-in book for exercise classes in the Fitness Center.
- Post a schedule for classes and walking times in the center. The children mark the times they participate in an exercise program.
- Create a fitness book.
- Keep a fitness journal.
- Help the children make a chart to keep a record of their exercise, weightlifting, walking, and jogging habits.
- Ask the children to create the signs for the obstacle course.

Other Printed Materials

- Create a book, using newspaper advertisements for health clubs or pictures from fitness magazines.
- Display magazines related to health and nutrition to provide additional opportunities for children to use printed material in meaningful ways.

Books for the Fitness Center

Crews, D. 1985. *Bicycle Race.* New York: Greenwillow. *Vivid illustrations and repetitive numbered text count the 12 racers as the race progresses.*

Milne, A. A. 1996. *Pooh's Little Fitness Book.* New York: Dutton. *Children learn physical fitness and workout tips from Pooh and his friends, who illustrate how easy it can be to incorporate exercise into the daily routine.*

Murphy, S. J. 1998. *The Greatest Gymnast of All.* New York: HarperCollins. *While performing an energetic gymnastic routine, Zoe demonstrates spatial opposites, such as* on *and* off, inside *and* outside, *and* over *and* under.

Nelson, R. 2005. *Exercising.* Minneapolis, MN: Lerner. *Children run, jump, skip, and climb in this book that is all about exercising!*

Newcome, Z. 1996. *Toddlerobics.* Cambridge, MA: Candlewick Press. *A group of toddlers has fun, as they stretch high, bend low, clap their hands, bump bottoms, and generally enjoy exercising.*

Thomas, P. 2001. *My Amazing Body: A First Look at Health and Fitness.* New York: Barron's. *This colorful and lively picture book explores various aspects of health and fitness. This book looks at the importance of maintaining a good diet and getting plenty of exercise in a simple and informative way.*

Evaluation of the Fitness Center

(This form is on the CD that comes with this book.)

Ask yourself the following questions to evaluate the Fitness Center in your classroom:

- Are children participating in large motor activities?
- Are children discussing healthy practices, including nutritious eating and exercise?
- Are children recording their fitness activities when they are in the Fitness Center?
- Are children helping each other as they set up activities or participate in groups?
- Are children enjoying their participation in physical activities?

Observation of the Individual Child

(This form is on the CD that comes with this book. Always date observations of each child.)

- Is the child choosing to go to the Fitness Center?
- What activities is she doing in the center? Describe.
- Is the child keeping a personal fitness journal? What is she including and how is she recording the information?
- What vocabulary and language is the child using in the Fitness Center and with peers?
- What aspect of the center seems most enjoyable to this child? What specifically have you observed her enjoying?

Summary

Young children need many opportunities to problem solve and think in creative ways. The Box Center provides children with several ways to engage in this special kind of thinking. Boxes, in a variety of sizes and materials, will challenge the children who work in the center to see differences, make combinations, and create new structures. Because the boxes are versatile, the children can use them repeatedly, with unique combinations. The variations possible with boxes provide the perfect setting for the development of fluency, a key element of creativity. This fluency is demonstrated by the children's use of the boxes in many different ways. The tools placed in this area can help children construct in diverse ways, which will stimulate ideas and original possibilities.

Introducing the Center

Stimulate interest in the Block Center by adding large boxes. In a discussion with the children, ask questions about the new boxes that are in the Block Center. Make sure the boxes you add are large and take up a great deal of space. As the children become concerned about all the boxes, move them out to form a new Box Center. Ask the children what tools they need to work with the boxes (examples include masking tape, clamps, scissors, contact paper, large paper clips, and so on). Label these tools and let the children help store them in the newly established Box Center.

Learning Objectives for Children in the Box Center

1. To recognize and name the variations of size: large, small, and medium.
2. To develop fluency, originality, flexibility, and elaboration in their thinking.
3. To use problem-solving skills to find different ways to combine and attach boxes.
4. To develop an ability to effectively use small and large motor skills.
5. To design, name, and label structures.

Time Frame for the Box Center

This unique center can be set up in the Block Center or in a separate space. Because it challenges thinking in new ways, it will work best if it is set up later in the year. This way, children have already had many opportunities to create, so that this center builds on those experiences. Observe when children's interest begins to fade and add another box that varies from the other boxes in an interesting way. If this does not reenergize the children's interest in the Box Center, close it down.

 Note: The attached CD contains a sample letter to send to families, introducing them to the Box Center.

Boxes in a variety of sizes challenge a child's problem-solving abilities.

Vocabulary Enrichment

box
cardboard
clamp
combine
creative
differently
duct tape
foam
glue
inside
lacing
large
masking tape
materials
medium
nesting
paper
plastic
possibility
problem solving
size
small
string
support phrases:
  "wow," "amazing,"
  "unbelievable," "I
  wish I had thought
  of that," "what if?"
  and so on
teamwork
thinking
tool
yarn

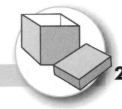

Web of Integrated Learning

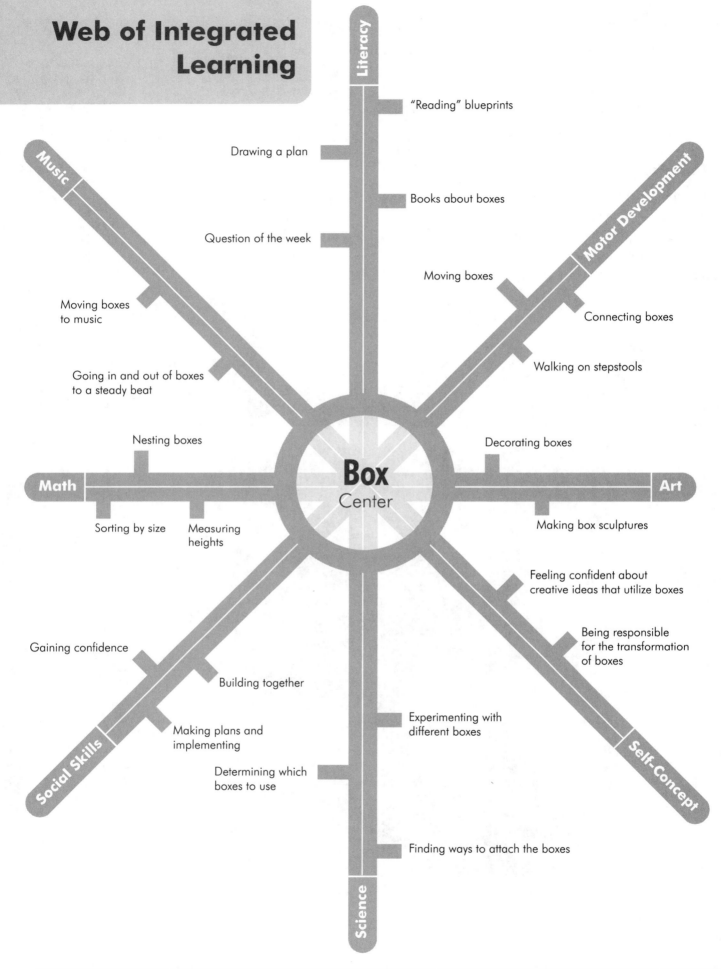

Box Center

Literacy
- "Reading" blueprints
- Drawing a plan
- Books about boxes
- Question of the week

Music
- Moving boxes to music
- Going in and out of boxes to a steady beat

Motor Development
- Moving boxes
- Connecting boxes
- Walking on stepstools

Math
- Nesting boxes
- Sorting by size
- Measuring heights

Art
- Decorating boxes
- Making box sculptures

Self-Concept
- Feeling confident about creative ideas that utilize boxes
- Being responsible for the transformation of boxes

Social Skills
- Gaining confidence
- Building together
- Making plans and implementing
- Determining which boxes to use

Science
- Experimenting with different boxes
- Finding ways to attach the boxes

- ❏ glue, clamps, twine, heavy string
- ❏ large appliance and piano boxes
- ❏ items for attaching boxes:
    - ❏ adhesive tape
    - ❏ duct tape
    - ❏ electrical tape
    - ❏ masking tape
- ❏ medium boxes:
    - ❏ canned food boxes
    - ❏ cereal boxes
    - ❏ gift boxes
    - ❏ storage boxes
- ❏ small boxes:
    - ❏ jewelry
    - ❏ lingerie
    - ❏ toothpaste
- ❏ things to use in decorating:
    - ❏ construction paper
    - ❏ contact paper
    - ❏ markers
    - ❏ paint
    - ❏ shoe polish
    - ❏ tissue paper
    - ❏ wallpaper

Child-Created Props for the Box Center

A Decorating Box   ART

> items and materials to decorate boxes such as colored cellophane, construction paper, fabric, foil,
>   pieces of contact paper, stamp and pad, stickers, and yarn
> markers

- Place the collection of items in a clear container.
- Label the container to indicate the items that are inside: fabric, foil, yarn, and so on.
- Place the container in the Box Center so the children can easily access it as they work with the boxes.
- Children can choose what and where to add decoration.

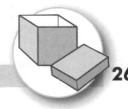

items that help make combinations such as big paper clips, clamps, clothespins, dowel rods, stapler, tape, and twine

- Collect several items like those in the list above and put them in a clear container in the Box Center.
- Some children may need demonstrations on how to use the various items.
- Be sure to move out of the center as soon as you finish your demonstration. This way the children can come up with their own procedures and ways to use the items.
- Check in occasionally to see if the children need help or prompting. Ask, "What about this?" "What do you think?" "Is there another way?" and "Wow, how does it work?"

Activities for the Box Center

Box Creations Book LITERACY

digital photographs or illustrations of box creations
shallow boxes, such as gift boxes, jewelry boxes, shoeboxes, and so on
scissors
hole punch (adult only)
markers or crayons
white paper
yarn, ribbon, or macramé rope

- Invite each child to select a box and cut several sheets of paper so it fits inside the bottom of the box. Make sure the cut sheets of paper are large enough that the children can still turn the pages.
- The children punch holes on the left side of their paper, with corresponding holes on the inside left bottom of their boxes.
- The children decide what they want to name their books and then decorate their boxes accordingly.
- Over time, the children make drawings and collages and "write" letters on the sheets of paper. If necessary, help them include these pages in their books. If their creations cannot fit into the box books, take pictures of their creations and help the children attach the pictures into the books.
- Continue to add pages over the entire period that the Box Center is in use.
- When the books are complete, demonstrate how to lace the pages of the books to their boxes using yarn, ribbon, or macramé rope.
- The lids of the boxes will serve as their covers. Show the children how they can open and close. The children can decorate their box lids.
- Place the box creations books in the Box Center.
- Later, put the box creations books in the Library Center so the children can share them with their families.

large boxes: piano, appliances, shipping, storage, or moving containers

small boxes: toothpaste, food coloring, makeup, jewelry, and so on

unique boxes: unusual shapes, materials, or design, as with round tubes used for rugs, flooring, or packing dishes for moving

tools: scissors, tape, pipe cleaners, markers

decoration materials: tissue paper, stickers, pieces of contact paper, old magazines

- Place a variety of boxes in the Box Center.
- Give the children time to experiment with moving, manipulating, and playing with the boxes.
- Set out tools and decorations the children can use on the boxes.
- Observe and record the children's building activities.
- Ask the children to tell you when they create something very unusual, and photograph the treasure.
- On the wall of the Box Center, display the photos with the names of the creations and their designers.

Higher Building
SCIENCE

large pieces of heavy-duty corrugated cardboard or lumber

2 small stepstools

- One week before the Box Center opens, place two stools about 2'–3' apart.
- Place heavy-duty cardboard or lumber across the stools, so the cardboard forms a platform, and let the children experiment with ways to build on or use the platform.
- If the children do not take the initiative with the platform, place a few boxes on the platform to stimulate their thinking.

Nesting Boxes
MATH

3–4 boxes that can fit inside other boxes

nesting blocks or toys

- Set out some nested boxes and toys in the Box Center with which the children can experiment. Allow the children to discover the nested items, while they begin to look for other boxes that they can combine in similar ways.
- Children can open, close, or place a treasure inside the smallest boxes they find.

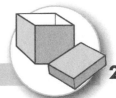

boxes   markers, pencils, erasers, and so on

digital camera   sample blueprints

drawing paper

- Set out various sample blueprints along with drawing paper, markers, pencils, erasers, and so on, so the children can create design plans for an object or thing they would like to create from the boxes.
- The children may want to name their creations. When the children decide upon the names they want to use, they label their blueprints with those names.
- After the children finish making their creations, take photographs or make drawings of them.
- Display the creations in the Block Center.
- Some of these photographs and drawings of their creations can be included in their box creations books.

Question of the Week   LITERACY

chart paper, white board, or drawing board   markers or crayons

- Write down a question for the children to answer in the Box Center.
  Examples include the following:
    - "Can you find the biggest box? Can you find the smallest?"
    - "How tall can you stack the boxes?"
    - "How can you use the boxes to move things?"
    - "Can you pack boxes for moving?"
- Display the "question of the week" in the Box Center.
- Discuss the children's questions and responses when the children are reflecting on their work in the Box Center.

Adding Spark to the Box Center

Add plastic tubing to the Box Center. This could include clear tubing, dryer vent tubing, a piece of garden hose, or rubber tubing. These new materials will stimulate the children and encourage them to look for new ways to combine and use the boxes.

The Essential Literacy Connection

Reading/Writing Opportunities

- There are several books (see the following list) that explain some of the possible uses of boxes in the classroom.
- The children can use markers, tempera paint, and scissors to "write" in the box creations book.
- The children "read" and think about the question of the week.

Other Printed Materials

- The children create blueprints and signs for various creations of theirs.

Books for the Box Center

Gauch, P. 1971. *Christina Katerina & the Box*. Illustrated by Doris Burn. New York: Putnam. *A new refrigerator arrives at Christina's house. Both Christina and her mother are excited, but for different reasons. Christina uses the refrigerator box to go on many imaginative adventures.*

Hillenbrand, W. 2006. *My Book Box*. Orlando, FL: Harcourt. *A elephant wonders what he can do with a plain cardboard box. He comes up with all sorts of ideas, transforming the object into a hat, a container for toys, and a hide-and-seek haven. The story provides insight to limitless possibilities of creativity.*

McAllister, A. 2003. *Harry's Box*. Illustrated by Jenny Jones. New York: Bloomsbury. *Accompanied by his dog, Harry carries a cardboard box to different places in his home and pretends that it is a store, a lion's den, a pirate ship, and underwater cave, and a castle.*

Portis, A. 2007. *Not a Box*. New York: HarperCollins. *A rabbit goes on an imaginative journey using a cardboard box.*

Russo, M. 2000. *The Big Brown Box*. New York. Greenwillow. *As Sam plays in a very large box in his room, he turns it into a house, then a cave, then a boat. He is reluctant to let his little brother, Ben, join him, but then he finds the perfect way for them to share.*

Evaluation of the Box Center

(This form is on the CD that comes with this book.)

Ask yourself the following questions to evaluate the Box Center in your classroom:

- Are the children using a variety of boxes in their play?
- Are the children talking and collaborating with others?
- Are the children using literacy materials, such as books, writing tools, and questions?
- Are the children developing problem-solving skills through their use of the center?
- Have the children moved beyond the exploratory and manipulation stage?
- Are the children making plans and combinations; are they developing possibilities?

Observation of the Individual Child

(This form is on the CD that comes with this book. Always date observations of each child.)

- What language is the child using? Provide specific examples of vocabulary, sentences, and conversations.
- Have you observed the child making a creative construction? Describe.
- Is the child working individually, beside other children, or collaboratively?
- How is the child using boxes to explore, stack, combine, and create new constructions?
- How would you describe this child's small and large motor skills? Give specific observed examples.

Summary

The Dance Studio Center provides a wonderful space for young children to experiment with movement. Here, they will be able to become dancers, costume designers, or choreographers. Fill the Dance Studio Center with music, mirrors, and costumes that relate to dance. There are many opportunities to combine movement with music while enjoying dance. This center provides a place where young children can be active and involved in experiences that are interesting to them and encourage their creative thinking.

Introducing the Center

Introduce this center by discussing some of the unique costumes that will be in the Dance Studio Center. Be sure to have costumes that both boys and girls will enjoy. Visit the Dance Studio Center with a small group of children who chose to play there during center time. Talk with them about the operation of the CD or tape player, the music, and the costume possibilities. Children who select this center will be able to dress as dancers, select music, and watch their bodies move in new ways.

Learning Objectives for Children in the Dance Studio Center

1. To gain control of their bodies as they participate in dance.
2. To create movements that will accompany music.
3. To refine their large motor skills.
4. To discover creative ways of using props.
5. To activate in the children a kinesthetic approach to learning.

Time Frame for the Dance Studio Center

Set up this center in the classroom for two to three weeks at a time. Also, consider rotating it back into the classroom several times during the year. It can be especially helpful to include the Dance Studio Center during the winter months, when the weather may limit outdoor play opportunities. In this center, children can dance, jump, spin, and slide, activating both their minds and bodies.

 Note: The attached CD contains a sample letter to send to families, introducing them to the Dance Studio Center.

Vocabulary Enrichment

ballet

choreographer

clap

costume

dance

high and low

jazz

rap

rhythm

shake

slow and fast

steps

tap

Interesting props inspired these children to move and dance.

Web of Integrated Learning

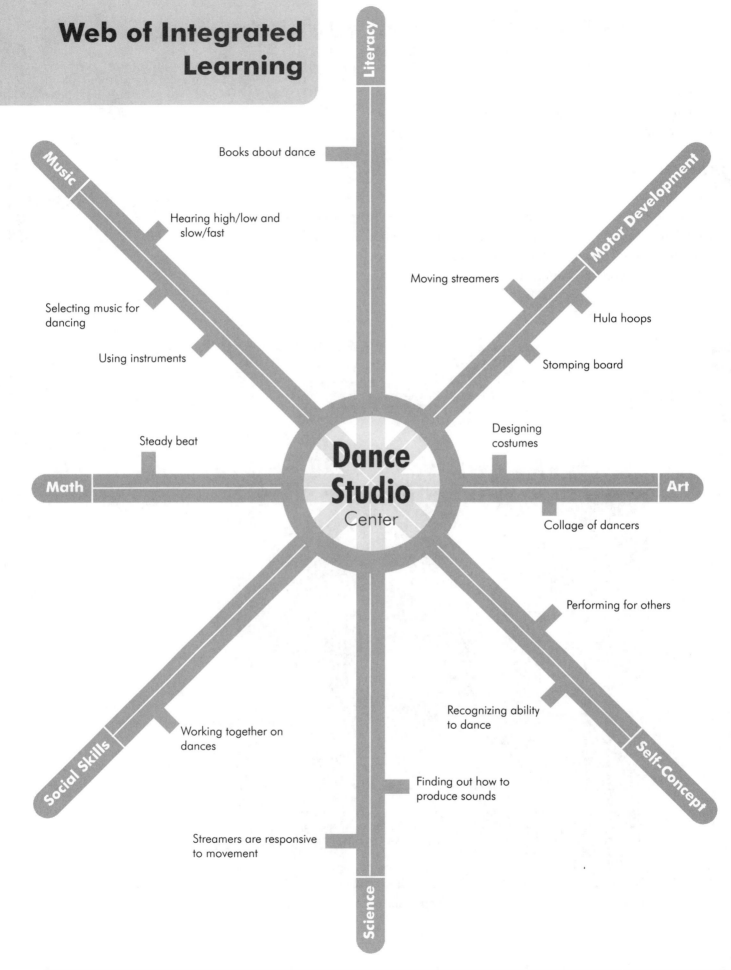

Literacy

Books about dance

Music

Hearing high/low and slow/fast

Selecting music for dancing

Using instruments

Moving streamers

Motor Development

Hula hoops

Stomping board

Steady beat

Math

Designing costumes

Dance Studio Center

Art

Collage of dancers

Performing for others

Working together on dances

Social Skills

Recognizing ability to dance

Self-Concept

Finding out how to produce sounds

Streamers are responsive to movement

Science

- ❏ ballet shoes
- ❏ bells
- ❏ boots
- ❏ Christmas tree lights
- ❏ dance costumes
- ❏ hula hoops
- ❏ music (include slow, fast, and rocking recordings)
- ❏ pictures of dancers to be displayed in the center
- ❏ pieces of transparent, lightweight fabric
- ❏ small suitcases or carry bags
- ❏ tap shoes
- ❏ tutus (several)
- ❏ vests, hats, and gloves

Admiring her dance costume in the mirror

Bells on Strings

colorful shoelaces
holiday and jingle bells with holes in the top

- Show the children how to string shoelaces through the tops of the bells and then tie the ends together. Some children may need help with tying.
- Children can wear the strung bells around their ankles or wrists. Longer string can be used to allow strung bells to reach around the waist.
- As the children play, the bells will jingle and ring. The children will likely become more active as they try to make their bells ring longer and louder.

Collage of Dancers

Dance recital programs
glue
old magazines
paper (large sheets)
pictures of dancers from art classics
pictures of dancers from diverse cultures
scissors

- Set out several old magazines, dance recital programs, and other materials that contain images of dancers.
- Ask the children to find, cut out, and attach pictures of dancers to a large sheet of paper, making a dancers' mural.
- Display this mural in the Dance Studio Center.
- Consider taking pictures of the children as they dance in the Dance Studio Center. Add these pictures to the mural.

Design Dance Costumes

belts (elastic and buckled)
clothespins
unbreakable floor-length mirror
pieces of interesting fabric cut in ¼- and ½-yard pieces
ribbon or elastic pieces

- Hang fabric pieces on pegs next to a floor-length mirror, so children can see their choices and combinations.
- Using the materials, children can create, design, and make dance costumes.
- Show the children how to drape, tie, and belt the fabric around themselves.

Streamers

aluminum foil

cardboard rolls (paper towel or wrapping paper)

child-safe scissors

glue

shiny/silver contact paper

stapler

tape

tissue paper or crepe paper

- Show the children how to cover the cardboard rolls with foil or contact paper.
- Set out pieces of tissue or crepe paper for the children to cut into long strips.
- After the children finish making the long strips of paper, they can glue, staple, or tape the strips to one end of the cardboard roll.
- The children can experiment with the streamers to make their arm movements more visible.

Activities for the Dance Studio Center

Dand Bar

drill and bits

hack saw

large unbreakable wall-mounted mirror

plywood (2' x 8' x ¾"; 1 piece)

PVC glue

PVC piping (use 1" or larger for extra support):

    90° connectors (2)

    end caps (3)

    T-connector (1)

    3 ½' pieces (2)

    2' pieces (3)

screwdriver

screws ½" in length (9–12)

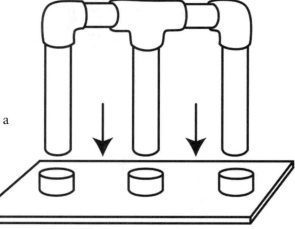

- Follow the adult-only steps below to create a dance bar for the children:
    - Using the hack saw, cut the PVC to desired lengths. These lengths can range from 3'–6' depending on the space you have in the center.
    - Use the drill to make 3–4 holes in the cap side of each of the three end caps.

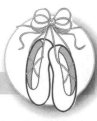

- Using screws, attach the end caps to hold the 2' supports along the longest midline of the plywood, with one on each end, and one in the center. Place the openings in the end-cap supports vertically.
- Insert three of the 2' pieces of PVC into the end-cap support openings, perpendicular to the plywood base, and glue into place.
- Cut the 3 ½' pieces of PVC to fit between the side supports. Insert the ends of each piece into the T connector, placing a 90° connector on each end.
- Place the 90° connectors on the PVC supports at each end and the T-connector on the center support.
- After you fit all the pieces into their proper places, glue the joints into place.
- Check to be sure that the bar is secure before letting the children use it.
- After you finish making the dance bar, set it out across from a wall-mounted, full-length mirror for the children to use for exercising and for practicing their balance.

Hula Hoops

ART & MOTOR DEVELOPMENT

hula hoops (2)
ribbon, fabric, or crepe paper streamers

- Set out ribbon, crepe paper, and fabric strips for the children to use to decorate the hula hoops.
- The children can move the Hula hoops in a variety of ways. For example, one child may move the hoop independently or two children can cooperate to move the hoop.
- The decorations on the hula hoops can serve as a challenge to the children, encouraging them to think of new ways to get their hula hoops turning.

CD or tape player (easy-to-operate design)

5–6 music recordings: include marching, ballet, folk, dance, rock, and yoga (the recording cover should communicate the type of music)

- Put the CD or tape player in the Dance Studio Center, along with the various recordings.
- Children will be able to listen to the various recordings and select the music to use in their dance.
- Children can create a dance to accompany the recording with a partner or individually.

Props are needed for boys who want to dance.

Stomping Board

boards (two 4' 2" x 4"; two 8' 2" x 4")

nails or screws and tools needed for assembly of platform

plywood sheet (½" 4' x 8')

- Construct a raised platform for dancing. Be careful to round all corners to avoid injury. Or consider using pallets to create a simple stage.
- This new dance floor will inspire leg and foot movement, because tapping and stomping on it will produce sounds that are more audible.
- Provide tap shoes, ballet shoes, and boots with which the children can experiment. The children can explore the different sounds that each kind of shoe produces.

Adding Spark to the Dance Studio Center

A few new dance costumes will encourage new activities in the Dance Studio Center. Place them in an exercise bag, so the children can retrieve and return the costumes to the container.

Reading/Writing Opportunities

- Create charts of ballet or jazz movements.
- Read the information on CD covers to the children.
- Make books about dance and dancers available for the children to explore.
- Provide paper and markers with which the children can create programs or "write" out dance movements (choreography).

Other Printed Materials

- Make programs from dance performances and photographs of dancers available to the children.

Books for the Dance Studio Center

Brisson, P., & Cote, N. 2005. *Tap-Dance Fever.* Honesdale, PA: Boyds Mills Press. *Nothing, it seems, can stop the tappity-tap of Annabelle Applegate's dancing feet.*

Helldorfer, M. C. 2004. *Got to Dance.* New York: Doubleday. *Set in the city on a hot summer day, this joyful book presents a high-energy portrait of a young girl. With her mother at work and her brother at camp, she has "nothing to do" and a case of "the summertime blues" that can only be cured by dancing.*

Holabird, K., & Craig, H. 2006. *Angelina Ballerina.* New York: Viking. *Angelina Ballerina is a little mouse who loves to dance. She dances all over the schoolyard, and through the house. Finally, her parents enroll her in a ballet class, where she becomes one of the best students.*

Ross, K. 1996. *The Little Ballerina.* New York: Random House. *The little ballerina practices hard with the others in her class and experiences the thrill of a big dance recital.*

Walton, R, and Lopez-Escriva, A. 2001. *How Can You Dance?* New York: Putnam. *This book combines playful illustrations with rhymes that hop, skip, and jump. The text features short verses about different situations or emotions and the dances that could go along with them.*

Wilson, K. 2004. *Hilda Must Be Dancing.* Illustrated by Suzanne Watts. New York: Margaret K. McElderry Books. *Hilda the hippo loves dancing more than anything. But, whether she's tangoing, square dancing, boogying to the disco, doing the rumba, or samba, Hilda makes a lot of noise.*

Evaluation of the Dance Studio Center

(This form is on the CD that comes with this book.)

Ask yourself the following questions to evaluate the Dance Studio Center in your classroom:

- Are the children dancing and moving in the center?
- Are the children using the props in creative ways?
- Is there evidence that the children are working cooperatively?
- Do the children exhibit a sustained interest in their play?
- Are the children using books and other literacy materials?

(This form is on the CD that comes with this book. Always date observations of each child.)

- Is the child able to coordinate the movement of her arms, legs, and body?
- Have you seen the child create a dance or a sequence of movements?
- Have you seen the child collaborating on any activities in the center?
- What language and literacy materials is the child using?
- Does the child seem to enjoy the center and choose to return to it?
- Can you identify any movement/motor problems the child may be having?

An elaborate costume created for dancing

Summary

Young children love hats. Hats allow them to talk in different ways, act silly, and pretend. Hats are also a favorite topic for children's books, such as the classic *Caps for Sale* and *Jennie's Hat*. Each story is capable of inspiring creative play. The activities in the Hat Center include making hats, using hats in play, and dramatizing stories about hats. In this Hat Center, children can be creative as they design and make hats. They can also use stories from books involving hats to dramatize, taking on roles and repeating repetitive phrases.

Introducing the Center

During circle or group time, sharing a collection of unusual hats is just what young children need for selecting the Hat Center for their play. Suggestions include a police hat, beanie, and feathered hat. Try on various hats as the children gather to make their center choices. Read the children a book about hats at this time, making an important connection to literature.

Learning Objectives for Children in the Hat Center

1. To take on roles and participate in play sequences.
2. To develop small motor skills as they make hats in the center.
3. To enhance their creativity as they use their imagination and flexible thinking in the Hat Center.
4. To enjoy new stories about hats and retell them in the Hat Center.
5. To learn and use new vocabulary that relates to making and wearing hats.

Time Frame for the Hat Center

This center will function effectively for at least two weeks. The books and stories encourage children in the center to move beyond simply trying on the hats, becoming involved in sociodramatic play that includes roles, play sequences, and cooperative conversations. When the center is first set up, the children may need guidance to move from simply wearing different hats to more complex play that involves taking on roles or developing a story.

 Note: The attached CD contains a sample letter to send to families, introducing them to the Hat Center.

A helmet inspires this child's role-play as an emergency worker.

Vocabulary Enrichment

baseball cap

bonnet

braid

brim

cap

collage

crown

decoration

design

earmuffs

emblem

fancy

feather

felt

firefighter's helmet

flowers

fruit

hat

hatbox

ribbon

secure

straw

toboggan

trim

veil

Web of Integrated Learning

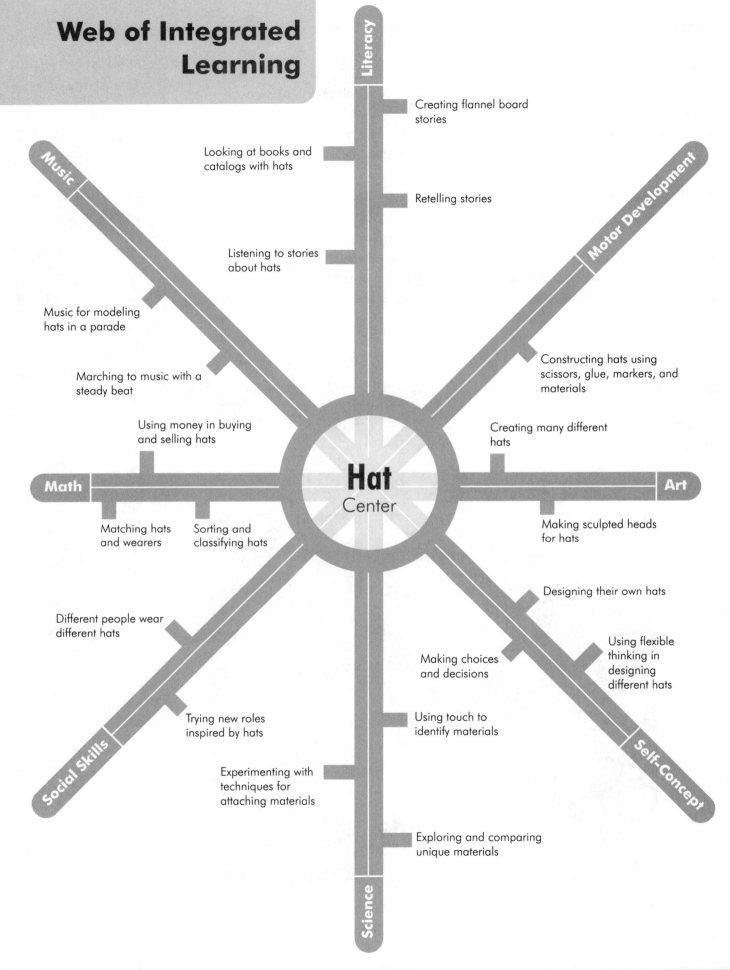

Hat
Center

Literacy
- Creating flannel board stories
- Looking at books and catalogs with hats
- Retelling stories
- Listening to stories about hats

Music
- Music for modeling hats in a parade
- Marching to music with a steady beat

Math
- Using money in buying and selling hats
- Matching hats and wearers
- Sorting and classifying hats

Social Skills
- Different people wear different hats
- Trying new roles inspired by hats

Motor Development
- Constructing hats using scissors, glue, markers, and materials

Art
- Creating many different hats
- Making sculpted heads for hats
- Designing their own hats

Self-Concept
- Using flexible thinking in designing different hats
- Making choices and decisions
- Using touch to identify materials

Science
- Experimenting with techniques for attaching materials
- Exploring and comparing unique materials

- ❏ cash register
- ❏ child-size dolls
- ❏ hat boxes
- ❏ low coat tree for hats
- ❏ low table
- ❏ various kinds of hats: men's and women's; hats of community helpers, such as firefighters or police officers, add variety to the collection
- ❏ materials needed for making hats:
  - ❏ bubble paint
  - ❏ buttons
  - ❏ chenille stems
  - ❏ fabric pieces
  - ❏ feathers
  - ❏ foil
  - ❏ glitter
  - ❏ glue
  - ❏ large pieces of paper
  - ❏ markers
  - ❏ metallic contact paper pieces
  - ❏ net
  - ❏ newspaper
  - ❏ scissors
  - ❏ scraps of fabric
  - ❏ stapler
  - ❏ tape
  - ❏ trim
  - ❏ yarn
- ❏ mirror

"What can I be when I wear this hat?"

Hat Boxes   ART

cardboard boxes
crayons
fancy trim
markers

- Set out several deep cardboard boxes, along with crayons, markers, and fancy trim, and for the children to use to transform the boxes into hat containers.
- After the children finish decorating the boxes, use them to display and store hats.

Hat Making   ART & SELF-CONCEPT

newspaper
colored paper

- Set out the various materials listed above. Show the children a few examples of hats that could be made from the materials.
- The children experiment with the materials to make different kinds of hats.
- Encourage the children to use the materials to create their own unique hat-.

Head for a Hat   ART

crayons
child-safe scissors
fabric glue or child-safe needle and thread
fabric that represents different skin colors
markers
newspaper or pantyhose
paint
paintbrushes

- Make sculpted heads to display designer hats.
- Set out pieces of fabric so children can make their selection
- Help each child trace her head on two pieces of fabric and cut out the outline on each piece.
- The children use child-safe scissors to cut out the traced outlines of their heads.
- Provide glue or thread and a child-safe needle so the children can attach the two outlines of their heads together.
- Once the children finish sewing their outlined heads together, or the glue connecting them dries, set out old pantyhose or sheets of newspaper the children can use to stuff their fabric heads.
- Provide paint and paintbrushes so the children can decorate their sculpted heads however they like.

Colonial Hat

child-safe scissors
large, child-safe plastic needles
white fabric or crepe paper
yarn

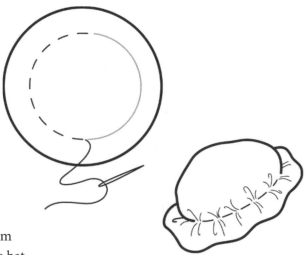

- Show the children how to make colonial hats.
- First, help the children cut circles out of white fabric or crepe paper.
- With yarn and large, child-safe plastic needles, the children sew stitches around the fabric piece, about 2" from the edge.
- When the children finish sewing, help them gather the stitches together to produce the hat.
- Secure the yarn by tying the ends together.

Fabric Cards

pieces of fabric (various textures)
basket
hatbox or shoebox with small opening cut in the lid
scissors
index cards
glue

Preparation
- Place various pieces of fabric and a basket next to the box.
- Cut two 2" x 2" squares from fabric (adult step).
- Attach one square from each type of fabric to an index card.
- Place the cards inside a box that has a small opening in the top.
- Place the matching squares of fabric in a basket next to the box.

Activity
- Set out the box and basket containing the matching pieces of 2" x 2" fabric.
- The children can take turns feeling a piece of fabric from the basket, then putting their hands through the opening in the box and feeling around for the piece of fabric that feels the same.
- When the child thinks she has the matching piece of fabric, she can pull it out and compare the pieces.

decorating materials:

		glue
crayons	glitter	masking tape
fabric	markers	newsprint
feathers	paint	plastic hat cage (use when washing baseball caps)
flowers	tissue paper	tape

- Create groups of two children. Give each group six sheets of newsprint and some masking tape.
- Show the children in each pair how to place three large sheets of newsprint on their partners' heads.
- After putting the paper on their partners' heads, show the children how to form a hat crown by wrapping masking tape around the paper until it takes on the shape of the child's head. This assures a custom fit. (Alternately, consider using a plastic hat cage to create the crowns.)
- Show the children how to roll the edges of the paper to produce the brims of their hats. The children can experiment with crunching and taping the edges to produce different looks.
- The children switch positions and repeat the steps until everyone has a hat.
- The children decorate their hats with various materials like those in the list above.

Flannel Board Story

Caps for Sale by Esphyr Slobodkina	plastic zipper-closure bag
colored felt	scissors
flannel board	washable markers
interfacing (available from fabric stores)	

- *Caps for Sale* is a wonderful story that young children enjoy. It is easy to adapt for use on a flannel board by following the steps below:
  - Place interfacing over the illustrations in the book and trace the outlines of the important characters and props.
  - Cut out and color the pieces with washable markers.
  - Make the hats from interfacing or color felt.
  - Place all the pieces in a plastic zipper-closure bag.
- Once all the pieces are ready, put the plastic bag with the flannel board in the Hat Center and invite children to explore retelling the classic folktale using these items.

Plastic Fruit Basket Hats

| plastic fruit baskets (from strawberries, for example) | scissors |
| strips of crepe paper | |

- Set out several plastic fruit baskets that can be used as the base for an unusual hat.
- The children weave strips of crepe paper in a variety of colors through the basket openings. Leave a few strips of crepe paper dangling for streamers.
- Model for the children how to wear their fruit basket hats, leaving the opening on the top so the children can place items inside their hats.
- Attach strips of crepe paper to each side of the baskets and tie the strips under the children's chins to keep the hat on their heads.

fabric glue
old adult-sized socks
trim, yarn, fringe, ribbon, and so on

- Set out several old socks for the children to use to create interesting caps. (Adult-sized athletic socks, with a top that stretches, work well because they will easily fit a child's head.)
- Set out various materials, like those listed above, and invite the children to decorate their sock caps with trim, yarn, fringe, ribbon, pompoms, and so on. Also, show the children how to stuff the feet of their socks if they want to make tight caps, or let them leave the feet hanging loose to create Santa-type hats.

Story Hat   ART & SELF-CONCEPT

Aunt Flossie's Hats by Elizabeth Fitzgerald Howard
selection of hats

- Set out a collection of hats.
- Read *Aunt Flossie's Hats* by Elizabeth Fitzgerald Howard to the children and engage them in a discussion about the story.
- Ask each child to select a hat from the collection, or help the children make hats to use as props to tell a story.
- *Aunt Flossie's Hat* by Elizabeth Fitzgerald Howard is a wonderful inspiration for the children to retell in their own words.
- Record the storytelling, so other children can listen to the story.

Three-Cornered Hat   ART & SELF-CONCEPT

construction paper
paint, stickers, and other decorative materials
pencil
ruler
scissors
stapler or tape

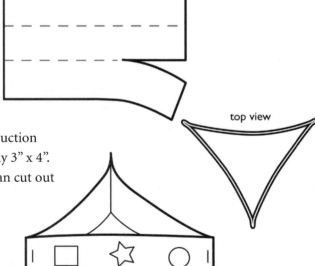
top view

- Using a ruler and pencil, draw lines on construction paper, making three strips, each approximately 3" x 4".
- Give the children child-safe scissors so they can cut out the strips of paper.
- The children staple or tape the three strips together on each end to produce a triangle-shaped, three-cornered hat.
- Adjust the length of the strips to fit the size of the child's head.
- The children decorate the hats with paint, stickers, and other materials.

pictures of hats and people who wear them   plastic container

- Collect pictures of hats and the people who wear those particular hats. Using pictures of people who wear hats while working in the school will make this activity more meaningful. Examples include the following: cooks, janitor, nurses, crosswalk guards, or public safety officers.
- Place the images of the hats and the people who wear them in a plastic container.
- The children match each hat to the person who would wear it.

Adding Spark to the Hat Center

Hold a musical hat parade, complete with children wearing their hats. A recording of band music with a steady beat will encourage the children to march in the hat parade.

The Essential Literacy Connection

Reading/Writing Opportunities

- Children take orders to create specific, custom-made hats.
- Use catalog order forms, giving the children the opportunity to pretend to place orders by phone.

Other Printed Materials

- Display clothing catalogs that include pictures of people wearing hats.

Books for the Hat Center

Cooper, S. K. 2006. *Whose Hat Is This? A Look at Hats Workers Wear: Hard, Tall, and Shiny.* Illustrated by Amy Bailey Muehlenhardt. Mankato, MN: Coughlan Publishing. *This book presents seven community jobs by looking at the hats worn by a variety of workers.*

Fox, M. 2006. *The Magic Hat.* Illustrated by Tricia Tusa. New York: Voyager. *A magic hat sweeps into a park, turning each adult into a different animal. Rhymed verses add to the humor and allow listeners to predict what happens next.*

Howard, E. 1995. *Aunt Flossie's Hats (and Crab Cakes Later).* Illustrated by James E. Ransome. Boston, MA: Houghton Mifflin. *Aunt Flossie shares the many stories of her youth with all the young children around her. Aunt Flossie wears a new hat each time she tells a different story.*

Keats, E. J. 2003. *Jennie's Hat.* New York: Puffin. *Jennie receives a hat from her aunt, but it is rather plain and not as she expected. Keats' colorful illustrations show how Jennie transforms her hat into one of the prettiest ever.*

Polacco, P. 1998. *Chicken Sunday.* New York: Penguin. *Children from different cultures become friends and eat Sunday dinner together at Miss Eula's. To thank her, they sell decorated eggs to buy her a beautiful hat.*

Rumford, J. 2007. *Don't Touch My Hat.* New York: Knopf. *A 10-gallon hat is important in defining a cowboy's persona. When Sheriff John wears his hat he can round up outlaws. Without it, he is not sure he can do anything. Later, he finds out that it is his heart, not his hat, that is important.*

Slobodkina, E. 2006. *Caps for Sale* (Book and CD). New York: HarperCollins. *This classic folktale relates a story about a peddler who balances many caps upon his head and sells them for 50 cents. When he stops to rest, he awakens to find that monkeys have taken all but one cap.*

Evaluation of the Hat Center

(This form is on the CD that comes with this book.) Ask yourself the following questions to evaluate the Hat Center in your classroom:

- Are the children showing interest in hats and their construction?
- Are children using creative thinking as they determine the hat designs and decorations they will use?
- Are the children enjoying the stories about hats?
- Do the stories inspire the children to create specific hats and play sequences that relate to a theme?
- Are children sharing ideas about hats and the people who wear them?

A teacher interacting with a child.

Observation of the Individual Child

(This form is on the CD that comes with this book. Always date observations of each child.)

- Is this child making hats? Which ones?
- Is the child being creative in the design of an original hat, or does her hat look like the hats the other children made? Either way is acceptable, but each demonstrates this child's level of creative development.
- How is this child using tools to make her hats? This can help determine the development of the child's small motor skills.
- Is the child talking with others as she works on her hat? What is she saying?
- Do you see evidence of the child using ideas, words, or roles from books about hats?
- Is the child successfully working cooperatively to make hats or on other projects?

Summary

Today's children live in a world filled with dark messages: war, crime, disruptions in family life, violent TV and videos, and so on. The Laughing Center explores the "lighter" side of life. This center encourages children to laugh and play with a variety of different fun possibilities. The props and materials in this center allow children to make choices, find things that interest them, and enjoy active participation. Children using the Laughing Center play, create, hatch ideas, and enjoy laughing.

Introducing the Center

During circle or group time, share some "crazy" items with the children that will be in the Laughing Center. For example, share a big nose, a Jack-in-the-box, a clown wig, or other fun and interesting props. Encourage the children to discuss how the items make them feel, how people react to them, and what they make us want to do. Provide a mirror, so children can see themselves when they try on the items. After the discussion, put the items in the Laughing Center, which will encourage the children to visit the center and expand their play.

Learning Objectives for Children in the Laughing Center

1. To expand the range of props and materials with which the children imagine and explore.
2. To incorporate humor and laughter into their play.
3. To stimulate language that relates to humor and laughing.
4. To encourage the development of social skills through collaborative play.
5. To use "reading" and "writing" in meaningful and enjoyable ways.

Time Frame for the Laughing Center

Set up the Laughing Center in the classroom for two to three weeks at a time, reintroducing it throughout the year. It may be especially helpful during the winter months when days might be shorter and tend to be drearier.

Note: The attached CD contains a sample letter to send to families, introducing them to the Laughing Center.

Vocabulary Enrichment

amusing
audience
clown
comedian
costume
giggle
humorous
joke
laugh
mask
mirror
perform
play
script
show
silly
smile
story
surprise
trick

Wearing mismatched house slippers is fun and funny!

Web of Integrated Learning

Laughing Center

Literacy
- "Writing" funny stories
- "Reading" jokes
- Listening to the stories of others

Motor Development
- Making clown acts
- Dress and undress in costumes

Music
- Creating funny jingles
- Singing funny songs

Art
- Creating funny faces
- Making costumes
- Drawing funny pictures

Math
- Counting objects
- Seeing more and less
- Adding items to costumes

Self-Concept
- Gaining confidence in oral skills
- Having others value ideas
- Repeating stories and jokes

Social Skills
- Determining roles in collaboration
- Listening to others' ideas
- Developing a skit

Science
- Mixing paint
- Focusing on details
- Observing changes

- ❏ cardboard boxes
- ❏ clip-on lights
- ❏ clown props
- ❏ clown costume
- ❏ colorful wig
- ❏ hat
- ❏ nose
- ❏ umbrellas
- ❏ costumes
- ❏ dance
- ❏ Halloween
- ❏ party
- ❏ hand mirror
- ❏ hula hoop
- ❏ joke books and funny stories
- ❏ posters/art that show funny happenings
- ❏ small plastic chairs
- ❏ sturdy stepstool

A pair of glasses with a big nose is funny.

Funny Hands

3–4 pairs of cotton work gloves
decoration for gloves: markers, fabric,
  chenille stems, buttons, ribbon, colored
tape
glue

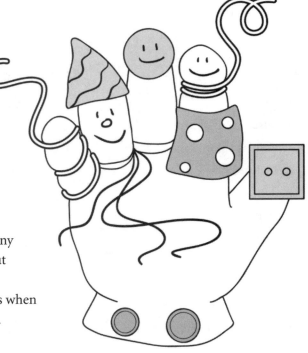

- Set out several pairs of cotton work
  gloves, along with various materials the
  children can use to decorate their "funny
  hands."
- The children use their imaginations when
  decorating the gloves.
- After the children finish making their "funny
  hands" and the glue on the gloves dries, put
  them in a container marked "gloves." The
  children can use them as parts of costumes when
  they want to put on various performances.

Funny Mask

construction paper or paper plates
decorative trim: rickrack, edging, pompoms, tassels, ribbon, tinsel
glue
mirror
moveable eyes
scissors
scrap pieces of foil, wrapping paper, newspaper, magazines, colored paper, contact paper
  yarn, twine, elastic

- Children can examine the collection of masks in the center and look at books that include
  pictures of different types of mask.
- Provide children with paper plates or sheets of construction paper to use as the bases for their
  masks. The children attach string, twine, or elastic to the edges of their masks so they can wear
  them on their faces. If necessary, help them cut out eye, nostril, and mouth holes if they want
  them in their masks.
- Placing a large mirror in the center will allow children to see how they look in their own masks.
- Once the children finish making their masks, take pictures of the children wearing them, and
  display the photographs in the Laughing Center.
- Help the children sign both the insides of their masks and the photographs of the children
  wearing their masks.

Old Baseball Hats

glue

materials that can be attached to hats: feathers, yarn, sequins, chenille stems, fabric scraps, felt
  pieces, and so on

old baseball hats or other types of hats

stapler to attach items to hat

clothespins to hold trim in place while it dries. (keep this, please)

- Set out various decorative materials and several old baseball hats, or other various types of hats.
- The children select hats and decorate them with some of the materials that are displayed in the center.
- Clothespins can be used for items to dry or connect to the hat.
- Funny hats can be placed in a small suitcase for children to try on and encourage play.

Activities for the Laughing Center

Cleaning Up the Fun

brooms	shredded paper
dustpans	trash can or small plastic buckets

- Consider demonstrating the steps in this activity before the children try it.
- Set out several buckets or trashcans, as well as piles of shredded paper.
- The children fill buckets or trash cans with shredded paper.
- Children can feel the shredded paper, and toss it in the air.
- After the children finish tossing all the paper, pass out some brooms and dustpans so the children can sweep up the paper, then return the props to their proper place.
- For young children, the cleanup is as much fun as the tossing.
- A chart of the steps in this activity would add a literacy opportunity to the activity.

Creating a Clown

½-yard pieces of interesting fabric: textured, stripes, bright colors, and so on

clown-related materials:

big glasses	pictures of clowns
face paint	stuffed animals
noses	washable markers
wigs	

large, unbreakable mirror

- Set out various interesting and funny materials.
- Children can select items that make them look like a clown.
- The children can see how they look by using a mirror.

exterior latex paint (bright colors)

markers

old shower curtain

paintbrushes

pieces of contact paper

scissors

sprinkles or glitter

spring-loaded shower curtain rod

- The children can decorate an old shower curtain with paint, markers, and sprinkles or glitter. The children will be creative in developing designs and decorations on the curtain.
- Big paintbrushes can be used to create large designs and decorations.
- Once the children finish decorating the curtain, and after it dries, securely attach it to a corner of the Laughing Center using a spring-loaded shower curtain rod. Make sure it can open and close easily.
- With the curtain up, the children can use it to present funny performances.

Adding Spark to the Laughing Center

Invite a guest clown, mime, or funny storyteller to visit the children and perform in the Laughing Center. Later, the children can imitate the visitor and create their own humorous shows.

The Essential Literacy Connection

Reading/Writing Opportunities

- Read joke books with the children.
- Look at funny pictures in magazines and advertisements with the children.
- Collect humorous stories and jokes from various print materials.

Other Printed Materials

- Make humorous magazines and newspapers available for the children to practice "reading."

Books for the Laughing Center

Ahlberg, A., & Ingman, B. 2006. *The Runaway Dinner*. Cambridge, MA: Candlewick. *What happens if a dinner decides it does not want anyone to eat it? It is a plight that can only result in a breathless escape—and what a chase it is! This is a fast and funny tale with kid-friendly illustrations that add visual comedy to the chase.*

Arnold, T. 2004. *Catalina Magdalena Hoopensteiner Wallendiner Hogan Logan Bogan Was Her Name.* New York: Scholastic, Inc. *This colorful book follows the life of a unique child while growing up.*

Bateman, T. 2004. *April Foolishness.* Illustrated by Nadine Bernard Westcott. Morton Grove, IL: Albert Whitman. *Grandma, Grandpa, and the grandkids enjoy April Fools' Day on the farm.*

Curtis, J. L. 2007. *Today I Feel Silly & Other Moods That Make My Day.* Illustrated by Laura Cornell. New York: HarperCollins. *Rhyming text describes the different emotions of a little girl.*

McBratney, S. 2004. *Once There Was a Hoodie.* Illustrated by Paul Hess. London, UK: Hodder Children's. *While trying to make friends, a Hoodie manages to scare off some sheep, cows, and children before finding the one thing that will make him truly happy.*

O'Connor, J. 2005. *Fancy Nancy.* Illustrated by Robin Preiss Glasser. New York: HarperCollins. *For Nancy, there's no such thing as too, too much. She loves her frilly bedroom, her lace-trimmed socks, and her pen with a plume. Nancy teaches her family how to be fancy, too.*

Evaluation of the Laughing Center

(This form is on the CD that comes with this book.)

Ask yourself the following questions to evaluate the Laughing Center in your classroom:

- Are the children participating in the Laughing Center?
- Are the children using the props and materials in funny ways?
- Are the children collaborating to produce a performance or act?
- Are the children using new vocabulary and language as they play?
- Are the children using literacy-related materials in the Laughing Center?

Observation of the Individual Child

(This form is on the CD that comes with this book. Always date observations of each child.)

- Is the child enjoying the Laughing Center? Give an example that demonstrates how she is enjoying it.
- What has the child created that relates to the Laughing Center (such as a silly hat, silly gloves, a joke, a performance, and so on)?
- Have you seen the child working independently, beside other children, or collaboratively? Explain.
- Is the child performing, involved with, or observing most of the activities in the Laughing Center? How?
- Is the child using any of the literacy materials in the center? Which materials, and in what ways?

Summary

Nighttime is interesting for young children. The world looks different in the dark and many special activities occur at night. Nighttime can also be a fearful time in the minds of young children. Children can imagine monsters hiding in dark places and ordinary sounds can be very frightening. In this center, young children will have the opportunity to work through some of their fears. There are a number of wonderful books and stories about nighttime that the children can discuss and enjoy.

Introducing the Center

During circle or group time, engage the children in a discussion about the different times of the day. Young children like to understand a typical day's sequence of events and often like to repeat them in the same order each day. Talk with the children about what they do early in the morning, when they get home from school, at meal time, and during the night. It may be helpful for you to write their ideas about what happens during the night on chart paper. This not only helps them remember what they have shared but also lets them see the written versions of the words they say.

Learning Objectives for Children in the Nighttime Center

1. To experience pleasant activities that relate to nighttime.
2. To give the children the opportunity to work through some of their experiences and fears.
3. To learn that other children have positive and negative feelings about nighttime.
4. To enjoy quality children's books that relate to nighttime.
5. To use new vocabulary words as the children talk about nighttime and related experiences.

Time Frame for the Nighttime Center

This center can be in operation for two to three weeks, depending on the amount of interest the children demonstrate. If children are actively participating in the center, use additional nighttime books and extend the period in which the center is in use.

 Note: The attached CD contains a sample letter to send to families, introducing them to the Nighttime Center.

A flashlight and a lamp encourage experimentation.

Vocabulary Enrichment

bedtime
bedtime story
calm
change
dark
dream
flashlight
moon
moonlight
night
nightlight
nightmare
quiet
relax
restful
routine
scary
shadow
sleeping
snoring
sounds
star
street light

Web of Integrated Learning

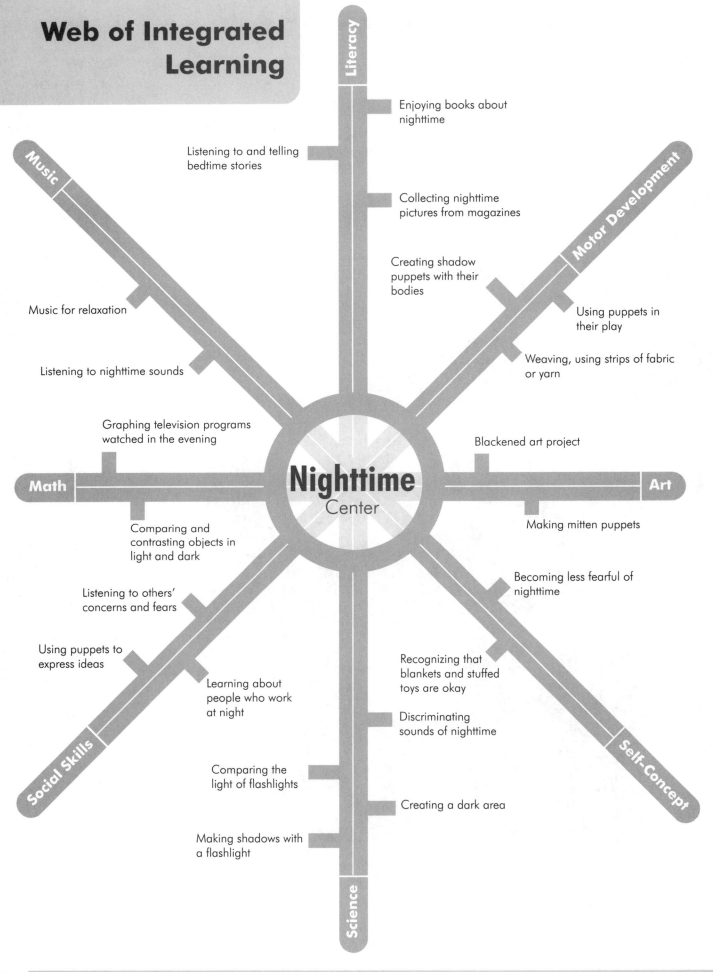

Literacy
- Enjoying books about nighttime
- Listening to and telling bedtime stories
- Collecting nighttime pictures from magazines
- Creating shadow puppets with their bodies

Music
- Music for relaxation
- Listening to nighttime sounds

Motor Development
- Using puppets in their play
- Weaving, using strips of fabric or yarn

Math
- Graphing television programs watched in the evening
- Comparing and contrasting objects in light and dark

Art
- Blackened art project
- Making mitten puppets

Social Skills
- Listening to others' concerns and fears
- Using puppets to express ideas
- Learning about people who work at night

Self-Concept
- Becoming less fearful of nighttime
- Recognizing that blankets and stuffed toys are okay
- Discriminating sounds of nighttime
- Creating a dark area

Science
- Comparing the light of flashlights
- Making shadows with a flashlight

Nighttime Center

❏ air mattress

❏ baby blankets

❏ fuzzy fabric and fabric glue

❏ glow-in-the-dark stickers in shapes such as moon and stars

❏ lamp

❏ large appliance box with many holes cut in the shapes of stars (to let in light)

❏ pillows, beanbag chair, or lawn chair pads

❏ recordings of soft, relaxing music and CD or tape player

❏ rocking chair

❏ roll of black shade cloth (This inexpensive fabric used to keep grass from growing under walks or to provide shade for plants can be bought at garden or home improvement stores.)

❏ sheet, rope, and clamp-on light to make a shadow stage

❏ small flashlights

❏ stuffed toys

A blanket was used to create a darkened area.

Fuzzy Puppets   ART

fuzzy, soft fabric
scissors
fabric glue
felt, fabric scraps, lace, trim, and so on
markers

- Make mitten puppets from fuzzy, soft fabric.
- Cut out child-size mitten shapes from a variety of soft fabrics of different colors and place them in the center.
- The children choose two mitten shapes to glue together with fabric glue.
- Once the glue finishes drying, the children decorate the puppets with felt, fabric scraps, lace, trim, or markers.
- Mitten puppets are easy for young children to manipulate and use in their dramatic play about nighttime.

The Dark Place   SCIENCE

black paper
black shade cloth
glow-in-the-dark stickers
tape

- Create a dark place in the corner of the Nighttime Center by taping pieces of black shade cloth across one corner of the center. The fabric will let some light into the area, so it will not be too dark.
- Put black paper on the walls of the center. Place glow-in-the-dark star stickers in the dark area.
- Encourage the children to help create the dark space. Working to create and decorate the space will make it less frightening for the children and will help them be more comfortable and courageous when they use the corner. The children enter and leave this section of the center whenever they choose.

Woven Blanket   MOTOR DEVELOPMENT

large piece of burlap or other loosely woven material
large plastic needles
pieces of thick yarn

- Use a large piece of burlap or other loosely woven fabric as the foundation for a child-made blanket.
- Provide the children with large plastic needles that have big eyes and blunt tips so they can sew thick yarn through the burlap or fabric.

- Demonstrate the weaving process to the children. Also, tie large knots at the end of lengths of yarn for the children when they begin sewing.
- After learning the basics of weaving, encourage the children to create abstract designs and patterns on the fabric.

Activities for the Nighttime Center

Bedtime Stories

LITERACY

blank recording media
CD or tape recorder

- Encourage the children to tell their favorite bedtime stories in the center.
- As the children retell their stories, record them for other children to hear.
- Leave the recording equipment out for other children to listen to and enjoy, as well as to encourage them to make their own recordings.

Black Art

ART

black construction paper
colorful chalk

- Set out black construction paper and several pieces of colorful chalk.
- Children can create their own night scenes on the black paper.
- Display the pictures on a black wall in the Nighttime Center.

City Nights

LITERACY

Goodnight Moon by Margaret Wise Brown
markers
paper

- Read *Goodnight Moon* to the children, and then engage them in a discussion of nighttime in the city, including people who work when others are sleeping.
- With the children, use markers and paper to create a list of jobs and responsibilities that people do at night.

basket

black paper

chalk

chart paper

collection of flashlights

large appliance box

markers and crayons

scissors

- Set out a large appliance box.
- Cut holes in the top of the appliance box so light will filter in and make the area less frightening (adult step).
- Collect flashlights of different sizes and shapes and place them in a basket outside the entrance to the appliance box.
- The children can select a flashlight and go inside the dark box to determine the amount of light it produces.
- Set out chart paper, markers, and crayons for the children to make drawings of the various flashlights.
- On the side of the appliance box, post a chart of the children's drawings of the different flashlights.
- At the top of the chart, write, "Which flashlight would you use on a dark night?"
- Ask the children to mark the drawing of which flashlight they would use.
- With chalk, draw circles, squares, or letters on black paper. Attach the drawings on the inside of the box. When the children go into the box they can use the flashlights to trace around the patterns.

It Looks Different   MATH

basket of objects, such as a cooking pot, plastic water bottle, ball, and forks or spoons

hat

flashlights

large appliance box

- Place a basket of objects outside the large appliance box.
- Encourage the children to look at the objects in the light and then take them inside the box to look at them again.
- The children can use a flashlight to observe the objects in the dark.

child-safe scissors
glue or tape
old magazines
scrapbook or sheets of paper stapled together

- Set out several magazines and catalogs that contain images of nighttime activity.
- The children cut out pictures that show nighttime happenings from old magazines.
- The children glue or tape the images in a scrapbook.
- Put the scrapbook in the Nighttime Center for the children to examine and discuss.

Restful Music   MUSIC

CD or tape player
collection of musical recordings, including selections of soft and slow music
small pillowcase

- Place a CD or tape player and collection of musical recordings in a small pillowcase next to a CD or tape player.
- As the children listen to the music, they select the recordings they find most relaxing.

Shadow Frame   MOTOR DEVELOPMENT

clothesline
white sheet
clip-on light

Note: This activity encourages creative dramatics through the use of a shadow stage.
- Hang clothesline across a corner of the center.
- Place a white sheet across the clothesline, with space left at one end to permit the children to enter and exit easily.
- Attach a clip-on light to the other wall, behind the sheet. Experiment with the light's angle to ensure that the children can produce clear shadows.
- One or two children at a time produce shadows from behind the sheet, while the other children watch from the audience in front of the sheet.
- The creative dramatics can be as simple as individual pantomime or as complex as a small group acting out an entire story.

Adding Spark to the Nighttime Center

Record sounds the children might hear at night. Add the recording to the center for the children to listen and identify the sounds they hear. Encourage the children to draw pictures of some animals and objects that make the sounds they hear on the recording at night.

Reading/Writing Opportunities

- The children "write" or dictate what they like about nighttime.
- Make a graph to represent the children's favorite nighttime books.
- Read the children enjoyable books about nighttime.
- Make recordings of what the children say about nighttime.
- Listen for nighttime sounds.
- Children "read" to baby dolls or other children before bedtime.
- The children create and use puppets in their play.
- The children develop visual skills by tracing a pattern with a flashlight.

Other Printed Materials

- Start a collection of nighttime pictures.

Books for the Nighttime Center

Berger, B. 1996. *Grandfather Twilight*. New York: Philomel. *At the day's end, Grandfather Twilight walks in the forest to perform his evening task, bringing the miracle of night to the world.*

Brown, M. W. 1975. *Goodnight Moon*. New York: HarperCollins. *This is a popular and soothing nighttime book for children.*

Fox, M., & Denton, T. 1992. *Night Noises*. London: Voyager. *While her family celebrates her 90th birthday with her, a woman remembers scenes from her youth.*

Rylant, C. 1991. *Night in the Country*. New York: Aladdin. *Text and illustrations describe the sights and sounds of nighttime in the country.*

Wise Brown, M. 2005. *Goodnight Moon*. Illustrated by Clement Hurd. New York: HarperCollins. *A short poem of goodnight wishes from a young rabbit preparing for or attempting to postpone his own slumber.*

Yolen, J. 1994. *Owl Moon*. Torrance, CA: Frank Schaffer. *A girl and her father go owling on a moonlit winter night near the farm where they live. In harmony with the art, the melodious text brings to life an unusual countryside adventure. A Caldecott Medal Award winner.*

Evaluation of the Nighttime Center

(This form is on the CD that comes with this book.)

Ask yourself the following questions to evaluate the Nighttime Center in your classroom:

- Are the children talking about nighttime and some of the personal experiences they have had at night?
- Are books and stories providing the children with positive ideas about nighttime?
- Are children discovering that they and others enjoy and dislike certain aspects of nighttime?
- Does the center's nighttime theme provide an opportunity for children to engage with their ideas and feelings about nighttime?
- Are the children gaining confidence in dealing with nighttime?

Observation of the Individual Child

(This form is on the CD that comes with this book. Always date observations of each child.)

- What is the child saying about nighttime? What words does the child use? What feelings does the child express?
- Is the child returning to this center or avoiding the area?
- What sort of play is the child engaging in while in the Nighttime Center? Does the child exhibit a sense of routine or schedule with her play?
- Are there special books that the child enjoys and returns to in the Nighttime Center?
- What sort of night-related images is the child drawing? What does she have to say about the drawing?

Summary

Young children enjoy participating in parties. Of course, their favorite party is their own birthday celebration. The Party Center is designed so that all children can participate in activities, rather than having a party focusing on one child. In this center, children wrap and give presents to themselves or others. They participate in making costumes and preparing food for a party, enjoying the social experiences repeatedly.

Introducing the Center

In circle or group time, sing the Birthday Song. Ask if anyone has a birthday today? Then, explain that there is a big party going on in our new Party Center. We are going to celebrate everyone's birthday, even if it is not today. Share an invitation with them that asks them to come to the new center to celebrate.

Learning Objectives for Children in the Party Center

1. To develop language skills as they communicate with others.
2. To enjoy listening to quality children's books and "rereading" them in the center.
3. To enhance their social skills as they cooperate and share at the "party."
4. To develop small motor skills while wrapping, cutting, and decorating.
5. To learn to appreciate ways that children are the same and different.

Time Frame for the Party Center

Set up the Party Center for approximately two weeks. This will provide sufficient time for all of the children to visit the Party Center and participate in the activities occurring there. At the end of this period, encourage the children to help you pack the party things away, so they can be brought out at another time. Store items in large plastic containers and label when the center was used.

 Note: The attached CD contains a sample letter to send to families, introducing them to the Party Center.

Vocabulary Enrichment

appreciate

Birthday Song

calendar

caring

celebration

classify

decorate

enjoy

friend

game

gift

host

invitation

noisemaker

party hat

present

refreshments

RSVP

scavenger

search

share

thank you

wrapping

Playing rhythm patterns together is great fun!

Web of Integrated Learning

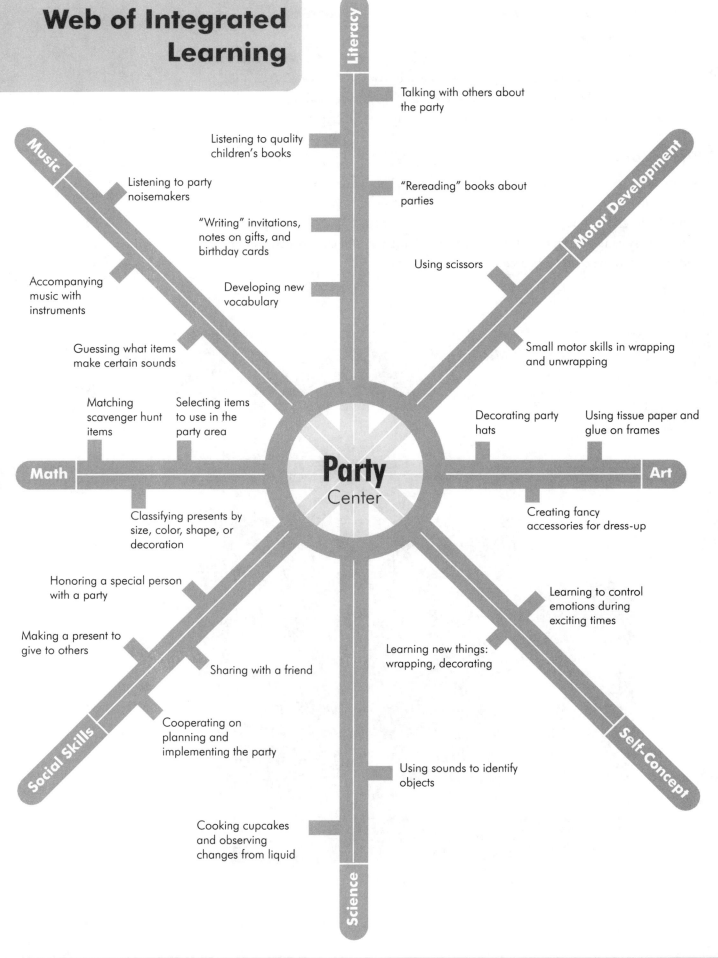

Literacy

- Talking with others about the party
- Listening to quality children's books
- "Rereading" books about parties
- Listening to party noisemakers
- "Writing" invitations, notes on gifts, and birthday cards
- Developing new vocabulary

Music

- Accompanying music with instruments
- Guessing what items make certain sounds

Motor Development

- Using scissors
- Small motor skills in wrapping and unwrapping

Math

- Matching scavenger hunt items
- Selecting items to use in the party area
- Classifying presents by size, color, shape, or decoration

Art

- Decorating party hats
- Using tissue paper and glue on frames
- Creating fancy accessories for dress-up

Party Center

Social Skills

- Honoring a special person with a party
- Making a present to give to others
- Sharing with a friend
- Cooperating on planning and implementing the party

Self-Concept

- Learning to control emotions during exciting times
- Learning new things: wrapping, decorating

Science

- Using sounds to identify objects
- Cooking cupcakes and observing changes from liquid

- ❑ bows
- ❑ fancy dress-up clothes
- ❑ markers and pens
- ❑ old invitations and birthday cards
- ❑ photos from family parties
- ❑ plastic tablecloths or sheets
- ❑ scissors
- ❑ small cardboard boxes
- ❑ stickers and tags
- ❑ tape
- ❑ two low tables
- ❑ wrapping paper

A birthday hat for a party

Decorating the Party Place

MOTOR DEVELOPMENT

balloons
flowers
streamers

- Let the children determine the decorations they would like to use in the Party Center.
- Use balloons, streamers, or flowers to add to the party atmosphere.

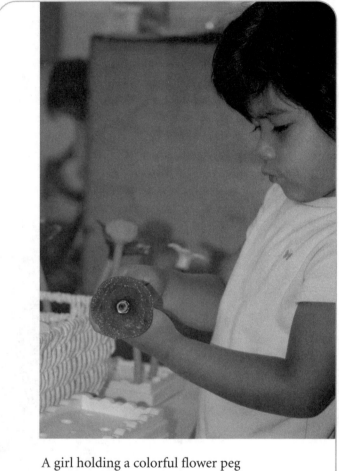

A girl holding a colorful flower peg

Fancy Clothes

ART

cardboard
glue
inexpensive shiny metallic fabric
scissors
shells, shiny stickers, and so on

- Let the children use clothes from the Home Living Center to dress up for the party.
- Add a few accessories made by the children in the Party Center.
- Make ties and scarves by cutting pieces from inexpensive shiny, metallic, or unusual fabric.
- Make sparkling necklaces and/or buckles by gluing shells and attaching stickers to a cardboard shape. Paint or sprinkle with glitter for additional decoration.
- The children can select outfits and accessories they want to wear to the party.

construction paper

feathers, pieces of silver contact paper, pompoms, and so on

glue

stapler or tape

- The children can make simple party hats by rolling a piece of construction paper into a cone shape.
- If necessary, help children staple or glue the seam together.
- The children can decorate the hat, using feathers, pieces of silver contact paper, pompoms, glitter, trim, ribbon, yarn, or wallpaper scraps from the junk box.

Activities for the Party Center

Birthday Cake   SCIENCE

colorful frosting, colorful sugar, sprinkles, gumdrops, or birthday candles

recipe and ingredients for cupcakes or prepared cupcakes

- For a cooking activity, the children make and decorate cupcakes.
- After the cupcakes are baked, the children decorate a cupcake with frosting, sugar, sprinkles, gumdrops, or a birthday candle.

Recycled Birthday Cards   LITERACY

child-safe scissors

envelopes

glue

markers

old birthday cards or party invitations

old stamps

stickers

tape

white paper, construction paper, or newsprint

- If there is a name or personal information on a recycled card, the children can cover it by cutting and gluing a white sheet of paper to the old card.
- The children can draw or "write" invitations to the party on the old cards.
- Children can either draw or "write" their invitees' names on the envelopes.
- The children can attach stickers or old stamps to the envelopes.
- The invitations may be delivered to the cubbies in the classroom.

5–8 different sizes of boxes wrapped in different colors, with some matching
large box

- Place five to eight wrapped presents that vary in size, shape, color, and decoration in a large box.
- The children sort the presents, using one characteristic: color, size, or shape. Remember that the young children will not be able to sort by two characteristics at the same time–that skill comes later in their development.
- They discuss their approach and observe other children who may group the presents in a different way.

Making a Present   ART

colorful tissue paper
glue or tape
markers
mixture of white glue and water
paintbrushes
paper
pictures painted by the children
Styrofoam trays

- Explain to the children that not all presents are bought at a store.
- Children enjoy making a present to give to a family member or friend.
- Pictures painted by the children can be framed in the Party Center for a very special gift.
- Glue or tape the picture to the inside of a Styrofoam tray.
- Cut, crunch, or tear colorful tissue paper.
- Paint the crumpled paper onto the Styrofoam tray with a thick mixture of white glue and water. This technique produces a blending of colors and a texture of paper resulting in an attractive frame for the picture.
- After the frame is completed, the children "write" or dictate a message and attach it below their framed picture.

Party Book   LITERACY

construction paper
instant-print camera and film or digital camera, printer, and photo paper
markers
scissors

- Cut a book cover and paper in the shape of a birthday cake or party hat.
- Use an instant-print or digital camera to take and print pictures of the children participating in the Party Center.
- Put the children's photographs in the party book. The photographs will act as the illustrations for the book.

- Encourage the children to "write" or dictate an accompanying story.
- The children name their books.
- List the authors of the book on the title page, along with their book title.

Party Music MUSIC

collection of noisemakers: horns, clappers, plastic bottles, lids

- Set out a collection of noisemakers for the children to use to create party music. Horns, clappers, plastic bottles, and lids produce interesting sounds.
- After the children experimenting with the noisemakers, the children decide which sounds they will use to accompany the Birthday Song and other party songs.
- The children can sing the songs using different sounds to accompany each song.

Scavenger Hunt MATH

items from around the room
markers
paper with pictures of hidden items (1 copy for each child)

- Hide some items from the classroom.
- On one sheet of paper, draw pictures of the items that have been hidden.
- Each child has a copy of this sheet and a marker.
- When a child finds an item, she places a mark next to the picture of the item on her sheet.
- Children can work individually or with a partner on this scavenger hunt.
- Some children may repeat the scavenger hunt using the same items or venturing to try new items.

Surprise Boxes SCIENCE

4–5 cardboard boxes
4–5 objects to place in each box
tape
wrapping paper

- Wrap four or five cardboard boxes so the lids can be taken off, even after wrapping.
- Hide an object inside each box.
- The children shake the boxes to guess the contents.
- When they open the boxes, they see if they guessed correctly.
- After the children open the box, they can rewrap it and allow another child a turn, or put a new item inside the box for another child to guess.

bows, yarn, and small decorations
cardboard boxes
child-safe scissors
newspaper
paper
ribbon
tape
tissue
wrapping paper

- Set up a place in the Party Center where children can wrap presents.
- Place a selection of materials on a low table.
- Include scissors, tape, wrapping paper, tissue paper, newspaper, ribbon, bows, yarn, and other decorations.
- Provide cardboard boxes that are easy for small hands to wrap, such as small shoeboxes, cereal boxes, lingerie boxes, and toothpaste containers.
- The children select a box, place a "gift" inside, and wrap the present.
- They can open the present or give it to a friend and watch them open the surprise package.

Adding Spark to the Party Center

Let the children select a special person in their school whom they would like to honor with a party. They can plan the celebration, make the invitations, and entertain the special person in the Party Center. After the party, the children can "write," dictate, or draw pictures about the party experience. The children's "writings" can be given to the honoree, as a gift.

The Essential Literacy Connection

Reading/Writing Opportunities

- Children "write" invitations to the party and "write" names on gifts.
- Children send birthday cards to friends and create banners for the party.
- Children wrap and unwrap presents.
- Children create a party book.
- Children enjoying books about birthday parties.
- Children draw logos and pictures of items for a scavenger hunt.

Other Printed Materials

- Bring in catalogs that include gift items.
- Display toy advertisements or gift flyers from newspapers or stores.

Books for the Party Center

Bridwell, N. 1993. *Clifford's Birthday Party.* New York: Scholastic, Inc. *Emily Elizabeth, Clifford's owner, has a birthday party for him and many humorous adventures occur.*

Freeman, D. 1977. *Dandelion.* New York: Puffin. *Dandelion is invited to a tea and taffy party.*

Keats, E. J. 1998. *A Letter to Amy.* New York: Puffin. *Peter wants to invite Amy to his birthday party, but he wants it to be a surprise.*

Rempt, F. 2007. *Snail's Birthday Wish.* Illustrated by Noelle Smit. London, UK: Boxer Books. *It's Snail's birthday! All his forest friends have gathered to celebrate. Here comes Beaver, Squirrel, Duck, Mole, Frog, and Ant, all carrying colorful balloons and brightly wrapped presents.*

Rylant, C. 1991. *Birthday Presents.* Illustrated by Sucie Stevenson. New York: Scholastic, Inc. *A five-year-old girl listens, as her parents describe her previous birthdays and how they celebrated each occasion.*

Willems, M. 2007. *I Am Invited to a Party!* New York: Hyperion. *Piggie is invited to her very first party. But what will she wear? Gerald, the party expert, knows just how to help, or does he?*

Evaluation of the Party Center

(This form is on the CD that comes with this book.)

Ask yourself the following questions to evaluate the Party Center in your classroom:

- Are children participating in activities in the center?
- Are children working together on wrapping presents, scavenger hunts, making music, or "writing" invitations?
- Are children using the theme and children's books in their play?
- Are children talking and sharing ideas in the center?
- Are children able to celebrate someone else's birthday? Are they able to express positive feelings toward the child and give her a gift?

Observation of the Individual Child

(This form is on the CD that comes with this book. Always date observations of each child.)

- Is the child participating in the party activities? In what ways?
- How does the child respond when the birthday party is for someone else?
- Has the child used small motor skills when wrapping presents, "writing" invitations, cutting paper, or decorating packages? How would you describe the development in this area?
- Is the child conversing with others in this center? What was said?
- Is she beginning to understand that everyone (at least everyone in the class) has a birthday?

Summary

A topic of global concern is caring for the environment. The Recycling Center is designed to nurture children's interest in environmental issues. In this center, children learn that they can have a positive impact on the environment. It is important to provide concrete experiences that are related to young children's lives. If the activities or projects are too abstract, young children will not accomplish the objectives of the Recycling Center or apply the learning to their world.

Introducing the Center

To introduce the Recycling Center to the children bring junk or discarded items to circle or group time. Brainstorm the many ways this junk could be reused by the children and society.

Learning Objectives for Children in the Recycling Center

1. To expand their knowledge of the environment through hands-on experiences.
2. To develop vocabulary related to environmental issues and concerns.
3. To develop their feelings of competence as they participate in activities.
4. To heighten their awareness of how to care for their environment.

Time Frame for the Recycling Center

After the children have enjoyed the Recycling Center for two weeks, incorporate the activities and recycling in the classroom for the remainder of the year.

 Note: The attached CD contains a sample letter to send to families, introducing them to the Recycling Center.

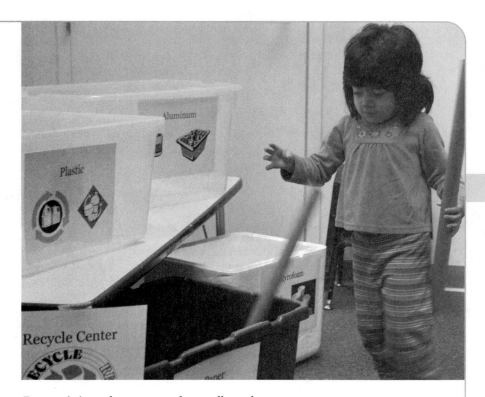

Determining where to put the cardboard

Vocabulary Enrichment

aluminum
bale
biodegradable
collect
conserve
crush
disposable
ecology
environment
garbage
greenhouse
landfill
nature
ozone layer
package
plastic
pollution
recycle
replant
resource
sorting
Styrofoam
toxic
trash
treasure

Web of Integrated Learning

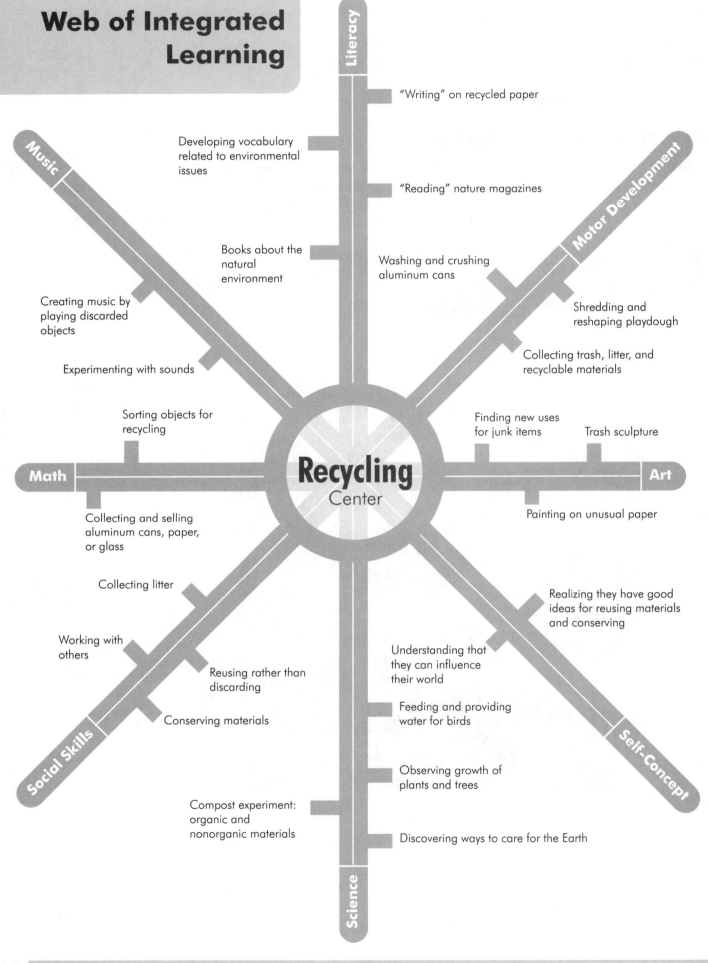

Literacy
- "Writing" on recycled paper
- Developing vocabulary related to environmental issues
- "Reading" nature magazines
- Books about the natural environment
- Washing and crushing aluminum cans

Music
- Creating music by playing discarded objects
- Experimenting with sounds

Motor Development
- Shredding and reshaping playdough
- Collecting trash, litter, and recyclable materials

Math
- Sorting objects for recycling
- Collecting and selling aluminum cans, paper, or glass

Art
- Finding new uses for junk items
- Trash sculpture
- Painting on unusual paper

Recycling Center

Social Skills
- Collecting litter
- Working with others
- Reusing rather than discarding
- Conserving materials

Self-Concept
- Realizing they have good ideas for reusing materials and conserving
- Understanding that they can influence their world

Science
- Feeding and providing water for birds
- Observing growth of plants and trees
- Compost experiment: organic and nonorganic materials
- Discovering ways to care for the Earth

Family- or Teacher-Collected Props for the Recycling Center

- ❏ can crusher
- ❏ charts that show the growth of a tree
- ❏ large bins or cardboard boxes to hold recyclable items
- ❏ photographs of forests, landfills, forest fires, and litter

Working together to decide how to recycle

Child-Created Props for the Recycling Center

Litter Bag

SOCIAL SKILLS

crayons   paintbrushes
markers   plastic or paper shopping bags
paints

- Use plastic or paper shopping bags, usually thrown away, as containers to hold litter.
- The children paint or decorate trash bags with markers.
- The children use the decorated bags when they go on a "trash hunt" around the school or neighborhood.

Recycle

LITERACY

chart paper   scissors
crayons   tape
markers

- With the children, make a chart showing pictures of objects that the class can recycle.
- When the class starts recycling, make labels for the bins that will hold these items, such as glass, metal, and paper.
- Throughout the day, encourage the children to determine what classroom materials they should put in the Recycling Center.

Aluminum Cans

can crusher
collected aluminum cans

- Encourage the children to collect aluminum cans.
- Wash and crush the cans in the Recycling Center.
- The children can sell the cans to a local recycling center (depending on your state).
- Use the money from their recycling project to purchase something for the classroom.
- This is a lesson in economics, as well as a concrete example of the rewards of recycling.

Compost Experiment

leftover food and serving pieces
shovels

- Collect leftover food from lunch, such as lettuce, apple cores, or bread crusts (no meat products).
- Include several trash items, such as Styrofoam trays, milk cartons, and plastic utensils in the collection.
- Let the children bury these items in an area outside and label the site.
- Return to the site after one week and uncover the items.
- Compare and contrast the changes to the organic matter and the Styrofoam, aluminum, or plastic items.
- Bury the materials again and return periodically for another look.

Environmental Wallpaper Books

crayons
markers
paper
stapler and tape
wallpaper sample book

- Make a book about the environment that includes pictures or writing about ways to protect the earth.
- Use a discontinued wallpaper sample book to make attractive covers for the books.
- Ask the children to select the wallpaper they want to use, determine the size of their book, and insert the paper.
- Help the children by stapling or taping the cover and pages together.
- Be sure each author and illustrator includes her name in the environmental wallpaper book.

discarded items:

aluminum pie pans	plastic wrap
bottle caps	small milk cartons
cans of different sizes	Styrofoam trays
margarine dishes	yarn
plastic cups	

large plastic container

- Collect junk items and place them in a large plastic container in the Recycling Center.
- Encourage the children to use these junk items to create new products or make art projects. Items that are versatile work best for this activity.
- This activity encourages children to conserve materials, reuse items, and think creatively.

Music from Junk   M U S I C

discarded items   music recording

- The children make a musical instrument collection from discarded items. Possible instruments include aluminum can shakers, coffee can drums with lids, baby food lid clappers, twig wood sticks, plastic plates with mallets for cymbals, and wooden clothespins attached to a wooden board to use as a scraper.
- Place the instruments in a music box in the Recycling Center for the children to use.
- Individual children or groups of children use these instruments to make their own music.
- After children discover what sounds the instruments produce, they play the instruments to accompany a musical recording.

Newspaper Paintings   A R T

newspaper, packing paper, computer printouts, wallpaper, and so on
paint, and paintbrushes

- Let the children paint on paper that is not usually used for painting.
- Papers that could be used include newspapers, packing paper, computer printouts, wallpaper, paper bags, wrapping paper, and gift wrap.
- This activity encourages children to consider the different ways they can use a particular material, and in doing so, they develop flexible thinking.

Plant a Tree   S C I E N C E

reference books containing tree types
tree to plant

- Look at reference books about trees with the children to determine which tree will grow best in the school's environment.

- With the children, select a tree to plant in the outdoor area of the school.
- Ask a local forestry service or nursery to donate a tree or seedling.
- Encourage the children to water, protect, observe, and value the tree throughout the school year.

Shredding Materials   MOTOR DEVELOPMENT

| garlic or dough press | playdough |
| plastic knives | rolling pin |

- Let the children experiment with the concept of shredding by using playdough. Roll the dough into thin sheets with a rolling pin and cut into small pieces or push the playdough through a playdough press or garlic press.
- The children shape the shredded playdough into another form, demonstrating the reuse of a material.
- They can reuse the dough many times.

Trash Sculpture   ART

| collected trash | piece of wood |
| glue or tape | |

- Collect trash from the playground or in areas around the school.
- Use a piece of wood as a substantial base for the trash sculpture.
- Glue or tape pieces of trash onto the wood to produce a tall structure.
- This demonstrates clearly to young children the volume of trash found around their school.

Adding Spark to the Recycling Center

Add a new project that relates to caring for birds. Because birds need both food and water, the children can make bird feeders and birdbaths in the Recycling Center. Make feeders by covering pinecones or grapefruit rinds with peanut butter and seeds. Hang the coated cones with string from a tree branch. Make a simple birdbath from a ceramic or plastic flower pot saucer. Metal pans are not recommended, because they will get too hot during warm weather. Place the feeder and bath outside the classroom window and observe the birds' activities. Keep a record of the number of birds that eat from the bird feeders and use the birdbaths.

The Essential Literacy Connection

Reading/Writing Opportunities

- Use recycled paper for "writing" or drawing.
- Display examples of the children's "writings" and drawings in the center.

Other Printed Materials

- Share articles and pictures from magazines and newspapers on issues related to the environment.

- Copies of *Big Backyard* and *Ranger Rick*, published by the National Wildlife Federation, have beautiful photographs of animals and habitats, which will help children understand connections between nature and their environment.

Books for the Recycling Center

Gibbons, G. 1992. *Recycle: A Handbook for Kids*. Ontario: Little Brown. *This book explains the process of recycling, from start to finish, and discusses what happens to paper, glass, and plastic when they are recycled into new products.*

Green, J. 2005. *Why Should I Recycle?* Illustrated by Mike Gordon. Hauppauge, NY: Barron's. *Mr. Jones is a teacher who sets a good example for his students by separating his trash for recycling. When he takes them on a class trip to a recycling plant, they learn the value of recycling.*

Landau, E. 2002. *Earth Day—Keeping Our Planet Clean*. Berkeley Heights, NJ: Enslow. *This book discusses the origins of Earth Day, its history, and how it is observed in the United States today.*

Mackenzie, A. 2007. *Let's Recycle!* Pebble Books. Mankato, MN: Capstone Press. *Easy to read book and great photographs that describe recycling, why it is important, and simple ways children can recycle.*

The Earthworks Group. 1990. *50 Simple Things Kids Can Do to Save the Earth*. Berkeley, CA: Earth Works. *This book provides ideas to use in the classroom that will help children learn to recycle.*

Evaluation of the Recycling Center

(This form is on the CD that comes with this book.)

Ask yourself the following questions to evaluate the Recycling Center in your classroom:

- Are children talking about environmental issues in the Recycling Center, in the classroom, and/or on the playground?
- Do children use new vocabulary as they participate in the Recycling Center?
- Are children demonstrating a concern for their environment by participating in recycling projects?
- Are children beginning to understand that they can have an influence on the environment in which they live?
- Are children coming up with creative uses for junk items they have found?

Observation of the Individual Child

(This form is on the CD that comes with this book. Always date observations of each child.)

- Is this child participating in recycling items in the center? How?
- Have you observed the child sorting items? How accurately did she sort?
- Has she used vocabulary that relates to recycling? What was said?
- Is the child able to find ways to attach the boxes? How?
- Have you seen this child conserving materials in other areas of the classroom? Where?
- Have you observed a time when this child collaborated with others in the center? If so, in what way did she work with others?

Summary

Young children learn many things through their senses. Seeing provides them with an avenue to examine their world. Hearing determines unique features of the sounds in their environment. By touching and manipulating, children begin to identify differences and similarities of materials. Smells also lead to new understandings as children examine the diverse aromas of their world. The Sensory Center provides many activities and materials that allow children to use their senses, as they make distinctions and comparisons through hands-on, meaningful experiences.

Introducing the Center

Before opening the Sensory Center, discuss with the children sensory experiences that occur during their regular classroom activities. When the children wash their hands, ask, "Does the water feel hot or cold?" When they go to lunch, ask them to guess what they will be having by using their sense of smell. When they use playdough, ask them to describe how it feels. While they are playing outside, encourage them to notice the blue sky, rain clouds, or a smooth stone. Developing this awareness will lead the children to anticipate the opening of the Sensory Center.

Learning Objectives for Children in the Sensory Center

1. To expand children's understanding of the world in which they live.
2. To allow children to use their senses in discriminating between the materials they use each day.
3. To participate in activities that will enhance children's sensory abilities.
4. To use new vocabulary as children discuss the senses that they are using in the Sensory Center.
5. To encourage children to become more aware of the sights, smells, sounds, and textures in their environment.

Time Frame for the Sensory Center

This center will interest young children for several weeks. During this time, there will be sufficient opportunity for children to visit the center several times and explore the materials.

 Note: The attached CD contains a sample letter to send to families, introducing them to the Sensory Center.

Clay with an unusual texture is difficult to roll.

Vocabulary Enrichment

bright/dark

compare

describe

discover

examine

experiment

explore

focus

group

hard/soft

hear/auditory

loud/quiet

manipulate

notice

order

rough/smooth/shiny

senses

sight/see

similar/different

small/large

smell/olfactory

sort/classify

touch/tactile

Web of Integrated Learning

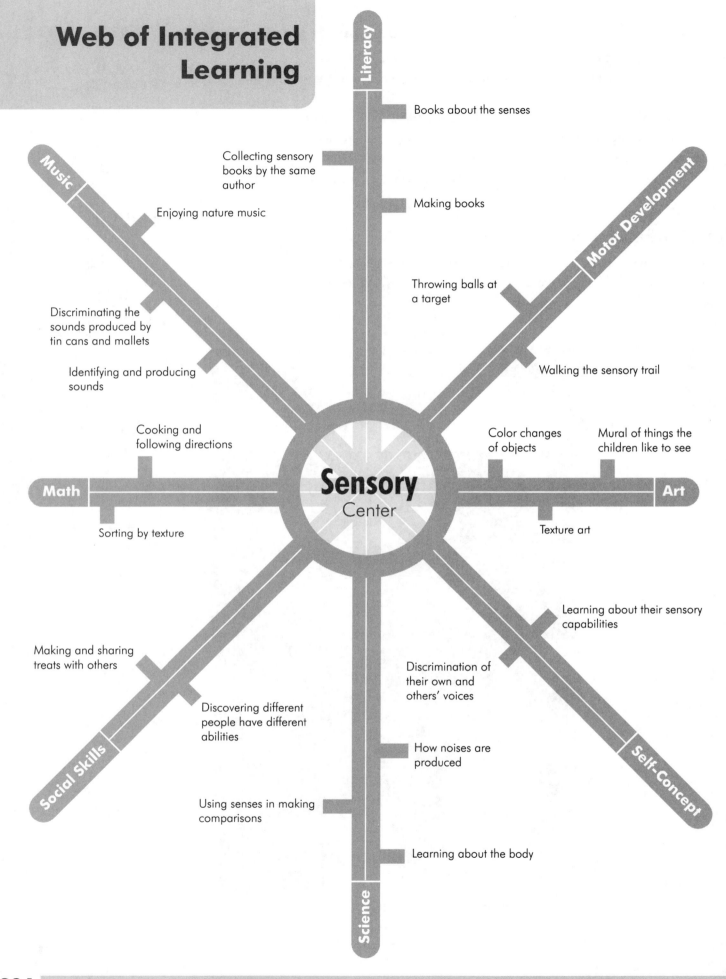

Sensory Center

Literacy
- Books about the senses
- Collecting sensory books by the same author
- Making books

Motor Development
- Throwing balls at a target
- Walking the sensory trail

Music
- Enjoying nature music
- Discriminating the sounds produced by tin cans and mallets
- Identifying and producing sounds

Art
- Color changes of objects
- Mural of things the children like to see
- Texture art

Math
- Cooking and following directions
- Sorting by texture

Self-Concept
- Learning about their sensory capabilities
- Discrimination of their own and others' voices
- How noises are produced

Social Skills
- Making and sharing treats with others
- Discovering different people have different abilities
- Using senses in making comparisons

Science
- Learning about the body

- ❏ cardboard boxes
- ❏ ingredients for a variety of playdough recipes
- ❏ items with distinctive smells:
  - ❏ flower
  - ❏ milk
  - ❏ onion
  - ❏ orange
  - ❏ peppermint
  - ❏ perfume
  - ❏ soap
- ❏ materials with a variety of textures:
  - ❏ fabric
  - ❏ food items
  - ❏ nature items
  - ❏ pieces of carpet
  - ❏ plastic bags
  - ❏ sandpaper
  - ❏ scrapbooks with magnetic pages
  - ❏ small plastic wading pool

- ❏ sorting items in a variety of sizes:
  - ❏ balls
  - ❏ blocks
  - ❏ books
  - ❏ buttons
  - ❏ cans
  - ❏ plastic jars
  - ❏ screws
- ❏ taste items:
  - ❏ apple pieces
  - ❏ chocolate
  - ❏ dill pickle
  - ❏ pretzels
  - ❏ salt
  - ❏ sugar
- ❏ trays or muffin tins for sorting
- ❏ visual materials:
  - ❏ colorful fabric for sorting
  - ❏ paint samples
  - ❏ unusual pictures

Colored water looks different, but how does it respond?

Class Voices

SELF-CONCEPT

CD or tape recorder
pictures of noises
recording media

- The children make a recording of some of the voices they hear in the classroom.
- Provide pictures of children and teachers in the classroom in the Sensory Center.
- The children use the recording in the center to try to match pictures of classmates, teacher, principal, and others to the voices they hear.
- For variation, record some of the sounds the children hear in the classroom or school, such as the door shutting, a chair moving along the floor, laughter, and so on.

I Found It

ART

butcher paper or any long piece of paper
catalogs or magazines
glue

- The children create a large mural to cover one of the Sensory Center walls. They can cut pictures out of catalogs or magazines that show items that they like to see. Let the children glue pictures to the mural for several days or until the mural is full.
- Place a sign by the mural that says, for example "Do you see [picture of eyes] a tree [picture of a tree]?"
- The children try to find a tree on the mural.
- For variation, the children can look for a different item, or ask a child to look for a specific picture. These searches can become more difficult during the Sensory Center's operation.

Rough, Smooth, and Shiny Book

LITERACY

Is it Rough? Is it Smooth? Is it Shiny? by Tana Hoban
glue or tape
loose-leaf binder rings
poster board (colored)
rough, smooth, and shiny materials
scissors

- *Is it Rough? Is it Smooth? Is it Shiny?* stimulates the children's creation of their own book using this theme.
- Cut four pieces of colored poster board in half. This substantial board will provide a base for children to attach items that have a distinctive feel.
- Glue or tape the items to the pages.

Sense Boxes

4 containers
marker
four plastic containers with lids
items collected in the classroom
four plastic containers with lids

- Label four containers with symbols for "see," "feel," "smell," and "hear."
- Children can go on a hunt for sensory items in the classroom and on the playground.
- They can determine and place items in the sense box that indicates the sense needed to identify the material.
- The children use their senses to determine into which sense container they should place the item.
- After the hunt, place these containers in the sensory center for other children to examine.

Activities for the Sensory Center

Changing Colors (sight)

cellophane in four colors
4 matching shoeboxes
items from the classroom
scissors
tape

- Find four matching shoeboxes of the same size with interchangeable lids.
- Cut a large circular opening in the top of each lid, for viewing the contents.
- Tape a piece of cellophane on the inside of the lid, making sure that each box has a different color.
- Have a collection of familiar objects that will fit inside the shoeboxes, so the children can see how they look in different colors. Some possible items for viewing could include a wooden block, doll, plastic fork, piece of paper, white mug, envelope, and a small plastic bottle.

Musical Cans (hearing)

duct tape
dull, child-safe table knife
large nail
metal cans
rhythm sticks
rubber ball

- Provide a collection of different sizes of metal cans children can use for discrimination of sounds.
- Cover the tops of the empty cans with duct tape to cover sharp edges.
- The children can tap on the cans to produce a variety of pitches and rhythm patterns.
- Provide a variety of items children can use to produce different sounds on the cans: a table knife, rhythm stick, large nail, and rubber ball.

Listening for the sound to come through the can

Nature Music (hearing)

CD or tape player
recordings of nature sounds

- Place nature recordings and a CD or tape player in the Sensory Center. Recordings that include classical music combined with sounds of nature, such as the ocean, woodlands, and animals, provide interesting listening experiences in the Sensory Center.
- When children listen to the recording together or using headphones, they begin to discriminate the nature sounds from the musical sounds.

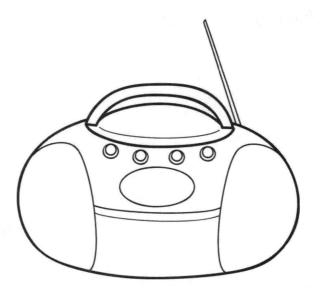

Roller Paint (touch and sight)

butcher paper   paper towel or wrapping paper rolls
fabric   tempera paint
glue

- Show the children how to glue different textures of fabric on paper towel or wrapping paper rolls.
- After the glue dries, the children can apply tempera paint to the rolls.
- Children can move or roll the wet painted rolls across a large sheet of butcher paper to produce textured designs.

Sensory Box (touch)

item to put in the box or container
shoebox, small cardboard box, or small margarine container and a sock

- Construct a sensory "feely" box using a shoebox or small cardboard box.
- Place mystery items inside the box for the children to examine.
- Let the child remove the top to determine if her tactile sense helped identify the item inside.

Alternative Box
- Make a simpler construction by inserting a small plastic margarine container (without the lid) inside a sock. Push the container all the way in, filling the toe of the sock.
- Drop the mystery object into the margarine container.
- Encourage children to reach inside the sock to examine the object by touch only.
- Ask the children to identify the object using only their sense of touch.

Sensory Stepping Stones (touch)

cardboard (heavy)
gelatin and play foam
glue
materials: fabric, carpet, bubble wrap, pebbles, and so on
scissors
2 zipper-close bags

- Create a path of stepping stones.
- At the beginning of the path, place a tub or designated area for children to put their shoes and socks.
- Place stepping stones on the floor so children can feel them with their feet.
- Create the stones by cutting large circles out of heavy cardboard.
- Glue materials onto the circles, such as fabric, carpet, bubble wrap, pebbles, and so on.
- Place two zipper-close bags at the end of the path. Put play foam in one bag and gelatin in the other. Close the bags and allow children to feel the materials through the bag as they finish walking on the path.

Sensory Tub (touch and sight)

plastic wading pool

shredded paper, fabric scraps, or Styrofoam packing peanuts

- Set out a plastic wading pool in which children can sit and feel different substances.
- Place shredded paper, Styrofoam packing peanuts, or fabric scraps in the tub for the children to sit in, feel, and rub.
- Let the children observe the changes that occur through their manipulation of the materials.
- Write words that children dictate to you that describe how it felt, how it looked, and the entire experience.

Smell Only (smell)

blindfolds

box or tub

items with strong scents

- Place a collection of "smelly" items in a box or tub.
- With blindfolds on, children try to identify the items using only their sense of smell.
- When children name the item they think they smell, they remove the blindfold to check if they were right.

Sorting by Texture (touch and sight)

materials with different textures

plastic tub or cardboard box

- Place a collection of materials with different textures in a plastic tub or cardboard box.
- The children feel and sort the materials by touch.
- To extend interest, add pairs of the same fabric or texture, and let the children put the matching items together.

Target Practice (sight)

contact paper

old socks, yarn balls, ping pong balls, and so on

- Attach a large piece of contact paper on the wall with the sticky side out.
- The children throw items at the large target, such as old socks rolled into a small ball and held together with rubber bands, yarn balls, ping pong balls, balls made out of old pantyhose legs, and balls made out of masking tape.

- Let the children prepare recipes that have an unusual combination of ingredients or taste variations.

- Use recipe cards or charts that allow the children to work alone or in small groups.

- Interesting snacks include the following:

Trail Mix
Children choose the ingredients to combine into a trail mix in zipper-close bags. Suggestions for ingredients include marshmallows, pretzels, raisins, chocolate chips, Chinese noodles, goldfish crackers, and dry cereal.

Fruity Art
Use fruit and other edible items to create edible art on aluminum pie pans or Styrofoam meat trays. Suggestions include apple slices, cherries, cheese, oranges, bananas, raisins, marshmallows, grapes, kiwi, and olives.

Adding Spark to the Sensory Center

Set up a table with unusual painting substances to renew interest in the Sensory Center. Some choices include making prints on wax paper, putting play foam on the table top with food coloring added, painting with coffee on a white sheet, dropping food coloring on paper towels or coffee filters, painting with sponges on wallpaper lining, and mixing sand in tempera paint and painting on corrugated cardboard pieces.

Reading/Writing Opportunities

- Children make labels for containers.
- Children developing visual and auditory discrimination.
- Children learn descriptive vocabulary while experimenting with sensory items.
- Children make a texture book.
- Children can record what they see, hear, smell, or touch on large sheets of paper.
- Children can "write" or illustrate what they experience in books made from construction paper, textured wallpaper, or rough fabrics.

Other Printed Materials

- Children focus on a visual target.
- Children follow recipes when making different snacks to taste.

Books for the Sensory Center

Hoban, T. 1984. *Is It Rough? Is It Smooth? Is It Shiny?* New York: Greenwillow. *Color photographs without text introduce objects of many different textures, such as pretzels, foil, hay, mud, kitten, and bubbles. All the objects in this book are textured--they are rough, smooth, shiny, sticky, wet, or furry.*

Martin, B, and Carle, E. 2007. *Baby Bear, Baby Bear, What Do You See?* New York: Henry Holt. *Baby bear goes on a quest to find his Mama. Young readers will revel in identifying each of the native North American animals that appear long the way.*

Miller, M. 1998. *My Five Senses.* New York: Aladdin. *This book provides a simple introduction to the five senses and how they help us experience the world around us.*

Evaluation of the Sensory Center

(This form is on the CD that comes with this book.)

Ask yourself the following questions to evaluate the Sensory Center in your classroom:

- Are children using their senses as they participate in the Sensory Center?
- Are children using new vocabulary words when they are involved in center activities?
- Are children developing an understanding of their sensory environment?
- Are children demonstrating improved ability in identifying similarities and differences in materials and experiences?
- Are children using their sensory abilities as they participate in other classroom activities?

(This form is on the CD that comes with this book. Always date observations of each child.)

- Is the child fearful or overly sensitive to any of the activities in this center? Which ones?
- Have you heard new vocabulary or descriptive language being used in the Sensory Center? What was said?
- Is this child able to use all of the senses in the activities? Have you identified any difficulties? In what area?
- Can the child recognize sounds and voices on a recording?
- During center play, is the child talking with other children? Working with others? Describe.
- Is the child choosing to return to the Sensory Center or avoiding going to the area?

Is this child cautious about touching the gelatin?

Summary

Space is an intriguing topic for children. On television, they see spaceships with astronauts taking off from Earth and returning from space adventures. The Space Center is designed to encourage children to play with some of their ideas about space. It is designed to expand children's interest in space and current events. In the Space Center, children can assume the role of astronaut or an alien from outer space. They can talk about weightlessness or "research studies" that will be conducted in the "spaceship." The Space Center is transformed by the children to include topics of interest to them in a way they can understand.

Introducing the Center

Talk with the children about outer space, spaceships, and astronauts. Listen to what they say about space and determine their level of understanding. Ask if they would like to fly into space. Then, introduce the new place in their classroom where they can pretend to travel into space: the Space Center. Visit the center with the children and talk about the materials and props that can be used in their imaginative play.

Learning Objectives for Children in the Space Center

1. To try out new roles and play experiences.
2. To become more interested in space and current events that relate to this topic.
3. To use problem-solving skills as they explore outer space and space travel.
4. To expand their language as they use new vocabulary related to space.
5. To learn about scientific research as they participate in experiments in the Space Center.
6. To collaborate with others in designing a rocket, a trip, or conducting an experiment.

Time Frame for the Space Center

The Space Center will encourage pretend play for several weeks. If children are still choosing to go to this center after three weeks of play, continue the Space Center operation for a few more days.

 Note: The attached CD contains a sample letter to send to families, introducing them to the Space Center.

A space helmet and goggles created for space travel.

Vocabulary Enrichment

astronaut
balance
controls
Earth
experiment
gravity
helmet
lift-off
mission control
moon
orbit
oxygen
oxygen tank
parachute
planet
radio
research
return
rocket
satellite
space
space capsule
spaceship
space suit
speed
star
transmit
weightlessness

Web of Integrated Learning

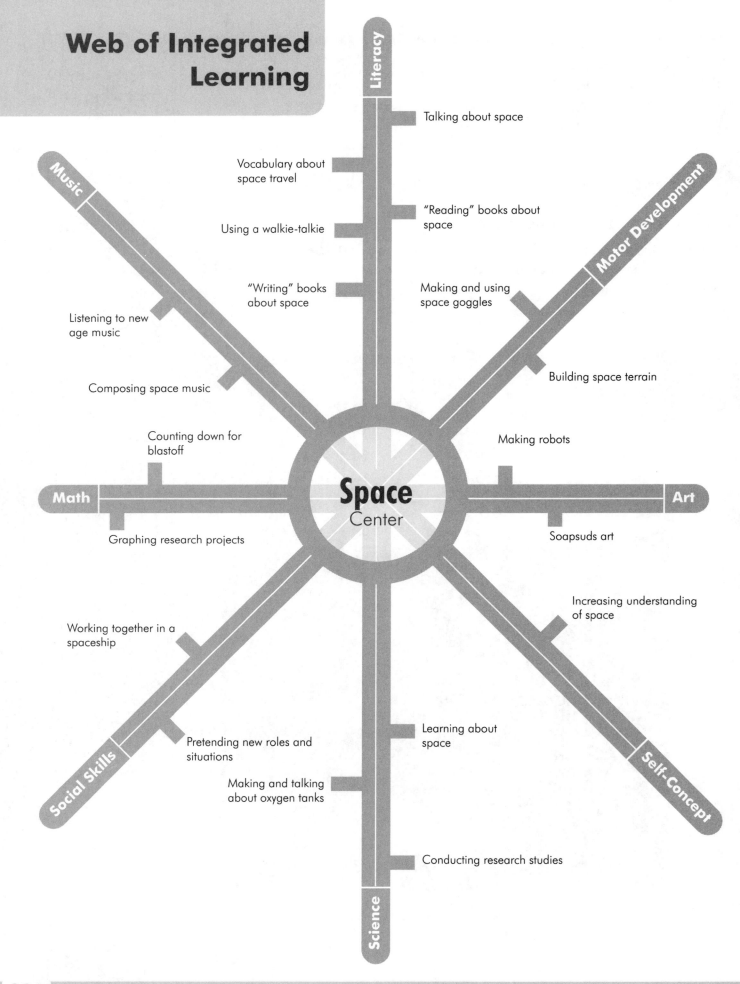

Space Center

Literacy
- Talking about space
- Vocabulary about space travel
- "Reading" books about space
- Using a walkie-talkie
- "Writing" books about space
- Making and using space goggles

Music
- Listening to new age music
- Composing space music

Motor Development
- Building space terrain

Math
- Counting down for blastoff
- Graphing research projects

Art
- Making robots
- Soapsuds art

Self-Concept
- Increasing understanding of space

Social Skills
- Working together in a spaceship
- Pretending new roles and situations
- Making and talking about oxygen tanks

Science
- Learning about space
- Conducting research studies

- ❏ balance scale
- ❏ computer/monitor
- ❏ dress-up clothes:
  - ❏ coveralls
  - ❏ gloves
  - ❏ goggles
- ❏ large cardboard boxes and small jewelry boxes
- ❏ new age music recording and CD or tape player
- ❏ pieces of foam and Styrofoam
- ❏ sheets of bubble wrap
- ❏ silver and/or metallic nontoxic spray paint
- ❏ strobe light and strings of twinkling lights

(**Note:** Some children may be sensitive to the use of a strobe light—it may trigger a seizure. Use caution.)

- ❏ tops from spray cans, lids, and knobs

Aluminum is shaped into a rocket ship.

Space Helmets Made from Plastic Milk Jugs

ART

foil or nontoxic silver spray paint

gallon milk jug

items for decorating: stars, contact paper, chenille stems, and so on

masking tape or electrical tape

scissors

- Trim the neck off the milk jug and cut an opening for the child's face.
- Cut a slit from the bottom of the face opening to the neck so the child can get the helmet on easily.
- Cover the edges with masking or electrical tape.
- When the children are not present, spray the jug with nontoxic silver paint or cover with foil.
- If desired, the children can add decorations to the helmets, such as clear tubing, stars, pieces of contact paper, or chenille stems.

Child-Created Props for the Space Center

Control Panel

SCIENCE

cardboard box (large)

glue

materials for decorating:

    clear plastic tubing

    electrical wire

    foam board

    jewelry boxes (small)

    tops from spray cans, lids, and knobs

    string of twinkling lights

- The children draw a design for the control panel.
- Set out materials such as plastic tubing, electrical wire, and lids from bottles for the children to use to attach to foam board to create controls and connections.
- Add a string of twinkling lights to the panel.
- Provide two small chairs so children can sit in front of the controls after the design has been completed.

Oxygen Tanks

cardboard boxes
foil
paint
paintbrushes
stapler
strips of fabric or elastic

- Explain to the children that astronauts need oxygen to survive in outer space.
- The children make portable oxygen tanks out of cardboard boxes to use in the Space Center.
- Cover the boxes with foil or paint them.
- Staple strips of inexpensive fabric or elastic to each side of the tank so the children can put their arms through the openings and wear the tank to "breathe" during the time they are in the Space Center.

Space Terrain

glue
plastic bubble wrap
Styrofoam, packing pieces, and foam
tape

- Create a sensory experience to explore in the outer space portion of the Space Center.
- Cover the floor and walls with plastic bubble wrap.
- Construct unusual structures or mountains using large pieces of Styrofoam, packing pieces, and foam.
- Glue or tape together.
- The children continue to add to these space structures while the center is in operation.

Walkie-Talkie

plastic tubing
Styrofoam cups
tape

- Make a space-age walkie-talkie by using a long piece of ½" clear plastic tubing for the line.
- Attach Styrofoam cups to each end to serve as the earpiece and mouthpiece.
- This design allows two children to talk and listen to each other in the outer space area of the center.

Soapsuds Art

A R T

bowl
cardboard
food coloring or glitter (optional)
hand or electric mixer
hot water
powdered laundry detergent

- Combine white powdered laundry detergent and water in a very large plastic bowl and beat with a mixer.
- When the suds become stiff, similar to whipped cream, use them for creating paintings and sculptures.
- The suds work best when they are placed on pieces of cardboard to provide a substantial base.
- If desired, color the suds or add glitter.
- The suds dry quickly. However, as with many art activities for young children, the creative process is more important than the finished product.

Recipe for "Soapsuds Finger Painting"
1 cup of hot water in a deep bowl
¾–1 cup powdered detergent, such as Ivory Snow™

- Gradually add detergent, while beating with a mixer, until it is the consistency of whipped cream.
- Separate mixture into equal parts.
- Add a few drops of food coloring or tempera paint. Place the mixture on the table.
- The children use their hands to make designs on white, colored, or foil-covered cardboard.

Space Goggles

S E L F - C O N C E P T

chenille stems
color cellophane
glue
plastic six-pack rings
scissors

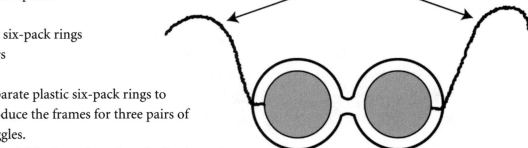

chenille sticks

- Separate plastic six-pack rings to produce the frames for three pairs of goggles.
- Each child selects the color of cellophane she wants to glue in for the lenses.
- Attach chenille stems to each side of the frame, so they will stay on the child's face.
- Encourage the children to look at their space world through multicolored lenses.

Space Mission Book

       colored paper

       foil or metallic wrapping paper

       hole punch

       silver and gold star stickers

       silver wire and metallic chenille stems

- Cut out book covers in the shape of stars, moons, or suns.
- Provide foil or metallic paper for the children to glue on their covers.
- Punch holes in the book cover, including four to five sheets of colored paper to put inside.
- String the book together will silver wire or metallic chenille stems.
- Children can use stars to decorate the book and "write" about or draw pictures of their trip into outer space. Or, they may prefer to "write" or draw about a possible mission in space.

Research Studies: Science Experiments Children Explore Independently

Oil and Water

       buckets of colored water

       funnels and plastic measuring cups

       glue or tape

       oil

       plastic drink bottles (small)

       stars, glitter, sequins, and beads (if desired)

- Provide funnels, small plastic drink bottles, buckets of colored water, and a container of oil.
- The children use plastic measuring cups and funnels to pour the colored water and oil into the drink bottles.
- If desired, add stars, glitter, sequins, and colored beads to the mixtures.
- Help the children tighten the jar lids.
- Glue or tape the lid closed so the top is secure when the children shake the mixture.
- Ask the children, "What happens when you shake the bottle?"

Weighing a Moon Rock

       balance scale

       chart to record findings

       large plastic container

       rocks

       silver spray paint (adult only)

       Styrofoam pieces, blocks, pebbles, and so on

- Spray paint rocks silver to make "moon rocks." (This is an adult-only step that should be done when the children are not present.)
- Set up a table with a balance scale in the research area of the Space Center.
- On one side of the balance scale, place one moon rock.
- The project is to find what will balance the moon rock.
- Place an assortment of items in a large plastic container. Suggested items include Styrofoam peanuts, blocks, pebbles, jar lids, plastic pieces, bottles of sand, small balls, small blocks, plastic fruit, and magnets.
- The children determine how many of each item or what assortment of items balances each moon rock.
- The children record the results on the chart.

Adding Spark to the Space Center

Building robots is a fascinating project for the Space Center. Unusual construction materials challenge the creativity of the children. Suggested materials include plastic six-pack rings, frozen food containers, packing pieces, wood scraps, strips of aluminum, plastic containers, various sizes of cardboard boxes, aluminum foil, tinsel, plastic wheels and gears, colored electrical wire, nuts, bolts, and coils. Children can name the finished robots and display them beside the Space Center.

The Essential Literacy Connection

Reading/Writing Opportunities

- Children can "write" labels for the control panel.
- Children can look at reference books about space, planets, and the moon and sun.
- Children can use measuring scales.
- Children can "write" about their space adventures in individual space mission books.
- Children can design, make, and "write" "mission reports," a record of travels and findings.
- Children chart and record information from space experiments as they participate in the Space Center.

Other Printed Materials

- Provide reference books with high-quality pictures of space, rockets, and the earth.

Books for the Space Center

Barker, H. 2003. *It Came from Outer Space.* Illustrated by Barry Gott. New York: Kane Press. *Three friends who are having a sleepover see a bright object shoot across the sky and the next morning, they venture into the woods to see if they can find what the mysterious object.*

Barton, B. 1988. *I Want to Be an Astronaut.* New York: Thomas Y. Crowell. *A wish allows a child to become an astronaut in this book, where he participates in adventures in outer space.*

Cole, N. 1994. *Blast Off! A Space Counting Book.* Illustrated by Marshall Peck, III. Watertown, MA: Charlesbridge. *This book introduces children to numbers by describing various space items. Information is included about each item and its purpose.*

Jeunesse, G., & Verdet, J. P. 1989. *Earth and Sky.* Illustrated by Sylvaine Perols. New York: Scholastic, Inc. *This book allows children to see the phases of the moon, explore inside the earth, see a volcano erupt, and discover many other wonders of the sky and earth.*

Kirk, D. 1999. *Moondogs.* New York: Putnam. *A boy flies to the moon to get a moondog for a pet, but finds true happiness back home on Earth with a loyal dog named Scrappy.*

Landry, L. 2007. *Space Boy.* Boston: Houghton Mifflin. *Children can escape to the moon with Nicholas in this delightful picture book. This world, decides Nicholas, is too noisy. Time to take a trip. He packs a snack, puts on his suit, and takes off to the utterly quiet craters and vast deserts of the distant moon.*

Evaluation of the Space Center

(This form is on the CD that comes with this book.)

Ask yourself the following questions to evaluate the Space Center in your classroom:

- Are children using the materials and props in the center in appropriate ways?
- Are children expanding their vocabulary as they talk about space and operations?
- Are children participating in the research studies set up in the Space Center?
- Are children trying out new roles and play that you have not observed in other centers?
- Are children demonstrating new interest in current events and happenings related to space?

Observation of the Individual Child

(This form is on the CD that comes with this book. Always date observations of each child.)

- Is the child showing interest in the Space Center? What props does she like to use?
- Does this child have knowledge of concepts related to space and space travel? What has been shared?
- Is the child playing interactively with other children? In what way?
- Has the child demonstrated creativity in construction of any of the props? What have you seen?
- Has the child used literacy materials in the center? Which ones and in what way?
- Is the child taking on a role? If so, what is she doing?

Summary

Telling stories is an important tradition in many cultures. Stories are a way for young children to learn about the world of their ancestors. Stories capture the interest of young children, because the listening material is both entertaining and enlightening. Stories that are told allow children to be both the audience and participant. After hearing stories, young children like to repeat them for others. In this retelling process, they begin to understand how stories work and use these elements in their oral telling. These experiences provide a strong oral foundation for emerging literacy. The Storytelling Center establishes a special place in the classroom where teacher, children, or guests can enjoy telling stories.

Include many different recordings, props, and books in the Storytelling Center to inspire storytellers. In this center, young children listen to others and build the confidence to begin retelling stories. Later, they may create their own stories. Tell a story in this center as the exciting happening that will lead to the opening of the Storytelling Center.

Introducing the Center

The fall of the year is a great time to set up the Storytelling Center. During this time, many communities, schools, and libraries have a storytelling festival that children can attend. Because some will not have this opportunity, invite a storyteller to share a story with the group during circle or group time or in the new Storytelling Center. Learn a folktale or story that you can share with the group without using a book. This experience with a teller demonstrates how stories people tell are different from stories they read in books. For many of the children, this will be their first storytelling experience.

Learning Objectives for Children in the Storytelling Center

1. To have the opportunity to hear stories told by the teacher, guests, and peers.
2. To experience stories told in many ways.
3. To expand their oral language as they listen, participate, and tell stories.
4. To begin to understand the form, characters, and moral of stories.
5. To enjoy and expand their interest in literature.

Time Frame for the Storytelling Center

This center can inspire "budding storytellers" for many weeks. It functions most effectively after it has been in operation several days, giving children the time to examine the contents and move on to becoming storytellers. Set up the Storytelling Center several times during the year.

 Note: The attached CD contains a sample letter to send to families, introducing them to the Storytelling Center.

Stories capture the interest of young children.

Vocabulary Enrichment

ancestor
audience
beginning
character
dialog
dynamics: loud/soft
emphasize
ending
folktale
hand motion
listener
location
long ago
pattern
pretend
puppeteer
repeating phrase
retell
sequence
shadow puppet
sound effect
storyteller
tempo: slow/fast
voices

Web of Integrated Learning

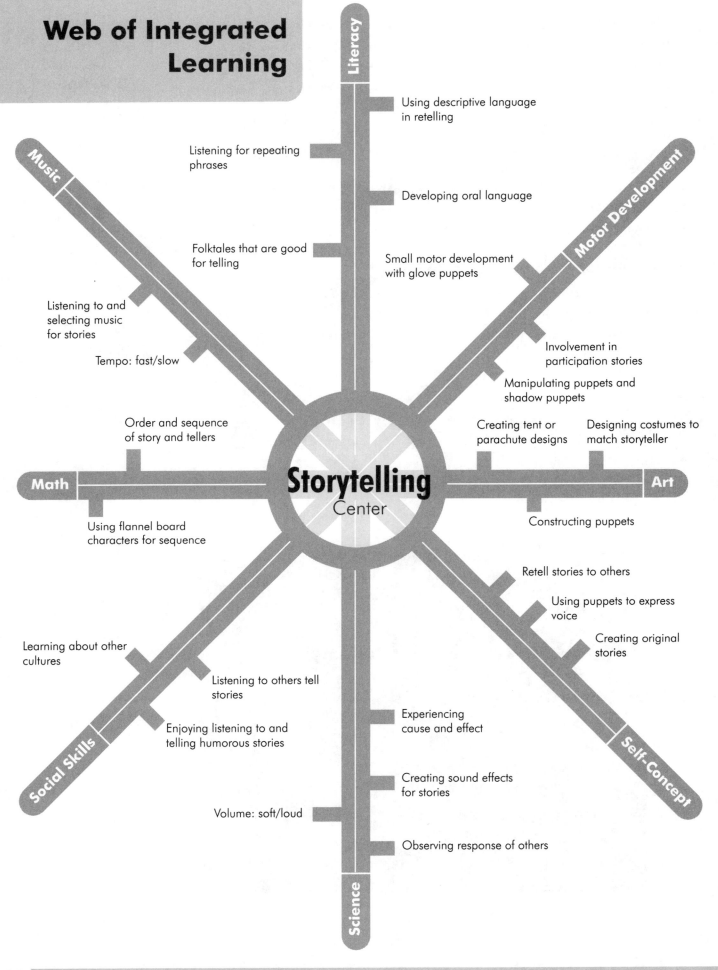

Storytelling Center

Literacy
- Using descriptive language in retelling
- Developing oral language

Music
- Listening for repeating phrases
- Folktales that are good for telling
- Listening to and selecting music for stories
- Tempo: fast/slow

Motor Development
- Small motor development with glove puppets
- Involvement in participation stories
- Manipulating puppets and shadow puppets

Math
- Order and sequence of story and tellers
- Using flannel board characters for sequence

Art
- Creating tent or parachute designs
- Designing costumes to match storyteller
- Constructing puppets

Social Skills
- Learning about other cultures
- Listening to others tell stories
- Enjoying listening to and telling humorous stories

Self-Concept
- Retell stories to others
- Using puppets to express voice
- Creating original stories

Science
- Experiencing cause and effect
- Creating sound effects for stories
- Volume: soft/loud
- Observing response of others

- ❏ tent or parachute
- ❏ CD or tape player
- ❏ wigs
- ❏ hats
- ❏ earphones
- ❏ recordings of stories
- ❏ dress-up clothes:
  - ❏ hats
  - ❏ pieces of bright colored fabric
  - ❏ scarves
  - ❏ shawls
  - ❏ unusual clothing items

Puppets help these children tell their stories.

Glove Puppets

MOTOR DEVELOPMENT

cotton gardening gloves

markers

trim materials and glue (for decorating, if desired)

- Cotton gloves are a very inexpensive way to create puppets.
- Use one glove to create five finger puppets a child can manipulate.
- The children can draw a face on each finger with a marker.
- Some children may want to add pompoms and decoration.
- Use the glove to tell the story of the Five Little Monkeys or let the child tell her own version of a familiar story using this glove puppet.

Puppet Stage

MOTOR DEVELOPMENT

blanket or sheet

clothesline

large appliance box

paint and brushes (if available)

- Construct a very simple puppet stage by placing a blanket or sheet over a low piece of clothesline.
- Make a more elaborate stage out of appliance boxes, painted for additional effect.
- Use either stage in the Storytelling Center.

Sock Puppets

MOTOR DEVELOPMENT

glue

scraps of fabric, yarn, feathers, and so on

socks

- Make a puppet with a moving mouth.
- Each child places the sock over her hand with the heel over her thumb.
- With the other hand, she pushes the toe into her cupped hand.
- Create the top of the puppet's head by stitching the top of the toe to the middle of the sock, between the toe and the heel.
- Glue or tack the mouth in place, so the puppet's mouth will move during the telling.
- Decorate with scraps of fabric, yarn, strips of trim, movable eyes, small hats, feathers, or flowers to create any puppet character.
- These simple puppets are very versatile and can be used by the children for many different stories.

heavy yarn
hole punch
large sheet of paper
markers

- The children can have a storytelling festival.
- Children can design a chart to schedule the order of the storytellers.
- Children can also make a flyer to hang in the Center or around the classroom announcing the festival.
- Children can make other posters or advertisements to post in the center as desired.

Activities for the Storytelling Center

Child-Size Flannel Boards   ART

construction paper
glue
pieces of flannel or felt
recorded stories
sandpaper
child-safe scissors
small, shallow boxes or individual pizza boxes

- Make individual flannel boards for children by using a small shallow box, such as a lingerie box.
- Cut several pieces of flannel in different colors and place them in the Storytelling Center.
- Each child selects and glues a flannel piece inside the top of her box.
- The children make characters from construction paper.
- When the children complete their characters, they can cut out the characters and glue small pieces of sandpaper on the backs of their characters so they will adhere to the flannel.
- Play recorded stories or encourage the children to tell stories using the flannel board characters.
- This small portable board can be taken home for the children to share their stories with their families.

Once upon a time...

recording of simple jokes

- Young children enjoy listening to and telling jokes; you can create a humorous recording of simple jokes children will enjoy in the Storytelling Center.
- Label the recording with smiling faces.
- After the children have had a good laugh, they may want to add one of their favorite jokes to the recording.

Listening to Storytellers   LITERACY

various recordings by storytellers

- The children will enjoy hearing recordings of professional storytellers in the Storytelling Center.
- Children can select the recording they want to hear and listen to it individually or with several other children.
- Jackie Torrance's *Classic Stories* is a good example of the many wonderful recordings available.

Participation Stories   MUSIC

chart of stories
musical instruments
recordings of music

- List stories the children know that invite them to add sound effects or make hand motions on a chart in the Storytelling Center.
- The children select a story and create the appropriate accompaniment for the telling.
Stories to begin with include "The Little Red Hen," "The Gingerbread Boy," "The Three Billy Goats Gruff," and "Fat Cat." Be sure to include stories that the children enjoy and know.

Shadow Puppets   MOTOR DEVELOPMENT

chart of simple shadow puppets
spot or clip-on light

- Set up a spot or clip-on light in the Storytelling Center to produce shadows on the wall.
- Display a chart of simple shadow puppets that the children can make with their hands.
- Allow the children to experiment with and discover how to make the shadow puppets.
- Later, encourage the children to use these puppets to tell or accompany stories.

box
foil or gold wrapping paper
glue
jewelry or sequins
story items: a beautiful rock, feather, old picture, and so on

- Cover a box with foil or gold wrapping paper and glue old jewelry or sequins on the top.
- Place interesting items that may stimulate a story inside the box. Items that could start a story include a beautiful rock, a feather, a glass marble, a flower, old lace, an old picture, a baby toy, or a silver coin.
- The children open the box, take out one item, and begin a story. They use the other items as needed during the story.

Story Pictures   LITERACY

picture album
scissors
unusual pictures from magazines

- Place unusual pictures in a picture album.
- The children look at the pictures and create a story to accompany the events they see happening in the pictures.

Adding Spark to the Storytelling Center

Invite a grandparent or senior citizen to be the guest storyteller in the center. Ask them to tell stories about what life was like for them when they were young children. Children find these stories fascinating and this often inspires the teller to tell "new" stories. This also provides a very positive way for young children to interact with older adults.

"Let me tell you a story."

Reading/Writing Opportunities

- Books of folktales with many pictures stimulate children to tell stories.
- Children "write" or record their own stories. Keep these stories in the Storytelling Center for other children to enjoy.
- Wordless books can encourage children to tell stories.
- Children "reread" stories told to them.

Other Printed Materials

- Use flannel boards with books that contain a good story for telling but may have dated illustrations.
- Show the children festival programs or articles about storytellers.

Books for the Storytelling Center

Christelow, E. 2006. *Five Little Monkeys Jumping on the Bed*. New York: Clarion. *A counting book in which, one by one, the little monkeys jump on the bed only to fall off and bump their heads.*

Duke, K. 1995. *Aunt Isabel Tells a Good One*. New York: Puffin. *Penelope and her Aunt Isabel make up an exciting bedtime story about the adventures of Prince Augustus and Lady Penelope.*

Edgson, A. 2006. *Three Billy Goats Gruff*. Swindon, England: Child's Play International. *A classic folk tale about three goats who outwit a big, ugly troll that lives under the bridge they must cross on their way up the mountain.*

Isbell, R., & Buchanan, M. 2004. *Everyone Has a Story to Tell*. Jonesborough, TN: Olde Towne. *Two children search for stories in Jonesborough, Tennessee, the storytelling capital of the world.*

MacDonald, M. R., & Paschkis, J. 2001. *Fat Cat: A Danish Folktale*. Little Rock, AR: August House. *A greedy cat grows enormous as he eats everything in sight, including his friends and neighbors who call him fat.*

Pinkney, J. 2006. *The Little Red Hen*. New York: Dial. *This is the familiar story of the hen unable to get help. There is the rat, the goat, the pig, and the dog, who refuse to help Hen make the bread but are perfectly willing to share the finished product.*

Sierra, J., & Vitale, S. 1996. *Nursery Tales Around the World*. New York: Clarion. *This book is an international collection of 18 nursery tales for young children, illustrated with full-color borders and grouped by theme, such as Runaway Cookies, Slowpokes and Speedsters, and Chain Tales.*

Evaluation of the Storytelling Center

(This form is on the CD that comes with this book.)

Ask yourself the following questions to evaluate the Storytelling Center in your classroom:

- Are children interested in listening to stories in the center?
- Are children telling stories orally with or without props?
- Are children telling stories that include expressive language, gestures, or sound effects?
- Are children demonstrating interest in different types of literature?
- Are children making props or puppets to use in their storytelling?

(This form is on the CD that comes with this book. Always date observations of each child.)

- Is the child choosing to go to the Storytelling Center? What is she doing there?

- Is the child listening to the stories of others or on recordings? Which ones?

- Is the child retelling or creating a story? What vocabulary, language, or gestures is she using?

- Does the child seem confident in her abilities? What have you observed that leads you to this conclusion?

- Has the child demonstrated creativity in the telling or story creation? How?

A girl "reading" a book

Summary

The Project Center provides a working space for children who are focused on a specific project or idea. Center time is the perfect time for a small group of children to work on ideas that might come from class themes, creative ideas, or special interests. While the other children are working in centers, these children can focus on a project that needs more time and that they can return to for an extended period of several days or weeks. This center allows children to experiment with interesting and challenging ideas and more in-depth and complex projects.

Introducing the Center

When children want to continue investigating an idea, they need a place to work. Sometimes, you may observe a budding project. At other time, the children may need you to ask questions to help them think in more complex ways. The Project Center is where they can do this work. You can suggest that certain children go to this area or provide them the option of choosing to go to this center. There may be times when no one is in the Project Center and other times when it is buzzing with activity. By providing this center, you are encouraging children who are intrigued by a project to remain with the work for longer periods.

Learning Objectives for Children in the Project Center

1. To identify ideas and questions that they want to explore.
2. To develop problem-solving and research skills to find information.
3. To build persistence by working on a project for a long time.
4. To participate in a team that is working together on an idea.
5. To examine and complete more complex projects and investigations.
6. To strengthen their self-confidence as they work on their ideas and long-term projects.

Time Frame for the Project Center

Keep this center in the classroom for most of the year or set it up later in the year to encourage more in-depth investigations. If there is limited space, set it up in the Art Center area when project ideas are thriving.

Note: The attached CD contains a sample letter to send to families, introducing them to the Project Center.

How can this material be used in their project?

Vocabulary Enrichment

(**Note:** New vocabulary will emerge during each project.)

chart

collaborate

construct

creative

find out

idea

investigate

planning

possibilities

problem

question

record

references

research

search

teamwork

unique

Web of Integrated Learning

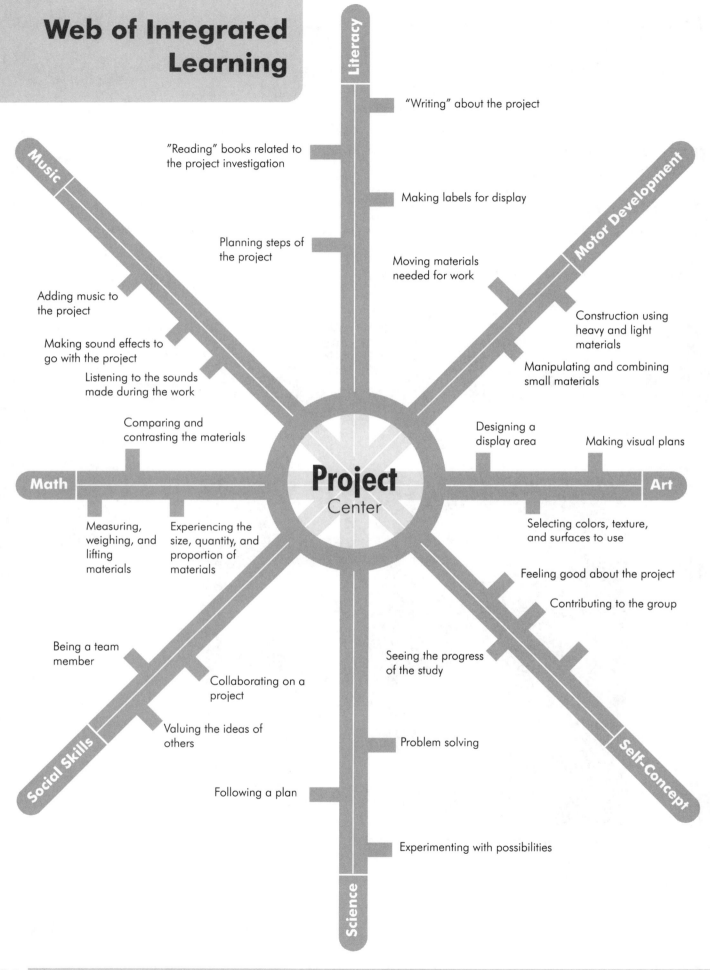

Project
Center

Literacy
- "Writing" about the project
- "Reading" books related to the project investigation
- Making labels for display
- Planning steps of the project

Music
- Adding music to the project
- Making sound effects to go with the project
- Listening to the sounds made during the work

Motor Development
- Moving materials needed for work
- Construction using heavy and light materials
- Manipulating and combining small materials

Math
- Comparing and contrasting the materials
- Measuring, weighing, and lifting materials
- Experiencing the size, quantity, and proportion of materials

Art
- Designing a display area
- Making visual plans
- Selecting colors, texture, and surfaces to use

Social Skills
- Being a team member
- Collaborating on a project
- Valuing the ideas of others

Self-Concept
- Feeling good about the project
- Contributing to the group
- Seeing the progress of the study

Science
- Problem solving
- Following a plan
- Experimenting with possibilities

❏ building materials:
  ❏ boxes
  ❏ cardboard
  ❏ fabric
  ❏ large sheets of paper
  ❏ scraps of lumber
❏ computer, digital camera, and printer
❏ food trays (for working on messy projects and storing)
❏ materials for holding things together:
  ❏ electrical tape
  ❏ glue
  ❏ masking tape
  ❏ wire clamps
❏ junk box:
  ❏ chenille stems
  ❏ foil
  ❏ paper scraps
  ❏ pieces of fabric
  ❏ pieces of screen
  ❏ wire
❏ large and small clear plastic storage containers with lids
❏ plastic bottles and jars of various sizes
❏ roll of plastic
❏ toolbox:
  ❏ clamps
  ❏ hammer/nails with large heads
  ❏ ruler
  ❏ scissors
  ❏ screwdriver/screws
  ❏ measuring tape

❏ variety of papers:
  ❏ cardboard pieces
  ❏ foam board
  ❏ newspapers
  ❏ magazines
  ❏ wallpaper
❏ writing tools:
  ❏ pens
  ❏ markers
  ❏ chalk
  ❏ colored pencils

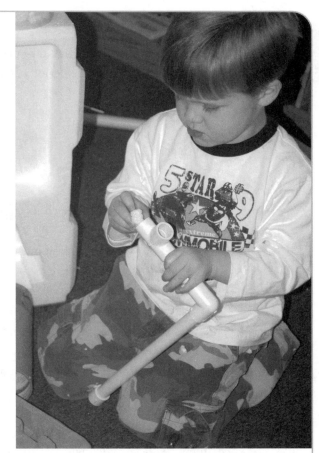

Unique materials, such as plastic pipes, inspire thinking in new ways.

Child-Created Props for the Project Center

These will match the projects and the investigations. Each will be different based on the project and the ideas developed by the children.

Organizing the Space for the Project Center

Consider the following when setting up space for children to explore projects:
- Create a work area.
- Group materials for projects.
- Determine where materials will be stored.
- Select an area for storing long-term projects.
- Explore the possible areas where the children's work will be displayed.
- Have clean-up materials in the project area.

Activities for the Project Center

The projects and activities that take place in this area will vary based on the specific interests and work of the children over a period of time. The following activities may relate to many projects.

Planning the Project   LITERACY & SCIENCE

chart paper
marker

- The teacher talks with the children who are interested in a specific project and asks them questions, such as
  - What do you want to find out?
  - What do you want to learn?
  - What do you want to try?
  - How are you going to do this?
  - How can you show your classmates what you discovered?
- The teacher can write these questions on chart paper and then record the children's responses to each question. This chart can be displayed in the Project Center.

What Materials Are Needed?   SELF-CONCEPT & SOCIAL SKILLS

- Identify the specific materials, tools, or books that are needed to develop this project.
- Children can collect these materials from the classroom or from their homes, or they can find a source for the materials.
- The children organize and store the materials in the project area.
- Be sure the materials include paper, pencils, art supplies, and books.

chart paper
marker

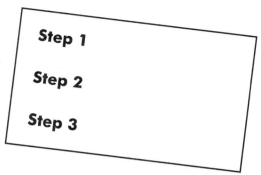

- The children talk and discuss the project and then draw or "write" the steps that need to be followed.
- Be sure the steps include how work will be displayed and shared.

Reference Items for the Project LITERACY

books and reference material related to the project

- Each project will have books and reference materials that will help the children in their work. Some standard items could be a picture dictionary, informational books, old reference books, how-to books, and books about how things work. Other reference materials will focus on the topic of the project.

Documenting the Project LITERACY & SELF-CONCEPT

digital camera

- Children can use a digital camera to document their work. These photographs should show each step of the process as it is developing, especially the early stages.
- Children can include their names on the list of workers that will accompany the documentation for a display of the project.

Adding Spark to the Project Center

When children seem to be stalled on a project, pose new questions to them. "What else could you do? Is there another way of doing it? What if you added _____?" Sometimes, the most creative ideas come after a period of difficulty. It may be helpful to encourage another child to join the work—a fresh perspective can help solve problems. If nothing happens, it may be time to bring the project to completion, document what was done, and display the work for others to enjoy.

Reading/Writing Opportunities

(These will vary based on experiences related to a specific project.)

- Children can record information by "writing," charting, and graphing.
- Children can examine references and books on a topic.
- Children can name, label, and list team members involved in a project.
- Children can determine ways to display and describe their work.
- Children can use oral language and new vocabulary to tell others what they are doing.

Books for the Project Center

Crews, N. 2006. *Below.* New York: Henry Holt. *Jack and his action figure, Guy, have many adventures together, until one day when Guy falls into a hole in the stairs and it's up to Jack to rescue him.*

Lum, K. 1998. *What! Cried Granny: An Almost Bedtime Story.* Illustrated by Adrian Johnson. New York: Dial. *It's a boy's first sleep-over at his Granny's, but he doesn't have a bed to sleep in. Granny does whatever it takes to care for the boy's needs.*

Robertson, J., & Robertson, B. 2004. *The Kids' Building Workshop: 15 Woodworking Projects for Kids and Parents to Build Together.* North Adams, MA: Storey. *Fifteen projects are explained for parents and children to work with wood.*

Singer, M. 2006. *Let's Build a Clubhouse.* Illustrated by Timothy Bush. New York: Clarion. *Rhyming text describes how a group of children work together to build a clubhouse, using a variety of tools.*

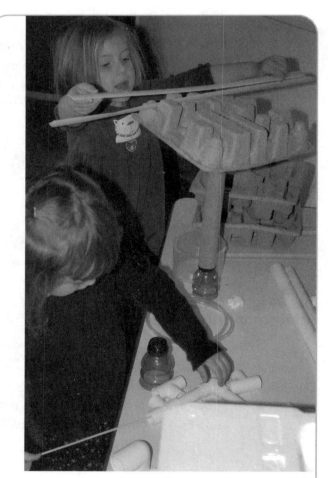

Construction with new materials helps these girls think creatively.

Evaluation of the Project Center

(This form is on the CD that comes with this book.)

Ask yourself the following questions to evaluate the Project Center in your classroom:

- Are children choosing to work in this area?
- Do children have specific ideas about what they want to do in the Project Center?
- Do you see evidence of more complex investigations?
- Are children carrying creative ideas to completion?
- Have some children returned to the project over time?
- Is teamwork occurring on projects in this center?
- Are sufficient tools and materials available to support the children's research and construction?

Observation of the Individual Child

(This form is on the CD that comes with this book. Always date observations of each child.)

- Is this child choosing to work on projects? Which ones and in what ways?
- What problem solving have you observed by this child?
- Has this child used new vocabulary and language related to projects, investigations, or research?
- Is the child persistent on the project? Is she returning to work on the same project?
- Have you seen this child using reference materials? Which ones and how?
- Is this child participating as a team player? Is she displaying leadership or following the ideas of other? Describe.

CHAPTER 5

Outdoor Centers:

A New Place for Centers

This new chapter in this revised edition includes learning centers that can work effectively outdoors or in the playground area. These centers activate young children's minds while helping provide experiences they need to help develop their motor skills. During outdoor play, children will also have opportunities to choose their activity, work with others, and participate in play that challenges their body and thinking. The outdoor centers included in this section are easy to set up, require a minimum amount of materials, and can be used many times during the year. By moving a few props outdoors into a planned learning center, the teacher can provide another place for young children to learn through play.

Adventure Center

Beach Center

Camping Center

Car Wash Center

Farm Center

Greenhouse Center

Outdoor Drama Center

Summary

The outdoors is a great place to set up an adventure area that invites physical activity and problem solving. The design for this center space is very flexible and adaptable to any playground area where equipment is already in place. Adjust this center to specific environmental features, such as trees, sand, water, and so on, that are in your outdoor area. With a few changes, implemented with moveable parts, the Adventure Center can be used throughout the months children play outside. The adventure area will encourage large motor activity, while challenging children to think and use symbols in their physical play activities.

Introducing the Center

An Adventure Center outdoors can provide many choices for young children to use in their physical play. This area will include new and unique materials that will encourage dramatic play, large motor activities, creative thinking, and collaboration. In this center, children will follow trails, build buildings, design props, and restructure when new challenges are needed. Some of the props can be left outside, others moved from inside, and others placed in storage when not in use.

Learning Objectives for Children in the Adventure Center

1. To develop and refine large motor skills.
2. To use creative ideas while selecting materials that will work in the outdoor center.
3. To collaborate with others about changes, adaptations, and uses of props in the center.
4. To combine symbols and sociodramatic play in their activities in this area.
5. To gain confidence in their ability to use and control their bodies.

Time Frame for the Adventure Center

The Adventure Center has many possibilities and a variety of designs that can be used on the playground. Because you can change and reconfigure this versatile center, you can use it for a long time outdoors. When children tire of an existing design, changing it into a new challenging area requires a minimum amount of work. Children can also assist in planning the new design, moving and arranging props so that they can use them in new ways.

 Note: The attached CD contains a sample letter to send to families, introducing them to the Party Center.

It is an adventure to push a riding car.

Vocabulary Enrichment

adventure
bees
birds
bugs
butterflies
crawling
design
detour
directions
fishing
flying/motion
frogs
hiking
hopping
map
moving
plan
running
slow
snakes
sounds
spiders
stop
swimming
trail
transporting/moving
treasure
wet/dry
wind

Web of Integrated Learning

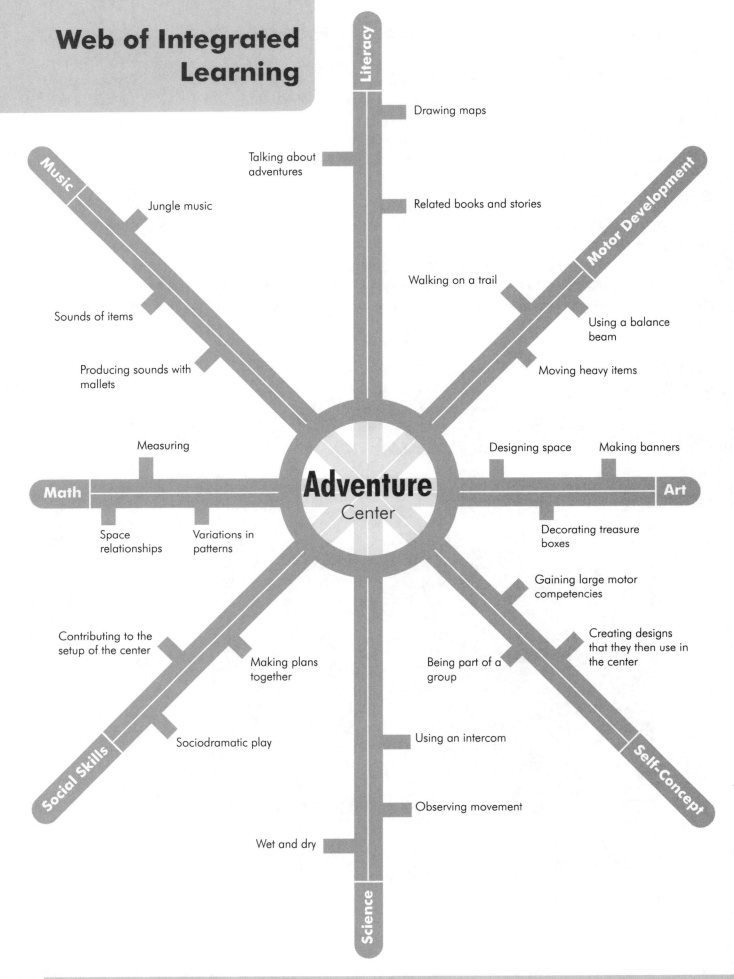

Adventure
Center

Literacy
- Drawing maps
- Talking about adventures
- Related books and stories

Motor Development
- Walking on a trail
- Using a balance beam
- Moving heavy items

Music
- Jungle music
- Sounds of items
- Producing sounds with mallets

Art
- Designing space
- Making banners
- Decorating treasure boxes

Math
- Measuring
- Space relationships
- Variations in patterns

Self-Concept
- Gaining large motor competencies
- Creating designs that they then use in the center

Social Skills
- Contributing to the setup of the center
- Making plans together
- Sociodramatic play

Science
- Being part of a group
- Using an intercom
- Observing movement
- Wet and dry

- ❏ Loose parts:
  - ❏ bricks
  - ❏ collection of pieces of lumber, plywood, or plastic siding
  - ❏ garden hose
  - ❏ hammers and large-head nails
  - ❏ large plastic blocks (moved from inside)
  - ❏ pallets collected from a warehouse or storage site (8–10)
  - ❏ plastic buckets (4–5)
  - ❏ plastic crates (6–8 large)
  - ❏ plastic wading pool
  - ❏ riding toys
  - ❏ rocks
  - ❏ roll of clear plastic
  - ❏ stumps from large trees
  - ❏ telephone line spools of varying sizes
  - ❏ wagons
  - ❏ wheelbarrow
- ❏ Other materials:
  - ❏ dome tent
  - ❏ fabric (several pieces of 1-yard lengths in a variety of color, texture, and thickness)
  - ❏ old fancy jewelry (be sure to remove pins)
  - ❏ old fishing boat (donated)
  - ❏ old tires: small and automotive tires (be sure to drill ½" holes through the tire, so water can run out when left on the playground)
  - ❏ plastic step stools
  - ❏ wind chimes

These children have figured out how to reach the bars—use buckets!

Adventure Trail

MOTOR DEVELOPMENT & SELF-CONCEPT

pieces of gray or brown vinyl fabric cut into circles, squares, rectangles, and so on
small pebbles or stones
wagon/wheel barrow
small shovels

- Child can plan, draw, and set up a walking trail in the adventure center.
- They can collaborate to determine the design for the trail.
- When the children finish their design, they can set out the vinyl stepping stones according to their design.
- If the vinyl pieces move, add dirt at the edges to hold them in place or weigh them down with small rocks.
- The children can test the walkway and redesign it if needed.
- During the design process, talk with the children about keeping the walkway away from the swings and other moving equipment.

Flying Banners

ART & SCIENCE

clothesline
color electrical tape
colorful fabric/or pieces of colored plastic
fence or trees
markers
old flags
PVC pipe pieces (1")
scissors
small dowel rods (¾")

- Cut pieces of fabric and or plastic into different sizes and lengths. Share these with children so that they can create and decorate the flags.
- The children can work individually or collaboratively on the banner.
- When the flags are completed, hang them from the clothesline, fence, climbing structures, or trees.
- Another way to display banners is by placing the PVC pipe pieces in the ground or on a fence. The banner can be attached to a small dowel rod and inserted into the pipe. These can be placed along a trail or around the play area.
- Children can observe the movement of flags, as the wind varies, when they are wet or dry, and they can compare the designs of different flags.

collection of trim: ribbon, pebbles, metallic paper or fabric, jewels, yarn, cellophane paper, old
  jewelry, and so on

colored electrical tape   scissors

glue   small vinyl or plastic containers with lids

markers

- Provide materials that children can use to create treasure boxes for hiding treasures in the
  Adventure Center.
- The children attach interesting materials to their boxes with glue.
- After the glue dries, children can place treasures in the boxes and hide them along the
  adventure trail.
- These boxes can add interest for the children because they can use the trail to look for hidden
  treasures.
- Possible treasures include old jewelry, coins, miniature toys, beautiful rocks, and so on.
- Some children may want to create a treasure map children can use to find the box.

Activities for the Adventure Center

Adventure Dress-Up   MUSIC & SOCIAL SKILLS

CD or tape player (battery operated)

collection of dress-up clothes:

    big hats

    boots

    capes

    fishing vest

    outdoor clothing

    raincoats

    safari jacket

    sunglasses

    umbrella

    walking stick

empty, clean bottle of bug spray/sunscreen (put water inside)

plastic container (large with air-tight lid)

recordings of animal sounds or jungle music

- Provide an assortment of dress-up clothes for children to choose from to wear on their
  adventure.
- The children determine roles, characters, and actions that they want to
  use in their dramatic play.
- The dress-up items can be stored outside in a weather-proof container.

hammer, large nails, and other tools   plastic containers
large plastic blocks   plastic dump trucks
pieces of lumber, plywood, and siding   wagons
plastic buckets   wheelbarrows

- Help the children chose an area for building outside.
- Next, encourage children to move the plastic blocks and/or containers outside using the wagons, wheelbarrows, buckets, and so on.
- The transportation of these building materials requires that they use large motor muscles as they load, pull, and build.
- Children can move the building materials around the playground and use them to create new structures for adventure play.

Musical Sounds in the Great Outdoors MUSIC

aluminum pie pans
aluminum soda cans
large bells
large metal nails
metal cooking utensils: large serving spoon, spatula, wooden spoons, and so on
metal pots and pans
various pieces of metal pipes

- Any of these items can be hung from the fence, tree, or low climbing structure.
- Children can experiment with the sounds these items produce.
- A variety of sounds can be made by using different mallets: wooden spoon, dowel rod, rubber mallet, and so on.

Outdoor Intercom SCIENCE

electrical tape or duct tape
hand garden tools
2 plastic funnels
PVC pipe (½"–long enough to reach from one end of the trail to the other)
shovel

- Dig a trench from one end of the trail to the other.
- Put PVC pipe in the trench. The pipe in the trench can be left uncovered so the children can see the connectors. Later on, later dirt can be used to cover the pipe.
- Insert a funnel into each end of the PVC pipe.
- Children can communicate with each other through their new intercom.
- Children find this activity most interesting when they cannot see the person they are talking to.

drill and 1" bit

2–4 small tires

4–6 large tires

- Tires can be arranged in different patterns around the adventure area.
- Children can move smaller tires, jump into tires, and step out of the tires.
- If the children show interest in doing so, let them paint the tires with exterior latex paint. (Cleanup will be easier if they wear latex gloves.)
- Be sure tires have holes throughout, so that water can drain out.

Walk the Plank   MOTOR DEVELOPMENT

blue plastic or vinyl

balance beam used indoors (4" wide) or long pieces of lumber (4" or more wide) and 4 bricks

- Place the plank on a section of the adventure trail.
- Put the blue plastic under the beam to represent water.
- The easiest way for children to walk the plank is with it lying flat on the ground. After they have more experience with walking and balancing on the plank, it can be raised 2"–4" off the ground.
- Some children may be able to walk across using different patterns: forward, sideways, backward, hopping on two feet, balancing on one leg, carrying objects across the plank, and walking and dipping their toes into the pretend water.

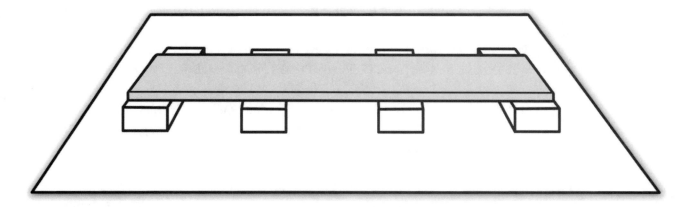

Adding Spark to the Adventure Center

Provide plastic buckets and a water source. Children can carry water from the source to a small wading pool. Next, they can add plastic frogs, snakes, or bugs. Other items from indoor water play can be used, such as plastic cups, sifters, plastic spoons, and plastic soda bottles. The addition of water to the area changes the play and includes science/math exploration as well.

Reading/Writing Opportunities

- Children make signs for the path ("stop," "slow," "one way," turn including word and/or symbol).
- Children draw plans and designs.
- Children "write" a story about the adventure.
- Children use oral language in communicating through the pipe-and-funnel intercom.
- Children gain control of their hands and bodies (essential for writing).

Other Printed Materials

- Children make a treasure map to search for hidden treasures on the adventure trail.
- Children follow directions on signs.

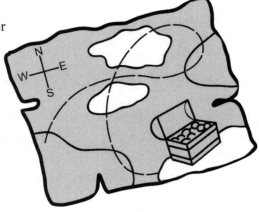

Books for the Adventure Center

Esbensen, B. 2000. *Jumping Day*. Illustrated by Maryann Leffler. Honesdale, PA: Boyds Mill. *A girl celebrates the joy of jumping from the moment she wakes up until it is time to jump back into bed.*

Eckart, E. 2003. *I Can Go Hiking*. New York: Children's Press. *When a father and son go hiking, the young boy shows the reader how to have fun exploring nature, properly and safely.*

Gordon, S. 2003. *Exercise*. New York: Children's Press. *This book explains to young readers the benefits of exercise and how it is good for our bodies.*

Greyson, B. 2001. *The outrageous outdoor games book*. Grand Rapids, MI: Frank Schaffer. *This book contains over 130 projects, games, and activities geared to outdoor play with preschoolers. These activities support multiple intelligences and accommodate a variety of learning styles.*

Hayes, C. 2003. *Playtime Is Exercise*. Illustrated by Tom Dineen. New York: Jayjo Books. *Children learn that having fun while playing outside is good exercise for their bodies.*

Love, P. 2005. *Two Feet Up, Two Feet Down*. Illustrated by Lynne Chapman. New York: Children's Press. *In this rhyming story, a girl describes how she jumps rope.*

Rockwell, L. 2004. *The Busy Body Book: A Kid's Guide to Fitness*. New York: Crown Books. *This book illustrates how our bones, muscles, heart, lungs, nerves, and brain all work together to keep us on the go.*

Evaluation of the Adventure Center

(This form is on the CD that comes with this book.)

Ask yourself the following questions to evaluate the Adventure Center in your classroom:

- Are the children using the adventure theme in their outdoor play?
- Have the props been used to inspire physical activity?
- Has sociodramatic or pretend play occurred in the area?
- Have the children discussed new ways of building or changing the trail?
- What are some ways the physical play can be expanded? What moveable materials can be added to the area?

Observation of the Individual Child

(This form is on the CD that comes with this book. Always date observations of each child.)

- How is the child using his body in physical activity? Describe his use of legs and arms, balance, climbing, walking, hopping, and so on.
- Is the child using pretend play in the Adventure Center? What is happening?
- Have you observed this child participating with others in making decisions or talking about plans?
- What new vocabulary is the child using during play in the adventure area?
- Is the child using unique and creative ideas while developing the adventure play?

Summary

Visiting the beach is an annual event for some children. Others have never had the opportunity to see a beach or play in the sand. But, all children will enjoy exploring sand, seashells, and water in the Beach Center. The equipment and materials in this center will inspire them to pretend they are lounging on the beach or building sandcastles. While in the center, the children will use new vocabulary that relates to the beach, ocean, and sand. This environment will also encourage cooperative play and the development of small motor skills.

Introducing the Center

To introduce the Beach Center, hide shells in the sand table in the Sand and Water Center. During circle or group time, ask the children if they found shells and ask them to guess what center will be opening soon.

Learning Objectives for Children in the Beach Center

1. To expand their knowledge of the beach, sand, and water.
2. To develop their oral language as they talk about the beach and participate in related activities.
3. To appreciate and value the natural environment and the elements, which are part of their world.
4. To encourage cooperative play while using materials in the Beach Center.
5. To learn about the need for protection from the sun.

Time Frame for the Beach Center

The Beach Center will interest young children for two to three weeks. If the children have visited the beach frequently or live near the beach, their play may continue for a longer time. For children unfamiliar with the beach, it will be helpful for the teacher to enter the center and participate in the play, then leave the center when the children no longer need help.

Note: The attached CD contains a sample letter to send to families, introducing them to the Beach Center.

An outdoor Beach Center can use a lot of sand.

Vocabulary Enrichment

beach ball

crab

dolphin

fishing/boat

float

jellyfish

lifeguard

lighthouse

motel/
    accommodations

ocean

pail

pavilion

pier

postcard

sailboat

salt water

sand

sand castle

seafood

shell

shovel

snorkel

sunburn

surf

surfboard

umbrella

wave/tide

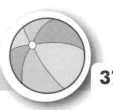

Web of Integrated Learning

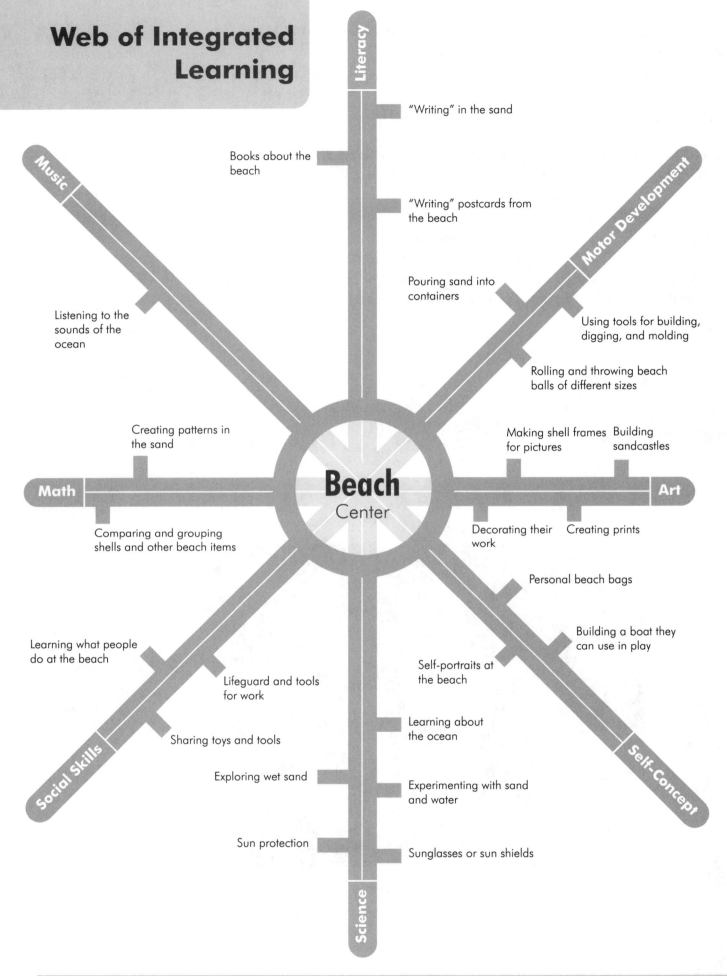

Literacy
- "Writing" in the sand
- Books about the beach
- "Writing" postcards from the beach

Motor Development
- Pouring sand into containers
- Using tools for building, digging, and molding
- Rolling and throwing beach balls of different sizes

Music
- Listening to the sounds of the ocean

Art
- Making shell frames for pictures
- Building sandcastles
- Decorating their work
- Creating prints

Math
- Creating patterns in the sand
- Comparing and grouping shells and other beach items

Beach Center

Self-Concept
- Personal beach bags
- Building a boat they can use in play
- Self-portraits at the beach

Social Skills
- Learning what people do at the beach
- Lifeguard and tools for work
- Sharing toys and tools

Science
- Learning about the ocean
- Exploring wet sand
- Experimenting with sand and water
- Sun protection
- Sunglasses or sun shields

❏ beach balls (many different sizes)

❏ beach chairs and umbrella

❏ beach hats and visors

❏ beach towels/air mattress

❏ empty sunscreen bottles

❏ flip flops, goggles, and fins

❏ lifesaving ring, floats, life jackets

❏ radio/CD or tape player and music recordings

❏ sand toys:

   ❏ buckets

   ❏ rakes

   ❏ sand wheels

   ❏ shovels

❏ shells

❏ sunglasses

❏ swim clothes

❏ wading pool (for sand or water)

A pan was used to make a sand sculpture.

Boats

appliance boxes
child-size life preservers (if available)
crayons

markers
paint
paintbrushes

- Provide appliance boxes for children to use to make fishing boats, sailboats, or speedboats.
- Make the boats large enough for children to sit inside during role-play.
- Encourage children to paint and decorate each boat.
- Add child-size life preservers to the boat for a realistic element. This is a good time to discuss boat safety and the need for children to wear life jackets whenever they are in a boat.

Personal Beach Bags

fabric scraps
glue
markers
paper
plastic bags

- Collect plastic bags from a grocery or clothing store for the children to use to make beach bags in the Beach Center.
- Each child selects a bag, decorates it, and uses it to hold personal items that are needed at the beach. They fill the beach bags with items from the center.

Sunshields or Sunglasses

chenille stems
clear plastic sheets
markers
scissors

chenille sticks

punch holes

- As children learn about the sun, they can learn about eye safety.
- Give the children a choice to make either sunshields or sunglasses for use in the Beach Center.
- Cut the sunshields out of clear plastic sheets into the desired shape, color the plastic with markers, make holes for attaching, and attach in the back with a chenille stem.
- Make sunglasses by cutting circles or squares out of clear plastic. Make holes for the nose. Color the plastic with markers and use chenille stems to attach the lenses and make earpieces.
- Children wear the sunglasses or sunshields on a "sunny" day in the Beach Center.

A Bottle of Sand   A R T

dry sand

small funnels

dry tempera paint or food coloring

small plastic dishpans

plastic bottles

spoons

- Mix sand with dry tempera paint to make colored sand, or add food coloring to bags of white sand.
- Place the colored sand in small plastic dishpans. These dishpans catch spills while the children are working.
- Each child can select a plastic bottle and choose the sand colors they'd like to use.
- The children can use a spoon or their hands to pour the sand into the bottle. They can experiment with using different amounts and colors of sand in the bottles.
- For young children, provide bottles with large openings and funnels.
- This is not an activity in which the children create perfect sand paintings, but rather, they are enjoying the creation of an interesting bottle that contains colored sand.

Beach Ball Party   M O T O R   D E V E L O P M E N T

beach balls of two different sizes

- Add two beach balls of different sizes to the Beach Center.
- The children roll, throw, or pass the beach balls.
- Place a beach ball on a small blanket, while several children hold the sides of the blanket and make it move from side to side by moving their arms.
- This activity helps develop important motor coordination for young children.

Beach Pictures   A R T

cardboard

markers

crayons

paper

glue

shells

- Provide materials for the children draw pictures of themselves at the beach and glue them to pieces of cardboard.
- When they finish their beach pictures, make frames for their pictures by gluing shells to the cardboard.
- Display these beach pictures in the center.
- After closing the center, encourage children to take the pictures home for their families to enjoy.

Lifeguard Post

beach umbrella, rescue board, life preserver, and megaphone (if available)
classroom chair
empty sunscreen lotion bottles
paper and glue or pieces of contact paper

- Transform a classroom chair into a lifeguard stand.
- Decorate the chair using paper and/or pieces of contact paper.
- If possible, include items a lifeguard needs, such as an umbrella, rescue board, life preserver, and a megaphone.

Listen to the Sounds of the Shell

chart paper and markers
large and small conch shells

- Place a large and small conch shell in the Beach Center.
- Make a sign that asks, "What do you hear?" and place it next to the shells.
- Draw a rebus on the sign of a child listening to the shells. The children hold the shells to their ears.
- This helps children listen, discriminate sounds, and enhances vocabulary as they discuss the sounds they hear.
- The children dictate, "write," or draw a picture of what they heard.

Music for Relaxing

CD or tape player   earphones (if possible)
beach bag   music recordings

- Put a CD or tape player in a beach bag.
- Include recordings of a variety of types of music in the bag.
- Encourage children to select a recording to hear while relaxing at the beach.
- Earphones make the selection and listening more private for the child.

Palm Trees

glue   paint and brushes
green crepe paper   scissors
large cardboard rolls

- Construct palm trees using large cardboard rolls (from carpet and linoleum stores).
- The children paint the rolls.
- Then, construct large green leaves from crepe paper and glue the leaves to the inside top of the rolls.

plastic cups, gelatin molds, margarine tubs, and so on

sand

small shovels, spoons, and plastic knives

wading pool

water

- Add water to sand in a wading pool.
- Explain to the children how they can use the moist sand to create sandcastles or other structures.
- Children can use shovels, spoons, and plastic knives to decorate the work.
- Some children like to use molds to create their "castles." Suggestions for molds include plastic cups, gelatin molds, plastic glasses of different sizes, and plastic margarine containers.

Sand Printing   MATH

items from the beach

spray bottle of water

- Collect items the children might find on the beach.
- Spray the sand in the Beach Center with water, so the children can make imprints easily.
- Materials to make imprints include shells, tennis shoes, aluminum cans, seaweed, bare feet, wheels, horseshoes, sand dollars, coral, starfish, and palm fronds.

Sun Protection   SCIENCE

empty bottles of sunscreen or plastic containers labeled "sun protection" with logo of sun

hats (boy and girl)

old shirts

small umbrellas

sunglasses

unbreakable mirror

- In circle or group time, tell the children who have chosen the Beach Center that they will need sun protection.
- Place sunscreen, hats, shirts, and sunglasses at the entrance of the Beach Center.
- Children can select hats, sunglasses, shirts, and umbrellas to use as they enter the center.
- They can also look in the mirror and pretend to put the sunscreen on their face and body.

old postcards of beach vacations

pencils

pens

stamps/sticky labels

- Collect old beach postcards and stamps or make stamps on sticky labels. Cover old messages with paper.
- Children can select a postcard on which to "write" messages or draw pictures of their Beach Center.
- Help the children "send" the postcards to families or friends.

Adding Spark to the Beach Center

Play a recording of music with beach and ocean sounds in the center. These beach sounds are intriguing for young children and will draw them back to the Beach Center for more activity.

The Essential Literacy Connection

Reading/Writing Opportunities

- Children print designs or letters in the sand.
- Children "read" brochures of beach vacations.
- Children "write" messages on postcards.
- Children use cake pans filled with sand for drawing and "writing." They can use sticks, plastic knives, or seashells as tools for "writing" messages in the sand.
- Children "write" their own ideas about the beach on postcards and send them to classmates or their families.

Other Printed Materials

- Provide motel stationery and motel brochures.
- Bring in travel magazines with pictures of the beach.
- Hang sea life posters on the classroom walls.
- Show the children sun protection factor (SPF) levels on sunscreen bottles.

Books for the Beach Center

Cooper, E. 2006. *Beach.* New York: Orchard Books. *As the day begins, the beach is empty, waiting to be filled. A pleasant portrayal of beach patrons enjoying a day by the ocean.*

Rockwell, A., & Rockwell, H. 1987. *At the Beach.* New York: Macmillan. *A little girl visits the beach. The book provides descriptions of what she takes with her, what she sees, and how she plays in the sand.*

Roosa, K. 2001. *Beach Day.* Illustrated by Maggie Smith. New York: Clarion. *Delighted Families rush onto the beach. Parents and children water-ski, bury themselves in the sand, splash and cavort in the water, play ball, and build colossal sand castles. The excitement and enthusiasm of the day are captured by the artist's bright, lively watercolors and the author's active, playful text.*

Rotner, S., & Kreisler, K. 1993. *Ocean Day*. New York: Macmillan. *This book describes a little girl's day at the beach. Clear and vivid photographs show many features of the beach and ocean.*

Wiesner, D. 2006. *Flotsam*. New York: Clarion. *A boy goes to the beach to collect anything that has been washed ashore. Bottles, lost toys, small objects of every description are among his usual finds. But there's no way he could have prepared for one particular discovery. A Caldecott Medal Award winner.*

Wood, A., & Wood, B. 2004. *Ten Little Fish*. New York: Blue Sky Press. *This rhyming and counting book features fish that gradually disappear from the reader's view. Colorful and bright illustrations capture children's attention as new images are introduced.*

Wood, A., & Wood, B. 2005. *The Deep Blue Sea*. New York: Blue Sky Press. *Bold and vivid illustrations are incorporated in this book that explores the many different aspects of the sea as well as the surrounding environment and animals.*

Evaluation of the Beach Center

(This form is on the CD that comes with this book.)

Ask yourself the following questions to evaluate the Beach Center in your classroom:

- Are children expanding their understanding of the sand, water, and sea life?
- Are children expressing their ideas and thoughts using new vocabulary related to the Beach Center?
- Are children working cooperatively on activities and projects in the Beach Center?
- Are children demonstrating that they appreciate and value their environment?
- Are children using sunscreen?

Observation of the Individual Child

(This form is on the CD that comes with this book. Always date observations of each child.)

- What materials and props is the child using in the Beach Center? How?
- Is he talking about the beach, sand, or water? Provide examples of vocabulary he uses.
- Has this child looked at any of the books about the beach? Which?
- Is the child "writing" in the sand, on a picture, or on postcards?
- Ask the child to describe what he saw.
- Is the child enjoying participating in the sand and water play? How was this demonstrated?

Summary

The Camping Center provides a place where young children can pretend they are sleeping, cooking, and being with friends in the great outdoors. Some children in the classroom have had these experiences, but many have only "dreamed" of the excitement. This Camping Center includes many opportunities for the children to work together as they "build a campfire" and prepare a campsite.

Introducing the Center

During circle or group time, introduce the camping equipment to interest the children in participating in the Camping Center. A flashlight, backpack, or compass can provide an intriguing way to begin a discussion about the center and its possibilities. Later, the children can use these props in their imaginative play.

Learning Objectives for Children in the Camping Center

1. To develop an appreciation for nature and the outdoors.
2. To expand their oral language as they discuss and work together while camping.
3. To learn about nature, including plants, animals, and birds.
4. To "read" books and keep journals about their camping experiences.
5. To gain confidence in their abilities as they learn to take care of their needs in the "great outdoors."
6. To work cooperatively while setting up a campsite, preparing meals, and going on hikes.

Time Frame for the Camping Center

Set up this center indoors or outdoors. This center will work effectively for at least two or three weeks. If children are continuing to choose the Camping Center after this time, add another week or move some of the more interesting activities to an outside area with easy access from the classroom.

 Note: The attached CD contains a sample letter to send to families, introducing them to the Camping Center.

Problem solving: How do you hold down a tent?

Vocabulary Enrichment

backpack
binoculars
bird-watching
bug spray
campfire
canteen
cooking
energy
equipment
fire
fishing pole
flashlight
heavy
hiking
hiking boots
insects
lantern
map
nature
outdoors
picnic
poncho
rope
sleeping bag
stove
survival
tent
trail/path
wildflower
wildlife
wood

Web of Integrated Learning

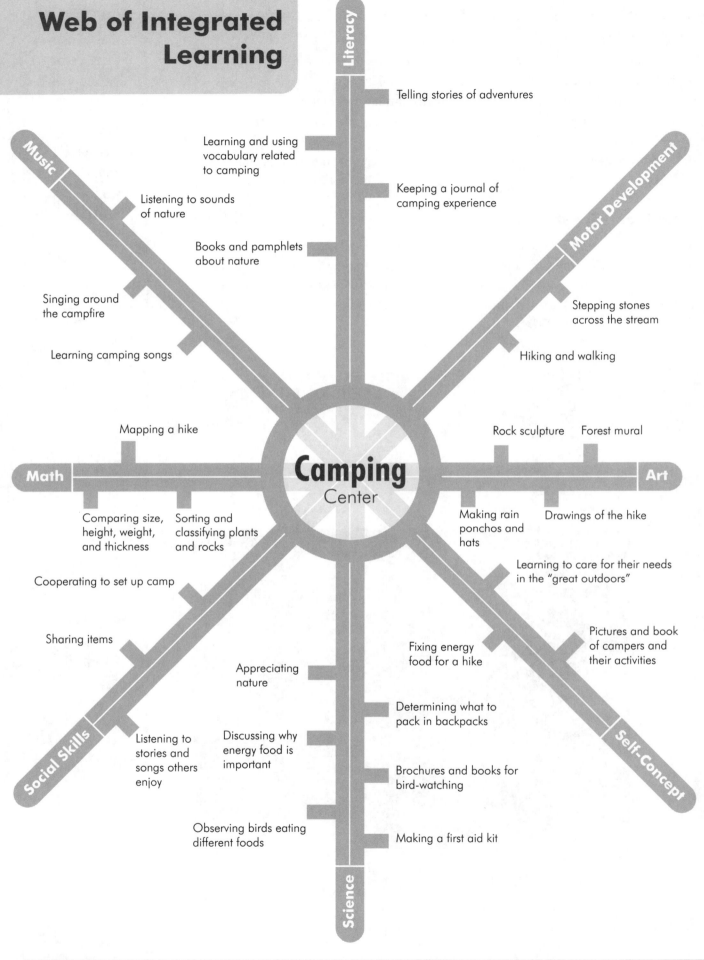

Literacy
- Telling stories of adventures
- Learning and using vocabulary related to camping
- Keeping a journal of camping experience
- Books and pamphlets about nature

Music
- Listening to sounds of nature
- Singing around the campfire
- Learning camping songs

Motor Development
- Stepping stones across the stream
- Hiking and walking

Camping Center

Math
- Mapping a hike
- Comparing size, height, weight, and thickness
- Sorting and classifying plants and rocks

Art
- Rock sculpture
- Forest mural
- Making rain ponchos and hats
- Drawings of the hike

Social Skills
- Cooperating to set up camp
- Sharing items
- Listening to stories and songs others enjoy

Self-Concept
- Learning to care for their needs in the "great outdoors"
- Pictures and book of campers and their activities

Science
- Appreciating nature
- Fixing energy food for a hike
- Discussing why energy food is important
- Determining what to pack in backpacks
- Brochures and books for bird-watching
- Observing birds eating different foods
- Making a first aid kit

THE COMPLETE LEARNING CENTER BOOK | REVISED

- ❏ air mattresses
- ❏ backpacks
- ❏ battery operated lantern and/or flashlight
- ❏ canopy or large piece of plastic that can be used to cover the eating area
- ❏ dress-up clothes:
    - ❏ flannel shirts
    - ❏ gloves
    - ❏ hats
    - ❏ heavy boots
    - ❏ heavy pants
    - ❏ jackets
- ❏ pieces of logs to construct a campfire
- ❏ pots and pans (from the Home Living Center)
- ❏ rocks to use in making a stream's path
- ❏ sleeping bags
- ❏ two-person tent or one made from a sheet and rope

A Forest Mural

ART

brown wrapping paper   paintbrushes
green, brown, and black paint   tape

- Cover one wall of the center with brown wrapping paper.
- Give the children paint and paintbrushes so they can paint trees on the paper, creating a forest using green, brown, and black paint. They can also attach strips of paper to add dimension to the forest.
- Leave out the art materials so children can paint additional trees or plants each time they work in the Camping Center.

Backpack

SCIENCE

backpacks   large box
items from the Camping Center

- Show the children how to use their backpacks in the Camping Center by packing their bags with items they may need on a camping trip.
- Children can select what they want to pack from a large box in the center containing such items as paper cups, plastic forks, small flashlights, combs, empty cans of food, plastic bag for collecting nature items, and water bottles (small pint-size plastic drink bottles with screw-on top).

Binoculars

SCIENCE

paper rolls (wrapping paper or paper towels)   tape
scissors   yarn

- Binoculars help children watch birds while on a hike.
- Make binoculars by attaching two paper rolls together with tape. Make a hole in each side and attach a piece of yarn on both sides.
- The children wear the binoculars around their necks when they are on a hike.
- Include books about birds in the Camping Center. They will help the children when they are bird watching.

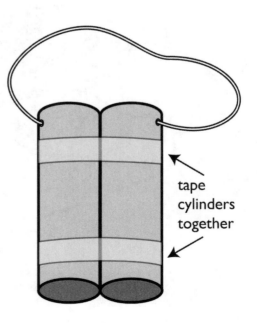

tape cylinders together

first-aid items
small plastic containers with a lid

- Use small plastic containers with lids to hold first-aid materials.
- Items available for the children to put into their kit include adhesive bandages, cotton, roll of gauze, masking tape, cotton swabs, and small plastic bottles with hand cream (representing bug repellent or sunscreen).
- The children carry the kits in their backpacks when in the Camping Center.

Rain Ponchos   A R T

duct tape or masking tape
markers, stickers, and scraps of contact paper (optional)
scissors
shower curtain liners
stapler

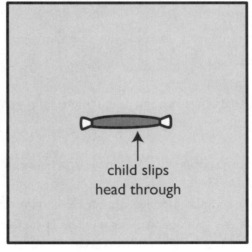

- Make ponchos for hiking in the rain by cutting inexpensive shower curtain liners into rain ponchos.
- Cut the liner into four squares, each one large enough for a child-size poncho.
- Cut a slit in the center of each square for the child's head.
- Reinforce the opening by placing a piece of duct or masking tape at the ends of the slits to make the opening more durable.
- Use other small pieces of plastic for a hat.
- Fold a square piece of plastic into a triangle two-cornered hat. Staple or tape the open sides together to create a waterproof hat.
- If desired, the children can add special decoration to the hat and/or poncho using markers, stickers, and scraps of contact paper.

child slips
head through

Bug Catcher   SCIENCE

baby food jars, or aquarium with moss, twigs, and dirt (with a net/wire top and tape)

- Use baby food jars to hold bugs that the children catch on the playground or on a hike.
- Alternatively, display the bugs in the Camping Center in an aquarium with moss, twigs, and dirt.
- Tape a net or wire top to the aquarium to contain the bugs in the aquarium.
- After a short stay in the Camping Center, the children release the bugs to the outdoors so they can return to their natural environment.

Energy Food   SCIENCE

dried fruit and nuts in bowls
small plastic bags
spoons

- Make trail mix for a camping trip.
- Encourage the children to select the dried fruits and nuts they want in their trail mix.
- Using spoons, they place their choices in small plastic bags.
- Provide labels so that children can label their mix with its contents and who made it.
- Children can eat the mix while hiking.

Feed the Birds   SCIENCE

chart
glue
markers
sunflower seeds, bread scraps, peanut butter, and so on
twigs, craft sticks, or tongue depressors

- Set out twigs, craft sticks, or tongue depressors for the children to use to build a bird feeder or birdhouse.
- Place the completed project outside close to the classroom window so the children can feed the birds different foods and observe the birds' preferences.
- Some foods to test are sunflower seeds, bread scraps, peanut butter, orange slices, and pieces of banana.
- Record the results on a bird food chart. Which food did the birds like best?

crayons
maps of walking trails
markers
paper (large and small sheets)

- Tell the children they will be planning a hike in the Camping Center.
- Encourage them to draw a map for the hike on a large piece of paper and display it in the Camping Center.
- Children should draw or mark points of interest they will see on the hike.
- If possible, give a reduced copy of the map to each child.
- When the children return from their hike, they draw pictures of the things they saw along the way onto the big map.

Rock Sculpture   A R T

glue
instant-print camera (optional)
piece of plywood or lumber
rocks

- Collect rocks on the school grounds, at home, or on a hike. Sort and classify the rocks in the Camping Center.
- Build a rock structure using a piece of plywood or lumber for the base of the structure.
- The children select and glue the rocks they would like on their "mountain."
- This structure develops as the children add rocks during the time the Camping Center is open.
- Instant-print camera shots of the growing structure, with the builders, provide a chronicle of the progress.
- The children will enjoy looking at the pictures and placing them in sequence.

Sounds of Nature   M U S I C & S C I E N C E

battery-operated CD or tape player
recording of outdoor sounds or a recording of sounds the children produce

- Play the recording in the Camping Center.
- Encourage children to guess what the sounds are.
- They can echo or create their own nature sounds.
- Some sounds that could be used are an owl hooting, crickets chirping, a stream bubbling, a fire crackling, and so on.

blue and brown construction paper

scissors

tape

- Use blue construction paper to represent water in a stream. Make stepping stones from brown paper.
- Explain to children that in the stream, they should try to stay out of the water by walking on the stepping stones.
- Lay the stones in a pattern that is easy for the children to follow. (If the floor is slippery, attach the construction paper to the floor with tape so the children will not slip.)
- The children can move the stones to create other patterns to follow.
- This activity develops motor coordination as the children maneuver their bodies from stone to stone.

Adding Spark to the Camping Center

A campfire will stir new interest in the Camping Center. Indoors, make a "campfire" by stacking several logs over a battery spotlight with red cellophane paper covering the lens. Or borrow a set of electric logs and plug them in. Tell stories about the day's adventures or sing songs around the campfire.

The Essential Literacy Connection

Reading/Writing Opportunities

- Read books about camping with the children.
- Children make a hiking map and "read" other maps.
- Children match items for the first aid kit.
- Children label their camping snacks.
- Children "read" and tell stories around the campfire.
- Children develop auditory discrimination while listening to the nature sounds on the recording.

Other Printed Materials

- Provide maps, brochures, and a first-aid kit with first-aid instructions in the Camping Center.

Books for the Camping Center

Eastman, P. 2005. *Fred and Ted Go Camping.* New York: Beginner Books. *Two loveable dogs are good friends, although they are very different. When they go camping they have their own preferences and ways of doing things. All in all, the pals enjoy activities that go along with camping: pitching a tent, fishing, cooking, canoeing, and eating berries and nuts.*

George, K. O., & Kiesler, K. 2001. *Toasting Marshmallows: Camping Poems.* New York: Clarion. *Everything that happens when you go camping can be an adventure, from getting dressed inside your sleeping bag on a chilly morning to meeting a moose to sharing secrets in a tent at night. The captivating poems and pictures in this book will leave readers with wonderful memories of a camping trip—even if they've never been on one!*

Harvey, R. 2007. *Caillou Goes Camping.* Montreal, Canada: Chouette Publishing. *Caillou goes camping with his grandpa. What an adventure they have together!*

Henkes, K. 1985. *Bailey Goes Camping.* New York: Greenwillow. *Bailey is too young to go camping with the Bunny Scouts, but his parents take him on a special camping trip—in the house.*

James, H. F. 2007. *S Is for S'mores: A Camping Alphabet.* Illustrated by Lita Judge Chelsea, MI: Sleeping Bear Press. *From what to pack, where to go, and what to do when you get there, this book takes readers on an A-Z trail exploring this outdoor pastime.*

Ruurs, M., & Kiss, A. 2004. *When We Go Camping.* Toronto, Canada: Tundra Books. *This book evokes the sights, sounds, and smells of camping. Family members pitch a tent by a lake, hike, swim, canoe, and interact with their surroundings. The text celebrates the pure wilderness, and the characters are depicted as responsible campers.*

Evaluation of the Camping Center

(This form is on the CD that comes with this book.)

Ask yourself the following questions to evaluate the Camping Center in your classroom:

- Are children learning how to care for personal needs on a camping trip?
- Are children working cooperatively on tasks in the Camping Center?
- Are children talking about camping, equipment, and nature with new vocabulary and longer interactions?
- Are children developing coordination as they build props and/or participate in the activities of the Camping Center?
- Are children using books and "writing" when they are involved in the Camping Center?

Observation of the Individual Child

(This form is on the CD that comes with this book. Always date observations of each child.)

- Is the child interested in the Camping Center? What leads you to that conclusion?
- Is he talking with others using the vocabulary related to the Camping Center? Give examples.
- Has the child looked at the hiking maps and/or participated in making a map?
- Have you observed this child cooperating with others in any task related to the Camping Center? Describe.
- Is the child posing questions about camping, setting up a site, or cooking meals? What questions did he ask?
- How coordinated is the child when stepping on the stones, building the fire, or putting up the tent? Explain.

Summary

One of the most intriguing outdoor centers is the Car Wash Center. In this center, the children are able to combine two things they enjoy, water and soap, to clean their riding toys and other plastic trucks and cars. Doing this outside enables the children to work and clean without the restrictions they might have when inside. This more open and flexible environment invites active participation and collaboration as they determine what to use for cleaning, what to wash, and how to dry the vehicles.

Because water and soap responds to the movement of the children, it provides immediate feedback for their work. This center also includes opportunities to use large motor skills in washing and small motor skills when they are working on the details. The built-in reward is seeing that their work has produced a clean and shiny toy.

Introducing the Center

On a warm day, take the children outdoors and examine the riding toys that are available for their use. Ask them how they might clean, dry, and wax these toys. Write down their suggestions. Tell them that tomorrow the Car Wash Center will be available as one of the areas where they can choose to work. It is a good idea to emphasize that, even if they are not able to work in the Car Wash Center tomorrow, it will be set up long enough for every child to participate in this center. You can make sure this happens by keeping a record of which children have chosen to work in this center.

Learning Objectives for Children in the Car Wash Center

1. To learn about the workings of their environment while washing.
2. To develop motor skills while washing and drying cars.
3. To use new vocabulary and language that relate to the Car Wash Center.
4. To experience working as a team to accomplish a task.
5. To gain an understanding of a sequence of events that relates to cleaning.
6. To develop self-concept by completing a job and seeing the results.

Time Frame for the Car Wash Center

This is a popular center that most children will want to experience. Some will want to return repeatedly. For this reason, it is necessary to be sure that every child who wants to work in the Car Wash Center has the opportunity to do so. Observe the children's choices, and when all of the children have participated, decide if this is the time to close the Car Wash Center.

 Note: The attached CD contains a sample letter to send to families, introducing them to the Car Wash Center.

Dipping and pouring develop coordination.

Vocabulary Enrichment

brush

bucket

change

clean

cloth

cost

customer

drying cloth

full-service

hubcap

inside/outside

money

polish

rhythm

riding toys: tricycle, scooter, wagon

soap

sunshine

team

ticket/bill

tire

water

wax

worker

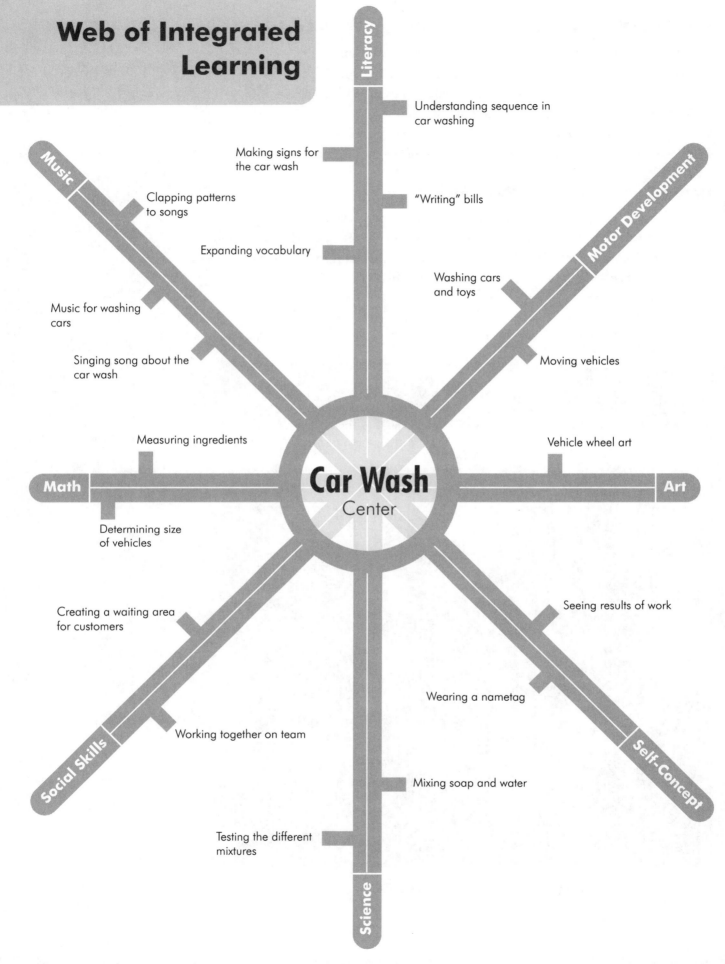

Web of Integrated Learning

Car Wash Center

Literacy
- Understanding sequence in car washing
- Making signs for the car wash
- "Writing" bills
- Expanding vocabulary

Motor Development
- Washing cars and toys
- Moving vehicles

Music
- Clapping patterns to songs
- Music for washing cars
- Singing song about the car wash

Art
- Vehicle wheel art

Math
- Measuring ingredients
- Determining size of vehicles

Self-Concept
- Seeing results of work
- Wearing a nametag

Social Skills
- Creating a waiting area for customers
- Working together on team

Science
- Mixing soap and water
- Testing the different mixtures

Family- or Teacher-Collected Props for the Car Wash Center

- ❏ brushes and sponges (variety of sizes)
- ❏ clothesline (for drying cloths)
- ❏ hand nozzle
- ❏ hose
- ❏ large and small plastic buckets
- ❏ old children's plastic raincoats
- ❏ old rags

The bottom of the truck gets washed.

Signs for Car Wash

markers

paintbrushes: large and small

plastic chairs

roll of butcher paper

scissors

string/twine

tempera paint

- Children can make and decorate signs for the car wash. Possibilities include signs that indicate the name of car wash, entrance, exit, waiting area, no smoking, and so on.
- When the children finish making the signs, they can choose where to put the signs up outdoors.
- At the end of center time, they will need to collect the signs and bring them inside.

Soapy Water

bars of soap

plastic cups for measuring

mild dishwashing detergent

plastic buckets with handles

sponges

water

- Children can combine soap and water to create a soapy mixture.
- This will be mixed in plastic buckets.
- Ingredients can be measured.
- The soapy water will be used to wash the riding and plastic toys.

Moving soapy water in buckets

Waiting Area

books/brochures, newspapers, and magazines

car accessories: small broom, plastic mirrors, CDs

cash register

money/change

plastic chairs

- The children can set up the waiting area using chairs, reading materials, and a cash register.
- Here, "customers" can wait for their car while other children in the center wash the vehicles.
- When the car is clean, the customer will pay for the service.

Music for the Car Wash

MUSIC

CD or tape player (battery operated)

CD/recordings of fast music (example: "Car Wash" song by Christina Aguilera and Missy Elliott from the *Shark Tale Motion Picture Soundtrack*. Lyrics are available online at sing365.com.)

- Children can select the recording they want to play while washing the cars.
- They can listen to several and then determine which one would work best.
- Encourage children to wash and dry cars to the rhythm of the music.

Steps to Follow

LITERACY

markers

paper (large sheet)

- In this activity, the children will determine the steps required to wash a car.
- Together, chart the work: the customer enters, workers ask the customer what type of car wash he wants (full service or outside only), workers wash the car, and so on. For example:
  - take order from the customer
  - wash vehicle with soapy water
  - rinse with water
  - dry
  - take money
- Display the chart close to the car wash.

Team of Workers at the Car Wash

SOCIAL SKILLS

camera

hole punch

nametag

paper (several sheets)

wire or ribbon

- Take pictures of the team members working in the Car Wash Center.
- Glue the pictures on separate sheets of paper.
- On each sheet, write the worker's name and what times he works.
- Punch holes in the paper.
- Lace the pages together with wire or ribbon or make nametags by stringing ribbon through holes in two corners so the children can wear nametags around their necks.

bar of soap
bottle of dishwashing detergent
container of laundry detergent
water

- Show children how to mix one container of each of the following in a bucket:
  - Soap and water
  - Dishwashing detergent and water
  - Laundry detergent and water
- Label the bucket containing the mixture with words and picture symbols.
- Encourage children to use the mixture to wash different toys.
- Ask children questions, such as, "Which is toy is cleaner?" "Which one was washed off most effectively?" "Which looked the best after the entire car wash?"
- Children can discuss, vote, and chart their opinions and answers to the questions.

Wheel Art   ART

aluminum roaster pans
large old sheet
paintbrushes: large and small
tempera paint
vehicles of various size and with wheels of varying size

- Explain to the children that they will be creating art with wheels and ask them to select which vehicles they want to use.
- Using different colors, paint the tires of the children's chosen vehicles with tempera paint, and encourage the children to roll the wheels across the sheet.
- Hang the artwork in the Car Wash Center.
- After the artwork is complete, ask the children to wash the wheels in the car wash.

Adding Spark to the Car Wash Center

Add sponges to the tools that can be used for washing. These new items respond differently and absorb water in a new way. This will encourage expanded play and participation in the Car Wash Center.

The Essential Literacy Connection

Reading/Writing Opportunities

- Children make signs for the car wash that give directions.
- Children "write" orders and bills.
- Children "read" and "write" labels on cleaning products and mixtures.
- Read books with the children about washing cars.
- Discuss with the children and encourage them to "write" the sequence required to wash a car.
- Children create nametags for team members.

Other Printed Materials

- Children "read" numerals on a cash register.
- Children experiment with money and making change.
- Provide a phonebook in the waiting area, or show children car wash listings.

Books for the Car Wash Center

Christelow, E. 2000. *Five little Monkeys Wash the Car.* New York: Houghton Mifflin. *Five little monkeys wash the family car before trying to sell it, but that is only the beginning of the adventure.*

Dingus, B. 1997. *Jeffery the Jeep.* Illustrated by Carol Bates Murray. Johnson City, TN: The Overmountain Press. *Jeffrey the Jeep wishes to become a fire truck, and realizes that he is not big enough to be a fire truck. He decides to help people in other ways by becoming a Forest Service fire jeep.*

Murphy, S. J. 2002. *Slugger's Car Wash.* Illustrated by Barney Saltzberg. New York: HarperCollins. *The Sluggers baseball team has a car wash to earn money for new T-shirts. CJ serves as the accountant, sips lemonade, and makes change for the customers. At the end of the day, the workers turn the hose on the one member of the carwash team who never got his hands wet.*

Evaluation of the Car Wash Center

(This form is on the CD that comes with this book.)

Ask yourself the following questions to evaluate the Car Wash Center in your classroom:

- Are children participating in the washing and drying of the toys?
- Have children moved beyond experimenting with water and soap to actually using the material in their play?
- Are the workers talking to each other and the customer?
- Are children developing literacy by making signs, charts, and "reading" books?
- Have some children begun working together and separating the responsibilities?

Observation of the Individual Child

(This form is on the CD that comes with this book. Always date observations of each child.)

- Is the child interested in and using soap and water? How?
- Is the child working with others to wash toys? Who?
- Have you seen the child be "proud" of his work? In what way?
- Has the child participated in making and using signs? Describe.
- How would you describe this child's large and small motor development? What did you see him do that helped you with this determination?
- Is new vocabulary and/or language being used in this center? What?

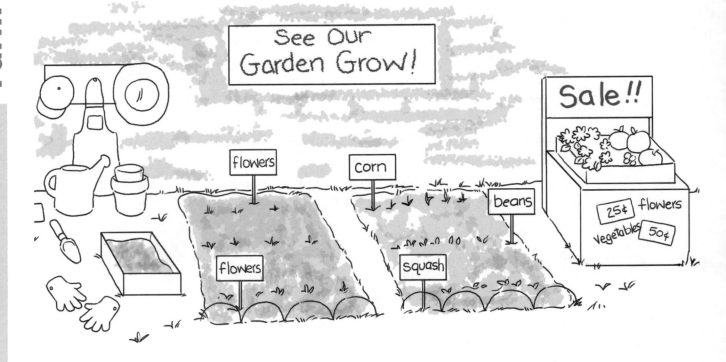

See Our Garden Grow!

flowers

corn

beans

Sale!!

flowers

squash

25¢ flowers

Vegetables 50¢

Summary

A farm is a fascinating place—farmers grow and harvest plants, care for and feed animals, and use tools. Children who have lived on a farm have some understanding of the work involved in the operation of the farm. Children who have only seen pictures in books or television programs about farms have very little knowledge of farm life. The Farm Center lets children try out some of the roles and responsibilities related to farm life. Set up this center inside the classroom or outside on the playground.

Introducing the Center

Spring is an excellent time to set up the Farm Center. During this season, children can observe the changes that are occurring in nature around the school or neighborhood. These beginning signs of spring encourage discussion of plants and growing things.

Learning Objectives for Children in the Farm Center

1. To learn about plants and animals on a farm.
2. To grow plants and keep a record of the growth progress of the plants.
3. To expand their vocabulary to include words related to farm life.
4. To appreciate the work of farmers and the importance of farm products in their lives.
5. To gain understanding of the world in which they live and use products.

Time Frame for the Farm Center

Keep the Farm Center in operation for about two weeks. Some of the growing projects you start in this center, however, will retain the children's interest for a much longer time. Some of the plants and activities can be moved outside when the Farm Center is closed in the classroom.

 Note: The attached CD contains a sample letter to send to families, introducing them to the Farm Center.

Seeds were planted in a wooden barrel.

Vocabulary Enrichment

barn
conserve
crops (Use names of crops grown in the local area, including corn, hay, wheat, cotton, soybeans, vegetables, and fruit.)
farm animals (and their young):
  cow/calf
  pig/piglet
  chicken/rooster/chick
  duck/duckling
  goose/gosling
  turkey/poult
  horse/colt/filly
  donkey/mule/foal
  sheep/lamb
  dog/puppy
  cat/kitten
farm tools:
  hoe
  mower
  rake
  saw
  seeder
  shovel
  tractor
  plow
  wagon
feed bin
fence
fertilizer
gate
planting
seed
watering trough
weeding

Web of Integrated Learning

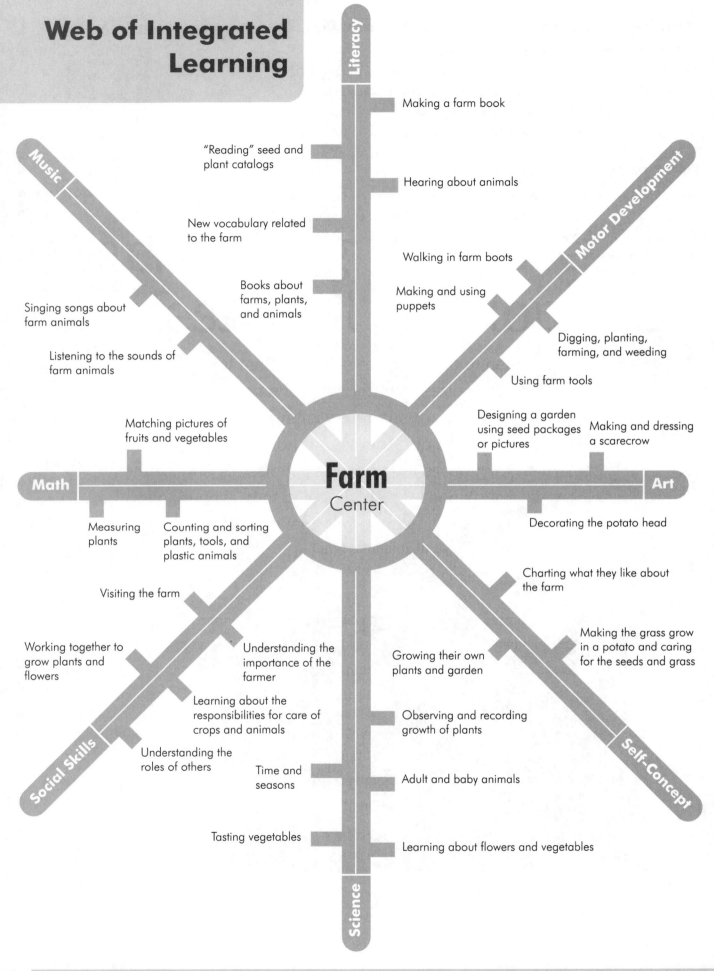

Literacy
- Making a farm book
- "Reading" seed and plant catalogs
- Hearing about animals
- New vocabulary related to the farm
- Books about farms, plants, and animals

Music
- Singing songs about farm animals
- Listening to the sounds of farm animals

Motor Development
- Walking in farm boots
- Making and using puppets
- Digging, planting, farming, and weeding
- Using farm tools

Math
- Matching pictures of fruits and vegetables
- Measuring plants
- Counting and sorting plants, tools, and plastic animals

Art
- Designing a garden using seed packages or pictures
- Making and dressing a scarecrow
- Decorating the potato head

Farm Center

Self-Concept
- Charting what they like about the farm
- Making the grass grow in a potato and caring for the seeds and grass

Social Skills
- Visiting the farm
- Working together to grow plants and flowers
- Understanding the importance of the farmer
- Learning about the responsibilities for care of crops and animals
- Understanding the roles of others

Science
- Growing their own plants and garden
- Observing and recording growth of plants
- Time and seasons
- Adult and baby animals
- Tasting vegetables
- Learning about flowers and vegetables

- ❑ bulbs
- ❑ cuttings for planting
- ❑ dress-up clothing:
    - ❑ aprons
    - ❑ baseball caps
    - ❑ boots
    - ❑ overalls
    - ❑ straw hats
    - ❑ work gloves
- ❑ farm tools to use outside:
    - ❑ bucket
    - ❑ hoe
    - ❑ rake
    - ❑ shovel
- ❑ large plastic tray with soil (or use a cardboard box lined with plastic)
- ❑ seeds
- ❑ toy barn with small plastic farm animals, tractor, and plastic toy farmers

Digging in hard-packed dirt is a challenging activity.

Child-Created Props for the Farm Center

Barn Yard

MOTOR DEVELOPMENT

large cardboard boxes
paint
paintbrushes
scissors
tape

- Find boxes large enough that children can go inside while taking on the roles of the farm worker or the animals.
- Encourage the children to make barns, lots, and fences from large cardboard boxes.
- Children can paint their creations with tempera paint.

construction paper, contact paper, feathers, yarn, and so on
glue and tape
small brown paper bags

- Children create puppets for the Farm Center using small brown paper bags as the puppet base.
- Attach construction paper, contact paper, feathers, yarn, and fabric to make an animal, such as a chicken, rooster, bunny, cat, pig, cow, or horse.
- Using the puppets in the Farm Center encourages the children's language as they participate in creative dramatics.
- Use the barn the children built for the Farm Center as the puppet stage.

Farm Boots   MOTOR DEVELOPMENT

markers
paint and paintbrushes
scissors
shoeboxes (the lids are not needed)

cut hole in
bottom of box

- Explain to children that when they are working on a farm or in a barn, they need boots.
- Give each child two shoeboxes to make farm boots.
- Cut a hole in the bottom of each shoebox that is large enough to allow a child's foot to fit inside. Discard the lid and turn the box over with the newly cut hole facing up.
- Children insert their foot through the hole, to put on the farm boot. The children's feet are actually walking on the floor, making the boots more durable.
- Encourage the children to paint and decorate their boots.
- The children wear these farm boots when they are working in the Farm Center.

Individual Farms   SCIENCE

marker   seeds
masking tape   Styrofoam tray, plastic dish, or aluminum pie pan
potting soil

- Each child can select a Styrofoam or plastic dish to use to make his own miniature farm for growing seeds.
- Label each individual farm with the child's name.
- The child puts dirt in his tray and selects seeds to plant.
- The child is responsible for "farming" the crop: placing it in sunlight, watering it, weeding, and observing changes.

A Book About Baby Farm Animals

Big Red Barn by Margaret Wise-Brown

- Young children are very interested in both adult and baby animals. *Big Red Barn* introduces children to farm animals and expands their language by presenting the names of baby animals as well as the adult names they may already know.

A Fish Tale

galvanized pan or large plastic tub
magnets
paperclips
paper or plastic
pieces of cane or small dowel rods
scissors
string

- Create a fishing pond in the Farm Center using a galvanized pan or large plastic tub to represent the pond.
- Make fishing poles from pieces of cane limbs or small dowel rods with a magnet on the end of each string line.
- Make various sizes of fish from plastic or paper, attaching a paperclip to each fish, and place the fish in the pond.
- The children can catch fish and make up fish stories about "the big one that got away."

Designing a Garden

empty seed packages or pictures from gardening magazines
glue
large sheet of paper
scissors

- Collect empty seed packages or pictures from a gardening magazine or catalog, to design gardens.
- The children can design the gardens individually or in small groups.
- Use a large sheet of paper to represent the garden plot.
- The children cut and glue their picture selection to their garden for display in the Farm Center.

cash register
items to include in the co-op:
    bridles and harnesses
    feed for cattle, horses, pigs, or chickens
    fertilizer
    hoe
    hose
    overalls and work gloves
    plants
    seeds
    shovels
    tires

- Explain to the children that many farmers buy their supplies at a cooperative market, or co-op
- Adding a co-op to the Farm Center stimulates new learning, as the children explore some of the materials farmers actually use.
- Include an assortment of items from the suggestions above.
- Place a cash register in the co-op so children can discuss prices and make purchases.

Field Trip to the Farm   SOCIAL SKILLS

books about a farm
visit to a farm

- A wonderful spring field trip is a visit to a farm. Talk about the farm before the visit and read books about farms. During the visit, the children experience farm life first hand.
- After returning to the classroom, their play in the Farm Center will have new meaning with their increased understanding of the workings of a farm.
- Discuss and write about what happened on the trip.

Finding Baby Animals   SCIENCE

Animal Babies on the Farm by Vicky Weber
crayons
markers
wallpaper scraps

- Let the children examine *Animal Babies on the Farm*.
- Children can create their own animal baby pictures using wallpaper pieces for their drawings.
- Children can ask their friends to look for the animals in their drawings.

Growing Grass

grass seed	scissors or clippers
potato	paper cups
potting soil	spoon

- Cut the tops off several potatoes, scoop out the pulp, and place dirt inside the hollowed potatoes. These potatoes can be place in a plastic jar or cup.
- Plant grass seed in the dirt. Use a variety of grass seed that germinates and sprouts quickly.
- Place the potatoes in a sunny spot and water the seeds regularly.
- When the grass begins to grow, encourage the children to keep a record of the progress and observe the changes that occur. They can graph the growth of the grass.
- When the grass gets tall, the children trim it using scissors or clippers.

Love of the Land

chart table paper	markers

- Develop a chart that lists children's reasons for enjoying the farm.
- Title the writings "Why I Like the Farm."
- Include their names next to their statements.
- Display this chart in the Farm Center or use it as a thank you note to the farmers who invited the children to visit their farm.

Notebook of Farm Pictures

farm magazines	photo album
glue (if necessary)	scissors

- Select pictures from farm magazines that show crops, animals, or farmers.
- Place pictures in a photo album and label for children to "read" in the Farm Center.
- Include pictures of the children on their visit to the farm.

Scarecrow

clothing for the scarecrow	old sheet or butcher paper
marker or crayon	stapler or needle and thread
newspaper	

- Make a scarecrow to protect the crops.
- Trace around a child while he lies on an old sheet or butcher paper.
- Cut out two patterns and staple or sew them together to create a life-size doll.
- The children can use crumpled newspaper or other scrap materials to stuff the scarecrow.
- Dress the scarecrow by selecting clothing articles from a collection of overalls, work gloves, bandannas, bonnets, shirts, straw hats, dresses or skirts, aluminum pie pans, boots, shawls, and fabric scraps.
- The scarecrow can be placed by the children's garden to stand guard.

bowls of vegetables cut into small pieces

pictures of the vegetables

tray

- One way children learn is through using their senses.
- Prepare vegetables in small pieces for the children to taste.
- Include both familiar and new vegetables for the tasting party, so the children can taste and identify the vegetables they know and try new vegetables.
- Place pictures of vegetables next to the tasting tray so the children can match the real vegetable with the symbol.

Adding Spark to the Farm Center

Nothing adds a new spark to the Farm Center like a short visit by a baby farm animal. A kitten, puppy, chick, or bunny warms the heart of a child and creates renewed interest in the Farm Center. Ask a family member or friend who has a new animal to bring the animal to the class. During the visit, children can learn about the animal and the care it requires. Pose questions about what the animal eats, how it is cared for, and where it lives.

The Essential Literacy Connection

Reading/Writing Opportunities

- Include books and/or paper to keep a record of plantings and observed changes in the center.
- Encourage the children to make labels for the names of seeds planted.
- Create a language experience chart on "Our Trip to the Farm."
- Children create labels for plants and tools.
- Children "read" books of that teach the names of baby animals.
- Children create signs and prices for farm products at the co-op.
- Children design a garden.
- Children create a chart of things they like about the farm.

Other Printed Materials

- Include seed and plant catalogs in the Farm Center.
- Bring in magazines that include information about farms, animals, and machinery.

Books for the Farm Center

Amery, H. 2006. *What's Happening on the Farm?* Illustrated by Stephen Cartwright. Eveleth, MN: Usborne Books. *This book is designed to amuse young children and stimulate them to talk, to encourage them to learn new words, and to distinguish visual differences. Detailed illustrations of farm animals provide many incidents to talk about, things to find, and things to count.*

Florian, D. 1994. *Vegetable Garden.* New York: Harcourt. *In this book, a family shares in planting a garden. Illustrations demonstrate the steps in preparing and growing a garden.*

Hill, E. 2003. *Spot Goes to the Farm*. New York: Puffin. *Puppy Spot searches for new babies among the farm animals, each of which greets him with its own distinctive noise. Movable flaps conceal portions of the illustrations.*

Kightley, R. 1989. *The Farmer*. New York: Macmillan. *The farmer goes through daily farm tasks. These jobs range from feeding the animals to repairing machinery.*

Kutner, M. 2004. *Down on the Farm*. New York: Holiday House. *Simple rhyming text describes the sounds and activities of animals during a day on the farm.*

Weber, V. 2005. *Animal Babies on the Farm*. Boston, MA: Kingfisher. *This book shows seven young farm animals and is the perfect introduction to farms for young children.*

Wise-Brown, M. 2001. *Big Red Barn*. Illustrated by Felicia Bond. New York: HarperCollins. *In the barnyard, there are roosters and cows, horses and goats, and a pink piglet that has just learned how to squeal. Beautiful illustrations accompany this text about a day in the life of a barnyard.*

Evaluation of the Farm Center

(This form is on the CD that comes with this book.)

Ask yourself the following questions to evaluate the Farm Center in your classroom:

- Are children interested in learning about plants and animals?
- Are children growing plants and providing the care they need?
- Are children using new vocabulary and terms that relate to farming, plants, and farm animals?
- Are children working together and sharing ideas as they implement the projects in the center?
- Are the children gaining an appreciation for the responsibilities of the workers on a farm?

Observation of the Individual Child

(This form is on the CD that comes with this book. Always date observations of each child.)

- Does the child have any knowledge or experience with a farm? What?
- Is the child interested in growing plants in the farm center? In what ways is this demonstrated?
- What are the words and language that the child is using to describe the workings of a farm, care of animals, or growing plants?
- How is the child using the tools included in the Farm Center? How would you describe his small motor and/or large motor coordination?
- Is the child able to role-play in the Farm Center? In what way?

Summary

The development of a seed into a blooming plant is a marvelous process to observe. Young children, who naturally are young scientists, enjoy watching the changes that take place in their environment. In the Greenhouse Center they plant, water, and care for plants while observing changes as they occur. They dig in the dirt, design their garden, and weed the growing plants.

Introducing the Center

Springtime, when new plants and flowers are beginning to grow, is the perfect time to set up a Greenhouse Center. Take a short walk with the children around the neighborhood or school to observe new plants growing. In addition, consider a trip to observe greenhouse, nursery, or garden workers caring for vast numbers of plants. At springtime or throughout the year, children can plant seeds and grow plants in the classroom.

Learning Objectives for Children in the Greenhouse Center

1. To learn about growing plants through real experiences.
2. To observe plants and record information about plant growth.
3. To learn to appreciate the beauty in the world around them.
4. To develop confidence as they participate in growing plants and operating the greenhouse.
5. To work cooperatively in growing, displaying, and selling plants.

Time Frame for the Greenhouse Center

The time for this center to be open and operating will vary. If the greenhouse is set up outside, children can start plants and grow them in the classroom before it is warm enough to move them outdoors. When these plants have sprouted, children can take them to the greenhouse. Other plants can be started in the outdoor space. Because growing plants require time to mature, the Greenhouse Center can be set up and remain open outside for an extended period.

 Note: The attached CD contains a sample letter to send to families, introducing them to the Greenhouse Center.

Misting plants helps them grow.

Vocabulary Enrichment

bulb
cutting
fan
fertilizer
florist
flower pot
gardener
greenhouse
hanging basket
hoe
light
measure
plant
potting soil
propagate
rake
seedling
seed
shovel
sprinkler
temperature
transplant
tray
watering
weed

Web of Integrated Learning

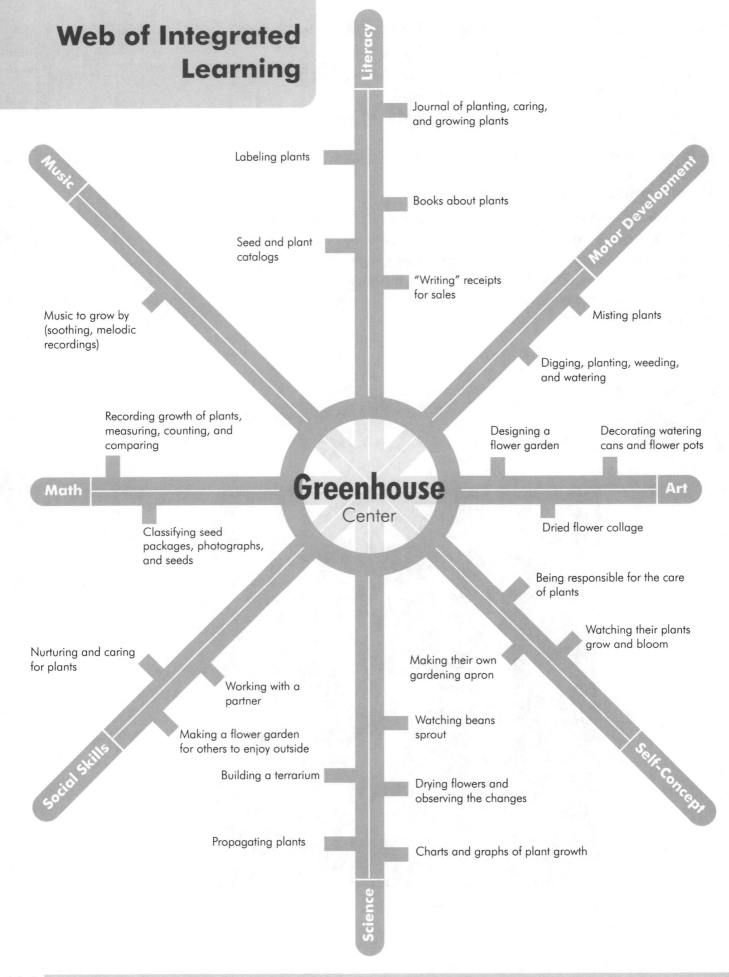

Greenhouse Center

Literacy
- Journal of planting, caring, and growing plants
- Labeling plants
- Books about plants
- Seed and plant catalogs
- "Writing" receipts for sales

Music
- Music to grow by (soothing, melodic recordings)

Motor Development
- Misting plants
- Digging, planting, weeding, and watering

Math
- Recording growth of plants, measuring, counting, and comparing
- Classifying seed packages, photographs, and seeds

Art
- Designing a flower garden
- Decorating watering cans and flower pots
- Dried flower collage

Social Skills
- Nurturing and caring for plants
- Working with a partner
- Making a flower garden for others to enjoy outside

Self-Concept
- Being responsible for the care of plants
- Watching their plants grow and bloom
- Making their own gardening apron

Science
- Building a terrarium
- Propagating plants
- Watching beans sprout
- Drying flowers and observing the changes
- Charts and graphs of plant growth

- ❏ craft sticks
- ❏ gardening tools:
  - ❏ clippers
  - ❏ hand spade
  - ❏ small shovel
- ❏ gravel
- ❏ large plastic trays for catching dirt when planting or transplanting
- ❏ potting soil
- ❏ roll of clear plastic for covering the growing area
- ❏ seeds/plants: flowers, vegetables, and herbs
- ❏ small plastic pots and trays
- ❏ spring bulbs
- ❏ soaker/sprinkle hose
- ❏ watering can and mister

Plants in the Greenhouse Center need labels.

Decorator Flower Pots

ART

     fabric paint

     glue

     markers

     small pieces of contact paper, foil, or wrapping paper

     Styrofoam cups or used plastic pots

     yarn and pieces of fabric

- Set out materials for children to use to decorate Styrofoam cups or pots of various sizes that they can use to hold plants.
- Children can color their pots with markers, glue yarn around the rim, glue pieces of fabric to the sides, attach contact paper pieces, or cover the pot with foil wrapping paper.
- Each pot will be different and special for the child who created it.

Gardening Apron

SELF-CONCEPT

     large green garbage bags

     scissors

     string or yarn (optional)

- Transform large green garbage bags into waterproof gardening aprons.
- Cut a hole in the bottom of the garbage bag for the child's head and slits in the side for arm holes.
- Cut an additional slit from the center of the opening for the head, down to the open end of the back of the bag so the child can slip the gardening apron on without having to pull the plastic bag over their head.
- The children wear these when planting and watering.
- If necessary, secure the apron by tying string or yarn around the bag at the child's waist.

Plant Labels

LITERACY

     construction paper

     craft sticks

     glue or stapler

     pictures of plants or crayons and markers

- The children draw or glue pictures on construction paper to identify the plantings.
- Glue or staple the pictures to craft sticks. The children can use them to label plants in the garden.

Sprinkling Plants

aluminum pie pans: pie-size or individual-size   pencil
buckets   water

- Help the children punch holes in the bottom of the pie pan they select.
- Provide small buckets of water so they can experiment with pouring water into the pan. By doing so they can determine the relationship between the number of holes in the pan and the amount of water coming through.

Watering Plants

contact paper or markers   gallon or quart plastic milk containers

- Use half-gallon or quart plastic milk containers to hold water for plants.
- The children decorate these containers with pieces of contact paper or markers.
- The children may create designs or drawings that indicate the container holds water and that it is a flower garden watering jug.

Activities for the Greenhouse Center

A Terrarium

large plastic drink bottles with black or clear plastic base
small plants: moss, ferns, grass, donated cuttings, vines, violets, and wildflowers
potting soil
scissors
small stones

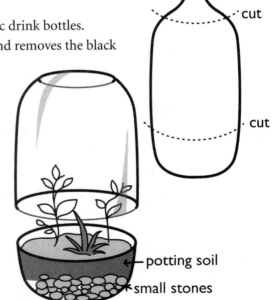

- Construct individual terrariums using large plastic drink bottles.
- The teacher cuts the top 3" off the plastic bottle and removes the black plastic base from the bottom.
- The children place a layer of small stones in the bottom of the black plastic piece.
- Cover the stone layer with approximately 2" of potting soil.
- Next, the children select plants that they would like in their terrarium and plant them in the dirt. Small, low-cost plants are suggested above.
- Mist the plants lightly.
- Inserts the clear plastic top of the bottle into the plant base.
- Place the terrariums in a lighted area away from direct sun.
- This plant greenhouse gives children an opportunity to see plants grow in a balanced ecological system.

Baggie Plants

bean seeds
paper towels
plastic bags

- An interesting way to start a plant is in a plastic bag.
- Beans will sprout easily if you place them on a damp paper towel and inside a closed plastic bag.
- The children can watch daily as the bean breaks apart and produces a sprout.
- Transplant the sprout into a pot or Styrofoam cup to watch more growth occur.

Bulbs in Water

fertilizer
small plastic bottles with necks that are smaller than bulbs
spring bulbs: jonquils, hyacinth, or narcissus (10 or more)
water

- Each child in the Greenhouse Center can select a bulb to grow.
- The child can choose a bottle with a neck that allows the bulb to sit on the neck of the bottle with its bottom portion touching the water when the bottle is filled.
- Children can place their bulb and bottle in a sunny spot in the classroom.
- As the bulb sprouts, the children will be able to watch the roots grow.
- Some children may choose to add fertilizer to the water.
- Compare and contrast the growing of the bulb and its roots, with and without fertilizer.

Designing a Flower Garden

box
brown paper
craft sticks
crayons
markers
paper
pictures of flowers (use old seed catalogs and seed packets)

- Partners work together to select the flowers they want in their garden.
- They glue pictures, drawings, or old seed packages onto craft sticks.
- Make a raised flower plot by using the top of a box and covering the open side with brown paper.
- The children stick their flower labels in this plot to create a three-dimensional flower garden plan.
- Label these cooperatively developed flower gardens with the children's names and display them in the Greenhouse Center.

Dried Blossoms

cardboard or poster board
flower blossoms
glue
heavy books or bricks
heavy cardboard (2 pieces)

- Collect flower blooms on a walk or from plants growing at home or visit a greenhouse and collect the blooms that have been snipped from the greenhouse plants.
- Dry these blooms by placing them between two pieces of heavy cardboard.
- Place heavy books or bricks on the cardboard.
- This experiment gives children the opportunity to see the difference between live plants and dried blooms.
- When completely dried, the children can glue the flowers onto pieces of cardboard or poster board to make cards or pictures to take home.

Potato Vine

clear plastic jar or cup   toothpicks
sweet potato or white potato   water

- The children will enjoy growing a vine from a sweet potato or white potato.
- Insert toothpicks around the midline of the potato and place it in the top of a clear plastic jar or cup.
- The water in the jar/cup should cover the bottom portion of the potato.
- The upper portion of the potato should be above the top of the jar.
- A pinch of plant food in the water will speed up the growing process.
- The children will be able to observe the growth, measure the length of the vine, and graph the progress.

Propagating a Plant

potting soil   small pots
scissors   spider plant, piggyback plant, ivy, or coleus

- Some plants are easy to propagate by simply cutting a leaf or "baby" plant from the large plant.
- By participating in this activity, the children learn about another way to grow plants.
- Plants that are easy to propagate in this way are spider plants, piggyback plants, ivy, and coleus.
- These plants grow quickly, so young children will soon see the results of their work.

large plastic tray or flower box   small plants that are ready to bloom

- Buy small plants that are ready to bloom and help the children plant them in a large plastic tray or flowerbox.
- These plants provide quick results for impatient young gardeners.
- Marigolds and zinnias are hardy and can survive drought and flood, which sometimes occur when children are responsible for the watering.

Those That Are Alike   MATH

basket   pictures of plants from magazines
old seed packages   pictures of plants from plant catalogs

- Collect old seed packages, pictures from plant catalogs, and photographs from magazines.
- Place this collection in a gardening basket in the Greenhouse Center.
- Encourage the children to group the pictures of flowers by color or another characteristic they identify for classification.

Adding Spark to the Greenhouse Center

Set up a flower garden outside the classroom or on the playground. Have the children plan the flower garden and start the plants inside. Transfer the seedlings to the outside site when they have matured. The children care for the plants and share their beauty with others. Once plants are growing, the Greenhouse Center can be expanded by providing a place to sell the plants, or the area could be expanded to include a florist area where flowers can be arranged, wrapped, sold, and delivered.

The Essential Literacy Connection

Reading/Writing Opportunities

- Children "read" and select from among different seed packages.
- Children create labels for the pots and trays of plants.
- Children explore plant catalogs.
- Provide informational books about plant growth for the children to "read."
- Help children chart the effects of sun, water, fertilizer, and temperature on growing plants.
- Children determine and "write" prices of plants.
- Charts, graphs, and journals will help children record plantings and the growth that occurs.
- Children can fill out blank catalog order forms for seeds and/or plants.
- Cash register receipts for "writing" bills extend the writing experience.

Other Printed Materials

- Bring in seed, bulb, and plant catalogs.
- Hang up wall charts from plant companies that show layouts for flower gardens, including pictures and names of flowers.
- Display books and magazines about flower gardening.

Books for the Greenhouse Center

Bunting, E. 1994. *Flower Garden*. Illustrated by Kathryn Hewitt. San Diego, CA: Harcourt. *Hewitt's beautiful illustrations and Bunting's direct text tell the story of a young girl's efforts to make a flower garden for her mother's birthday.*

Ehlert, L. 1988. *Planting a Rainbow*. San Diego, CA: Harcourt. *A mother and child plant a rainbow of flowers in the family garden.*

Garland, S. 2004. *Eddie's Garden and How to Make Things Grow*. London, UK: Frances Lincoln Children's Books. *After watching his mother plant a garden, Eddie and his sister, Lily, ask for a garden of their own.*

Heller, R. 1992. *The Reason for a Flower*. New York: Putnam. *The story and illustrations show the young reader how a flower is helpful to us and other living things. Different kinds of flowers and their parts are introduced to the reader in interesting new vocabulary.*

Jordan, H. 1992. *How a Seed Grows*. Illustrated by Loretta Krupinski. New York: HarperCollins. *This story tells of the various ways seeds can be planted and what is produced from them. It also demonstrates planting in a garden as well as in other containers.*

Evaluation of the Greenhouse Center

(This form is on the CD that comes with this book.)

Ask yourself the following questions to evaluate the Greenhouse Center in your classroom:

- Are children expanding their language and using new vocabulary in the Greenhouse Center?
- Are children accepting responsibility for the care and maintenance of the plants and the greenhouse?
- Are children "reading" and "writing" about their experiences in the center?
- Are the children learning what plants need to grow (light, water, and proper temperature)?

Observation of the Individual Child

(This form is on the CD that comes with this book. Always date observations of each child.)

- Is the child working in the Greenhouse Center? How?
- What language is he using in the center? Is he using new vocabulary?
- Have you observed the child talking with others and sharing in the work?
- Is he using tools to dig in the dirt? Describe his small motor coordination.
- Have you seen indications that the child is interested in learning more about plants? How?

Summary

Young children enjoy acting out stories and dramatizing events. This Outdoor Drama Center will provide the stimulation needed for them to become involved in creative dramatics. In this form of drama, there is no right or wrong way to perform—nor is there a memorized script. The children can determine which characters they want to be, say what they believe the character would say, and make the production as long or as short as they wish. Creative dramatics, indoors and outdoors, lets children have the opportunity to act in front of an audience. In these beginning creative dramatic experiences there is no stress for perfection or opportunity for failure. Rather, these activities are relaxed and unstructured and provide an appropriate and successful experience in drama for young children.

When you read the children a story, ask them about the characters, sequence of events, and how the story ended. When introducing the children to the Outdoor Drama Center, they can select the story they would like to dramatize. Remember that the children need to select the characters they want to play and the words they will use. Often, the more confident child will choose to be the main character, while a less confident child may choose to have a minor role. They have determined what they feel comfortable doing. Later, the less confident child may move to a more important role. This child may need more experience and, when successful, he may move on to more involvement.

Introducing the Center

In circle or group time, over several weeks, read stories to the children that would work well for a drama. For example, "The Three Billy Goats Gruff" or "Nail Soup" found in *Tell It Again!* by Shirley Raines and Rebecca Isbell and *The Gingerbread Boy* by Paul Galdone *or It Could Always Be Worse* retold by Margot Zemach. These stories have an easy-to-follow storyline, distinctive characters, and a clear beginning and end. Other stories, with similar characteristics, will work well in dramatizations, too.

Learning Objectives for Children in the Outdoor Drama Center

1. To develop creativity while developing costumes and sets.
2. To gain confidence in speaking in front of other people.
3. To learn the social rules for being in the audience of a production.
4. To gain understanding of the elements of stories.
5. To enhance "writing" abilities through the use of invitations, posters, and signs.
6. To select and use music in the support of stories.
7. To work with others in performing stage productions.

Time Frame for the Outdoor Drama Center

This center can be up for four to five weeks during the spring or summer months. If children are actively participating in the dramas, you may want to leave the Outdoor Drama Center up for a longer period. If no dramas are happening, you may want to read a new story with the children or revisit a book you have already shared. When you see a "great" production, ask the children involved if they want to invite classmates to come see their drama.

Note: The attached CD contains a sample letter to send to families, introducing them to the Outdoor Drama Center.

Vocabulary Enrichment

actor
amphitheater
bartering
beginning/ending
character
costume
decorating
emcee
entrance
exit
invitation
measure
microphone
musician
order
play
sequence
set
sound effect
stage
story

Hats support the development of an outdoor drama.

WELCOME TO OUR PLAY!

Web of Integrated Learning

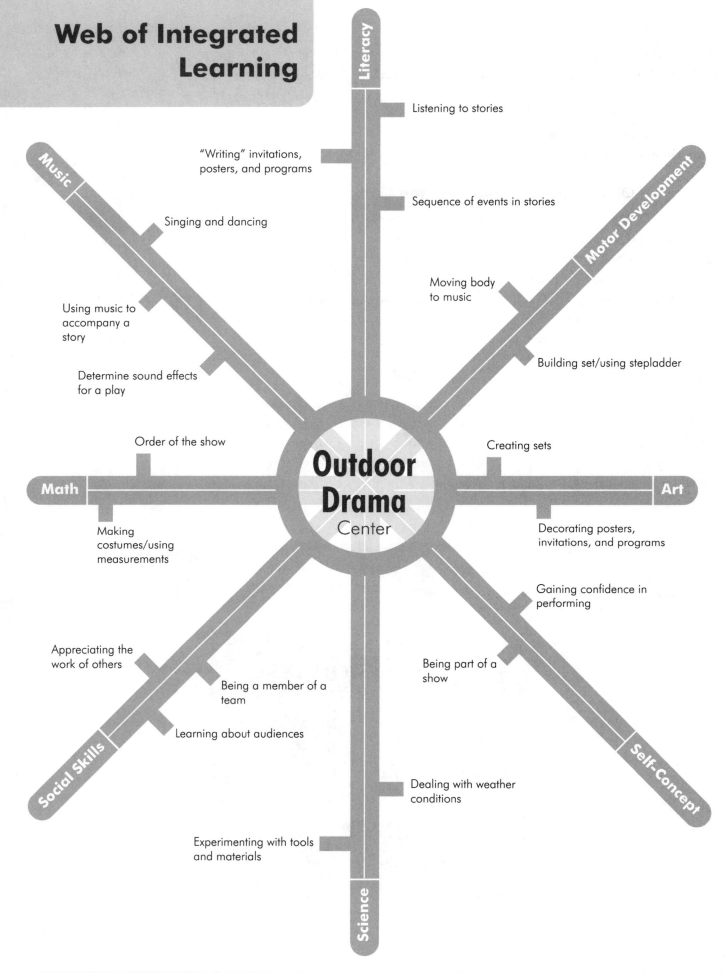

Outdoor Drama Center

Literacy
- Listening to stories
- "Writing" invitations, posters, and programs
- Sequence of events in stories

Motor Development
- Moving body to music
- Building set/using stepladder

Music
- Singing and dancing
- Using music to accompany a story
- Determine sound effects for a play

Math
- Order of the show
- Making costumes/using measurements

Art
- Creating sets
- Decorating posters, invitations, and programs

Self-Concept
- Gaining confidence in performing
- Being part of a show

Social Skills
- Appreciating the work of others
- Being a member of a team
- Learning about audiences

Science
- Dealing with weather conditions
- Experimenting with tools and materials

- ❏ different types of shoes:
    - ❏ boots
    - ❏ heels
    - ❏ silver slippers
    - ❏ tennis shoes
- ❏ gloves (both dress and work gloves)
- ❏ large plastic storage containers that can easily be brought inside and outside
- ❏ old hats
- ❏ old fancy clothes:
    - ❏ capes
    - ❏ scarves
    - ❏ shawls
- ❏ other props that are need for specific stories:
    - ❏ art supplies to make props for a story
    - ❏ old suitcases (for storing props and bringing inside)

A large piece of fabric can become a costume for the drama.

Audience Training
SOCIAL SKILLS

chart paper
markers
microphone
plastic chairs or bench

- Have a discussion with the children about audience participation.
- Write some rules of audience etiquette on paper. For example:
  - Clap when you like something.
  - Listen quietly during the drama.
  - Don't leave before the show is over.

Costumes
ART & MOTOR DEVELOPMENT

clothespins/clips
construction paper
pieces of fabric
scissors

- Children can select the materials they want to use for costumes.
- They can experiment with attaching pieces with clothespins/clips.
- Children can use other materials from the Art Studio Center or the Home Living Center.
- When they have completed their costumes, children can wear them during their creative dramatics activities.

Invitations and Posters
LITERACY

colored paper
colored pencils
glue
markers
pieces of colorful contact paper
scissors
stencils
stickers
tape
trim

- If children want to invite others to their performance, they can create invitations.
- They could also make posters advertising the drama.
- If they make invitations, they can put them in the children's cubbies or deliver them personally.
- After the show, display the invitations and posters with pictures of the drama in the classroom.

large brushes	scissors
long pieces of plastic	sheets of paper (large)
markers and/or tempera paint	wood stakes (to secure set in the ground)
masking and duct tape	

- Children can design the set needed for their drama.
- Encourage the children to use the markers and/or tempera paint to decorate the set.
- Stake and suspend the set behind the stage. Be sure to break the set down after the production.

Activities for the Outdoor Drama Center

Activities for Creative Dramatics   M U S I C

CD or tape player	shakers
bells	tambourine
CDs/recordings	triangle
drums	xylophone

- After the children have determined the story they will use, they can investigate sound effects or recordings they may wish to include with the dramatization.
- Characters may use the instruments or a "back-up group" can add the sounds or music needed.

Big Production   S E L F - C O N C E P T

colored paper	microphone
costumes (for specific show)	props
markers	scissors

- After the children have been dramatizing in the Outdoor Drama Center for several weeks, they may want to perform a show for their friends. This can include a drama, music, dance, and an emcee. You may need to get involved in helping organize this, or they may want total control. Either way is fine, depending on the children in your classroom.
- Determine the order of the show. Children will decide what is needed for the show and the order of the performances, and can "write" these on chart paper.
- One child may want to be the emcee. This can be as simple or complex as the children want.
- Children can create posters, programs, and invitations. However, remember that this is the children's production and it should be very relaxed—no pressure—after all, this is play.

WELCOME
TO OUR
PLAY!

suitcase
clear contact paper
dance costumes
large pieces of fabric
old colored sheet
recordings of music for dancing
scarves

- Label a suitcase "Dance" and add a picture of a dancer. Cover the label with clear contact paper.

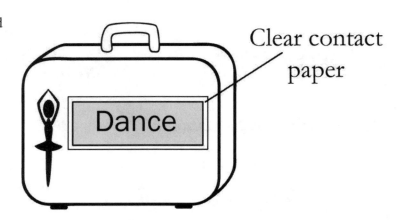

Clear contact paper

- Fill the suitcase with dance-related costumes. Children can select from these costumes for a dance performance.
- Provide several recordings that can be used for ballet, hoedown, or modern dance (with sheet and/or pieces of fabric).
- After selecting the music and costumes, the children can dance on the amphitheater stage.

Songs on Stage   MUSIC & SELF-CONCEPT

chart paper with list of songs
familiar songs/finger plays
rhythm instruments: drums, wood sticks, bells, triangle, wood blocks

- When children go outside, they can give a musical performance on stage. They can add instruments to the production.
- Display a chart of the songs they know in the Outdoor Drama Center.
- When a child selects a song, be sure to touch the name of the song on the chart.
- After singing several songs on the stage, the children can move into their active play outdoors.
- The experiences of singing on stage will build the confidence of the children who are unsure of what to do in this Outdoor Drama Center.

Adding Spark to the Outdoor Drama Center

Invite a storyteller, or other people to perform in the amphitheater. Children can practice being a good audience while their guest performs. Remind them to clap when the performance is completed. Afterward, they may talk, interview the performers, and take pictures. Often, this will lead to the children emulating the performer in the amphitheater.

Reading/Writing Opportunities

- Read stories for the children to listen to.
- Children experiment with sequence when planning their performance.
- Children learn to listen for their turn on stage.
- Children "write" invitations and posters.
- Children select and use music that relates to their performances.
- Children design a program, decide on the order of performers, and "write" or draw the information.

Other Printed Materials

- Collect and set out old programs and posters about professional groups and local performances.
- Provide pictures from magazines, newspapers, or shows for the children to look at.

Books for the Outdoor Drama Center

Cooper, P. 2007. *When Stories Come to School: Telling, Writing, & Performing Stories in the Early Childhood Classroom.* New York: Teachers & Writers Collaborative. *Placing stories at the center of the early childhood curriculum is a natural way to help young children begin to read and write. This book is for teachers and parents.*

Drachman, E. 2004. *It's Me!* Illustrated by Isabelle Decenciere. Los Angeles, CA: Kidwick Books. *Patricia's joyful creativity is infectious as she takes on different roles in her lively game of dress-up.*

Galdone, P. 2006. *The Gingerbread Boy.* Boston, MA: Houghton Mifflin. *This is the classic tale of the old couple, with no children, who bake a gingerbread boy to keep them company. This wonderful hectic cross-country chase is humorous and insightful.*

Isbell, R., & Raines, S. C. 2000. *Tell It Again! 2: Easy-to-Tell Stories with Activities for Young Children.* Beltsville, MD: Gryphon House, Inc. *This book includes compilation of 16 stories children love to hear and dramatize, presented with storytelling tips and activities.*

Jassart, S., & Courtney, G. 1996. *Story Dramas: A New Literature Experience for Young Children.* Tucson, AZ: Good Year. *This book, for grades K-3, explores how children can become active participants in the stories and poems they hear and read. The text includes 28 story dramas, with ways to explore and expand the story without fancy costumes, stage props, or written scripts.*

Prendiville, F. 2000. *Drama and Traditional Story for the Early Years.* New York: RoutledgeFalmer. *This book provides tried and tested example dramas based on numerous traditional stories.*

Raines, S. C., & Isbell, R. 1999. *Tell it Again! Easy-to-Tell Stories with Activities for Young Children.* Beltsville, MD: Gryphon House, Inc. *A compilation of the best tips and tricks of expert storytellers who retell 18 popular children's stories that are suitable for dramatization.*

Ward, W. 1981. *Stories to Dramatize.* Anchorage, KY: Anchorage Press. *This is a collection of stories that are suitable for dramatization by children of all ages. The stories are grouped by age.*

Zemach, M. 1990. *It Could Always Be Worse.* New York: Farrar, Straus, and Giroux. *A poor man, who lives with his family in a very crowded house, complains about his circumstances to the Rabbi, who advises him to bring in the farm animals, as well, and he realizes how lucky he really is.*

WELCOME TO OUR PLAY!

Evaluation of the Outdoor Drama Center

(This form is on the CD that comes with this book.)

Ask yourself the following questions to evaluate the Outdoor Drama Center in your classroom:

- Are children choosing to participate in the Outdoor Drama Center?
- What stories and characters are children dramatizing?
- Are children using the props that are available or creating their own?
- Do children need more materials or specific props added, to help with the story dramatizations?
- Are the children working together to prepare the dramatization?
- Are children creating sets, invitations, or posters?

Observation of the Individual Child

(This form is on the CD that comes with this book. Always date observations of each child.)

- Is the child playing a character in the story production? Which one?
- Have you seen the child as part of the audience? How did he act?
- Is the child gaining confidence in his ability to speak before others?
- Have you seen the child demonstrating creativity by making sets, sound effects, posters, costumes, or invitations?
- Has the child cooperated with others on any task related to the outdoor theater? Describe.
- Is the child learning about stories, characters, and plot? Give an example of this understanding.

CHAPTER 6

Evaluation of Centers and of Children in Centers

There are two important parts of center evaluation: the evaluation of the center and evaluation of the children's participation in the center.

Evaluation of the Center

When selecting a learning center to include in your classroom, it is important to think about the children who will be using the space. Consider their developmental levels, experiential backgrounds, individual interests, special needs, and cultural values. After including the centers, evaluate how the centers are functioning, how children are participating, and evaluate the learning that is taking place. This chapter provides methods and tools to use during the continuing process of evaluating centers and children.

Grand Opening

Before opening a center, take a moment to examine the area. Use the following questions as a quick checklist to identify potential problems with the design of the center.

- Is the center attractive and appealing to the young children in this classroom?
- Does the center match the interests and experiences of the children in your classroom?
- Are there enough materials and options available so that four or five children can use the center effectively?
- Is the center organized? Are the materials in the center labeled so that things are easy for the children to locate and return to the correct places when they finish playing?
- Are the activities and materials flexible and open-ended, to allow children to work at different levels and with diverse ideas?
- Are children's books, writing, and other literacy opportunities integrated into the center?
- Will the center invite young children to play?

After using this quick checklist, make last-minute changes and additions before the children begin work in the center.

Take Another Look

After the children use it for several days, evaluate the center again. This second look gives you an opportunity to see the center in operation and make any changes that are necessary to ensure the center continues to engage the children.

- Are children choosing to go to this center?
- Are children accomplishing the objectives you identified in the center plan?
- Are children working together on projects in the center?
- Are children talking about the center and activities that occur in the area?
- Are children demonstrating sustained interest in the center's activities and in playing in the center?
- Are children creating new ways to expand the center play?

Teacher's Role in the Center

Center time provides the perfect opportunity for you to evaluate how well specific centers function, how children are using the centers, or what new materials might encourage the continuation of play. The "adding spark" section in each center in this book contains ideas that will renew the children's interest in a specific theme. Each center plan also includes questions to use in determining the effectiveness of the center as well as whether the children are accomplishing the center's learning objectives.

Evaluation of the Individual Child

Center time is ideal for observing a specific child. Because center time is self-directed, you are free to move into different centers and observe individual children. In the centers, young children are using language, participating in activities, and playing in their own ways. This setting presents an ideal environment for you to see how children are progressing and using their skills. You can observe children in the following ways:

- Assess each child's cognitive, language, social, emotional, and physical development.
- Identify each child's personal strengths: language, social skills, math/science, the arts, emotional development, focus, attention, and so on. Center time provides the opportunity to observe individual children's behaviors, interests, and learning habits.
- Determine areas of concern, and what new learning experiences a child might need.
- Observe and record children's individual levels of interest in activities, books, props, and centers.
- Document observations to provide information that you can use to demonstrate how the child is learning, assist in an evaluation of the child, and provide specific examples for family conferences.

Children's Participation in the Center

Keep a record of which centers the children in the class prefer. This record provides an overview of the centers children find interesting and those that they seldom choose. Use a large center chart to create a quick visual record of the children's center interests. This record also identifies the children's individual patterns of selecting centers. Ask the children to mark the chart when center time is over. This recall period is an opportunity for children to discuss what they did in the centers. Some teachers make journals available in which the children can draw or write about their daily participation in centers. The following chart is an example of what you might use in the classroom (a copy of this chart is available on the CD that accompanies this book).

Center Choices

Week of _____

Child's Name	Home Living	Blocks	Art Studio	Music and Sound	Science and Nature	Grocery Store	Long Ago
Amilia Brown	x	x	xx		xx		xx
John Baxter		xxx	x		x		x
Cassy Ribe	xxx		x	xx		xx	
Herman Green		xxxx	xxxx		xx		
Maria Stevens	xxx	xx	xx				
Jack Scheren	x		x	xxx	xx		

Observing Children in Centers

Use the following form to lend focus to your observations of the children during center time. Be sure to observe children at the beginning of the year, and then again later in the year. Place the completed observation forms (this form is available on the CD that accompanies this book) in a child's folder or portfolio to review when preparing evaluations and family conferences.

What natural materials will invite exploration?

Individual Center Time Observation

Center _____ Observer

_____

1   Can the child identify the play theme for the center? | yes | no | sometimes

2   Is the child able to focus on a particular activity in the center? | yes | no | sometimes

3   Is the child using symbols in his or her play? In what way? | yes | no | sometimes

4   Is the child participating with other children in a positive manner? Describe. | yes | no | sometimes

5   Is the child experimenting with and exploring new ideas that relate to the center? | yes | no | sometimes

6   Is the child using new language when interacting with peers? | yes | no | sometimes

7   Is the child participating in the literacy opportunities included in the center? | yes | no | sometimes

8   Can the child explain or demonstrate what he or she accomplished during center time? | yes | no | sometimes

Other Observations:

_____

_____

_____

_____

Language Samples

Many experts believe that children's use of language mirrors their thinking, providing a way to observe the development of their thinking, as well as the manner in which they think. Center time is an excellent opportunity for teachers to listen to and record the language children use while they are involved in meaningful activity. This "real" language sample is another way of assessing a child's development.

Guidelines for obtaining a language sample:
- The child should be participating in an activity with other children.
- The sample should be 5–10 minutes in duration.
- Use an inconspicuous recorder to secure an accurate sample.
- Write down the child's language during the observation. Use the recording to check the accuracy of your notes.
- Collect samples for a child in different centers and activities to have a more accurate measure of the child's language.

Because collecting and transcribing language samples is very time consuming, teachers often do this with children who seem to be developing language skills at a different speed from the expected pattern.

After collecting a child's language sample, examine it while considering the following questions that focus on aspects of language:
- Is the child's speech understandable?
- Does the child exhibit interest in communicating with peers?
- Is the child taking turns communicating—talking, listening, and so on?
- How long is the child's average sentence or communication unit?
- What are some of the vocabulary words the child uses during the activities?

Sampling an individual child's language is another tool for assessing a child's development. Use this information to plan ways to maximize learning opportunities. (This observation form is also available on the CD that accompanies this book.)

Observation of Literacy Behaviors in Specific Learning Centers*

Center _____ Observer

_____

___

Oral language used by the child:

___

Vocabulary used by the child that relates to center and play:

___

Document the interactive conversations that occurred and with whom:

___

Writing materials the child used in the center (pencil, marker, "sticky" note, journal):

___

Printed materials the child used in the center (pamphlets, phone book, signs, specific literature):

___

How does the child use printed materials in the center?

___

What is the child's level of interest in literacy activities?

___

Can the child explain or demonstrate what he or she accomplished during center time?

___

Notes for future observations:

___

***Note**: Include examples of the child's language, selection, and use of literacy items.

Sociodramatic Play Checklist

In centers, young children demonstrate their levels of play, use symbols, enact roles, and develop play and communication skills. The following chart (also available on the CD that accompanies this book) is an adaptation of Sara Smilansky's characteristics of sociodramatic play and is a valuable tool to use when studying a child at play:

Individual Observation of Child's Play in a Center*

Center _____ Observer

_____

Role-play	Number of roles the child in play chooses	Child performs simple roles	Child demonstrates expanding concept of role	Comments
Using props	Manipulates objects	Uses prop in play	Use of "pretend" prop in play	Comments
Make believe	Little evidence of imaginative play	Imitation of simple actions in play	Creation of play episode	Comments
Time	Fleeting involvement	Involved for short periods	Child stays in play episode for 10 minutes	Comments
Verbal communication	Little verbalization	Talk focuses on props	Conversation with others about play and roles	Comments
Interaction with peers		Associative play	Cooperative play	Comments

Summary Comments:

_____

_____

* Adapted from the work of Sara Smilansky.

Focus on one child for approximately 10 minutes. Check the appropriate column that indicates the level of the child's play you observe during center time. Notice that the first observation column indicates the very beginning level of play, while the last observation column indicates play that is more advanced.

Write comments to clarify observations or specific statements that support the evaluation. This evaluation summarizes a child's play on a specific day in a particular center. Repeat this observation at another time and look for changes in the child's play.

Anecdotal Records

This type of observational record is a running account of what a child does in the center. During this observation, focus on a specific child for a minimum of 10 minutes. Record information that is factual and does not include any interpretation of the events. Use this detailed and accurate information in conjunction with other evaluations of the child. This type of information provides clear examples of a child's development in real situations.

Using Center Observations and Evaluation in Family Conferences

As more emphasis is placed on the assessment of learning, it is important to remember that appropriate evaluation includes observing what children can do in many different areas and how they use their abilities in real situations. Center time is a perfect time to observe how a child functions in the "real" world. Checklists, anecdotal records, and language samples provide meaningful evaluations that you can use to improve the program so each child can reach his or her potential.

Use your observations of the children in centers to help families understand the development of their children. Specific information is more effective in communicating to families than broad generalizations of a child's behavior. Observations can help clarify and support other information in a child's evaluation.

Index of Children's books

W

Index

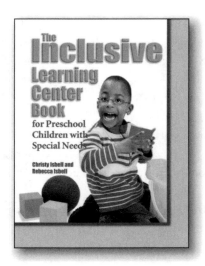

Sensory Integration

A Guide for Preschool Teachers

Christy Isbell and Rebecca Isbell

Do you have a child in your preschool classroom who:

- Climbs on top of furniture and jumps off?
- Covers his ears when children are singing?
- Refuses to touch clay, paint, or sand?
- Often falls down and skins her knees?
- Refuses to play on outdoor playground equipment?

If so, it is possible the child is having trouble with sensory integration. How can you help these children so they can enjoy learning and grow in positive ways? *Sensory Integration* helps identify children who have difficulties with their sensory processing, and offers teachers practical suggestions to support the sensory needs of young children in the preschool classroom. Easy-to-implement solutions include adaptations and activities for children with different types of Sensory Processing Disorder. 144 pages. 2007.

Gryphon House | ISBN 978-0-87659-060-7 | 16561

The Inclusive Learning Center Book

For Preschool Children with Special Needs

Christy Isbell and Rebecca Isbell

The Inclusive Learning Center Book is designed for teachers and directors who work with all young children, both those with special needs and typically developing children. The activities for each learning center have suggested adaptations to make them effective for children with a variety of special needs. The last two chapters of the book focus on assessment, evaluation tools, and building and creating items for centers that will be especially useful for children with special needs. 336 pages. 2005.

Gryphon House | ISBN 978-0-87659-294-6 | 19357

Also Available

Daily Preschool Experiences
For Learners at Every Level
Kay Hastings, Cathy Clemons, and April Montgomery

With 100 days of plans, *Daily Preschool Experiences* has learning center activities for learners at every developmental level. Organized by topic, each of the 20 units has a 5-day plan, taking teachers through an entire week of activities. Each plan includes:

- A morning circle activity
- Related children's book
- Vocabulary words
- Extension activities
- Activities for 4 different learning centers (Art, Math, Science, Language/Dramatic Play)

The learning center activities have three developmental levels of learning: for beginning, developing, and experienced learners. Because every child is unique, teachers can select activities that fit the developmental levels of the individual children in the class. With the learning center approach to teaching in *Daily Preschool Experiences,* children are involved in active exploration and sensory stimulation in a fun-filled learning environment. 448 pages. 2008.

Gryphon House | ISBN 978-0-87659-010-2 | 18765

Easy Daily Plans
Over 250 Plans for Preschool Teachers
Sue Fleischmann

In this curriculum based on the seasons and organized by month, teachers will find everything they need for a complete year's worth of daily plans. Each lesson plan is complete with:

- An opening group time activity
- Story time book suggestions
- Extension activities, such as small group activities, games, outdoor activities, and snack suggestions
- Activities for a variety of centers, including:
  - Art
  - Dramatic play
  - Fine motor
  - Math
  - Blocks
  - Music
  - Science

408 pages. 2007.

Gryphon House | ISBN 978-0-87659-005-8 | 13304

Also Available